WESLEYAN BELIEFS

WESLEYAN BELIEFS

Formal and Popular Expressions
of the Core Beliefs
of Wesleyan Communities

Ted A. Campbell

KINGSWOOD BOOKS
An Imprint of Abingdon Press
Nashville, Tennessee

WESLEYAN BELIEFS
FORMAL AND POPULAR EXPRESSIONS OF THE CORE
BELIEFS OF WESLEYAN COMMUNITIES

Copyright © 2010 by Abingdon Press

This book is printed on acid-free paper.

Library of Congress Cataloging-in-Publication Data

ISBN 978-1-4267-1136-7

US Cataloging-in-Publication data has been requested.

All scripture quotations unless noted otherwise are taken from the *New Revised Standard Version of the Bible*, copyright 1989, Division of Christian Education of the National Council of the Churches of Christ in the United States of America. Used by permission. All rights reserved.

Scripture quotations noted AV are taken from the King James or Authorized Version of the Bible.

The argument of the work as a whole was laid out in a preliminary fashion in "John Wesley and the Legacy of Methodist Theology," *Bulletin of the John Rylands University Library of Manchester* 85, no. 2–3: 405–20.

A version of chapter 1 was originally published as "The Shape of Wesleyan Thought: The Question of John Wesley's 'Essential' Christian Doctrines," *Asbury Theological Journal* 59, nos. 1–2 (Spring and Fall 2004): 27–48.

A portion of chapter 1 was previously published in "Conversion and Baptism in Wesleyan Spirituality," in Kenneth J. Collins and John H. Tyson, eds., *Conversion in the Wesleyan Tradition* (Nashville: Abingdon Press, 2001), 160–74. Used by permission.

A version of chapter 3 was previously published as "Charles Wesley, *Theologos*," Kenneth G. C. Newport and Ted A. Campbell, eds., *Charles Wesley: Life, Literature, and Legacy* (Peterborough: Epworth Press, 2007), 264–77.

A version of chapter 4 was originally published as " 'Pure, Unbounded Love': Doctrine about God in Historic Wesleyan Communities," M. Douglas Meeks, ed., *Trinity, Community and Power: Mapping Trajectories in Wesleyan Theology* (Nashville: Kingswood Books, 2000), 85–109. Used by permission.

A version of chapter 5 was previously published as "The 'Way of Salvation' and the Methodist Ethos beyond John Wesley: A Study in Formal Consensus and Popular Reception," *Asbury Theological Journal* 63, no. 1 (Spring 2008): 5–31.

A version of chapter 6 was previously published as "Methodist Ecclesiologies and Methodist Sacred Spaces," S T Kimbrough Jr., ed., *Orthodox and Wesleyan Ecclesiology* (Crestwood, N.Y.: St. Vladimir's Theological Seminary Press, 2007), 215–25.

10 11 12 13 14 15 16 17 18 19—10 9 8 7 6 5 4 3 2 1
MANUFACTURED IN THE UNITED STATES OF AMERICA

to
Richard P. Heitzenrater

CONTENTS

PREFACE

This book examines formal and popular expressions of core beliefs consistently affirmed by churches and other communities that identify themselves as Wesleyan or Methodist. It involves not only a study of the theology of John Wesley and the hymns of his brother Charles, not only a study of Methodist creeds and doctrinal statements, and not only a study of the beliefs of professional theologians who belonged to Methodist churches. This is a historical study of a persistent core of beliefs grounded in the work of John and Charles Wesley in the eighteenth century, confessed in the formal doctrinal statements of Wesleyan and Methodist churches, explicated and reflected on by Methodist theologians, and received and expressed in such commonly used sources as hymnals and catechisms, personal testimonies, and the architectures of Methodist worship spaces. This is an account of the beliefs of a cluster of Christian communities that have expanded and taken on new forms as they have developed over the last two hundred years, and which yet continue to profess certain consistent teachings as communities.

How can one describe historically and critically the core beliefs of Wesleyan communities? In the account that follows I offer some particular approaches to this question. These methodological approaches are described in more detail in the introduction, but are noted briefly here.

- This study describes the content of Wesleyan beliefs with reference not only to critical leaders and thinkers such as John and Charles Wesley and subsequent theologians but also with reference to key ideas and practices reflected in corporately affirmed denominational publications such as hymnals, catechisms, and works of systematic theology approved for the formation of preachers and in more popular expressions of a religious community such as personal testimonies and church architectures.

- This study seeks ways by which we can discern "core" critical doctrines, doctrines that have been described as "essential" (John Wesley's term) as well as distinctive teachings of the Wesleyan movement and of Wesleyan or Methodist churches.
- This study seeks to discern which beliefs have been expressed most consistently through the centuries in which Wesleyan communities have evolved through a range of Wesleyan literatures, music, and other expressions of faith.
- This study seeks to discern which teachings were understood to be common Christian teachings and which beliefs were understood to be distinctive contributions of Wesleyan or Methodist communities.

This work is intended primarily for a scholarly readership, especially for scholars in the fields of Wesleyan and Methodist studies, but it should be clear from the outset that I write from the perspective of a committed and active participant in the life of Wesleyan communities. I am an ordained elder (a minister of Word and sacrament) of the Texas Annual Conference of The United Methodist Church. I am aware of some of the dangers of "insider" descriptions of religious movements and institutions and I am also aware of some of the depths of understanding of Methodism that have been afforded by interpreters who do not identify themselves with Methodism, for example, Maximin Piette's study of *John Wesley in the Evolution of Protestantism* (1937), or Bernard Semmel's research on Methodism in relation to the social conditions of eighteenth-century Britain (1973).[1] I maintain that there is a certain giftedness in the perspective of those who view a religious community from a viewpoint outside of that community, and there is a different kind of giftedness for those who reflect on a religious community from the perspective of participants for whom the understanding of the community is a matter of deep urgency directly related to their own sense of religious vocation. Those of us who operate from a perspective from within the religious communities we study can gain considerable insight from those who have viewed our community from other perspectives.

I write, then, as a participant in the life of a contemporary Wesleyan community and I am keenly aware that participants face the danger of allowing their own perspectives and commitments to distort historical understanding. For this reason it has been written that "denominational histories, for the most part, do not belong to historical literature, but should be classed as apologetics, or possibly polemics."[2] This was written not by an outsider but by Episcopal historian Henry C. Vedder of Crozer Theological Seminary, reviewing in 1900 a book by Methodist church historian James Buckley. But Vedder went on to commend Buckley's historical honesty in dealing with difficult issues in Methodist history. I hope this work will display a similar honesty. I hope that this study may serve as a supplement or as an alternative to works currently used for reflection on the beliefs of Wesleyan communities, including studies of the theology of John Wesley and works that deal with formal Methodist doctrinal standards. It offers perspectives on the beliefs of Wesleyan communities grounded in a wider range of sources than these.

I want to offer thanks to many persons and institutions who have supported me in this work. I am grateful, first, to the academic institutions that have supported me, especially Perkins School of Theology, Southern Methodist University. The collections and the staff of Bridwell Library at Perkins have proved to be enormously helpful resources in this project. Earlier work on this project was carried out at Garrett-Evangelical Theological Seminary through December 2005 and at Claremont School of Theology in the spring of 2006. The Robert Guy McCutchan Collection of Hymnology at the Libraries of the Claremont Colleges proved to be an especially helpful resource for this research. I also acknowledge with deep gratitude a grant from the Summer Wesley Seminar at Duke Divinity School that gave me the opportunity to spend the month of June 2007 working in the libraries of the Divinity School and the University and conferring with other scholars in Wesleyan and Methodist studies concerning this project. I want to express special thanks to a number of individuals who have helped by reading drafts or discussing critical aspects of this project with me: Randy Maddox (Duke Divinity School), Richard P. Heitzenrater (Duke Divinity School), Rex D. Matthews (Candler School of Theology, Emory University, and editor of Kingswood Books), William B. Lawrence (Perkins School of Theology, SMU), Kevin Watson (Graduate Program in Religious Studies, SMU), and Phoebe Hambright Dishman (Beaumont, Texas).

Some of the chapters in the present work were developed as lectures and have been published as articles in journals or in collected works, as follows.

> The argument of the work as a whole was laid out in a preliminary fashion in a paper, "John Wesley and the Legacy of Methodist Theology," given for a conference at Manchester University in 2003 celebrating the tercentenary of John Wesley's birth. This paper was subsequently published in the *Bulletin of the John Rylands University Library of Manchester*.[3]

> An early version of chapter 1 was originally given as a lecture, "The Shape of Wesleyan Thought: The Question of John Wesley's 'Essential' Christian Doctrines," at a conference celebrating the tercentenary of John Wesley's birth held at Asbury Theological Seminary in October 2003. This was subsequently published in the *Asbury Theological Journal*.[4]

> A portion of chapter 1 that deals with John Wesley's views of baptism was included in an article, "Conversion and Baptism in Wesleyan Spirituality," in Kenneth J. Collins and John H. Tyson, eds., *Conversion in the Wesleyan Tradition*.[5]

> Chapter 3 is based on an article, "Charles Wesley, *Theologos*," published in a volume I co-edited with Kenneth G. C. Newport titled *Charles Wesley: Life, Literature and Legacy*.[6]

Chapter 4 is based on a plenary lecture given at the 1997 Oxford Institute of Methodist Theological Studies, subsequently published as "'Pure, Unbounded Love': Doctrine about God in Historic Wesleyan Communities" published in the collected papers of that Institute, *Trinity, Community and Power*.[7]

Chapter 5 is based on an article, "The 'Way of Salvation' and the Methodist Ethos beyond John Wesley: A Study in Formal Consensus and Popular Reception," published in the *Asbury Theological Journal*.[8]

Chapter 6 is based on a paper, "Methodist Ecclesiologies and Methodist Sacred Spaces," given at a consultation on Orthodox and Wesleyan Spiritualities held at St. Vladimir's Theological Seminary, Crestwood, New York, in January 2006 and subsequently published in the collected papers of that consultation, *Orthodox and Wesleyan Ecclesiology*.[9]

In referring to Wesleyan texts, I have tried consistently to give (a) a reference to the name of the text and an internal division that readers can find apart from volume and page numbers in a printed edition (for example, "John Wesley, sermon on 'Salvation by Faith,' I:2" or "John Wesley, *Journal* for 24 May 1738"), then (b) volume and page numbers in printed editions, with a preference for the most recent critical edition. However, I have also retained many references to loci in other editions that may enable readers to find the material in differing editions of the Wesley works.

The book is dedicated to my *Doktorvater* and mentor, Richard P. Heitzenrater. For decades now Dr. Heitzenrater has held the reputation of being the leading historical interpreter of the Wesleyan movement based on his meticulously careful scholarship and his dedicated oversight of the Wesley Works Editorial Project. He is known in other circles as an avid runner, a woodworker, a printmaker, a builder of mountain homes, and a sports car mechanic. I have come to know him as a friend and a Methodist believer who struggles personally with the contemporary meaning of Wesleyan faith and sings in the choir on Sunday mornings.

INTRODUCTION

THE CONTEMPORARY QUEST FOR THE HEART OF THE METHODIST MESSAGE

We find ourselves at a critical juncture in the historical study of Wesleyan and Methodist communities. Contemporary historians outside of Wesleyan communities have begun to recognize the prominent cultural influence of Methodism in the United States as well as Methodism's broader influence on Evangelical Christian movements throughout the world. Beginning with Nathan Hatch's *The Democratization of American Christianity* (1989), a series of historical studies has explored the cultural impact of the Methodist movement in the nineteenth century and beyond.[1] John H. Wigger's *Taking Heaven by Storm: Methodism and the Rise of Popular Christianity in America* (1998), Ann Taves' *Fits, Trances, and Visions: Experiencing Religion and Explaining Experience from Wesley to James* (1999), and David Hempton's *Methodism: Empire of the Spirit* (2005, among other studies) all depict Methodism as a vigorous popular spiritual movement that has had a decisive effect not only on North American religious culture (Wigger) but also on the global culture of Evangelical Christianity (Hempton).[2]

These newer historical studies provide a sharp contrast to conventional studies of Methodist history written from the perspective of denominational historians who were participants in Methodist churches. Works by denominational historians have tended to move from John Wesley in the eighteenth century to the

1

ecclesiastical growth of Methodism in the nineteenth century and beyond with relatively little attention paid to the broader popular culture that Methodism shaped and by which it was shaped.[3] Wigger, Taves, and Hempton, by contrast, begin with the work of the Wesleys and then move to popular spiritualities in the nineteenth century and beyond without the focus on Methodist churches and their institutional structures that characterized conventional Methodist histories. These narratives offer a depth of understanding of the experiences of ordinary Methodist people that had not been offered in conventional accounts, although they can give readers the impression that once the Methodist movement grew beyond John Wesley or the first generation of Methodist leaders, its popular spirituality had little connection to the more formal structures or stated doctrinal commitments of Methodist churches.[4]

David Hempton, to take one example, has a chapter, "The Medium and the Message," which offers "an attempt to get to the heart and center of the Methodist *message* and how it was *heard* and *experienced* in the eighteenth and nineteenth centuries."[5] The chapter itself proceeds by summarizing some aspects of John Wesley's theology, then moves to popular spirituality expressed in personal narratives, hymns, and sermons, mentioning the development of more formal systematic theologies at the end of the chapter.[6] Hempton describes "the heart and center of the Methodist *message*" in this chapter by identifying three consistent foci of Methodist spirituality: "conversion, sanctification, and holy dying."[7] Hempton comes close to the mark in this description, at least of some of the most distinctive marks of the Methodist movement. "Holy dying" was indeed an important aspect of Methodist spirituality, an expression of sanctification *in articulo mortis*. Methodists' own accounts of their central message, the message of the "way of salvation," tended to express the elements of this spiritual journey as involving "conviction, conversion, and [entire] sanctification," as a traveling preacher explained the Methodist message to Jarena Lee in an account considered in chapter 5 below.[8] "Conviction" (conviction of sin), the experience of a spiritual awakening prior to conversion, was also a critical moment in Methodist spiritual autobiographies. Hempton's account does move us toward perceiving the spiritual experience of Methodist

2

people, although it does not consistently recognize that many elements of this popular spirituality were consistently expressed in formal denominational literature.

In contrast to the work of Hempton, Thomas Langford's *Practical Divinity: Theology in the Wesleyan Tradition,* originally published in 1983, offered a very different perspective on Methodist beliefs by way of a study of the work of Methodist theologians.[9] In writing *Theology in the Wesleyan Tradition* Langford had delimited his subject matter to the work of theologians who were members of Methodist churches and this led him to very general conclusions about consistent theological themes or at least consistent issues or questions raised by Methodist theologians, general themes that are not at all as distinctive as the vivid Methodist experiences described by Hempton or Wigger or Taves.[10] Placing Langford's account of sophisticated Methodist theologians alongside Hempton's account of "the heart and center of the Methodist message" or Wigger's account of Methodists' "boiling hot religion" or Ann Taves's account of "shouting Methodists," one might feel they are describing vastly different universes.[11] One would perceive a chasm between accounts of popular Methodist spirituality and the formal teachings of Wesley and later Methodist theologians.[12]

I will argue, however, that this chasm is more a construction created by the ways in which contemporary historians and interpreters have delimited their subjects rather than a chasm in the actual experience of Methodist constituents. Popular spirituality consistently interacted with the formal teachings and practices of Methodist communities. Consider, for example, an American Methodist laywoman in 1855.[13] She would have sung hymns laid out in a pattern illustrating the "way of salvation" in the *Hymns for the Use of the Methodist Episcopal Church* (1848). She would have attended quarterly meetings or camp meetings where the preaching followed the sequence of the "way of salvation," keeping "a strict account" of how many souls were awakened, converted, and sanctified during these meetings. Her family might own a copy of one of the 1852 Methodist Episcopal catechisms detailing the "way of salvation" in questions and answers that could be posed to children and young people. The circuit-riding preachers she heard would have studied the "way of salvation" expressed in John Wesley's sermons and explicated in Richard Watson's *Theological*

Institutes (1823) or Thomas N. Ralston's *Elements of Divinity* (1847), textbooks that were required for study by preachers. She would have heard fellow Methodist people narrating their personal testimonies utilizing terminology learned through all of these sources.[14] If she abided with Methodists very long—and she would have been required to abide with them for between three and six months of probationary membership in a local society—she would have been well familiar with the "way of salvation" as Methodists understood it through a variety of sources, both formal ones as well as popular sources.

In attempting to illuminate a core of Wesleyan beliefs, then, this study will examine the range of sources suggested in the previous illustration. It will consider the writings of John and Charles Wesley and in doing so it will draw on a corpus of studies in the theology and spirituality of the Wesleys that has flourished since the 1970s. This study will also consider the formal doctrinal statements of Methodist and other Wesleyan churches, such as the Articles of Religion that John Wesley redacted from the Thirty-Nine Articles of the Church of England and sent to the American Methodists in 1784, Articles that are formally affirmed as doctrine today in the African Methodist Episcopal Church, the African Methodist Episcopal Zion Church, the Christian Methodist Episcopal Church, The United Methodist Church, and other denominations derived from the American episcopal pattern of Methodist churches. This study will also consider the teachings of Wesleyan and Methodist theologians, with an emphasis on those theologians whose works were prescribed for study by Methodist churches and thus were given some degree of corporate affirmation. In addition to these, it will consider contemporary Methodist theologians who have reflected on the contemporary meaning of Wesleyan beliefs.[15]

Beyond these sources, the chapters that follow will also make use of some crucial texts that have not been as well studied in scholarly communities but which do reveal and elucidate a core of Wesleyan beliefs, specifically, Methodist hymnals, catechisms, liturgies, and other official or quasi-official church documents such as tracts authorized by denominations. Randy L. Maddox has consistently argued for the nature of Wesleyan thought as "practical divinity" that should privilege such first-order theological activities as the singing of hymns, participation in liturgies, and forming children and young people by the use of catechisms.[16] The structures of Methodist hymnals, for example, consistently reveal a core of teachings involving the praise of the divine Trinity at the beginning of hymnals and then the "way of salvation," often under the category of hymns on "The Sinner" and "The Christian life." Methodist catechisms likewise reveal what beliefs Methodist churches chose to hand on to their children. But the content of Methodist hymnals, catechisms, liturgies, and other didactic materials has seldom been brought into dialogue with the teachings of Methodist theologians, the works of the Wesleys, and the formal doctrinal statements of Methodist churches. Nor has this theological and spiritual content been brought into a sustained dialogue with accounts of the religious experiences of Methodist people, the kinds of experiences on which David Hempton, Ann Taves, and John Wigger have focused. The study of hymnals, catechisms, liturgies, and other denominational literature will thus complement the study of more formal theological and doctrinal literature, on the one hand, and accounts of personal spirituality, on the other.

In this study, then, I hope to offer an alternative to contemporary accounts of the characteristic beliefs of Wesleyan communities and churches or at least a corrective to those accounts. To date, scholarly works utilized for the formation of Methodist clergy and other leaders have taken either the form of studies of John Wesley's theology or studies of the formal doctrinal standards of Methodist churches. In the former category, there has been a succession of books since the publication of Colin W. Williams's *John Wesley's Theology Today* (1960).[17] This volume focused on John Wesley's thought in dialogue with contemporary ecumenical issues in Williams's age and served for almost twenty years as the standard treatment of Wesleyan theology. It was followed by Albert C. Outler's brief study *Theology in the Wesleyan Spirit* (1975) that also focused on contemporary ecumenical issues, although Outler brought a much wider range of knowledge of Catholic, Eastern Christian, and Anglican sources in dialogue with John Wesley's thought.[18] These studies were followed in turn by Randy Maddox's *Responsible Grace* (1994), Theodore Runyon's *The New Creation: John Wesley's Theology Today* (1998), and Kenneth J. Collins's *The Theology of John Wesley: Holy Love and the Shape of Grace* (2007).[19] In the category of works explicating Methodist doctrinal standards are two contemporary publications: Scott J. Jones's *United Methodist Doctrine: The Extreme Center* (2002),[20] which focuses on the range of formally authorized doctrinal standards of The United Methodist Church, and my own study *Methodist Doctrine: The Essentials* (1999), which considers formally defined doctrine held in common between the African Methodist Episcopal Church, the African Methodist Episcopal Zion Church, the Christian Methodist Episcopal Church, and The United Methodist Church.[21] This study of Wesleyan beliefs will offer an additional perspective, considering the beliefs enunciated by the Wesleys, beliefs formally endorsed in Methodist doctrinal statements, beliefs expressed in Methodist systematic theologies, and beliefs expressed in more popular forms such as hymnals, catechisms, liturgical practices, personal testimonies, and even church architectures.

THE WESLEYAN MOVEMENT, RELIGIOUS TOLERATION, AND THE DEFINITION OF CORE BELIEFS

The Wesleyan movement was born in a particular era that left its mark on Wesleyan and Methodist communities as they engaged in the cultural enterprise of defining and handing on religious beliefs. Methodism was born in an era whose culture had begun to value religious toleration and which saw the dogmatic conflicts of the past century as destructive of Christian faith. Historians today are inclined to interpret the Thirty Years' War on the European continent (1618–48) and the English Revolution (1640–60) as conflicts between an older agrarian and feudal economy with the flourishing mercantile economy of Northern Europe.[22] This economic interpretation does not mollify the fact that these wars were also inter-Christian conflicts waged by political states and their state-supported churches over which forms of Christian faith would prevail within them. During these periods of inter-Christian carnage, Protestant as well as Catholic theologians had labored to define sharply the boundaries between their own professed beliefs and practices and those of opposing churches, producing a voluminous apologetic and polemical literature that includes the Protestant scholasticism of the seventeenth century. This period of extended theological as well as political conflict led to what has been called the *Verkonfessionalisierung* or hardening of confessional boundaries between European state churches.[23] Although Anglican theologians did not take up the genre of systematic theologies, they defended their own church establishment in this era by the elaboration of a patristic argument that the Church of England had replicated the teachings and practices of the primitive, pre-Constantinian church more authentically than other churches.[24] By the end of the seventeenth century, however, Europe in general and Britain in particular had entered a new era marked by the Act of Toleration of 1689 and John Locke's *Letter concerning Toleration* published in the same year.

Toleration did not mean jettisoning all traditional beliefs, but it did imply a restriction of the scope of doctrinal claims, especially the scope of claims that had been considered essential or necessary for defining state churches in the period of the religious wars. It implied that a religious community might define a relatively small nucleus or core of essential commitments, leaving other matters undefined and thus at the discretion of local communities or of individual believers. John Wesley advocated such a view of religious teachings in his sermon "Catholic Spirit" (1749). Christians could and should allow for differences in personal "opinions" and communally established "modes of worship," he argued, but, on the other hand, "A man of a truly catholic spirit, has not now his religion to seek. He is fixed as the sun in his judgment concerning the main branches of Christian doctrine."[25] Chapter 1 will explore in detail what John Wesley considered to be "the main branches of Christian doctrine," but the concept of defining a few essential teachings is noted at this point because it opens up the possibility of discerning a relatively small core or nucleus of beliefs or teachings transmitted in a religious community as its most central beliefs.

DISCERNING A CORE OF BELIEFS OF WESLEYAN COMMUNITIES

This book offers a critical account of a core of beliefs professed by and received in Christian communities that identify themselves as Wesleyan or Methodist. The Latin word *cor* means "the heart," and core beliefs are the beliefs that lie at the heart of a person or a community, the beliefs that express what an individual or a community fundamentally stands for. The term "beliefs" is used here to denote teachings that reflect formal consensus in a religious community (doctrine) and which have also been "received" and practiced in the popular life of these Christian communities.[26]

The present study takes the term "Wesleyan communities" to include churches that identify themselves as Wesleyan or Methodist, even if the terms "Wesleyan" or "Methodist" do not appear in the names of their denominations, and it also includes the Wesleyan movement between 1739 and 1784 when it existed not as a church or denomination but as a religious movement within the context of British Christianity and, in particular, the Church of England. In fact, we may need to speak of Wesleyan "movements" in the wake of the scholarly insight of Gareth Lloyd demonstrating the depth of the rift between Charles and John Wesley that became apparent around 1755–56 and resulted in the coalescence around Charles Wesley of a distinct "Church Methodist" party or movement.[27] Wesleyan communities share a common heritage in the Wesleyan movements of the eighteenth century. Distinctive Christian communities have grown from the Wesleyan movement associated with John Wesley, in particular, and these communities have handed on a pattern of core beliefs to contemporary Wesleyan churches. Wesleyan communities today include the denominations that make up the World Methodist Council and a few other groups that claim a connection to the Wesleyan movement.

The terms "Wesleyan" and "Methodist" connect participants in these communities to the eighteenth-century origins of the Methodist movement under the leadership of John and Charles Wesley. The use of the words *Methodist* or *Wesleyan* in the name of a denomination implicitly links that denomination to the narrative of the Wesleyan revival. The disciplines or constitutional manuals of many Methodist denominations begin with a historical statement explicitly linking themselves to the narrative of the Wesleyan revival,[28] and Methodist catechisms have typically included questions and answers forming the identity of children in the narrative of the Wesleyan revival and the content of Wesleyan beliefs.

This study of Wesleyan beliefs pays sustained attention to the fact that Wesleyan communities claim to be Christian communities. Wesleyan communities have been concerned with the central meaning of the Christian faith as well as the distinctive teachings and the distinctive mission of the Wesleyan movement. Much of the critical or scholarly literature on Methodism and Wesleyan theology has focused on what is distinctive about the Wesleyan movement such as the beliefs identified by David Hempton as expressing the heart of the Methodist message. But, as we shall see, it is characteristically Wesleyan to insist that the first identity of Wesleyans or Methodists is their identity as Christians, and therefore a critical study of core beliefs of Wesleyan communities must account for both the common Christian faith espoused by the Wesleys and by Wesleyan communities as well as the distinctive claims made by them.

A case will be made that there has been a distinctively Wesleyan way of thinking about what it means to be Christian, specifically, an "adiaphorist" approach that defines a relatively small but strong set of essential Christian beliefs and practices and leaves other matters (*adiaphora*) to the discretion of local communities or of individuals.[29] This adiaphorist approach to Christian faith and life is the ground of often-repeated claims of Methodist liberality in doctrine. As indicated above, this grew out of the mood of religious toleration following the period of European religious wars in the seventeenth century, and Wesley's sermon "Catholic Spirit" is a critical source for this adiaphorist approach to understanding what it means to be Christian. To discern the core teachings of Wesleyan communities, then, requires attention to the ways in which these communities define their identities as Christian communities.

Religious communities and other cultural communities often identify themselves with respect to their practices, their beliefs, and the distinctive narratives by which they tell their own stories. The present study focuses on the beliefs of Wesleyan communities. I hope in the future to offer similar studies that will examine the practices of Wesleyan communities and the narratives of Wesleyan communities, that is, the ways in which Wesleyan communities have defined themselves by way of historical narratives.

DISCERNING COMMUNAL BELIEFS:
FORMAL AND POPULAR SOURCES

The method employed in this study examines correlations between formal consensus about teachings on the part of Wesleyan communities and the popular reception and expression of those teachings. It does examine doctrine as formal, communal consensus on what to teach, but it also examines the critical role of what participants in the ecumenical movement have called the "reception" of teachings on the part of the whole people of God. This marks a departure from the way in which others and I have studied doctrine in the past, where we focused primarily on formal, authoritatively stated communal consensus.[30] As noted above, this book does not focus on practices except for teachings related to baptism and the Lord's Supper and points at which worship practices, for example, reflect other teachings. In addition to correlations between formal teachings (doctrine) and popular reception, this study also requires an examination of correlations between Wesleyan communities, which have developed a variety of ways of approaching doctrine and a variety of modes of reception in popular church cultures.

Formal Consensus about Core Beliefs

The terms "formal consensus" or "doctrine" denote the teachings of a community in whatever ways communities come to consensus about what to teach and practice, as contrasted with the opinions of particular individuals. There are five principal sources of formal consensus on the part of Wesleyan communities used in this study.

In the first place, this study examines the writings of John and Charles Wesley as sources of the beliefs of Wesleyan communities. They are sources of doctrine in the most formal sense because the "Model Deed" incorporated into the "Large Minutes" and subsequently into the constitution of the British Methodist Church and churches that follow its constitutional pattern held certain of Wesley's *Sermons on Several Occasions* and his *Explanatory Notes upon the New Testament* to be standards of Methodist teaching or doctrine.[31] Although American Methodist churches did not make explicit reference to the Wesleyan writings after 1784, the Wesleyan writings were referred to as doctrinal standards in the *Plan of Union* (1967) adopted by The United Methodist Church in 1968 and in the first *Discipline* of that denomination (1968).[32] From 1972, following the adoption of a new theological statement and an extensive revision of the preface to the doctrinal statements, the Wesleyan writings were not explicitly named among doctrinal standards in United Methodist *Disciplines*. There was a controversy over the disciplinary status of the Wesleyan standards in the 1980s, and since 1988 they have again been referred to among doctrinal standards in United Methodist *Disciplines*, but the constitutional status of the Wesleyan writings remains a topic of contention in The United Methodist Church.[33]

In a broader sense, the Wesleys' writings provide a ground for Methodist beliefs as they were instrumental in forming Methodism as a popular religious movement and subsequently have been a consistent source of Methodist theological reflection and spirituality. In this sense the Wesleyan writings are not limited to the constitutionally defined "doctrinal standards" of Wesleyan or Methodist churches. *The Book of Discipline of The United Methodist Church* notes that although Wesley's *Sermons and Notes* were not explicitly named in early American Methodist doctrinal statements, they nevertheless "continued to function as the traditional standard exposition of distinctive Methodist teaching."[34] I question the extent to which the *Explanatory Notes upon the New Testament* actually functioned as standards or guidelines for doctrine because they were eclipsed in popular Methodist use by Adam Clarke's *Commentary* from the early nineteenth century, but it is true that John Wesley's *Standard Sermons* continued to be studied and utilized in British and American Methodist communities and their missions throughout the world through the nineteenth century.[35] The United Methodist *Book of Discipline* has noted since 1988 that "the doctrinal emphases of these statements [the Wesleyan writings] were carried forward by the weight of tradition rather than the force of law. They became part of the heritage of American Methodism to the degree that they remained useful to continuing generations."[36] The use of the Wesleyan writings as sources of doctrine is not without problems (constitutional and theological problems) for Methodists, and requires some judgment as to which writings really constitute consistent sources of corporate consensus.

In the second place, this study uses formal doctrinal statements of Wesleyan and Methodist churches. This includes Articles of Religion (Methodist Episcopal Church and its successors), Confessions of Faith (United Brethren and successors), Articles of Faith (Church of the Nazarene), and some other doctrinal statements. Doctrinal standards are not uniformly utilized throughout Wesleyan churches, and formal statements of faith are most characteristic of North American Methodist churches and other Methodist churches that follow their constitutional (disciplinary) pattern. The British Conference and its successors have not adopted particular statements of faith but state in general terms in their constitutions their allegiance to historic Christian faith and Wesleyan teachings.[37]

In the third place, this study examines Methodist hymnals and liturgies as an indication of doctrinal consensus as well as an indication of the reception and expression of beliefs. Although hymns may be the compositions of individuals, their acceptance into a hymnal shows some degree of communal approval, and I have found that the creedal structure of Wesleyan hymnals—the way in which the hymns are organized giving an outline of beliefs— reveals consistent points of doctrinal consensus. As an example, the structure of Methodist hymnals typically begins with the praise of the Trinity before giving hymns celebrating the attributes of God. A consideration of Wesleyan beliefs about God in chapter 4 will follow this pattern. Moreover, the hymns celebrating the Trinity reflect common (ecumenically affirmed) Christian teachings, and it is appropriate that they appear in the first position, before hymns celebrating the more distinctly Wesleyan teachings on the "way of salvation." Chapter 5 will discuss hymns on the "way of salvation" and their typical arrangement in Methodist hymnals.

In the fourth place, the present study draws upon Methodist catechisms as indications of corporate teachings. There is a long and complex history of Methodist catechisms, down to the 1988 catechism sponsored by the British Conference. I note, however, that The United Methodist Church and its predecessors have not actively produced catechisms since the 1930s. Catechisms reveal in a particularly clear way what teachings and practices are considered important enough to transmit to children and other candidates for church membership, so they serve as important indicators of the core teachings of communities.

Finally, in the fifth place, this study uses the writings of Wesleyan and Methodist theologians whose works have been approved for study by preachers, and so have a degree of communal approval. In particular I shall have reference to Methodist theologians Richard Watson, Thomas O. Summers, William Burt Pope, Miner Raymond, John Miley, and the Nazarene theologian H. Orton Wiley. This category is problematic because one can question whether the simple inclusion of a book in a prescribed course of study implies approval of the book's content as a whole. In the twentieth century, it is particularly difficult to assess whether the inclusion of a work by such a theologian as Alfred Knudson implies broad communal consensus or simply indicates that the book is taken as a good example of modern theological method. This study also refers to the works of other Methodist theologians, even if their works have not been formally prescribed, as indicators of ways in which formal doctrines were being received in contemporary theological reflection.

Popular Reception and Expression of Beliefs

"Reception" goes beyond formal consensus and it means that even when teachings are formally affirmed through a community's own processes, they may not be "received" by communities themselves. That is, formally affirmed teachings might not actually be taught, and formally approved practices might not be actually effected in communities.[38] There are many cases in which teachings and practices have been formally affirmed but failed to be received in churches. Perhaps most notable as a classic instance of the lack of reception was the union between Eastern and Western churches supposedly put in place by the Council of Florence. This union insisted on the use of the *filioque* clause in the Nicene Creed, but this teaching and practice was not received and practiced in most of the Eastern churches. Hence it lacks in these churches the status of authoritative teaching and practice, despite the fact that Eastern church delegates (bishops) at Florence formally approved these measures.

It can be debated whether Methodist churches (including The United Methodist Church) formally acknowledge any role of reception in their own processes of doctrinal authority. But, taking my cue from the importance of reception in ecumenical life and the study of popular religious life more broadly, I argue that studying formal consensus and popular reception together offers a fruitful historical and descriptive methodology for getting at the core beliefs of Wesleyan communities. What I have sought in this study of core beliefs of Wesleyan communities, then, is to find correlations between formal consensus, on the one hand, and popular spirituality signaling reception of formal teachings and authorized practices, on the other hand. I have taken personal testimonies as an indication of the reception of teachings about the "way of salvation" in chapter 5, and I have taken church architectures as indicators of the popular reception of ecclesiologies in chapter 6. Correlations between formal doctrine and the popular reception and expression of doctrine yields a strong sense of the Christian and Wesleyan beliefs of Wesleyan communities.

OUTLINE OF CONTENTS

The following chapters, then, set out to examine formal and popular expressions of core beliefs of Wesleyan communities. Chapters 1 through 3 examine the spiritual and theological roots of Wesleyan communities in the teachings of John and Charles Wesley, especially in their understandings of the meaning of Christian faith and then their understandings of their own most distinctive teachings. Chapter 1 reflects on the question of John Wesley's understanding of common Christian doctrines, that is, doctrines that he believed to have been held almost universally in Christian communities. I focus in this chapter on identifying his "fundamental" or "essential" Christian doctrines, developing a methodology by which ten common Christian doctrines can be discerned. Chapter 2 reflects on the question of John Wesley's understanding of the distinctive teachings of the Methodist movement, finding this distinctive teaching consistently in Wesley's understanding of experiential religion and the "way of salvation." Chapter 3 examines Charles Wesley's role as one who handed on common Christian teachings as well as the distinctly Wesleyan spirituality of the "way of salvation" to Wesleyan communities by way of his hymn corpus.

Chapters 4 through 6 examine Methodist teachings as they are reflected in formal doctrinal consensus and in popular reception in Wesleyan communities after the time of the Wesleys. These chapters offer three "core samples" exploring in depth some particular beliefs. Chapter 4 examines the common Christian teaching about the divine Trinity with which Methodist hymnals traditionally begin. Chapter 5 examines the more distinctly Wesleyan teaching about the "way of salvation," showing how popular spiritual autobiographies, as well as more formal doctrinal statements on the part of Wesleyan and Methodist churches, reflect this teaching. Chapter 6 examines the tensions inherent in Methodist ecclesiologies, that is, the tension between identifying the Wesleyan movement as a "church" or as a religious movement, and it considers the ways in which local church architectures reflect these varying understandings of "church" on the part of Methodists.

Chapter 7 is my attempt to state fourteen consistent core teachings of Wesleyan communities in a more contemporary and ecumenical way. These include both common Christian teachings and some distinctive teachings of Wesleyan communities. The conclusion of the book reflects on the relevance of Wesleyan beliefs to the understanding and transmission of a "Wesleyan tradition" today.

CHAPTER 1

JOHN WESLEY AND COMMON CHRISTIAN BELIEFS

INTRODUCTION

Wesleyan communities today evolved from the Wesleyan movement led by John and Charles Wesley, who considered Methodism to be preeminently an expression of Christian faith. As John Wesley stated it in his sermon "On Laying the Foundation of the New Chapel, Near the City-Road, London" (1777): "Methodism, so-called, is the old religion, the religion of the Bible, the religion of the primitive Church, the religion of the Church of England."[1] John Wesley's immediate successors thought of his work as being preeminently a work of revival of Christian faith, thus the inscription on his tomb which claims that God had "raised up" John Wesley "To Revive, Enforce and Defend [t]he Pure Apostolical Doctrines and Practices of the Primitive Church."[2]

This chapter initiates a study of Wesleyan beliefs by asking what John Wesley himself believed to be the most essential, commonly held beliefs of the Christian faith. The next chapter will consider John Wesley's claims about distinctive teachings of the Methodist movement under his leadership, and the third chapter will consider how Charles Wesley transmitted these common Christian beliefs as well as distinctively Methodist beliefs by way of poetry that formed the nucleus of a body of hymnody utilized by Wesleyan communities. Comprehensive studies of John Wesley's theology since the 1980s have focused on particular ideas or "axial themes" in John Wesley's thought that serve as keys to interpreting Wesley's contemporary theological relevance, for example, the notion of "responsible grace" (Maddox), the liberation and redemption of creation (Runyon), and the axial theme of "holy love" (Collins).[3] The account of the origins of Wesleyan theology in this and the next two chapters does not aim to be as comprehensive as these early studies but examines two key questions regarding the theologies of John and Charles Wesley. First, what did they hold to be the most basic or fundamental beliefs of common Christian faith? Second, what did they hold to be the most distinctive beliefs of the Wesleyan movements they led?

"A man of a truly catholic spirit," John Wesley wrote in 1749, "has not now his religion to seek. He is fixed as the sun in his judgment concerning the main branches of Christian doctrine."[4] But what were "the main branches of Christian doctrine," as John Wesley understood them? Because Wesley never gave out a definitive list of essential doctrines, or so it has been claimed, scholars have given a variety of answers to this question. This chapter responds to these questions about John Wesley's understanding of "essential" or "fundamental"[5] doctrines by offering some criteria by which we may discern Wesley's understanding of essential Christian doctrines. With these criteria clarified, the chapter proceeds to examine ten doctrines central to John Wesley's understanding of the Christian faith. The next chapter will identify some doctrines that, in his view, were the distinct characteristics of the Evangelical movement and of the Wesleyan branch of that movement.

When I first approached this subject, I entertained the hypothesis that John Wesley made a clean distinction between doctrines that he considered commonly Christian ("catholic") and doctrines that he considered distinctive of the Methodist movement, which I supposed to be synonymous with the Wesleyan movement. Historical evidence has led me to modify this earlier hypothesis in two ways. In the first place, it has shown that there was a complex relationship between the doctrines Wesley considered to be commonly Christian and the doctrines he considered to be the distinct emphases of the Methodist movement. In the case of three doctrines he held to be essential or common—original sin, justification, and regeneration—Wesley maintained that each of these was a common Christian teaching and yet each had a distinctive emphasis within the Methodist movement, especially as they supply a basis for the Methodist teaching about the "way of salvation" involving repentance, faith, and holiness.

18

Moreover, the evidence showed that most of the distinctive emphases of the Methodist movement in the eighteenth century were not limited to the Wesleyan branch or side of the Methodist movement. The teachings of repentance, faith, and even holiness in a broad sense were consistently proclaimed by such Calvinistic Evangelical preachers as George Whitefield as well as the Wesleys and the preachers associated with them, and the term "Methodist" was applied to the Calvinist Evangelical preachers as well as to the Wesleys.[6] The next chapter will examine in more detail some of these common emphases of the Evangelical revival but it will also show that the teaching of entire sanctification was a unique and distinguishing mark of the Wesleyan sphere of the revival movement.

Methodists have come to regard the writings of the Wesleys as a canon of classical literature, but this way of understanding their work does not acknowledge the extent to which the Wesleys functioned as intellectual leaders of a popular religious movement in the eighteenth century. The literature produced by the Wesleys appears today in scholarly editions with footnotes and other academic apparatus, but when it appeared in the eighteenth century it took the form of cheaply printed tracts, pamphlets, fascicles of John Wesley's *Journal* sold for a penny, copies of single sermons, and small collections of hymns. The process of authorization or "canonization" began with the Wesleys themselves, for example when John Wesley arranged a collection of Charles's verse into the *Collection of Hymns for the Use of the People Called Methodists* in 1780, or in John Wesley's "Model Deed" that specified that the doctrines preached in Wesleyan chapels should be those contained in the first four volumes of his own *Sermons on Several Occasions*. The canonical status of the literature, however, should not blind us to the fact that it originated as popular literature, and thus there has been a long interplay between popular and formal expressions of beliefs, with some works originally intended for popular readership eventually taking the form of authorized texts.

DISCERNING JOHN WESLEY'S "ESSENTIAL" DOCTRINES

John Wesley's distinction of "essential" or "fundamental" beliefs, as contrasted with "opinions" or "modes of worship" over which disagreements could be allowed, reflected an ongoing discussion about Christian doctrine inherited from the time of the Protestant Reformation. One of the suggestions advocated by such Catholic humanists as Desiderius Erasmus and by such Protestant Reformers as Philipp Melanchthon was to affirm a relatively short list of central or "fundamental" beliefs that Christians should agree on that would allow wide latitude over nonessential doctrines or opinions. The term *adiaphora* was used in sixteenth-century and seventeenth-century theological disputes to distinguish "nonessential" or "indifferent" teachings.[7] This notion was taken up late in the seventeenth century and early in the eighteenth century by Protestant Pietists, who maintained that Christian piety should be a principal ground of unity and that Christian unity did not rely on detailed agreement in doctrinal matters.[8]

It is widely recognized that John Wesley distinguished between "essential" or "fundamental" doctrines, on the one hand, and nonessential "opinions" and "modes of worship," on the other hand, most notably in his 1749 sermon "Catholic Spirit,"[9] but also in a wide range of writings through his career.[10] Nevertheless, the question of what precisely his "essential" doctrines were has continued to puzzle his interpreters. In this section I will try to clarify some criteria by which essential doctrines can be discerned. In doing so, both this chapter and the next chapter attempt to identify what I will call the "ecclesial scope" of essential or fundamental teachings, that is, whether John Wesley understood a particular doctrine to be constitutive of Christianity per se, constitutive of Protestantism (in some cases), constitutive of the Evangelical revival ("Methodism" in the broadest sense),[11] or constitutive of the distinct ethos and message of his own branch of the revival movement. The identification of ecclesial scope will show that Wesley identified specific teachings as being essential to Christian faith in general, he identified other doctrinal emphases that were essential to the more particular definition or identity of the Evangelical revival, and in at least one case he identified a doctrine critical to the definition of the Wesleyan movement within the scope of the Evangelical revival.

Affirmation of Essential Doctrines in
Occasional Comments

Colin W. Williams's *John Wesley's Theology Today* (1960) influenced generations of Wesleyan scholars and students. In this work Williams attempted to identify John Wesley's essential doctrines by collating passages where Wesley himself indicated that a particular teaching was an "essential" or "fundamental" element of Christian faith that could not be abandoned without abandoning the Christian faith itself. Using this method, Williams took the following six items[12] to be essential doctrines for John Wesley:

(1) original sin,[13]
(2) the deity of Christ,[14]
(3) the atonement,[15]
(4) justification by faith alone,[16]
(5) the work of the Holy Spirit,[17] and
(6) the doctrine of the Trinity.[18]

Williams's list and his criterion of identifying doctrines explicitly stated by John Wesley to be essential or fundamental offers a useful beginning point, although as it stands, it is a rather unorganized combination of doctrines. Item 5 is especially problematic: one can argue that it refers to the distinctive teaching of the Methodist movement that insisted on "perceptible inspiration,"[19] although my own reading of the passages that Williams cites at this point is that Wesley did not insist in these loci that any *doctrine* of the work of the Holy Spirit is necessary; rather, Wesley insisted that *the work of the Holy Spirit* is itself necessary to Christian existence. On my reading, Wesley was not making a claim about an essential doctrine in this case. Belief in the work of the Holy Spirit required no more definition of doctrine than was already present in the doctrine of the Trinity defined in the ancient creeds. Moreover, as the text following will show, Williams omitted at least two doctrines that John Wesley did claim as fundamental or essential, namely, the doctrines of biblical authority and the doctrine of regeneration. Further still, Williams did not include in this list some teachings that John Wesley identified as describing necessary Christian institutions, namely, teaching about the Christian church and the Christian sacraments of baptism and the Lord's

Supper, although Williams did devote attention to John Wesley's beliefs about these institutions elsewhere in the book.

In contrast to Williams's list of John Wesley's essential doctrines, a very different list appeared two years after the publication of Williams's work in Lawrence Meredith's 1962 Harvard dissertation, "Essential Doctrine in the Theology of John Wesley with Special Attention to the Methodist Standards of Doctrine."[20] Meredith's dissertation focused on three essential doctrines in John Wesley's thought, namely:

> repentance,
> faith, and
> holiness.

This triad is grounded in a passage in John Wesley's "Principles of a Methodist Farther Explained" in which Wesley asserted that "Our main doctrines, which include all the rest, are three,—that of repentance, of faith, and of holiness."[21] It is clear that Meredith had conceived of the project of "essential doctrine" in a different way than Williams, whose book he had seen before the completion of his own thesis.[22] Rather than identifying passages in which Wesley had denoted a doctrine to be "essential" or "fundamental" or otherwise constitutive, Meredith tried to find a logical consistency or coherence to Wesley's claims about characteristically Methodist teachings, thus the significance of Wesley's claim about "*our* main doctrines" (my emphasis) in the passage cited. Despite the focus on "essential doctrine" in his dissertation, then, what he sought was rather different from Colin Williams's quest for the ecumenically significant core or fundamental doctrines in John Wesley's work. Using my own terminology, what Meredith did was to restrict the ecclesial scope of the claims he examined to distinctive claims emphasized by the Methodist movement. This is helpful in its own way and Meredith's work will be particularly important in developing the next chapter, which deals with distinctly Methodist teachings.[23] In this chapter, however, I will focus more on the kinds of doctrinal claims that Williams investigated and in doing so I shall try to examine texts with attention paid to their contexts, especially as contexts reveal the ecclesial scope of John Wesley's doctrinal claims, that is, whether he claims specific doctrines as necessary for Christianity in general, for Protestant identity, or for the identity of the Methodist or Wesleyan movement.

I have already noted a problem with these lists of essential doctrines, and that is the fact that they omit a range of teachings about necessary or essential Christian institutions and practices—specifically, teachings about the church and the sacraments of baptism and the Lord's Supper—that Wesley elsewhere identified as necessary for Christian existence. That is to say, he identified the Christian church itself as necessary, since there can be no "solitary religion,"[24] and he identified the sacraments as indispensable means of grace. As we will see, this raises the issue of identifying teachings about some of these indispensable practices and about the Christian community alongside the definition of strictly essential or necessary doctrines in John Wesley's thought.

Doctrinal Affirmations in the "Letter to a Roman Catholic"

There are two documents in which John Wesley did in fact give something like a list of essential or constitutive Christian teachings, and these are his "Letter to a Roman Catholic" (1749) and his redaction of the Articles of Religion of the Church of England (1784). Keeping the question of ecclesial scope in mind, I now want to examine some of John Wesley's specific claims about essential Christian doctrines that appeared in his "Letter to a Roman Catholic." This was a published (open) letter that he wrote in 1749 around the same time when he wrote his sermon "Catholic Spirit." It appears that Wesley actually began a statement of essential doctrines within the sermon "Catholic Spirit," when he asked about the nature of Christian unity with reference to his Scripture text, "Is thine heart right, as my heart is with thy heart?"[25] After dismissing inappropriate notions of Christian unity such as the notion that Christian unity depends on unity in "opinions" or "modes of worship,"[26] Wesley proceeded to state positively what Christian unity should imply, and the first two paragraphs in this statement begin as follows:

> The first thing implied is this: Is thy heart right with God? Dost thou believe his being and his perfections? [H]is eternity, immensity, wisdom, power? [H]is justice, mercy, and truth? Dost thou believe that he now "upholdeth all things by the word of his power" and that he governs even the most minute, even the most

noxious, to his own glory, and the good of them that love him? [H]ast thou a divine evidence, a supernatural conviction, of the things of God? Dost thou "walk by faith not by sight," looking not at temporal things, but things eternal?

13. Dost thou believe in the Lord Jesus Christ, "God over all, blessed for ever?" Is he revealed in thy soul? Dost thou know Jesus Christ and him crucified? Does he dwell in thee, and thou in him? Is he formed in thy heart by faith? [H]aving absolutely disclaimed all thy own works, thy own righteousness, hast thou "submitted thyself unto the righteousness of God," which is by faith in Christ Jesus? Art thou "found in him, not having thy own righteousness, but the righteousness which is by faith?" And art thou, through him, "fighting the good fight of faith, and laying hold of eternal life?"[27]

From this point, however, the sermon focuses on signs of Christian unity in heartfelt faith and in appropriate Christian practice. But I note that the passage begins by naming the importance of faith in God the creator and faith in Christ as God, that is, it appears to begin a trinitarian formulation of Christian faith although it does not follow through with this scheme.

John Wesley did follow through with such a scheme in a critical, extended passage in his "Letter to a Roman Catholic," written in Dublin on 18 July 1749. In this open letter, Wesley urged his Catholic reader to avoid disputes about "opinions," which here have the same meaning as in the sermon "Catholic Spirit," namely, nonessential beliefs.[28]

John Wesley employed in this passage a rhetorical device known as meiosis. Meiosis involves an apparently restricted claim that is later revealed to imply a much larger claim. In this case, Wesley made a series of claims about the beliefs of "a true Protestant," beliefs about which he might claim some expertise in dialogue with his Catholic reader and in discussing which he could temporarily sidestep the issue of his authority for describing Catholic beliefs. The problem is that if what he meant in these passages was only true of a Protestant, then the ecclesial scope of the claims he made here would apply only to Protestantism. "A true Protestant may express his belief in these or the like words," he wrote, and then in five numbered paragraphs he paraphrased the substance of the

Apostles' and Nicene Creeds.[29] With this summary complete, though, Wesley revealed his use of meiosis by asking,

> Now, is there anything wrong in this? Is there any one point which you [the Catholic reader] do not believe as well as we?
>
> But you think we ought to believe more. We will not now enter into the dispute. Only let me ask, If a man sincerely believes thus much, and practices accordingly, can any one possibly persuade you to think that such a man shall perish everlastingly?[30]

That is to say, Wesley revealed that what appeared to be a restricted claim limited to assertions of Protestant beliefs was actually a set of claims about common Christian beliefs. Bracketed as it is in the text by reference to division over "opinions," what Wesley identified here was what he took to be the essence of Christian belief—Protestant and Catholic. Thus although the passage is literally cast as reflecting the beliefs of "a true Protestant," Wesley's use of meiosis tried to convince his Catholic reader that what "a true Protestant" believes is in fact consistent with the essence of Christian faith that should be shared by all Christians. The ecclesial scope of the passage is ecumenical or "catholic" in the sense in which Wesley affirmed this term and so the passage offers what I believe is as close as John Wesley came to a statement of essential or fundamental Christian teachings.[31]

What specific teachings did John Wesley affirm as common Christian beliefs in this passage? The passage follows the trinitarian pattern of the Apostles' and Nicene Creeds. At a number of points, Wesley followed the language of Anglican Bishop John Pearson's *Exposition of the Creed,* a document well known to the Wesley family. The published works of Susanna Wesley include an extended commentary on the Apostles' Creed based on Pearson's *Exposition.*[32]

The first paragraph of this passage in the "Letter to a Roman Catholic" affirms belief in God the Father, affirming God's fatherhood in relation to Christ's divine sonship and God's fatherhood in relation to God's providence over all things.[33] The second paragraph affirms doctrine about Christ, including Christ's offices as prophet, priest, and king. It affirms the Nicene Creed's assertion that Christ is "God of God, very God of very God," and it affirms

Chalcedonian language about Christ "joining the human nature with the divine in one person."[34] This paragraph also includes a reference to Wesley's belief in the perpetual virginity of the Blessed Virgin, an odd point in describing the beliefs of "a true Protestant" but a point that heightened the meiosis employed in the passage. It also affirms the reality of Christ's work on behalf of human salvation, including Christ's suffering, death, burial, and resurrection, echoing the words of the Apostles' Creed and the primitive Christian gospel as expressed in 1 Corinthians 15:1-4.[35]

The third paragraph of this passage affirms belief in the Holy Spirit "equal with the Father and the Son" and the work of the Holy Spirit in bringing about human salvation.[36] The next paragraph affirms belief in the "catholic, that is, universal, Church" which comprises all who have fellowship with the divine Trinity, both the living and the dead.[37] The fifth and final paragraph of this creedal passage affirms that "God forgives all the sins of them that truly repent and unfeignedly believe his holy gospel," concluding with the affirmation that the unjust will suffer eternal torment and the just will "enjoy inconceivable happiness in the presence of God to all eternity."[38] The paragraph can be read as affirming a doctrine of justification by faith, although Wesley did not use this distinctly Protestant vocabulary in addressing his Catholic interlocutor.

Framed as it is by the trinitarian shape of the historic creeds, this extended passage affirms five of the six teachings that Colin Williams identified as essential doctrines for John Wesley: the doctrine of the Trinity (Williams's item 6), the doctrine of the full divinity of Christ (item 2), the atonement (item 3), teaching about the work of the Holy Spirit (item 5), and at least a glancing reference to the doctrine of justification by faith (item 4), though not couched in traditional Protestant language of justification by faith alone. Wesley's statement on justification appears in the last paragraph (on the Final Judgment), where Wesley asserted that "God forgives all the sins of them that truly repent and unfeignedly believe his holy gospel."[39] This passage from the "Letter to a Roman Catholic" also includes a reference to the doctrine of regeneration, asserting that God the Father "is in a peculiar manner the Father of those whom he regenerates by his Spirit, whom he adopts in his Son."[40] The "Letter to a Roman Catholic" also names teachings about the Christian church among the common teachings it discusses. Oddly enough, it is the doctrine of original sin

(Williams's item 1) that is absent from Wesley's sustained discussion of common Christian teachings here. John Wesley's concern with original sin as an essential doctrine did not develop until the mid to late 1750s, when he published his doctrinal treatise "The Doctrine of Original Sin: According to Scripture, Reason and Experience" (1757) and then his doctrinal sermon "Original Sin" (1759), though it seems odd that it is not mentioned in an extended description of common Catholic and Protestant teachings.

This passage from John Wesley's "Letter to a Roman Catholic" deserves sustained attention in a discussion of Wesley's essential doctrines. Williams did not deal with this passage in his own treatment of essential doctrines, but it gives a logical form to the group of "essential" items that Williams had identified in a haphazard fashion in John Wesley's writings. Because the letter was written in 1749, it gives an indication of Wesley's sense of the most important Christian affirmations early in the development of the Methodist movement, ten years after John Wesley's initial open-air preaching.

I also observe that John Wesley crafted this passage in such a way that characteristic emphases of the Methodist movement appear as integral aspects of the Christian faith in this account. Taking Meredith's list of characteristically Methodist doctrines, for example (repentance, faith, and holiness), we find repentance and faith asserted together ("God forgives all the sins of them that truly repent and unfeignedly believe his holy gospel")[41] and the need for holiness under the article on the Holy Spirit, whom Wesley describes as

> the immediate cause of all holiness in us; enlightening our understandings, rectifying our wills and affections, renewing our natures, uniting our persons to Christ, assuring us of the adoption of sons, leading us in our actions; purifying and sanctifying our souls and bodies, to a full and eternal enjoyment of God.[42]

The reader may also discern in this last quotation a reference to the distinctly Wesleyan teaching about the assurance of pardon. Even the paragraph on God the Father includes a reference to believers as "those whom he regenerates by his Spirit, whom he adopts in his Son."[43] The creedal passage from the "Letter to a Roman Catholic," then, weaves together themes of Christian doctrine inherited from the ancient church, from the Reformation (though expressed in a very modest manner), and from the Methodist movement (the subject of the next chapter).

Doctrines in Wesley's Recension of the Articles of Religion

Another important text for discerning John Wesley's beliefs about essential Christian doctrines is the recension of the Anglican Articles of Religion that Wesley sent to North America with Thomas Coke in the fall of 1784. This came thirty-five years after the "Letter to a Roman Catholic" and reflected Wesley's understanding of what doctrines were necessary for the organization of a Christian community as a church. It is possible that Thomas Coke or another of Wesley's coworkers may have prepared or edited the recension of the Articles and taken them to the printer, although the work went out under Wesley's authorship with his recension of the Book of Common Prayer under the title *The Sunday Service of the Methodists in North America*.[44] The recension of the Articles was based on the Thirty-Nine Articles of the Church of England, and it involves not only the omission of some whole articles (like the articles on predestination and on the three creeds) but also some significant alterations of the text of the Articles. For example, the first Anglican article states that there is one true God, "without body, parts, or passions." The Methodist article states that there is one true God, "without body or parts," leaving open the question of divine impassibility.[45] The Articles do not utilize the terminology of "necessary" or "essential" doctrine but the fact that they constitute a list of doctrines defining a church indicates that they were in some way considered necessary for defining a particular Christian community as a church.

Although it might appear that the Articles of Religion present a long list of necessary or essential doctrines (Wesley sent twenty-four Articles), the truth is that many of them were concerned with matters of Christian practices and ethics. Within the Methodist recension of the Articles, the first thirteen deal with doctrine per se and the last twelve deal with doctrine or teachings related to specific Christian practices including the sacraments, with Article 13 (on the church) as a transition from the earlier doctrinal material on God, the authority of Scripture, and salvation, to the later material concerned with the practices of the church. This book will be concerned with Articles 1 through 20, since it does consider teachings about the sacraments (Articles 16–20). If the Articles are arranged topically (see the next paragraph), we can discern twelve specific doctrinal topics dealt with in the Articles (excluding the material on the marriage of clergy, swearing oaths, and Christian goods).

In some cases, more than one of the Articles of Religion deals with a similar doctrinal topic. For example, Articles 16, 18, 19, and 20 all deal with theology related to the Lord's Supper. For the sake of comparison with other doctrinal material that appears in John Wesley's teachings, then, it might be helpful to group the doctrines and practices discussed in the Articles of Religion into the following general categories. In the table following I have utilized the numbering of the Articles of Religion as they appear in American Methodist Disciplines after 1784, but I have omitted Article 23 (on obedience to the government of the United States) since it was not among the articles that John Wesley sent with Thomas Coke:

Doctrinal Category	Articles
Trinity	1, 4
Divinity of Christ	2, 3
Humanity and Work of Christ	2, 20
Authority of Scripture	5, 6
Original Sin	7, 8
Justification by Faith	9, 11
Good Works and Pardon after Justification	10, 11, 12
The Church	13
Purgatory (denied)	14
Worship Practices (language, customs)	15, 22
Baptism	16, 17
The Lord's Supper	16, 18, 19, 20
Marriage of Clergy	21
Christian Goods	24
Swearing Oaths	25

It might be noted, further, that some of the Articles involve only a denial of a late-medieval Catholic belief or practice, such as Article 14, which denies belief in purgatory as this belief had been expressed in late-medieval Catholicism. A denial of a doctrine as contrasted with a positive affirmation of a doctrine will not be as relevant in discerning necessary or essential doctrines.

Beliefs about Essential Christian Institutions and Practices

John Wesley's "Letter to a Roman Catholic" and his recension of the Anglican Articles of Religion included references to teachings about the church and its sacraments that Wesley did not explicitly identify as "necessary" or "essential" teachings, although he did consistently identify the Christian community as necessary for Christian existence and he thought of the sacraments and some other "means of grace" as indispensable means for Christian existence. A case must be made, then, that some such teachings should be included within the scope of John Wesley's understandings of common Christian beliefs.

Although John Wesley did not use the expressions "necessary" or "fundamental" with respect to Christian practices, he did identify specific Christian practices as "means of grace" or "ordinances of God," and in some cases he made explicit that these practices held universal ecclesial scope. John Wesley's sermon "The Means of Grace" defines "means of grace" as denoting "*means ordained* of God, as the usual channels of his grace," or more specifically as "outward signs, words, or actions, ordained of God, and appointed for this end, to be the ordinary channels whereby he might convey to men, preventing, justifying, or sanctifying grace."[46] Writing in response to an eccentric group of London Moravians[47] who had claimed that those who had not yet experienced the full "assurance of pardon" must abstain from all means of grace (including the Lord's Supper), Wesley asked in this sermon if there were any means ordained by God within the scope of the New Covenant, and he offered scriptural evidence for prayer, "searching the Scriptures," and the Lord's Supper as means of grace.[48]

Within a short time after the sermon "The Means of Grace," John and Charles Wesley clarified expectations of members of Methodist societies in the "General Rules" (1743). In this set of rules that functioned as the original covenant for Wesleyan societies, "attending upon the ordinances of God" is a third general category after avoiding evil of all kinds and doing good of all kinds. The practice of each of the three "means of grace" defended in the earlier sermon "The Means of Grace" appeared in the General Rules as requirements for continuation of members in Wesleyan societies, and more items were added, so the full list of "ordinances of God" required in the General Rules is as follows:

> the public worship of God
> the ministry of the word, either read or expounded
> the supper of the Lord
> family and private prayer
> searching the Scriptures
> fasting, or abstinence[49]

The list of "ordinances" given in the General Rules thus includes all of the means specified in the earlier sermon "The Means of Grace" (prayer, the Lord's Supper, and "searching the Scriptures") and adds public worship, the ministry of the Word, and fasting (or abstinence). Similarly, John Wesley's *Instructions for Children* (1745) included a catechism that asked the question "Which are the chief Means of Grace?" The response was "The Lord's Supper, Prayer, Searching the Scriptures, and Fasting."[50]

John Wesley expanded his understanding of means of grace in the document historically called the "Large Minutes," a compilation of minutes of early Methodist conferences in which he made a distinction between "instituted" and "prudential" means of grace.[51] The "instituted" means include prayer, "searching the Scriptures," the Lord's Supper, fasting, and "Christian conference," by which Wesley meant carefully guarded conversation with other Christians. The "prudential" means include rules that individual Christians might make to be kept with the help of their societies, attending class and band meetings, occasions on which preachers could meet with society or class members, and even more specific items such as abstaining from meat or late meals, drinking water, and temperance in the use of wine and ale.

Although the "Large Minutes" do not elaborate on Wesley's terms, the "instituted" means were practices instituted in Scripture from the beginning of the Christian community, and thus Wesley understood them to be binding on the church in all times and places. That is to say, in my terms, the "instituted means" have universal ecclesial scope and thus can be regarded as essential or

fundamental practices for Christian communities.[52] The "prudential" means, by contrast, include specifically and distinctively
Methodist practices, that is, things that were not "instituted" in
Scripture but which were simply found to be prudentially helpful
by Methodist people. This contrast was made more explicit in
Wesley's open letter to the Reverend Vincent Perronet in 1748 entitled "A Plain Account of the People Called Methodists," in which
Wesley referred to particular Methodist practices as "merely prudential, not essential, not of divine institution."[53] The distinction
John Wesley drew between "instituted" and "prudential" means of
grace, then, seems to follow a pattern in his thought by which he
distinguished what is commonly Christian from those things that
marked the distinctive mission of the Methodist movement. The
identification of "instituted" means of grace is particularly helpful
in discerning what John Wesley considered to be practices common to Christians throughout the centuries, and comparing his
lists of "means of grace" (defended in 1739–41), "ordinances of
God" (defined in the "General Rules" in 1739), and the later definition of "instituted" means of grace (probably from the decade of
the 1750s) brings us close to understanding John Wesley's view of
essential Christian practices.

But there are problems with taking this cluster of "means of
grace" and "ordinances" as fully reflecting John Wesley's understanding of essential Christian practices. One is that this cluster of
practices does not include baptism, which elsewhere Wesley did
define as being a constitutive practice of Christian communities.
The Articles of Religion of the Church of England defined the
"church" as involving faith in Christ, the preaching of the Word,
and the right administration of the sacraments, which are specifically defined as including the Lord's Supper and baptism. Wesley
would later bequeath this same definition of "church" to American
Methodists in his recension of the Anglican Articles of Religion
along with articles defining baptism as a sacrament.[54] The absence
of baptism within the lists of "means of grace" or "ordinances" was
not an intentional omission on Wesley's part. The contexts in
which these lists were developed shows that they designated ongoing practices for Christian believers. John Wesley defined the
"means of grace," as noted above, in contention with the views of
a particular group of London Moravians who had deprecated the

means of grace for those who had not experienced the assurance of pardon.[55] His concern was to define and defend "means of grace" that were part of the ongoing life of Christians, both before and after they might experience assurance of divine forgiveness. John and Charles Wesley defined the "ordinances of God" in the "General Rules" as practices to be observed consistently by members of Methodist societies. In fact, since the context of the "General Rules" was the weekly meeting of Methodist classes into which societies were divided, the practices enjoined as "ordinances of God" were expected to be practiced weekly.

Baptism would not have appeared in such a list. But John Wesley did consider baptism to be constitutive of Christian churches, consistent with the definition of "church" given in the Articles of Religion, so a discussion of essential or definitive Christian practices, parallel to our earlier discussion of essential or definitive Christian doctrines, must include baptism as a definitive Christian practice in John Wesley's thought.[56]

A second issue in considering John Wesley's categories of the "means of grace" (especially the "instituted" means) and the "ordinances of God" as essential or definitive Christian practices is that the lists themselves are somewhat inchoate, giving as discreet items "public worship," "the supper of the Lord," and "the ministry of the word," which were typically combined in Anglican practice: the Anglican celebration of Eucharist involved all three of these elements, and the observance of Morning Prayer in an Anglican congregation would have involved public worship and "the ministry of the word." The latter ("the ministry of the word, either read or expounded") might also overlap "family and private prayer," especially if participants used the forms of daily morning and evening prayer in the Book of Common Prayer, as was customary among Anglican families. This was John Wesley's own custom and it had been the custom of the Wesley family in Epworth in his youth.[57] Combined with a devotional practice of Scripture study, these practices might again overlap the practice of "searching the Scriptures," also defended as a "means of grace" and listed as an "ordinance" to be followed by Methodists according to the "General Rules." So the categories that John Wesley gives as "means of grace" and "ordinances of God" are not strictly discrete, and in formulating an understanding of essential Christian practices in his thought we may need to consider how some (at least) of these categories might be combined.

Finally, the lists of "means of grace" and "ordinances of God," for the same reasons that they did not include baptism, do not acknowledge the privileged status of the Lord's Supper as well as baptism as sacraments. Again, this was not Wesley's intention in defining "means of grace" in the context of the controversy with London Moravians or in defining "ordinances of God" to be consistently followed by members of Methodist societies. But Wesley saw the sacraments as being related to means of grace: indeed, in his sermon "The Means of Grace," he cited the definition of a sacrament given in the Prayer Book Catechism as involving an "outward and visible sign" instituted by Christ which is a "means" of receiving an "inward and spiritual grace."[58] Sacraments, then, were organized in his thought as a subset of the larger category of "means of grace," but with the privileged status that Anglican and Protestant churches had accorded them.

With the preceding cautions in mind, I offer the following list of specific practices that John Wesley consistently taught as being both scriptural and nearly universal in Christian practice and thus as essential or definitive Christian practices. I do not include here the practices that Wesley considered distinctive of the Methodist movement (including "prudential" means of grace). The following list, like the list of ten essential doctrines given above, reflects my own arrangement of the Wesleyan essential Christian practices with the dominical sacraments heading the list:

> Baptism
> the Lord's Supper
> public worship (embracing the ministry of the Word and
>   frequently the Lord's Supper)
> Christian conversation ("Christian conference")
> family and private prayer
> devotional biblical study ("searching the Scriptures")
> fasting or abstinence

These practices are observed almost universally in Christian communities, even if fasting or abstinence is practiced rarely. The exception to more ecumenical Christian patterns of Christian practices we might note is the inclusion of Christian conversation or

"Christian conference." On this point we could say that Wesley wanted to elevate Christian conversation to *status confessionis*, that is, to the level of a teaching or practice that is necessary for the being of the church. Although this did not persist as a doctrinal claim in the subsequent development of Wesleyan communities, the idea of "conference" has structured Methodist church life, and Christian fellowship is enshrined as a central practice.

As we have seen above, John Wesley's "Letter to a Roman Catholic" and his recension of the Anglican Articles included teachings about the church and the sacraments of baptism and the Lord's Supper. The Articles also contain a passage about public worship (the Article asserting that worship customs do not need to be uniform, although ministers should observe the customs of their own church once established). Neither of these statements of common Christian teachings include specific reference to "Christian conference," family and private prayer, devotional Bible study, or fasting and the related practice of abstinence. I hope to take up these practices in a future study of Wesleyan practices, but for the purpose of the present study of Wesleyan beliefs, I will include beliefs about the church and the sacraments of baptism and the Lord's Supper as part of a core of common Christian beliefs taught by John Wesley. In chapter 3 I will examine these teachings as expressed in the verse of Charles Wesley.

Ten Common Christian Beliefs according to John Wesley

Given the above materials, then, we can now proceed to compare Wesley's description of Christian beliefs in the "Letter to a Roman Catholic" (1749), the recension of the Articles of Religion (1784), the various occasional passages through his writings where he indicated a teaching or belief to be necessary or essential or otherwise definitive of Christian faith, and occasions when he described beliefs about essential Christian institutions, specifically, the Christian church and the two dominical sacraments. In doing so, we can discern specific doctrines that John Wesley consistently taught as necessary or essential Christian teachings. In considering Colin Williams's list of six fundamental or essential doctrines, I have called into question the fifth item he listed (the work of the Holy Spirit), since it does not appear to be a *doctrine* or teaching that Wesley considered essential in the same sense as other common Christian doctrines. Utilizing Williams's own criterion, however, it would be fair to add another item to his list at least provisionally, namely, the doctrine of regeneration, since in one of the passages Williams cites, John Wesley stated that both the doctrines of justification and regeneration were "fundamental" for Christians.[59] That is to say, the doctrine of the regeneration should be an essential doctrine according to Williams's own criteria for discerning essential doctrines, even though Williams did not include it in his list. I shall argue by an expansion of Williams's criteria (see criteria above) that the doctrine of biblical authority can also be seen as essential or fundamental to Wesley. At least, he himself claimed that it was constitutive of Christian faith.[60] Moreover, as indicated in the previous section, I will also include beliefs about the church and the sacraments of baptism and the Lord's Supper within the scope of common Christian beliefs maintained by John Wesley. This, then, yields a list of at least ten core beliefs in John Wesley's understanding that I will now examine individually.

1. Belief in and Worship of the Divine Trinity

On belief in the Trinity, Williams cited a passage from John Wesley's sermon "The Trinity" (1775) stating explicitly that the doctrine of the Trinity is a necessary or essential doctrine. In the passage Williams cited, Wesley made the point that the praise of the one God in three divine Persons is closely tied to vital Christianity.[61] Wesley also made the point through the introduction to this sermon that there is a wide difference between fundamental beliefs and opinions, and the doctrine of the Trinity is indeed one of the fundamental beliefs of Christian faith.[62] Moreover, it is important to note that this sermon, like the "Letter to a Roman Catholic," was written during one of Wesley's visits to a traditionally Catholic region of Ireland (County Cork), and it is significant that in the first paragraph of the sermon he indicated that both Catholic and Reformed authors had been mistaken in many of their "opinions," but may nevertheless be saved by faith in Christ.[63] The context and the text of the sermon itself make clear that its ecclesial scope is ecumenical (trans-confessional), and its claim is that the doctrine of the Trinity is a doctrine essential to Christian faith as such, that is, not to the distinct identities of Catholics or Protestants. This is consistent with the observation in the previous section that the doctrine of the Trinity provided the overall framework of the creedal passage in John Wesley's "Letter to a Roman Catholic."[64] Moreover, the 1784 revision of the Anglican Articles of Religion that Wesley sent to North America with Thomas Coke included as its first article an affirmation of belief in the Trinity utilizing the language of the Nicene Creed.[65] There is consistent evidence, then, from throughout his career, that John Wesley considered the doctrine of the Trinity to be an essential Christian belief.

John Wesley understood the central meaning of the doctrine of the Trinity to lie in the claim that "these three [the Father, the Word and the Holy Spirit] are one," here quoting the so-called "Johannine comma" (1 John 5:7). To deny the unity of these three would make absurd Christians' worship of God as Father, Son, and Holy Spirit, and would make absurd the claim that believers receive assurance through the Holy Spirit that their sins have been forgiven by the Father on the basis of the atoning work of the Son.[66] Wesley did not insist that Christians needed to know the terms "Trinity" or "Persons," and he emphasized what contemporary theological interpreters have called the "economic Trinity," that is, the Trinity as revealed in the out-working of salvation.[67] Jason Vickers has shown that the doctrine of the Trinity was a contested teaching in the Wesleys' time and, moreover, many orthodox Anglican authors had responded to challenges to this teaching by philosophical defenses of the doctrine that abstracted the doctrine from the practice of devotion to or worship of the Trinity. The Wesleys, he shows, maintained the vital connection between the doctrine and its locus in the church's practices of worship.[68] Charles Wesley's doxological expressions of teachings on the Trinity will be taken up in chapter 3, and belief in the Trinity in John and Charles Wesley's works and in subsequent Methodist teaching and practice will be taken up in more detail in chapter 4.

2. Belief in the Full Divinity of Jesus Christ

Belief in the deity or full divinity of Jesus Christ was implied in belief in the Trinity. In asserting that the doctrine of the full divinity of Christ was an essential doctrine in the thought of John Wesley, Williams cited the introductory paragraph of John Wesley's tract, "The Character of a Methodist" (1742).[69] This warrants a bit of explanation since the tract was entitled "The Character of a Methodist" and one might think that it described the beliefs of a Methodist rather than common Christian teachings. But this is another case, as in the "Letter to a Roman Catholic," where it is necessary to understand John Wesley's use of meiosis to discern the ecclesial scope of the claim he makes. Although cast as a description of "The Character of a Methodist," it is clear from the outset that what Wesley offered in this tract was a description of a true Christian. The tract does not deal in any way with such distinctive Methodist teachings as assurance, entire sanctification, and the like. The first paragraph of the tract asserts that "the distinguishing marks of a Methodist are not his opinions of any sort..." and goes on to state grounds for unity with other Christians that amount to essential or fundamental teachings as contrasted with opinions.[70] One of these is Wesley's claim, quoted appropriately by Williams, that "we believe Christ to be the eternal, supreme God; and herein we are distinguished from the Socinians and Arians. But as to all opinions which do not strike at the root of Christianity, we think and let think."[71]

The context, in this case, is a claim about fundamental Christian beliefs, those beliefs that do indeed "strike at the root of Christianity," and so Wesley claims that the doctrine of Christ's complete divinity is essential to Christianity itself. The doctrine of the divinity of Christ is stated in the creedal passage in the "Letter to a Roman Catholic" in the paragraph on the work of Christ,[72] and is also asserted in the Articles of Religion that were sent to North America in 1784.[73]

The doctrine of the full divinity of Christ makes explicit with respect to Christ the claim of the doctrine of the Trinity that the second Person of the divine Trinity is equally and eternally God along with the Father and the Holy Spirit. It is the doctrine that became explicit in the early fourth-century conflict with Arianism, indeed, the doctrinal controversy that led to the formulation of the doctrine of the Trinity in the Nicene Creed. Arianism, as Wesley noted, was not a merely historical issue in his day since Arian teachings had been revived by William Whiston and others, and Deistic or

"Socinian" thinkers of the seventeenth and eighteenth century had likewise disputed the traditional trinitarian belief.[74] The doctrine of the full divinity of Christ was made most explicit in the first part of the second article of the Nicene Creed, which states that Christ is "God from God, light from light, very God from very God, of one being with the Father." Wesley argued for the complete divinity of Christ based on the Christians' worship of Christ, since worship of anything less than complete divinity would be idolatrous,[75] and on the need for God's own intervention and presence in the work of salvation.[76]

3. Belief in the Atonement and the Work of Jesus Christ

A third belief affirmed by John Wesley as necessary or essential has to do with the atonement or, speaking more broadly, with the saving work of Jesus Christ. In asserting that the doctrine of the atonement was an essential doctrine for Wesley, Colin Williams cites a letter from John Wesley to Mary Bishop, dated 7 February 1778.[77] Although this was a private letter, John Wesley did maintain in the letter that the doctrine of atonement distinguishes Christianity from Deism: "Indeed, nothing in the Christian system is of greater consequence than the doctrine of Atonement. It is properly the distinguishing point between Deism and Christianity....Give up the Atonement, and the Deists are agreed with us."[78]

Here the ecclesial scope of Wesley's claim is made clear by reference to "the Christian system" and by the contrast with Deists. The claim Wesley made here about Deism is somewhat odd: normally, one would think it was the doctrine of the full divinity of Christ that distinguished traditional Christianity from Deism, but Wesley also asserted the doctrine of atonement, including Christ's suffering and death on our behalf, as another critical distinction between Deism and historic Christian faith. Like the doctrine of the divinity of Christ, the doctrine of atonement is also stated in the creedal passage in the "Letter to a Roman Catholic," in the paragraph on the work of Christ, and it is also asserted in the second and twentieth Articles of Religion that were sent to North America in 1784.[79] These sources give us evidence, then, from 1749, 1778, and 1784 affirming that John Wesley viewed belief in the atonement an essential Christian teaching.

It may be important to note in this regard that in explaining Christ's work John Wesley pointed to many elements of Christ's saving work, including substitution, sacrifice, suffering, Christ's priestly intercession, and the notion of Christ's victory over the powers of evil (*Christus Victor*) as elements of Christ's work of salvation. Kenneth J. Collins has argued that the theme of substitution is primary among these various theories in John Wesley's thought on atonement,[80] and although it is true that Wesley refers frequently to the theme of substitution and to the cross as the center of Christ's work, the cross is for Wesley and for the longer Christian tradition before him a sign of the completion of Christ's whole life, a sacrificial life in which God poured out or "emptied" God's own being for the sake of human salvation. Wesley's variety of elements of atonement suggests that he regarded the atonement as involving the whole work of Christ in assuming humanity, including Christ's life and death. Thus Article of Religion 20 (in the Methodist recension) maintains that Christ's oblation was "finished upon the cross," and the language of "finished" or "completed" suggests that the cross was the culmination of the whole event of Christ's life through which God's salvation had been accomplished. This is consistent with the second section of the second article of the Nicene Creed, which asserts that Christ's incarnation was "for us [human beings] and for our salvation." In fact, John Deschner has pointed out that in Wesley's thought Christ's divine nature is a grounds of the atonement as well as Christ's human nature.[81] I would stress that although each of the historic "theories of atonement" focuses on one aspect of the work of Christ and tries to explain that aspect of Christ's saving work, what is important for the church to affirm is not a particular theory or a particular element of Christ's work, but rather the belief that our salvation has come about through the whole event of God's assuming humanity on our behalf through the events of Christ's life, death, and resurrection.

4. Belief in Biblical Authority

Belief in biblical authority ought to appear among John Wesley's "essential" beliefs. As noted above, however, it did not appear in Colin Williams's list, and perhaps did not because John Wesley's statements about this teaching did not explicitly include the key terms "necessary," "fundamental," or "essential." It is nevertheless on this point that I want to make the case for an extension of Williams's criterion. The passage in John Wesley's works that most clearly reveals his sense of a doctrine of biblical authority as constitutive of Christian faith is in the first paragraph of his tract "The Character of a Methodist," where Wesley wrote,

> We believe, indeed, that "all Scripture is given by the inspiration of God;" and herein we are distinguished from Jews, Turks, and infidels. We believe the written word of God to be the only and sufficient rule both of Christian faith and practice; and herein we are fundamentally distinguished from those of the Romish Church. We believe Christ to be the eternal, supreme God; and herein we are distinguished from the Socinians and Arians. But as to all opinions which do not strike at the root of Christianity, we think and let think.[82]

I have referred earlier to the latter sentences of this passage in discussing John Wesley's understanding of the doctrine of the full divinity of Christ as an essential Christian belief. John Wesley expressed this understanding of the divinity of Christ in parallel to his understanding of biblical authority: just as the doctrine of biblical authority distinguishes Christians from non-Christians (and Protestants from Catholics in the form in which Wesley states it), so the doctrine of the divinity of Christ distinguishes true Christians from Socinians and Arians. It may be that Williams took the last sentence quoted above (about "opinions which do not strike at the root of Christianity") to refer only to the doctrine of the divinity of Christ, but the parallelism involved here implies that John Wesley took both the doctrine of biblical authority and the doctrine of the divinity of Christ to be essential Christian doctrines, not indifferent opinions. He stated unequivocally in this passage that belief in biblical authority is constitutive of Christian faith in distinction from other religious traditions.

Although the doctrine of biblical authority does not appear in the creedal passage I have referred to in the "Letter to a Roman Catholic," the fifth and sixth Articles of Religion that were sent with Thomas Coke to the Methodists in North America in 1784 asserted the belief in biblical authority.[83] In this regard, it is critical to note in the passage from the "Character of a Methodist" cited above John Wesley's own sense of the ecclesial scope of beliefs about scriptural authority. Even though the passage is brief, it reveals some of the substance of his understanding of biblical authority. In the broad sense, he maintained that the doctrine of biblical authority is shared by all Christians including Catholics and in this sense is constitutive of Christian faith in general.

After a critical semicolon, however, Wesley went on to state that the doctrine of biblical authority involves the belief that the Bible is "the only and sufficient rule both of Christian faith and practice," and in this sense, he maintains, this doctrine distinguishes Protestants from Catholics. Putting the issue in this manner shows that Wesley reflected the apprehension typical of Protestants in his era that the Tridentine doctrine of ecclesial authority placed subsequent Christian traditions on an equal footing with Scripture. This same apprehension is reflected in Wesley's "Roman Catechism, with a Reply Thereunto."[84] Regardless of the accuracy of this apprehension or misapprehension (in the light of subsequent ecumenical dialogue), this makes it clear that John Wesley was committed to the Protestant notion of *scriptura sola* in the sense that the Bible contains all that is necessary for human salvation and for the reform of the church. Nevertheless, despite his claim that a more nuanced understanding of the doctrine was distinctive of Protestantism, we should not miss the point that Wesley maintained that the doctrine of biblical authority in the broad sense is itself constitutive of Christian faith.[85] Anticipating later developments of Methodist teaching, we can note that some elements of what would later be described as the "Wesleyan quadrilateral" were utilized by John Wesley in interpreting the Scriptures, including reason, Christian experience, the teachings of the early Christian church, and of the Reformation. But to none of these did Wesley accord the final authority that he associated with the Christian canon of Scripture.

5. Belief in Original Sin

I have noted above how peculiar it was that John Wesley's creedal statement in the "Letter to a Roman Catholic" did not refer explicitly to the doctrine of original sin. The letter was written in 1749, and it

42

was not until the middle of the 1750s that Wesley became concerned about the doctrine of original sin, producing both his lengthiest theological treatise, "The Doctrine of Original Sin, according to Scripture, Reason and Experience" (1757) and a shorter sermon, "Original Sin" (1759). Both of these works include explicit claims that the doctrine of original sin is an essential Christian belief.[86]

Two things should be noted about John Wesley's understanding of original sin. The first is that although "original sin" is typically the overarching category he utilized for describing the human need for divine grace, he also typically paired discussion of original sin with teaching about original righteousness. This was the case with the Anglican Articles of Religion and his recension of it, which holds that, due to the effects of sin, human beings are "very far gone from original righteousness."[87] John Wesley's sermons "Justification by Faith" and "The New Birth" both begin by showing that the ground of both of these doctrines is the original righteousness in which humans were first created and their subsequent lapse from this original righteousness.[88] Wesley even speaks of the perfection of the original creation: "'As for God, his way is perfect'—and such originally were all his works."[89] This notion of original perfection would lie in the background of John Wesley's understanding of the renewal of humankind and of all the creation. He follows this sentence with "And such they shall be again, when 'the Son of God' shall have 'destroyed the works of the devil.'"[90]

A second matter to be noted in regard to John Wesley's teaching about original sin is that Wesley's own belief about original sin was modified in one critical way from the Augustinian inheritance of the ancient Western church and the Reformation. Although he affirmed that the results of Adam and Eve's sin affect every human being, Wesley questioned the concomitant notion that every human being deserves damnation as a result of this inheritance of sin. Wesley did, for example, include the Anglican Article of Religion on Original Sin among the Articles he sent to America with Thomas Coke in 1784, affirming that original sin denotes "the corruption of the nature of every" person. But the version of the Article he sent omits a critically important phrase from the older Anglican Article stating that "in every person born into this world, [original sin] deserveth God's wrath and damnation."[91] A letter of John Wesley written in 1776 explained his doubt as to whether God would condemn anyone based on original sin alone.[92] This left Wesley affirming, as Eastern churches have historically affirmed, that all humans stand in need of divine grace, but that human culpability is due to our own involvement in sin rather than an inheritance of sin from our first human parents.[93]

For John Wesley the doctrine of original sin was very closely connected to the preaching of repentance, and specifically, the need for preaching "the repentance of sinners," that is, the acknowledgment of human sin and the need for divine help or grace that precedes Christian faith.[94] It is for this reason that in one place John Wesley had original sin as the first in a list of three doctrines that characterize the Methodist movement, and in a similar list in another place he had repentance in the first place.[95] When we examine his descriptions of original sin and repentance, we find them closely intertwined: the practical application of the doctrine of original sin is to call for repentance, and the presupposition of the call for repentance is the doctrine of original sin. In this case we can see how a common Christian doctrine also had a specific nuance within the ecclesial scope of the Methodist movement (by this I mean the Evangelical revival more broadly; see the next chapter). Wesley claimed that the teaching of original sin per se characterizes or should characterize all Christians; the implication of this, that preachers should call for heartfelt repentance on the part of sinners, was one of the consistent marks of the Evangelical movement.

6. Belief in Justification by Faith Alone

In asserting that the doctrine of justification by faith alone was a necessary doctrine for John Wesley, Colin Williams cited two passages from John Wesley's sermons. The first, from John Wesley's "The New Birth" (1760), bears quotation, since in fact it claims that not only justification but also regeneration[96] are "fundamental" for Christians:

> If any doctrines within the whole compass of Christianity may be properly termed "fundamental," they are doubtless these two,— the doctrine of justification, and that of the new birth: the former relating to that great work which God does for us, in forgiving our sins; the latter, to the great work which God does in us, in renewing our fallen nature.[97]

44

It is genuinely puzzling that, having cited this passage (in his notes), Williams would have listed only justification and not regeneration (the subject of the sermon he cited) as an essential doctrine for Wesley. It is on the basis of this passage that I have taken both justification and regeneration as necessary or fundamental for John Wesley's understanding of Christian faith. And yet in both cases Wesley's particular understandings of these doctrines differed in some significant respects from earlier expressions of them in the Augustinian and Protestant doctrinal traditions.

On the doctrine of justification by faith, Williams also cites a phrase from John Wesley's "The Lord Our Righteousness."[98] This citation strikes me as a less significant reference, however, because Williams took Wesley's reference to Luther's *articulus stantis vel cadentis ecclesiae* as a reference to the doctrine of justification by faith alone as Luther had used the expression, but in this instance Wesley, though borrowing Luther's expression, claimed that doctrine about *Christ* is "the article [or doctrine] on which the church stands or falls. "Nevertheless, there are other cases in which Wesley asserted the essential nature of the doctrine of justification by faith alone,[99] and this doctrine was maintained in the Articles of Religion that he sent to North America in 1784.[100]

In affirming justification by faith as an essential Christian doctrine, Wesley repeated one of the cardinal points of the Protestant Reformation and yet there is a distinctly Evangelical nuance to his understanding of justification and especially the understanding of "faith" that appears in the perorations of his sermons. "Faith" cannot simply mean assent, which could be "the faith of a devil": it must engage the heart and affections. In his lists of three key Evangelical teachings, John Wesley sometimes places "justification" in the second position and sometimes "faith," just as "original sin" and "repentance" could be swapped in the first position.[101] Thus a doctrine that has or should have universal ecclesial scope also has a specific nuance or emphasis within the scope of the Evangelical movement.

7. Beliefs about Regeneration and Holiness

I have justified my inclusion of the doctrine of regeneration or the new birth as an essential doctrine for John Wesley on the basis of the passage cited above from the sermon "The New Birth," where Wesley claimed that justification and regeneration were both constitutive of Christian belief.[102] The creedal passage in the "Letter to a Roman Catholic" refers to God as the Father of "those whom he regenerates by his Spirit, whom he adopts in his Son."[103] The 1784 Articles of Religion do not refer to regeneration as an essential doctrine since regeneration is mentioned only in the Article on baptism and this is a derivative reference that does not name regeneration per se as an essential teaching.[104] However, other Articles of Religion deal with broader aspects of the sanctification of believers following justification, such as the need for good works (Articles 10 and 11) and the possibility of sin and pardon after justification (Article 12). Although the evidence for regeneration per se as an essential doctrine is not quite as strong as the evidence for other doctrines considered above, this may be due to the fact that John Wesley took the term "regeneration" as a term denoting the gateway to the broader teaching of sanctification and holiness, and there is abundant evidence that he considered the need for holiness to be a common Christian teaching.[105]

The next chapter will show that John Wesley also considered the teaching of regeneration (leading to holiness) as being one of the three key doctrines of the Evangelical revival and indeed, he considered the teaching of entire sanctification to be perhaps the one clear distinguishing mark of the Wesleyan branch of the revival. At this point, however, we may note again the distinctive emphasis of Wesley's understanding of regeneration. Although he acknowledged the traditional teaching of baptismal renewal for infants consistent with the Anglican Articles of Religion and the liturgy for baptism in the Book of Common Prayer, he took the practical implication of the doctrine for adults to be that one must be born again or regenerate, whether or not one was formerly baptized.[106] In this respect, Wesley found himself in a position similar to that of Spener, Francke, and other Lutheran Pietists, namely, in affirming the grace received in baptism but insisting that fallen Christians need to experience divine grace anew.[107]

8. Belief about the Christian Church

Although John Wesley did not identify a doctrine of the church as a "necessary" or essential Christian doctrine, he considered the

Christian community itself to be necessary for Christian existence. The first point of his fourth sermon in a series on the Sermon on the Mount was that "Christianity is essentially a social religion; and that to turn it into a solitary religion, is indeed to destroy it" and he went on to claim that Christianity "cannot subsist at all, without society,—without living and conversing with other men."[108] This was directed, in the first place, against the practice of anchoritism, but the point he made here is that although a *doctrine* of the church might not be strictly necessary, the *church* as a "society" of believers is necessary for the Christian life. Consistent with this, he included teaching about the church among the Articles of Religion he sent to the American Methodists in 1784. The Methodist Article replicated the Anglican Article of Religion that was itself based on the wording of the Augsburg Confession. This Article states that "the visible Church of Christ is a congregation of faithful men, in which the pure Word of God is preached, and the Sacraments [be] duly ministered according to Christ's ordinance, in all those things that of necessity are requisite to the same."[109]

"Church" is constituted according to this Lutheran and Anglican definition by three elements: faith, preaching, and the sacraments. "Faith" in this Article has reference to a body or gathering (in the Latin of the article, *coetus*) of believers (*coetus fidelium*, "a gathering of the faithful" or "of believers"), although in a wider sense "faith" as definitive of the church could denote the profession of common faith on the part of a community, such as the Augsburg Confession or the Anglican Articles of Religion themselves. Moreover, the definition given here requires the preaching of the "pure" Word of God and it requires that the sacraments must be "duly" administered. John Wesley's "Letter to a Roman Catholic" also affirms the Christian church among the common teachings Wesley ascribed to the Catholic Church as well as Protestant churches:

> I believe that Christ by his Apostles gathered unto himself a Church, to which he has continually added such as shall be saved; that this catholic, that is, universal, Church, extending to all nations and all ages, is holy in all its members, who have fellowship with God the Father, Son, and Holy Ghost; that they have fellowship with the holy angels, who constantly minister to these heirs of salvation; and with all the living members of Christ on earth, as well as all who are departed in his faith and fear.[110]

Despite his strong assertion of the fellowship of the church on earth and in heaven in this description, with its notes of unity, apostolicity, catholicity, and holiness, Wesley did not mention the sacraments in this definition. This may seem surprising since in contemporary ecumenical thought the dominical sacraments are held in common by the Catholic Church as well as Anglican and Protestant churches. But Wesley may have been concerned that his intent of demonstrating unity in faith in this passage would have been imperiled had he ventured into sacramental theology. He also would have faced the problem of common language for speaking of the Eucharist, since in his time Catholics consistently referred to Eucharist as the "mass" and Protestant terms such as "holy communion" or "the Lord's Supper" would have been equally alien to Catholics.

Alongside the definition of the church given in the Article of Religion and the description of the church given in the "Letter to a Roman Catholic," we may compare John Wesley's general definition of the Church of England given in a manuscript cited by Frank Baker in which Wesley defined the Church of England as "that body of people, nominally united, which profess to uphold the doctrine contained in the Articles and Homilies, and to use Baptism, the Lord's supper and Public Prayer, according to the Common Prayer Book."[111] This has the elements of common profession of faith (in the Articles and Homilies) and the administration of the sacraments, and it implied the preaching of the Word that characterized Sunday celebrations of Morning Prayer in the Prayer Book tradition as it was implemented in the Wesleys' age.

To these three elements of "church" defined in the Anglican Article that Methodists used, the Reformed tradition had added a fourth element, namely, church discipline. This is discussed under the heading of "church censures" in the Westminster Confession of Faith, a confession that John Wesley knew and occasionally cited.[112] Discipline in small groups would become a distinguishing mark of the Methodist movement, but this raises a further complication in John Wesley's thought about the nature of the Christian community, namely, the issue of which elements of "church" Wesleyan communities claimed or needed as they existed initially within the Church of England and then as they came to exist as churches apart from the Church of England. We will see in chapter 6 that John Wesley's thought about the meaning of church was complicated by his sense of a distinctive mission or vocation of the Methodist movement, and that missional concerns often trumped traditional ecclesiological concerns, as in the case of the ordinations he performed in 1784.

9. Belief about the Sacrament of Baptism

The Articles of Religion that John Wesley sent to American Methodists in 1784 included an article stating that the two sacraments "ordained of Christ our Lord in the gospel" are baptism and the Lord's Supper.[113] Given his assent to the Article stating that the due administration of the sacraments is necessary to the existence of the church, this would imply that baptism is itself essential to the existence of the Christian church. A further Article of Religion that he included among those sent to North America in 1784 gave explicit teaching about baptism as discussed in the following. But despite this, we have already noted that Wesley did not mention sacramental teaching at all in his "Letter to a Roman Catholic," perhaps due to his perception that it was more a divisive issue than a unitive issue between Catholics and Protestants. He did not speak of teaching about baptism as a "necessary" or essential Christian teaching, and he did not include baptism within lists of the "means of grace." It was, I think, characteristic of Wesley to maintain that some Christian practices are necessary even if doctrine about them is not strictly necessary for the Christian life. But for the definition of a Christian community—and Wesley's Articles of 1784 were explicitly for the definition of a Christian community—it was important to have teaching about the sacrament of Christian initiation.

John Wesley's understanding of baptismal grace involved two claims that have seemed antithetical to some of Wesley's interpreters. On the one hand, he unequivocally stated that the baptism of infants does confer the grace of justification and regeneration. Wesley's account of his Aldersgate-Street conversion experience begins, "I believe, till I was about ten years old, I had not sinned away that 'washing of the Holy Ghost' which was given me in baptism."[114] Consistent with this, Wesley's sermon "The New Birth" (published in 1760) acknowledges that the grace of regeneration accompanies infant baptism.[115] Such passages about infant regeneration are consistent in Wesley's writings, and a train of Wesley interpreters has acknowledged Wesley's teaching in this regard.[116]

The other claim that John Wesley made about baptism, a claim that may appear to contradict his affirmation of infant regeneration and justification in baptism, is his consistently stated belief that adults could not rely on the fact of their being baptized as evidence that they were forgiven of their sins (justified) and born again (regenerate). Wesley's sermon "The New Birth" (mentioned above) draws these inferences: "And, first, it follows that baptism is not the new birth..." and second, the new birth "does not always accompany baptism."[117] At this point, Wesley cited the distinction between the outward rite and the inward grace in the Prayer Book definition of a sacrament.[118] It was in this sermon that Wesley allowed (as noted above) that baptism does confer regeneration in the case of infants.

In other places, John Wesley wrote at length about justification and regeneration without mentioning baptism. For example, his sermon "The Great Privilege of Those That Are Born of God" defines regeneration, contrasts it with justification, and describes its relationship to sanctification, with only the barest mention of the sacrament of Christian initiation.[119] His sermon "The Original, Nature, Properties, and Use of the Law" made the point that the second use of the Law is to bring believers to life in Christ (the language is the same that Wesley regularly used to describe the new birth), but does not mention baptism.[120] Two of his sermons described the way in which believers can know they are regenerate, both by the testimony of God's Spirit and the testimony of human conscience, but only one of them made a passing mention of baptism in relation to the new birth.[121] To speak of regeneration with only a nominal mention of baptism, as Wesley so often did, would have been incongruous within the sacramental tradition that regarded baptism as the instrumental means of justification and regeneration.

If the juxtaposition of these two views seems incongruous, we should observe that many subsequent Methodists did not see them as necessarily contradictory. An article published in 1824 in the *Wesleyan-Methodist Magazine* by an author who signed the article "T. J." (probably Thomas Jackson) offered the following summary of Wesley's views:

> [Wesley] not only acknowledged that a gracious communication is made to the minds of children in baptism, but to the effect of that communication he gave the name of the New Birth. . . . Mr. Wesley, nevertheless, denied that the same effect is invariably produced in cases of adult baptism; and believed that those children who receive that blessing in their infancy, generally lose it as they grow in years, and mix with the world. He also believed that when they are brought under the power of sinful affections and habits, the renewal of their minds in righteousness and true holiness, after the image of God, becomes a matter of indispensable necessity; and to that renewal, whenever it is effected, and how often soever it may be repeated, he used to give the name of REGENERATION, or of the NEW BIRTH.[122]

In a similar way, Charles R. Hohenstein has pointed out that Wesley's warnings against relying on baptism were in fact consistent with older spiritual and doctrinal traditions that had maintained that baptism is effective so long as an individual did not contradict the grace given in baptism by disbelief.[123]

There is a way of understanding Wesley's baptismal views as being within the main stream of Christian thought in the Anglicanism of his day, and that is to recognize the extent to which Georgian Anglicanism, and specifically its typical sacramental theology, reflected the sacramental theology of the Reformed tradition: not the left wing of the Reformed tradition (Zwinglianism) but the main stream of Reformed theology concerning the sacraments. The Reformed tradition had deeply influenced Anglicanism not only as it was seen in Puritan divines but in the broader doctrinal and liturgical inheritance of the Church of England. John Walsh and Stephen Taylor have made the point that eighteenth-century Anglicans could be Tories with respect to politics and yet Reformed with respect to their theological convictions.[124] Wesley's citation of the critical distinction between the outward sign and the inward grace, taken most immediately from the Prayer Book catechism, reflects a consistent hallmark of Reformed sacramental theology and spirituality.[125]

This distinction between inward grace and outward sign enabled the Reformed tradition to claim that although regeneration was normally "annexed" to baptism, it was not "invariably" so. Thus the Westminster Confession claimed with respect to baptism:

> V. Although it be a great sin to condemn or neglect this ordinance, yet grace and salvation are not so invariably annexed unto it, as that no person can be regenerated or saved without it, or that all that are baptized are undoubtedly regenerated.
> VI. The efficacy of baptism is not tied to that moment of time wherein it is administered.[126]

That is to say, in the Reformed understanding, the grace of regeneration normally accompanied baptism, but divine freedom required that this could not be "invariably" claimed, and insisted further that the moment of regeneration might not be the same moment when the water of baptism was applied.

John Wesley's revision of the rite of infant baptism omitted the prayer of thanksgiving that announced that the newly baptized infant was regenerate,[127] consistent with this Reformed understanding of regeneration and baptism. Moreover, his recension of the Articles of Religion that accompanied the *Sunday Service* of 1784 omitted a key phrase from the Anglican Article on baptism, which asserted that "as by an instrument, they that receive Baptism rightly are grafted into the Church; the promises of forgiveness of sin, and our adoption to be the sons of God by the Holy Ghost, are visibly signed and sealed; Faith is confirmed, and Grace increased by virtue of prayer unto God."[128] The deletion of this phrase from the Article allows for a broader understanding of the relationship between regeneration and baptism, since this phrase demanded a very specific "instrumental" understanding of this relationship.[129]

Thus although John Wesley's conjunction of baptismal regeneration and regeneration by way of a conversion experience makes little sense against the background of Catholic or Lutheran spirituality, it does make sense when understood against the background of the Reformed tradition in which the sacrament was understood as bearing divine grace and serving as a testimony of grace revealed. It is crucial to note in this regard that the Reformed tradition must not be identified with Zwinglianism either with respect to baptism or the Lord's Supper. The main stream of Reformed tradition had maintained a strong sense of the connection between baptism and regeneration. John Wesley would take a different direction than the Reformed tradition had done on issues related to human nature and grace, such as the issue of limited atonement, but his sacramental teaching was consistent with the Reformed theology characteristic of

Georgian Anglicanism. The next section will show that this was also the case with respect to John Wesley's understanding of the sacrament of the Lord's Supper.

10. Belief about the Sacrament of the Lord's Supper

Much of what has been said above about baptism applies also to John Wesley's beliefs about the sacrament of the Lord's Supper. Like baptism, the Lord's Supper was understood as a dominical sacrament that is necessary for the existence of the Christian church. Like baptism, Wesley believed that the supper conveyed divine grace and as such was necessary to Christian existence. There are four important sources for understanding John Wesley's belief about the Lord's Supper: (1) his recension of the Anglican Articles concerning the sacrament, (2) his comments on the sacrament in such sermons as "The Means of Grace" (between 1739 and 1741) and "The Duty of Constant Communion" (originally written around 1733 and republished in 1788), (3) the hymns that were published under his and his brother Charles's name under the title *Hymns on the Lord's Supper* (1745), and (4) an abridgment of Daniel Brevint's treatise *The Christian Sacrament and Sacrifice* (1673) that was included with the *Hymns on the Lord's Supper,* in the same volume published under the names of John and Charles Wesley. Although it may be the case that John Wesley was the author of some of the *Hymns on the Lord's Supper,* I will leave consideration of that corpus for a discussion of Charles Wesley's transmission of beliefs about the Lord's Supper in chapter 3. I begin here by a consideration of the Articles and sermons together, and then I will take up the Wesleys' abridgment of Brevint.

Three specific aspects of John Wesley's eucharistic theology become clear in his recension of the Articles and in his sermons. In the first place, consistent with what we have seen about baptism in the preceding section, John Wesley made a clear distinction between the outward sacramental signs of bread and wine and the inward grace signified by those signs, namely, the body and blood of Christ. The principal reason for the sacrament of the Lord's Supper is to call to mind the work of Christ by means of the "signs" of bread and wine. In his sermon "The Duty of Constant Communion" he wrote that "the design of this sacrament is, the continual remembrance of the death of Christ, by eating bread and drinking wine, which are the outward signs of the inward grace, the body and blood of Christ."[130]

Similarly in his sermon "The Means of Grace" he states that whenever Christians observe the sacrament, "Ye openly exhibit the same by these visible signs, before God, and angels, and men; ye manifest your solemn remembrance of his death, till he cometh in the clouds of heaven."[131] This is consistent with the understanding of the sacrament given in Article 18 of Wesley's recension of the Articles:

> The Supper of the Lord is not only a sign of the love that Christians ought to have among themselves one to another, but rather is a sacrament of our redemption by Christ's death, insomuch that to such as rightly, worthily, and with faith receive the same, the bread which we break is a partaking of the body of Christ; and likewise the cup of blessing is a partaking of the blood of Christ.[132]

Second, as the previous quotation indicates, Wesley's understanding of the Lord's Supper involves the belief that a distinctive divine grace is available in the sacrament. This, he argued, is a principal reason for the practice of "constant communion":

> 2. A Second reason why every Christian should do this as often as he can, is, because the benefits of doing it are so great to all that do it in obedience to him; viz., the forgiveness of our past sins and the present strengthening and refreshing of our souls....
>
> 3. The grace of God given herein confirms to us the pardon of our sins, by enabling us to leave them. As our bodies are strengthened by bread and wine, so are our souls by these tokens of the body and blood of Christ. This is the food of our souls: This gives strength to perform our duty, and leads us on to perfection. If, therefore, we have any regard for the plain command of Christ, if we desire the pardon of our sins, if we wish for strength to believe, to love and obey God, then we should neglect no opportunity of receiving the Lord's Supper; then we must never turn our backs on the feast which our Lord has prepared for us.[133]

The grace available in the sacrament is not simply the presence of Christ "wherever two or three are gathered" in Christ's name. The presence of Christ in the sacrament conveys "the forgiveness of our past sins and the present strengthening and refreshing of our souls." Neither his sermons nor his recension of the Articles of Religion specify a particular way of accounting for Christ's presence, but Wesley was abundantly clear that a distinctive divine grace is available in the sacrament.

Third, Wesley's understanding of the Lord's Supper expressed in the Articles and sermons maintains that the grace available in the sacrament is conditioned by the faith of the recipient. This is stated explicitly in the Article of Religion cited above, that "to such as rightly, worthily, and with faith receive the same, the bread which we break is a partaking of the body of Christ; and likewise the cup of blessing is a partaking of the blood of Christ." The Article goes on to state: "The body of Christ is given, taken, and eaten in the Supper only after a heavenly and spiritual manner. And the means whereby the body of Christ is received and eaten in the Supper is faith."[134] Similarly, in anticipating objections in his sermon "The Duty of Constant Communion," Wesley wrote, "But suppose a man has often been at the sacrament, and yet received no benefit. Was it not his own fault? Either he was not rightly prepared, willing to obey all the commands and to receive all the promises of God, or he did not receive it aright, trusting in God."[135] In other words, simply or mechanically receiving the sacrament did not guarantee that the recipient would receive divine grace. A recipient of holy communion could resist divine grace just as a mature (adult) recipient of baptism could resist divine grace.

If the Articles of Religion and John Wesley's sermons do not reveal a particular understanding of Christ's presence in the Lord's Supper, the Wesleys' recension of Brevint's treatise *The Christian Sacrament and Sacrifice* did. Brevint, who had been dean of Lincoln Cathedral, frequently spoke of the "virtue" of the sacrament or the "virtue" of Christ's body and blood present to those who rightly receive the sacrament.[136] In these cases, the term "virtue" was used in a very particular sense in which it had been utilized by Calvin and subsequent Reformed theologians. It denotes the distinctive power (Latin, *virtus*) available to faithful recipients of the sacrament, a power Calvin described as being "as if" Christ himself were bodily present.[137] Brevint followed this particular understanding of the mode of Christ's presence in the supper.

Brevint was, moreover, representative of Anglican thought of his day in this understanding of Christ's presence. Eric Richard Griffin has examined Daniel Brevint's eucharistic theology and shows that despite Brevint's identity as a "Caroline" Anglican divine, his eucharistic theology was thoroughly consistent with Calvinistic teaching on the sacrament, and especially on the manner of Christ's presence in the sacrament. In fact, the conclusion of Griffin's study of Brevint goes so far as to claim that this Calvinistic understanding of eucharist was common to Anglican divines of the late seventeenth century, both those identified as "Caroline" and those identified as Puritans:

> [Brevint's] *The Christian Sacrament and Sacrifice* typifies the thoroughly Calvinist eucharistic theology of the English divines of the Caroline period, and Brevint's devotional manual became so popular and influential precisely because it represented, and shared much in common with, the best eucharistic writing of the time. It witnesses to the significant theological consensus regarding the holy communion in its use of images and arguments which were the common currency of writers of the period, both those who have been classed as anti-Calvinist Caroline Divines and the reformed-scholastic Puritans. The division of the Church of England into two opposed theological camps, Anglican (or Laudian or Arminian, or Caroline) and Puritan, seems then to be largely artificial, at least in terms of the theology of the eucharist.[138]

The marks of the main stream of Reformed teaching on the sacrament of the Lord's Supper were (a) virtualism, belief in the distinctive power, *virtus*, available in the sacrament, and (b) receptionism, belief that the grace available in the sacrament is contingent on the faith of the recipient. John Wesley reflected both of these beliefs, and in doing so, as Griffin has shown, he reflected the common views of Anglican divines of his own era.[139] As we will see in chapter 3, Charles Wesley expressed these beliefs utilizing the technical language of virtualism and receptionism in his poetic corpus.

It might be appropriate to ask if in fact there were other theological options available for the explanation of Christ's presence in the Eucharist, given what Griffin has said about the "significant theological consensus" among Anglicans of various camps in favor of the Calvinistic understanding. It is the case that some Anglicans did not utilize the distinctly Calvinistic language of virtualism. For example, Anglican bishop William Nicholson of Gloucester (1660–72) claimed a "real presence" of Christ in the sacrament, and yet he denied that this meant a "corporal" or bodily presence.[140] One interpreter of the Wesleys, Franz Hildebrandt, tried to make the case that some of the language of the eucharistic hymns revealed the characteristically Lutheran understanding of the ubiquity of Christ's human nature. This theory allowed Lutherans to claim, in contrast to the Reformed views considered here, that Christ's humanity could be present anywhere (*ubique*) and thus in the eucharistic elements. But Ole Borgen has examined Hildebrandt's claims and concludes that although the eucharistic hymns do speak of Christ's ubiquity, they do not at all make it clear that this refers to the ubiquity of Christ's humanity, which would constitute the distinctive Lutheran doctrine.[141]

The consistency of the Wesleys' sacramental beliefs with Reformed or Calvinist tradition may come as a surprise to some Wesleyan interpreters. In recent decades there has been a strong tendency to identify the Wesleys' theology broadly as Anglican and as also reflecting elements of Catholic and Byzantine theological traditions. This is not to be denied, but "Anglican" cannot simply be equated with post-Tractarian Anglican beliefs and spirituality. The Wesleys reflected the Caroline theological inheritance of the late seventeenth century and worked within the framework of eighteenth-century (Georgian) Anglicanism, an era in which the Church of England was clear about its identity as a Reformed church.[142] In this respect, then, it should not be surprising that the Wesleys reflected the sacramental theology that did in fact characterize Anglican theologians of their era.

GROUPS OR CLUSTERS OF COMMON CHRISTIAN BELIEFS

Given the evidence for these ten beliefs as standing consistently as "essential" or "fundamental" beliefs and teachings about essential Christian institutions and practices in John Wesley's thought, we may now ask if there is any discernible shape or logic to the ten doctrines identified here, especially as they are considered as common

Christian teachings. Based on the evidence given above (including the extended passage in the "Letter to a Roman Catholic"), we can say that John Wesley considered the first three doctrinal claims that we considered above (the doctrines of the Trinity, of the divinity of Christ, and of the atonement) to be fundamental or essential to Christian faith as expressed in the ancient creeds. The trinitarian form in which he gave these doctrines, following the outline of the creeds, gives a certain shape to them, with the doctrines of the divinity of Christ and of the atonement as sub-points under the second article of the creed. The doctrine of the full divinity of Christ and the denial of this by Arians was, after all, the beginning of the trinitarian controversy and of the churches' definition of trinitarian doctrine in the fourth century, including the Council of Nicaea (325). Belief in the atonement and the broader work of Christ in salvation underlay the further development of Christology as formulated in the third (431) and fourth (451) ecumenical councils.

It is consistent with the identification of these three doctrines as essential or fundamental doctrines that the 1784 revision of the Anglican Articles of Religion that Wesley sent to North America with Thomas Coke included as its first two articles an article affirming belief in the Trinity utilizing the language of the Nicene Creed (Article 1) and an article affirming belief in the divinity of Christ and the atonement using some of the language of the Chalcedonian Definition of Faith (Article 2).[143] It is consistent with his identification of these three doctrines as fundamental that they should appear at the very head of the doctrines defined in the Articles. It may be important to state that John Wesley affirmed these three doctrines very much as they had been affirmed historically (in contrast to the next group or cluster of doctrines we shall consider), and affirmed them consistently throughout his career.[144]

We may identify the next four beliefs that were also essential or fundamental for Christian faith, by Wesley's own admission (the doctrines of biblical authority, original sin, justification by faith, and regeneration) as a distinct cluster, although the doctrine of biblical authority is a more foundational doctrine and is distinct from the remaining three, which are concerned with issues of human nature and salvation. As noted above, although John Wesley claimed all of these as essential doctrines, the doctrine of biblical authority and the doctrine of regeneration do not appear in Colin

Williams's list, and the doctrine of original sin is absent from John Wesley's creedal affirmations in the "Letter to a Roman Catholic." The identification of these three or four doctrines as a cluster distinct from the previous three is my own distinction based on a comparison of Wesley's essential doctrines with similar teachings affirmed in twentieth-century ecumenical work, especially the work of Faith and Order groups; it does not reflect a scheme of organization that John Wesley himself utilized for them. Each of these doctrines reflected the distinct inheritance or at least the decided influence of the Western, Augustinian tradition, as contrasted with the previously identified three doctrines, which were affirmed in the ecumenical creeds of the ancient church. Moreover, John Wesley qualified in distinctive ways his affirmation of the doctrines of original sin, justification, and regeneration, and this suggests to me that we should see them in a somewhat different light than the previous three.

Yet another group of doctrines has to do with teachings about the necessary Christian institutions and practices discussed above. The doctrine of the church, in particular, is defined in Article 13 of the Wesleyan recension of the Articles of Religion and alluded to in the "Letter to a Roman Catholic." I am not aware of loci where Wesley specifically named a doctrine of the church as a necessary Christian doctrine, but he did claim that the fellowship of the church is necessary to Christian existence. In a similar position would be teaching about the dominical sacraments of baptism and the Lord's Supper as practices essential to the Christian community and indispensable means of grace.

If I could lay out these ten beliefs in a schematic way, then, they can be arranged as follows:

> beliefs about the divine Trinity
> beliefs about the full divinity of Jesus Christ
> beliefs about the atonement and the work of Christ
>
> beliefs about biblical authority
>
> beliefs about original righteousness and original sin (calling for repentance)
> beliefs about justification (calling for faith)
> beliefs about regeneration (leading to holiness)

beliefs about the Christian church
beliefs about the sacrament of baptism
beliefs about the sacrament of the Lord's Supper.

I have suggested above and will show in more detail in the next chapter that the three sets of beliefs about human nature and salvation bear a very close relationship to the three "grand scriptural doctrines" that John Wesley claimed as the distinctive emphases of the "Methodist" movement (meaning the Evangelical movement), namely, the doctrines of repentance, faith, and holiness. The latter three sets of beliefs about the church and the sacraments form a cluster by themselves.

CONCLUSIONS

This chapter has shown that John Wesley identified some specific doctrines as "essential" to or definitive of Christian communities and maintained other common Christian teachings related to essential Christian institutions and practices (the church and its sacraments). The manner in which John Wesley expressed these doctrines in the creedal passage from his "Letter to a Roman Catholic" and the patterns of doctrines I have tried to discern in the previous section suggest that there is a logic or shape to Wesley's understanding of central Christian teachings. The next chapter will extend this by showing how John Wesley's understanding of the distinctive doctrinal emphases of the Evangelical revival and of his own branch of the revival relate to his understanding of these central or essential Christian teachings.

What all of this indicates, considered together, is that John Wesley held a distinctive vision of Christian faith, a vision that can be described as "adiaphorist" or even minimalist by some standards, and this vision of Christian faith would come to characterize subsequent Wesleyan communities. Two things need to be said to make this point clear. On the one hand, this approach to Christian faith and life was indeed more "liberal" in the sense of being broad-minded or open-minded in contrast to restrictive versions of Christian confessionalism—Catholic as well as Protestant—that had flourished in the past and especially in the seventeenth century in the context of European wars of religion.

This general attitude is the ground of claims about Methodist "liberality" in doctrine, and there is more than a grain of truth to it. The second thing that must be said, however, is that this liberality did not denote for John Wesley, and very seldom denoted for subsequent Methodists, a thoroughgoing liberality, since it consistently affirmed specific doctrinal tenets both in its formal doctrine and in the central practices of Wesleyan communities, most notably, in their practices of worship.

Through the history of the Wesleyan movement, Methodist churches and Methodist leaders would claim that Methodist teaching was essentially that of the universal church. Methodist Episcopal bishop Matthew Simpson pointed in 1876 to the general insistence of Methodists on fidelity basic to Christian beliefs: "If [the Methodist preachers] preserve uncorrupted the doctrines of the Gospel, if they seek to bear the image of the blessed Saviour, and if they preserve the cardinal principles of their Church polity, the coming century will be full of glorious achievements."[145]

At the same time, consistent with John Wesley's description of a "catholic spirit," Methodists decried more elaborate and divisive dogmatic disputation. Thus Methodist Episcopal historian Abel Stevens wrote:

> [The narrative of Methodist history] presents, in full vitality, that original, that only, example of evangelistic propagandism, which, when all dogmatic conflicts and hierarchical pretensions, with their wasted passions and pomps, are recorded as historical failures, will bear forward to universal triumph the ensign of the Cross by a catholic, living, working Church of the common people.[146]

Even among more progressive generations of Methodist leaders in the late nineteenth and early twentieth centuries, Methodists consistently sounded this emphasis on common doctrines. Thus the progressive American Methodist historian James Buckley wrote:

> The *doctrines* taught by Wesley and his itinerant and lay preachers included the fundamental principles of Christianity as held by the Reformed churches generally, but excluded ritualism and sacramentarianism, and divided from Calvinism on unconditional election, predestination, final perseverance of the saints, and kindred doctrines.[147]

In a very similar vein the late nineteenth-century British Methodist theologian and social reformer Hugh Price Hughes asserted the essential fidelity of Christians of all traditional denominations to the christology expressed in the earliest ecumenical councils, as he wrote in a series of sermons on *Social Christianity*:

> It is a remarkable fact, as Mr. Gladstone points out, that ever since the fourth century the Christian conception of Christ has been absolutely unchanged. Amid all our controversies and schisms we have never doubted or disputed the claims of Christ. To-day, if you were to shut up in a room the Archbishop of Canterbury, [Baptist preacher] Mr. [C. H.] Spurgeon, [Roman Catholic] Cardinal Manning, [Salvation Army leader] General [William] Booth, the Chairman of the Congregational Union, and the President of the Methodist Conference, and tell them that they must remain there until they were all agreed in a common definition of the claims of Christ, they would not be detained for five minutes.[148]

Many of these common teachings were to take on distinctive nuances in Wesleyan teaching: the triad of original sin, justification, and regeneration will be seen as being directly related to the Methodist calling to preach repentance, faith, and holiness. The teaching about holiness would come to characterize the Wesleyan movement and Wesleyan churches in a very distinct way. The next chapter, then, will expand on this by considering John Wesley's claims about distinctively Methodist or Wesleyan beliefs.

CHAPTER 2

John Wesley's Claims about Distinctively Methodist Beliefs

INTRODUCTION

The previous chapter began to describe the core beliefs of Wesleyan communities in the works of John Wesley by asking about his understanding of common Christian faith, examining in particular his understanding of common "essential" or "fundamental" Christian beliefs affirmed in the Methodist movement. I turn in this chapter to consider John Wesley's claims about distinctive beliefs of the Methodist movement. As noted above, we have to distinguish, in the context of the eighteenth century, between the Wesleyan movement, the movement led by John and Charles Wesley,[1] and the broader Evangelical or "Methodist" movement that denoted the Evangelical revival including Calvinistic preachers and leaders as well as the Wesleys.[2] The distinctive teachings of the Methodist or Evangelical movement in the eighteenth century focused around the Christian's pilgrimage from sin to salvation, the pilgrimage described in the Reformed tradition as the *ordo salutis*, the "order of salvation," and which John Wesley preferred to call "the way of salvation" or "the way to heaven."[3] But as we shall see in this chapter, there were some other critical nuances to distinctly Methodist and Wesleyan teachings that will also be considered here, namely, a distinctive emphasis on religious experience ("perceptible inspiration") as a grounds for claims about the religious life, and the teaching of entire sanctification as a very distinctive mark of the Wesleyan branch of the Evangelical movement.

Scholarly literature on the theology of John Wesley has often pointed to the "way of salvation" as a distinctive mark of John Wesley's theology. In the previous chapter I attempted to discern doctrines that John Wesley understood to be "essential" or "fundamental" to Christian faith and life. That chapter examined Colin Williams's list of John Wesley's essential doctrines and contrasted Williams's list with that of Lawrence Meredith's 1962 Harvard dissertation "Essential Doctrine in the Theology of John Wesley with Special Attention to the Methodist Standards of Doctrine."[4] Meredith's dissertation focused on three essential doctrines in John Wesley's thought, namely:

> repentance
> faith
> holiness

This list is based on a passage in John Wesley's "Principles of a Methodist Farther Explained," in which Wesley asserted that "Our main doctrines, which include all the rest, are three,—that of repentance, of faith, and of holiness."[5] It is clear that Meredith had conceived of the project of "essential doctrine" in a different way than Williams, whose work he had indeed seen before the completion of his own thesis.[6] Rather than identifying passages in which Wesley had denoted a doctrine to be "essential" or fundamental," Meredith tried to find a logical consistency or coherence to Wesley's claims about characteristically Methodist teachings. Despite the focus on "essential doctrine" in his dissertation, then, what he sought was rather different from Colin Williams's quest for the ecumenically significant core or fundamental doctrines in John Wesley's work. Using my own terminology, what Meredith did was to restrict the ecclesial scope of the claims he examined to distinctive claims emphasized by the Methodist movement.

Just as Colin Williams's list of essential Christian doctrines was helpful in beginning our consideration in the previous chapter, so Meredith's work will be particularly important in this chapter where we consider distinctly Methodist doctrinal emphases. Here we are asking how John Wesley conceived of the distinctive marks of the Methodist movement under his leadership. Again, we have to exercise caution, for as we have seen in the previous chapter, there were occasions when John Wesley used the terms

"Protestant" and "Methodist" as part of a meiosis, revealing subsequently that by these terms he denoted what was simply or commonly Christian. But as we shall see here, there are other occasions when he more straightforwardly identified what is distinctly Methodist in texts where he did not use the term as part of a rhetorical device.

Although Colin Williams identified other doctrinal emphases consistent with his ecumenical concerns, he followed the general pattern of the "way of salvation" in describing John Wesley's theology,[7] and most Wesleyan scholars have shaped their considerations of John Wesley's theology within the general framework of the "way of salvation." A version of it structured Albert C. Outler's lectures and his subsequently published book *Theology in the Wesleyan Spirit* (1975), which has an introductory chapter followed by three chapters (originally lectures) on original sin, justification, and sanctification.[8] Randy Maddox's *Responsible Grace* (1994) has an extended discussion of salvation in "The Way of Salvation: Grace Upon Grace."[9] Theodore Runyon's *The New Creation: John Wesley's Theology Today* takes up teachings on the way of salvation in two sequential chapters.[10] Kenneth J. Collins has written at length on the subject in *The Scripture Way of Salvation: The Heart of John Wesley's Theology* (1997), which focuses, as the title suggests, on the "way of salvation," and he has returned to this subject as a central theme in his larger *The Theology of John Wesley: Holy Love and the Shape of Grace* (2007).[11]

Methodist scholars in the early twentieth century, however, did not focus on the way of salvation as a distinctly Wesleyan trait. Such scholars as Umphrey Lee and Herbert Brook Workman emphasized religious experience as the most distinctive aspect of Wesleyan life.[12] Teachings about the need for personal religious experience, the way of salvation, and entire sanctification would all become consistent marks of Wesleyan communities. Together with the common Christian teachings considered in the previous chapter, these more distinctive teachings form a nucleus of distinctive beliefs of Wesleyan communities as these beliefs were handed on from the Wesleys to later Wesleyan and Methodist communities.

BACKGROUND: THE REFORMED TRADITION, THE TESTIMONIUM INTERNUM, AND THE ORDO SALUTIS

The previous chapter has shown at a number of points that John Wesley's understanding of common Christian doctrines was shaped by his Anglican creedal, doctrinal, and liturgical heritage, and it has shown that the Anglicanism of his day was strongly influenced by the Reformed tradition, most notably in its sacramental theology. When we begin to consider the more distinctive teachings and practices of the Methodist movement, especially teachings about the central importance of religious experience and about the "way of salvation," we need to consider again the formative role of the Reformed tradition on John Wesley's thought and practice. Although John Wesley defined his theology over against that of the Reformed tradition at very crucial and specific points (for example, the doctrine of limited atonement), in other respects his thought and specific practices can be understood as elements inherited from the Reformed tradition. Chapter 1 has pointed out that Georgian Anglicanism was strongly Reformed in character and it was not until the Oxford or Tractarian movement of the nineteenth century that the ties between Anglicanism and the Reformed tradition began to weaken. Robert C. Monk cites Horton Davies's claim that Methodism's "evangelical passion and experimental religion were a revival of Puritan religion."[13] But although the importance of the Reformed tradition for Wesleyan theology has been widely acknowledged by scholars and has been explored in depth by Monk himself,[14] it has not figured prominently in recent interpretations of John Wesley's theology where there has been a strong interest in demonstrating Wesley's Anglican roots, often presuming that "Anglican" had to denote a high church Anglican culture such as that of Caroline Anglicanism or even of post-Tractarian Anglicanism. Similarly, contemporary studies of John Wesley have also emphasized his ties to Catholic writers and even his connections to ancient Eastern Christian writers. In what follows, then, I am not so concerned to show the relative strength of Reformed "influences" on John Wesley as I am concerned to show that many of the Wesleys' most distinctive teachings and practices are best understood against a background of Reformed teachings and practices.

In the first place, it was the Reformed tradition from Calvin on that had emphasized the "inward witness" (or "inward testimony") of the Holy Spirit (*testimonium internum Spiritus Sancti*), and this idea of the inward witness as a ground of the religious life would come to hold great prominence in the thought of John Wesley and the other leaders of the Evangelical movement. In Calvin's *Institutes*, the inward witness of the Spirit was spoken of primarily as the way in which the Spirit confirms the truth of the sacred Scriptures, so for Calvin it was the direct work of the Spirit and not the mechanism of the church and its traditions that confirmed the truths of the Scriptures.[15] But Calvin went on to associate the inward witness of the Spirit with the ways in which the work of Christ was applied to believers in the out-working of election[16] and it was in this sense that subsequent Reformed theologians were to elaborate the *ordo salutis* in a believer's experience of divine grace. This Reformed emphasis was certainly known in the Wesley family: John Wesley reported to the anonymous correspondent he called "John Smith" that he had heard his father say in the last eight months of the elder Wesley's life, "The inward witness, son, the inward witness, that is the proof, the strongest proof, of Christianity," harking back to the Reformed faith in which Samuel Wesley had been formed.[17]

In the second place, the Puritan movement of the late sixteenth and seventeenth centuries developed the motif of spiritual pilgrimage as an order of salvation (*ordo salutis*), describing in identifiable stages the soul's progress from sin to salvation. Developed at first by such theologians as William Perkins (1558–1602) and William Ames (1576–1633) as an understanding of the out-working of predestination, Puritans consistently outlined the stages of the Christian life following Romans 8:30 and a tradition of Calvinistic exegesis in four or five discernible "degrees" or stages. For William Perkins, these stages were as follows:

effectual calling
justification
sanctification
glorification[18]

To these four stages, William Ames added a fifth, "adoption," between justification and sanctification,[19] thus

> effectual calling
> justification
> adoption
> sanctification
> glorification

The Westminster Confession of Faith (1648) had listed the following stages as chapters 10–13 of the Confession:

> effectual calling
> justification
> adoption
> sanctification[20]

Thus the Westminster Confession followed Ames's order, although it did not deal with glorification in sequence with the other elements of the *ordo salutis*.

Puritan teachers described "effectual calling" (also called "conversion" by Ames), as that event in which men and women are brought to repentance and faith by means of the proclamation of the Law and the Gospel.[21] Both Perkins and Ames defined "justification" in characteristically Reformed language as the imputation of Christ's righteousness to the believer, and the believer's being "accounted" righteous before God on the basis of faith alone through the work of Christ.[22] They understood "sanctification" to denote the Christian's continuing death to sin ("mortification") and growth in life to Christ ("vivification").[23] Perkins and Ames defined "glorification" as the completion of the Christian's likeness to Christ that begins at death and is consummated at the time of the Final Judgment.[24]

Puritan teachers stressed the possibility that human beings can know of their election to eternal life, although they differed in their placement of this belief within their schemes. In his discussion of effectual calling, William Perkins distinguished several "degrees" of Christian faith. "The highest degree of faith," he wrote, "is plerophoria, a full assurance, which is not onely certaine and true, but also a full perswasion of the heart."[25] In the concluding chapter of *A Golden Chaine*, Perkins again returned to the question of the knowledge of election, and maintained that believers may know of their election both by "the Testimonie of Gods Spirit" and by the works of sanctification which give evidence of a believer's election.[26] Where Perkins had but briefly discussed "adoption" as one of the privileges bestowed by God on believers,[27] Ames developed the topic into a fifth section in his account of the order of salvation interposed between justification and sanctification.[28] Here Ames claimed that one of the principal benefits of adoption is "the witness of the Spirit which is given to believers" or the "assurance of salvation."[29] As with Perkins, this meant assurance that one was among the elect. As we shall see, these concepts and many of these very terms would be utilized by John Wesley and would be bequeathed by him to Wesleyan communities, although in the thought of John Wesley they would be severed from the groundwork of Reformed thought on predestination.

The exposition of the order of salvation comprehending effectual calling, justification, sanctification, and glorification that Perkins and Ames analyzed was popularized by Puritan preachers and spiritual writers who produced biographies of saintly Christians whose own lives illustrated the way of salvation. It was also popularized in the widespread practice of keeping diaries or journals recounting one's own spiritual experience. What these Puritan diaries accomplished was to make concrete the idealized order of salvation that Perkins, Ames, and others had described. They also served to illustrate the range of religious affections experienced by women and men as they traversed the order of salvation. Perhaps the crowning literary expressions of the Puritan understanding of the way of salvation were John Bunyan's autobiography, *Grace Abounding to the Chief of Sinners* (1666), and then his well-known allegorical account of *The Pilgrim's Progress from This World to the Next* (1678 with a second part published in 1684).

An understanding of the *ordo salutis* laid out in this Puritan pattern can be seen in the organizational scheme of a later but very influential collection of eighteenth-century English Evangelical hymnody that set a precedent for later Methodist hymnals. This was one of the best-known of English-language hymn collections, John Newton's and William Cowper's *Olney Hymns* (1779), the collection in which the text of the hymn "Amazing Grace" first appeared. It was published the year before John Wesley issued his *Collection of Hymns for the Use of the People Called Methodists* (1780). Book III of the *Olney Hymns* is entitled, "On the Progress and

Changes of the Spiritual Life." The headings in this section follow the traditional Calvinist understanding of the way of salvation, although elaborated at points. These headings are as follows:

I. Solemn Addresses to Sinners
II. Seeking, Pleading, Hoping
III. Conflict
IV. Comfort
V. Dedication and Surrender
VI. Cautions
VII. Praise
VIII. Short Hymns

With exception of the last section of "Short Hymns," we can see the Puritan *ordo salutis* comprising effectual calling, justification, sanctification, and glorification in these divisions and in the hymns within them. The first three divisions ("Solemn Addresses to Sinners," "Seeking, Pleading, Hoping," and "Conflict") deal with the state of sinners before conversion to Christ. The next two divisions deal with conversion itself, namely, "Comfort" and "Dedication and Surrender." The "Cautions" are directed toward believers and so comprise at least a part of the believer's sanctification, and "Praise" is the manner in which the believer on earth appropriates the glories of heaven to come, or, in other words, anticipates glorification.

Each of these Puritan beliefs would be transformed by the Wesleys and within the Wesleyan movement. The Reformed emphasis on the inward witness of the Spirit met the Moravians' own distinct religious experiences, especially the experience of the "assurance of pardon" that would be a critical element in the experiences of both John and Charles Wesley in 1738. As John Wesley explicated his understanding of religious experience, he would utilize language derived from contemporary philosophy, including the Cambridge Platonists and John Locke in addition to the ways in which Reformed thought had described the "inward witness." The Reformed understanding of the "order of salvation" was detached in the Wesleys' thought and experience from its Reformed moorings in the doctrine of election and was further modified by the Wesleys' insistence that entire sanctification is possible in this life.

JOHN WESLEY'S CLAIMS ABOUT THE DISTINCTIVE BELIEFS OF THE METHODIST (EVANGELICAL) MOVEMENT

With this Reformed background in mind, we now turn to consider John Wesley's claims about distinctive Methodist beliefs, beliefs that defined the self-understanding of the Evangelical movement and as a subset of that, of the Wesleyan movement. That is to say, the doctrines with which we are concerned here were expressed within a more restricted ecclesial scope that refers to the "Methodist" (in the sense of "Evangelical") movement or even more specifically to the Wesleyan movement under John Wesley's leadership. Lawrence Meredith's 1962 doctoral dissertation understood "essential doctrine" in this way. It focused on the Wesleyan standards of doctrine and identified the triad of doctrines about repentance, faith, and holiness as the key "essential" doctrines emphasized by the Methodist movement. I would note, however, that although Wesley did make claims about characteristically Methodist teachings (see the qualification in the next paragraph), he did not always use the terms "essential" or "fundamental" to describe doctrines consistently emphasized by the Methodist movement. As we have seen in the citations given in the previous two sections of this chapter, Wesley utilized these terms to describe commonly held Christian doctrines, that is, doctrines that were "essential" or "fundamental" to the Christian faith per se. The more characteristically Methodist teachings he called the "grand scriptural doctrines" or simply "our doctrines," though it is important to note that he believed most of these "Methodist" teachings to be characteristic of the Evangelical movement in its Calvinistic as well as Wesleyan or "Arminian" expressions.[30]

There is, however, a further qualification we must make at this point, and that is that John Wesley understood the characteristic claims of the Evangelical movement (for example, claims about the nature of repentance, faith, and holiness) to be closely linked to common Christian teachings. John Wesley sometimes appeared to claim that in fact there were *no* distinctly Methodist claims, as in the introductory paragraph of "The Character of a Methodist," where he wrote, "The distinguishing marks of a Methodist are not his opinions of any sort." The conclusion of the tract asserted that Methodist teachings were reducible to "the common, fundamental principles of Christianity."[31] In the former case, however, it was "opinions" with which Wesley was concerned, not with essential doctrines, and in the latter case, the device employed was meiosis in which Wesley made apparently restrictive claims (about "the Character of a Methodist") that were revealed at the end to be much more comprehensive claims about the nature of Christian faith. This was not merely rhetoric on Wesley's part: he genuinely believed that what the Methodist movement taught was in fact at the heart of Christian belief. Nevertheless, despite these claims that Methodism was reducible to common Christian principles, John Wesley did on numerous other occasions attempt to clarify what he understood to be the most consistent emphases or teachings of the Methodist movement, and these are the claims examined in this section.

"Perceptible Inspiration" as "The Main Doctrine of the Methodists"

Before considering Wesley's more familiar teachings about the "way of salvation," I want to point out that John Wesley often claimed that religious experience and the knowledge of God that comes via religious experience was a key emphasis of the Methodist movement. He employed a variety of terms to describe this characteristic emphasis. "Perceptible inspiration," he wrote to the anonymous correspondent he called "John Smith" in 1745, is "the main doctrine of the Methodists."[32] Similarly, his "Earnest Appeal to Men of Reason and Religion" (1743) begins with his explanation of "faith" in the broadest or most general sense as involving spiritual perception, following Hebrews 11:1.[33] Contemporary interpreters have shown that Jonathan Edwards and John Wesley both developed epistemologies utilizing Lockean categories but differing from Locke by claiming religious experience as a valid source of knowledge (a source of "simple ideas," in Locke's language).[34] This concern for religious experience cannot be seen as a point in the "way of salvation"; rather, like the Calvinistic notion of the inward witness of the Spirit, it must be seen as a consistent presupposition for the way in which the Methodist movement understood the Christian life and the stages involved in it. Thus repentance was understood as involving the spiritual perception of one's need for grace, Christian faith[35] was understood as involving the spiritual perception that Christ died "for me," and regeneration and sanctification following it were understood as involving the spiritual perception (as well as the outward marks or signs) that one is a new being in Christ.

As we will see in what follows, John Wesley consistently identified teachings about "the way of salvation" as being distinctive marks of the Methodist movement. His understanding of "perceptible inspiration" was a critical epistemological presupposition of teachings on the way of salvation, especially as he emphasized not only the objective facts of divine grace applied to human beings in the way of salvation but also the human apprehension or experience of divine grace at specific points in the way of salvation. Thus the repentance of sinners prior to justification was an experiential aspect of preventing or prevenient grace, and it could be understood as a species of "perceptible inspiration" whose object is the sinner's awareness of his or her own sin and need for grace. Similarly, Wesley spoke of the "assurance of pardon" as a correlate of justification (sometimes he spoke of it as a *necessary* correlate of justification), and assurance could be understood as a species of perceptible grace whose object was the believer's awareness of divine forgiveness. We now turn to the varied ways in which John Wesley explicated the "way of salvation" as distinctive of the Methodist movement.

Threefold Explication of the "Way of Salvation"

The "way of salvation" was John Wesley's counterpart to the Reformed understanding of the *ordo salutis*, and it was the topic on which John Wesley was to make his most distinctive contribution to Christian theology. Kenneth J. Collins has appropriately called this concept "the heart of John Wesley's theology,"[36] and it was to become enshrined in later Wesleyan tradition as it was taught in hymnals and catechisms and as it became a pattern by which Methodist people told their own stories of growth in grace and faith.

John Wesley's understanding of the "way of salvation" developed during the earliest decades of the revival movement as he developed a more and more consistent vocabulary and set of constructs by which he explained this set of teachings. The evolution of his technical vocabulary can be seen by comparing two of his best-known sermons, his 1738 sermon "Salvation by Faith" (traditionally the first sermon in collections of Wesley's sermons) and his 1765 sermon "The Scripture Way of Salvation," composed and delivered twenty-seven years later. Both of these sermons were on the epistle text Ephesians 2:8, "By grace are ye saved through faith" (AV), and they have similar structures. It is possible, then, to see the 1765 sermon as a much more mature version of the sermon from 1738. The 1738 sermon has the following three main points:

I. What faith it is through which we are saved.
II. What is the salvation which is through faith.
III. How may we answer some objections.[37]

The 1765 sermon has these main points:

I. What is salvation?
II. What is that faith whereby we are saved? And
III. How are we saved by it.[38]

Both sermons have main points in which John Wesley defines Christian faith and the salvation that comes by faith, although, as can be seen from the juxtaposition of these outlines, the positions of these two sections were reversed between the two sermons. Within the sermon sections defining "salvation," in particular, we can see indications of the development of John Wesley's thought between these two sermons. In the 1738 sermon "Salvation by Faith," Wesley first made the point that salvation is a present reality, not only the eternal destination of the believer. He made the same point in beginning the section on salvation in the 1765 sermon.[39] After this, the 1738 sermon went on to explain that salvation denotes salvation from sin (II:2), and then in three separate paragraphs it explained that this involves salvation from the guilt of past sin (II:3), from the fear that results from sin (II:4), and from the power of sin (II:5–6). In discussing freedom from the guilt of sin (II:3) he used the term "justified," and it would be tempting in the light of his later uses of theological terminology to see these three paragraphs as explicating what Wesley would call justification (II:3), assurance of pardon (freedom from fear, II:4), and sanctifica-

74

tion (freedom from the power of sin, III:5–6). However, in a summary paragraph following these (II:7), John Wesley explained that *all* of what he had described to that point could be summed up in the single term "justification" and its concomitant, the new birth in Christ. At the very end of this summary paragraph, Wesley stated that one who is thus justified and born again will progress "until at length he comes unto a perfect man, unto the measure of the stature of the fullness of Christ" (Ephesians 4:13 AV).[40] Wesley's language in the 1738 sermon, then, centered on justification, even though he suggested a connection with sanctification in speaking of the new birth, freedom from the power of sin, and the need to go on to perfection. The emphasis on justification in this sermon was consistent with Wesley's encomium on Martin Luther, "that glorious champion of the Lord of Hosts," in the conclusion of the sermon.[41] As Wesley came to focus more on sanctification, his estimation of Luther seems to have waned and he dropped this phrase from the sermon's 1746 printing.[42]

In the 1765 sermon, by contrast, the section on the meaning of salvation had a much more clearly delineated structure that utilized the terminology he had come to employ consistently in describing the "way of salvation." In fact, the term "way of salvation" as it is used consistently in Wesleyan studies comes from the title of this sermon, "The Scripture Way of Salvation." In this sermon, the section on salvation (which is section I) began with "preventing grace," which Wesley included as a component of salvation "in its utmost extent" (I:2). Preventing grace (later Wesleyan studies would utilize the expression "prevenient grace") denoted all the work of God in a person prior to justification and the new birth. Wesley then indicated that in a more restricted sense (the sense "which the Apostle is directly speaking of"), salvation had two parts: justification and sanctification. Justification denoted "pardon" or "the forgiveness of all our sins" (I:3). Sanctification began at the same moment as justification in the new birth and it was a "real" change in a person as contrasted with the "relative" change that occurred in justification (I:4). After an aside on the danger of imagining that sin had been completely done away with after justification (I:5–7), Wesley described the gradual work of sanctification (I:8) and the believer's hope for entire sanctification, "a full salvation from all our sins" (I:9).[43] The comparison of these two sermons, then, shows that in the twenty-seven years between 1738 and 1765 John Wesley had developed a more fully orbed vocabulary for describing the process of salvation, progressing in three recognizable stages from (1) "preventing" grace to (2) justification through (3) sanctification, culminating in entire sanctification.

But John Wesley would explain these stages of the way of salvation in different ways. This can be seen, to give another example, in John Wesley's claims about the characteristic teachings of the Methodist movement, given relatively early in the revival in his "Principles of a Methodist Farther Explained" (1746). The passage is as follows:

> Our main doctrines, which include all the rest, are three,—that of repentance, of faith, and of holiness. The first of these we account, as it were, the porch of religion; the next, the door; the third, religion itself.[44]

This triadic formulation served as the outline of Lawrence Meredith's discussion of characteristically Methodist teachings in his 1962 Harvard dissertation. The treatise in which this expression appeared had been written in response to a challenge from Anglican clergyman Thomas Church, who saw Wesley's movement as schismatic and had demanded Wesley's resignation from the priesthood.[45]

We may compare this reference to three primary doctrines (repentance, faith, and holiness) with later expressions where Wesley referred to a somewhat different set of doctrines. For example, in a letter to George Downing in 1761, John Wesley referred to three "grand scriptural doctrines" uniting the Evangelical clergy as the doctrines of original sin, justification, and the new birth.[46] Would we be justified in correlating the preaching of "original sin" (in the 1761 reference) with the preaching of "repentance" (in the 1746 reference)? John Wesley understood that a practical implication of the doctrine of original sin was the need for the repentance of sinners, that is, the acknowledgment that, because of the continuing effects of original sin, we as humans cannot save ourselves and we stand in need of divine grace. Another instance of this pattern, describing the way of salvation with respect to the divine grace that makes each of these stages possible, can be seen in John Wesley's claim in the sermon "The Means of Grace" that the means of grace are "the ordinary channels whereby [God] might convey to men, preventing, justifying, or sanctifying grace."[47] There is sufficient evidence to suggest a typical threefold pattern in his thought that can be laid out as follows.

1746 "Principles of a Methodist Farther Explained"	1749 sermon "The Means of Grace"	1761 Letter to George Downing	1765 sermon "The Scripture Way of Salvation"
Repentance	Preventing grace	Original sin	Preventing grace
Faith	Justifying grace	Justification	Justification
Holiness	Sanctifying grace	Regeneration	Sanctification

I do not mean to suggest that the items in each row are precise equivalents. The doctrine of original sin is the ground of preaching repentance to those who are not yet justified; prevenient grace includes repentance and awakening, regeneration is the beginning of sanctification. I am suggesting that in these four loci we can discern in Wesley's thought a typical threefold pattern that involves the work of grace prior to justification, the work of grace in justification itself, and the subsequent work of grace in sanctification beginning with regeneration or new birth.

Other Explications of the "Way of Salvation"

In the period between the middle of the 1740s and the middle of the 1760s, then, the threefold pattern of the "way of salvation" examined above appeared in Wesley's published works with some regularity. But there were different patterns that appeared simultaneously with these. John Wesley's sermon "The Way to the

Kingdom" was written around 1746 and its description of the progress of the religious life involved only two elements: repentance and faith.[48] Wesley's sermon "The Spirit of Bondage and of Adoption" was written in the 1740s,[49] and involves a different threefold pattern than that seen above. The structure of this sermon describes the following three "states" of the spiritual life:

> the state of a "natural man," or the natural state
> the state of a person "under the law," or the legal state
> the state of a person under grace, or the evangelical state[50]

In this scheme the first two states describe a person prior to justification, and the third state is the state of a justified person. Structuring the sermon in this way heightened the importance of "awakening," the moment when a person recognizes her or his fearful state in relation to God and thus passes from the "natural" to the "legal" state.

John Wesley's 1785 sermon "On Working Out Our Own Salvation" had yet a different pattern in a single paragraph, an expansion of the threefold pattern observed above with a fourth element added:

> preventing grace
> convincing grace
> justification
> sanctification[51]

The element that is added here is that of "convincing grace," between preventing grace and justification. Wesley stated that convincing grace is "usually in Scripture termed repentance; which brings a larger measure of self-knowledge, and a farther deliverance from the heart of stone."[52] Thus the distinction here between preventing grace and convincing grace seems parallel to Wesley's much earlier distinction of the "natural" state and the "legal" state in the sermon "The Spirit of Bondage and of Adoption," allowing Wesley to elaborate on the critical role of repentance in the progress of the soul toward justification, although elsewhere even this would have been included within the scope of prevenient grace.

John Wesley's most frequently used preaching text in the first year (1739) of the Evangelical revival was 1 Corinthians 1:30, "But of him are ye in Christ Jesus, who of God is made unto us wisdom, and righteousness, and sanctification, and redemption" (AV).[53] Although we do not have a published sermon from John Wesley on this specific text, he did cite it in the context of other sermons, and Wesley's comment on this text in his *Explanatory Notes upon the New Testament* takes "righteousness" to denote justification (Wesley knew that the words were the same in Greek), he took sanctification to denote "a principle of universal holiness," and he took "redemption" to denote "complete deliverance from all evil, and eternal bliss, both of body and of soul."[54] Although Wesley's comment on "wisdom" in this locus does not make it clear that it denoted the repentance of sinners (since "the fear of the LORD is the beginning of knowledge" or wisdom, Proverbs 1:7), it does appear that this frequently used preaching text gave Wesley another occasion to describe the "way of salvation." There is, moreover, a parallel with George Whitefield, who did publish a sermon on this text that explicated the "order of salvation" as repentance or effectual calling ("wisdom"), justification ("righteousness"), sanctification, and glorification ("redemption").[55]

John Wesley's organization of the influential 1780 *Collection of Hymns for the Use of the People Called Methodists* reflects yet another and even more complex understanding of the "way of salvation." We should note his comment on the organization of the 1780 *Collection*:

> [The *Collection*] is large enough to contain all the important truths of our most holy religion, whether speculative or practical; yea, to illustrate them all, and to prove them both by Scripture and reason. And this is done in a regular order. The hymns are not carelessly jumbled together, but carefully ranged under proper heads, according to the experience of real Christians. So that this book is in effect a little body of experimental and practical divinity.[56]

The main headings in the book are as follows:

Introductory Hymns (part I)
"Convincing" Hymns (part II)
Hymns for Mourners and Backsliders (part III)
Hymns for Believers (part IV)
Hymns "For the Society" (part V)

A perusal of the subheadings reveals that parts II, III, and IV comprise the essence of the "way of salvation," what Wesley apparently meant in referring to "the experience of real Christians." Moreover, parts II and III contain hymns addressed to "mourners" or "sinners," that is, persons who had not yet experienced justifying faith, or who had experienced justifying faith and had fallen away from it ("backsliders").[57] Part IV contains hymns specifically designated for "believers," that is, those who had experienced justification. Within this category are hymns for believers rejoicing, fighting, praying, watching, working, suffering, seeking full redemption (that is, seeking entire sanctification), "saved" (which here denotes those who have experienced entire sanctification), and "interceding for the world."[58]

We should not miss the parallels between this structure and that of the section of Cowper's and Newton's *Olney Hymns* described above, which had been published in 1779, the year prior to the *Collection of Hymns for the Use of the People Called Methodists*. The parallel is not at all precise or exact, but it may be that the idea of arranging a hymnal "under proper heads, according to the experience of real Christians" was inspired by Wesley's exposure to the *Olney Hymns*. Whatever the source, the 1780 *Collection* set a precedent followed by almost all subsequent Methodist hymnals in which a significant portion of hymns would be arranged according to the pattern of the "way of salvation" or more typically "the Christian life" (see chapter 5 below).

The sections within the 1780 *Collection* on believers "fighting" and "suffering" raise an issue within the Wesleyan explication of the "way of salvation." Wesley's shorter schemes of the way of salvation do not list this as a separate category, but Wesley and subsequent Methodists spoke frequently of the trials or problems faced by Christians in the process of sanctification. Wesley himself offered "Heaviness through Manifold Temptations," "Wandering Thoughts," and what he called "The Wilderness State," the state of a person who has abandoned their faith and thus forfeited their justification. This did in fact come to characterize later Methodist views of the religious life, and would appear in the testimonies of Methodist people and in the schemata of hymnals that were arranged according to the way of salvation (see chapter 5 below).

John Wesley's sense that this understanding of the "way of salvation" lay at the heart of the Methodist contribution can be seen in a sermon late in his career, "On God's Vineyard" (1785), in which he offered an extensive comment on the distinctive knowledge that Methodists had of the relationship between justification and sanctification:

5. It has been frequently observed, that very few were clear in their judgment both with regard to justification and sanctification. Many who have spoken and written admirably well concerning justification, had no clear conception, nay, were totally ignorant, of the doctrine of sanctification. Who has wrote more ably than Martin Luther on justification by faith alone? And who was more ignorant of the doctrine of sanctification, or more confused in his conceptions of it? In order to be thoroughly convinced of this, of his total ignorance with regard to sanctification, there needs no more than to read over, without prejudice, his celebrated comment on the Epistle to the Galatians. On the other hand, how many writers of the Romish Church (as Francis Sales and Juan de Castaniza, in particular) have wrote strongly and scripturally on sanctification, who, nevertheless, were entirely unacquainted with the nature of justification! Insomuch that the whole body of their Divines at the Council of Trent, in their *Catechismus ad Parochos,* (Catechism which every parish Priest is to teach his people) totally confound sanctification and justification together. But it has pleased God to give the Methodists a full and clear knowledge of each, and the wide difference between them.

6. They know, indeed, that at the same time a man is justified, sanctification properly begins. For when he is justified, he is "born again," "born from above," "born of the Spirit;" which, although it is not (as some suppose) the whole process of sanctification, is doubtless the gate of it. Of this, likewise, God has given them a full view.

8. It is, then, a great blessing given to this people, that as they do not think or speak of justification so as to supersede sanctification, so neither do they think or speak of sanctification so as to supersede justification. They take care to keep each in its own place, laying equal stress on one and the other. They know God has joined these together, and it is not for man to put them asunder: Therefore they maintain, with equal zeal and diligence, the

doctrine of free, full, present justification, on the one hand, and of entire sanctification both of heart and life, on the other; being as tenacious of inward holiness as any Mystic, and of outward, as any Pharisee.[59]

This passage does not follow the threefold pattern described above, since it did not deal with the state of persons prior to justification (that is, preventing grace, which would bring about awakening and repentance). It focuses on what John Wesley had described as "salvation" in the proper sense of the term twenty years earlier, that is, justification and sanctification. Wesley's claim here was that the careful and balanced relationship between the two was a distinctive mark of the Methodist movement. Toward the end of the passage cited above, in paragraph eight, Wesley moved from speaking of "sanctification" or "the whole process of sanctification" to speaking of "entire sanctification" as a distinctive mark of the Methodist movement when balanced with the teaching of "free, full, present justification." This brings us to another point about John Wesley's claims about distinctively Methodist teachings.

JOHN WESLEY'S CLAIMS ABOUT THE CHARACTERISTIC EMPHASIS OF THE WESLEYAN REVIVAL

Within the scope of John Wesley's teaching on the "way of salvation," one element stands out as being distinctive of the Wesleyan branch of the Evangelical revival, and that is his teaching on Christian holiness, and specifically his teaching about the possibility of entire sanctification prior to death. The Minutes of the early Wesleyan conferences asserted this belief as central to the Wesleyan movement. Questions three and four of the collection of Minutes historically described as the "Large Minutes" state the distinctive mission and history of the Wesleyan movement as follows:

Q. 3. What may we reasonably believe to be God's design in raising up the Preachers called Methodists?

A. Not to form any new sect; but to reform the nation, particularly the Church; and to spread scriptural holiness over the land.

Q. 4. What was the rise of Methodism, so called?

A. In 1729, two young men, reading the Bible, saw they could not be saved without holiness, followed after it and incited others so to do. In 1737 they saw holiness comes by faith. They saw likewise, that men are justified before they are sanctified; but still holiness was their point. God then thrust them out, utterly against their will, to raise a holy people. When Satan could not otherwise hinder this, he threw Calvinism in the way; and then Antinomianism, which strikes directly at the root of all holiness.[60]

The responses to both questions show that holiness was understood to be the distinct mission of the movement associated with "two young men," that is, John and Charles Wesley.

The teaching of holiness as the end of humankind was in itself hardly original: sanctification had been a consistent element in the Puritan *ordo salutis* and in the preaching of such Evangelical leaders as George Whitefield. In a broad sense, the teaching about the need for holiness had been part of the inheritance of the Reformation, the Catholic tradition before it, and the long reaches of Christian spirituality and theology in the East and the West. But there was a critical nuance in the Wesleys' teaching about sanctification that distinguished their teaching from other Protestant approaches to holiness and this lay in their claims about the possibility of entire sanctification in this life. John Wesley could be very clear about the fact that it was the teaching about entire sanctification that distinguished his movement. In his sermon "On God's Vineyard" (1785), John Wesley maintained again that the teaching of entire sanctification, balanced with the teaching of justification, was a distinctive mark of the Methodist movement under his guidance. The Methodists, he stated,

maintain, with equal zeal and diligence, the doctrine of free, full, present justification, on the one hand, and of entire sanctification both of heart and life, on the other; being as tenacious of inward holiness as any Mystic, and of outward, as any Pharisee.[61]

Similarly, John Wesley reiterated six months before his death the claim that the teaching of entire sanctification was the distinctive mission of the Methodists: "I am glad brother D—has more light with regard to full sanctification. This doctrine is the grand depositum which God has lodged with the people called Methodists; and for the sake of propagating this chiefly he appeared to have raised us up."[62]

The emphasis on entire sanctification was a distinctive emphasis of the Wesleyan branch of the Evangelical revival and it was rejected by the Calvinistic preachers of the revival. In chapter 7 it will be considered as one of the distinctive core teachings of Wesleyan communities.

CONCLUSION

Considering the range of distinctively Methodist teachings described in this chapter, I am struck by the fact that almost all of these developed in the crucial period, just slightly more than a decade, between 1738 and 1749. As we have seen, John Wesley's vocabulary for describing the way of salvation settled into regular patterns in this period, and his 1748 "Plain Account of the People Called Methodists" described a very wide range of distinctive activities and practices that had emerged in the previous decade. The distinctive nucleus of Wesleyan beliefs was formed in this brief span of time.

This chapter has shown that John Wesley claimed several distinctive teachings for the Methodist movement. He claimed that "perceptible inspiration" was "the main doctrine of the Methodists." Consistent with this, he frequently defined "faith" in the broadest sense as an evidence of "things not seen," an internal evidence of spiritual realities, and this notion of an empirical evidence of religious states underlay his teaching on the various experiences that Christians may have in the course of their religious lives. John Wesley taught, in general harmony with the broader Evangelical movement of his day, that the Christian life could be understood as a "way of salvation" or "way to heaven" that involved the work of divine grace prior to justification that led sinners to awakening and repentance, the work of divine grace in justification that comes by heartfelt trust in Christ and was normally accompanied, as Wesley understood it, by an inward assurance of pardon, and then the work of divine grace in the sanctification of persons leading to their final salvation. He also maintained as a distinct teaching of his own branch of the revival movement that it is possible for a person to experience entire sanctification, involving complete love for God, in this life.

In these cases, then, we have identified some core teachings of the Wesleyan movement that are much more distinctive than the common, ecumenically affirmed teachings described in chapter 1. In the next chapter, we turn to consider how common Christian teachings and distinctively Wesleyan teachings were expressed in the legacy of Christian verse that Charles Wesley handed on to Wesleyan communities.

CHAPTER 3

CHARLES WESLEY AND THE TRANSMISSION OF WESLEYAN BELIEFS

INTRODUCTION

The previous two chapters have described a nucleus of core beliefs of Wesleyan communities in the thought of John Wesley. Chapter 1 examined John Wesley's understanding of common Christian doctrines, and chapter 2 examined John Wesley's understanding of distinctive teachings that characterized the Methodist movement under his leadership. I now want to consider both of these elements—essential or common Christian doctrine, on the one hand, and distinctly Methodist doctrine, on the other hand, as they were expressed in the works of Charles Wesley. Gareth Lloyd has made interpreters of Wesleyan history aware of the serious rift between John and Charles Wesley that occurred around 1755 or 1756 when Charles expressed serious misgivings about the separatist tendencies of many of John Wesley's preachers and Charles himself ceased itinerating. Charles Wesley thus came to head a "Church Methodist" party or movement that remained within the canonical boundaries of Georgian Anglicanism, rejecting itinerant preaching, lay preaching, and the separate ecclesial structures that John had effected in the 1780s including John's ordinations and his revision of the Book of Common Prayer.[1] The rift was primarily over matters of church polity, and not over maters of common Christian beliefs or distinctively Wesleyan beliefs. In fact, a body of Charles's poetic work from the 1730s and 1740s would form the consistent nucleus of Wesleyan hymnody that John transmitted via his *Collection of Hymns for the Use of the People Called Methodists* (1780).

Despite the rift between the brothers and the separate Wesleyan movements they led, Charles Wesley played a crucial role in the transmission of Wesleyan beliefs, including the transmission of those beliefs in the societies led by his brother that eventually formed the nucleus of Wesleyan churches. Very few Methodist people have ever read a text by John Wesley unless they have seen a sentence or two of his account of Aldersgate. By contrast, thousands of Methodist people have sung repeatedly the hymn texts of Charles Wesley. The Charles Wesley texts, then, are the most common channel through which Wesleyan people directly encounter the eighteenth-century nucleus of Wesleyan beliefs. It is important, then, that a consideration of core beliefs of Wesleyan communities should consider how this nucleus of teachings was expressed in Charles Wesley's works that were handed on to Methodist people, and this means preeminently his poetical works that were taken up as hymnody by Methodist and other Wesleyan churches. The genre of poetry and hymnody did not lend itself to the listing of essential or common doctrines that John Wesley's prose works gave, so in what follows I will consider how Charles Wesley's works reflect the common Christian teachings and the distinctly Methodist teachings considered in the previous two chapters.

Charles Wesley's theological contributions have been thought of in Methodist and Wesleyan communities as giving voice to Christian experience, hence J. Ernest Rattenbury's claim that Charles Wesley was "the prince of experimental theologians."[2] But this reflects an authorized reading of Charles Wesley given shape most forcibly in John Wesley's *Collection of Hymns for the Use of the People Called Methodists* (1780), which served as the basis for subsequent Methodist hymnals.[3] It is not an entirely incorrect reading of Charles Wesley, since his hymns and other poems did explore the depth of Christian experience, and John's arrangement of them exposited the range of Christian experience. But the 1780 hymnal was a small selection of Charles Wesley's hymns out of a much larger corpus of hymns and other poetry.

Within the broader range of Charles Wesley's verse one can see not only the exposition of the "way of salvation" and the "evangelical doctrines" associated with it, but one can also see the exposition of other Christian teachings, the ecumenical inheritance of Christian faith that was transmitted in the creeds and reflected in the liturgical year. The Charles Wesley Society's publications of Charles Wesley's many volumes of poetry celebrating specific seasons in the Christian liturgical year (e.g., *Hymns for Our Lord's Resurrection*, 1746) or on specific Christian teachings (e.g., his *Hymns on the Trinity*, 1767) show the vast range of Charles Wesley's poetry that celebrated not only the out-working of salvation in Christian experience but also the common inheritance of ancient and Reformation Christian teachings. In this chapter, then, I shall consider Charles Wesley's contributions to the expression of Wesleyan beliefs in two senses: first, as he gave voice to common Christian teachings, and then second, as he gave voice to the distinctly Wesleyan understanding of the "way of salvation."

In both of these areas, the expression of common Christian beliefs and the expression of beliefs distinctive of the Wesleyan movement, Charles Wesley's verse was able to accomplish something that John Wesley's prose did not accomplish, and that was to perform or enact the teachings expressed. So, for example, Charles Wesley's verse on the divine Trinity not only teaches doctrine or belief about the Trinity but it also places words in the mouths of believers by which they praise the divine Persons. Charles Wesley's verse about justification not only conveys the belief that our justification is by faith alone but it also gives words by which the Christian can say "I believe" with the heartfelt religious conviction that the Wesleys described.

CHARLES WESLEY'S TRANSMISSION OF COMMON CHRISTIAN TEACHINGS

Like his brother John, Charles Wesley had been formed in an environment where he was exposed to the riches of historic Christian doctrinal and liturgical traditions. Both were formed in a particular culture—the inherited culture of Caroline Anglicanism—that had stressed the inheritance of doctrine and liturgy from the earliest Christian centuries.[4] This could be seen both in their mother, Susanna Wesley, who had written a commentary on the Apostles' Creed following the exposition of that creed by Anglican bishop John Pearson,[5] and in their father, whose tomb at Epworth carries an inscription commemorating his faithful transmission of "the true Catholick Faith."[6]

Charles Wesley often organized collections of hymns around specific doctrinal subjects, such as his *Hymns on the Trinity* (1767).[7] He also organized collections around liturgical celebrations, and these collections also deal with common Christian doctrine. He issued in 1745 and 1746 a series of books containing collections of hymns for specific celebrations in the Christian liturgical year, including *Hymns for the Nativity* (1745), *Hymns for Our Lord's Resurrection* (1746), *Hymns for Ascension-Day* (1746), and *Hymns of Petition and Thanksgiving for the Promise of the Father*, with the alternative title *Hymns for Whitsunday* given on the first page of text (1746). He also issued a further collection of *Hymns for the Great Festivals* in 1746. In the case of each of the major seasons of the liturgical year, Charles Wesley's hymns conveyed not only the formal meaning of the liturgical celebration but also its affective implications for the sinner or the Christian believer. John R. Tyson has examined in detail the *Hymns for Our Lord's Resurrection* and he has shown how this collection of hymns inculcates both traditional christological doctrine and its implications for the life of a believer, focusing on the power of Christ's resurrection as empowering the believer in the quest for sanctification.[8] The entire sequence of Charles Wesley's hymns for the Christian festivals from 1745 to 1746 explicates the fullness of christological teaching by way of the sequence of the liturgical year. In these cases, Charles did indeed weave together or "synthesize" (as Tyson says) the themes of human redemption and the out-working of the way of salvation with christological material, but Charles's organizing principle in this sequence was the liturgical celebration of the life of Christ, not the process of the way of salvation that John Wesley would take as the organizing principle for the 1780 *Collection*. In this regard, it might be noted that the two most popular hymns of Charles Wesley, both within and outside of Methodist circles, are "Hark, the Herald Angels Sing" (1739, as altered subsequently by George Whitefield and others) and "Christ the Lord Is Risen Today" (which appeared in the same collection of *Hymns and Sacred Poems*, 1739),[9] both of which celebrate christological themes appropriate to the Christian festivals of Christmas and Easter, respectively, and neither of which appeared in the 1780 *Collection*. My point is that Charles Wesley's verse served theological ends far beyond the explication of the way of salvation, but one can argue that in the 1780 *Collection* John Wesley gave a particular arrangement to Charles's verse in a way that led most subsequent interpreters, especially those of the Wesleyan family, to see his contribution as lying chiefly in the area of the experience of the way of salvation. Even in the 1780 *Collection*, before the sections on sinners and believers and the way of salvation, John Wesley included a selection of hymns "Describing the Goodness of God" as the presupposition of the theology of the way of salvation.[10]

Charles Wesley exercised his creative abilities to express traditional teachings but he also employed the traditional language that had been used to express those doctrines or teachings. He not only sought to put historic teachings (about the divine Trinity, or the presence of Christ in the Eucharist) in contemporary terms, he also insisted on bringing believers into the richness of the Christian church's distinctive language for speaking of the divine mysteries. In this way he functioned as one who gives us words about God, words by which Methodist people could confess the divine mysteries in the company of the historic Christian community. I turn now to consider the common Christian doctrines and common Christian practices identified in chapter 1 that John Wesley had seen as "essential" doctrines or practices, but considered now in their poetic and hymnic expression by Charles Wesley.

1. The Trinity

Charles Wesley's role in giving voice to historic Christian teachings can be seen in his collection *Hymns on the Trinity* (1767). This collection of 188 hymns was inspired by his reading of William Jones's *The Catholic Doctrine of the Trinity* (1756) and, as Jones's prose work did, Charles Wesley's volume of hymns explicated historic trinitarian orthodoxy under four general headings:

1. The Divinity of Christ (hymns 1–57, more than half of the first sequence in the book),
2. The Divinity of the Holy Ghost (hymns 58–86),
3. The Plurality and Trinity of Persons (hymns 87–109), and
4. The Trinity in Unity (hymns 110–136).

To these main four sections Charles added a further group, "Hymns and Prayers to the Trinity" (fifty-two hymns numbered in a separate sequence). As Wilma Quantrille points out in her introduction to *Hymns on the Trinity*, all of the hymns in this collection were written "in doxological style," that is, they were written as words to be sung to God in praise of the divine Trinity, and their intent was not primarily pedagogical or polemical as William Jones's *Catholic Doctrine of the Trinity* had been.[11] To use my own terminology, Charles Wesley's verse on the Trinity enacts or performs these beliefs. Charles Wesley wrote explicitly in this collection that

> Knowledge acquired by books or creeds
> My learn'd self-righteous pride it feeds;
> 'Tis love that edifies.[12]

And yet, despite the warning that the knowledge acquired through books or creeds might feed one's pride, Charles did not hesitate to utilize the precise, technical language of the creeds and of historic doctrinal statements in his poetic explication of the mystery of the divine Trinity. Thus he employed the terminology of historically defined doctrines in singing of the divine Trinity:

> Hail Father, Son, and Spirit, great
> before the birth of time,
> Inthron'd in everlasting state,
> Jehovah Elohim!
> A mystical plurality
> We in the Godhead own,
> Adoring One in Persons Three
> And Three in Nature One.[13]

Not only does this one verse make use of the technical terms "Nature" (or "substance," rendering οὐσία) and "Persons" (ὑπόστασεις or πρόσωπα) that had been hammered out in the trinitarian controversies of the fourth century, he also uses Hebrew names of God such as the plural form of *Elohim* suggesting the plurality of divine Persons, and he refers to the teaching of the co-eternality of the divine persons, the teaching that distinguished the orthodoxy of the first Councils of Nicaea (A.D. 325) and Constantinople (A.D. 381) from Arianism.

Another instance of Charles's role of giving voice to traditional

Christian doctrine can be seen in his transmission of the Western church's use of the *filioque* clause attached to the third article of the Nicene Creed, which holds that the Spirit proceeds "from the Father and the Son." Contemporary ecumenically minded Wesleyans might prefer that he had known that the *filioque* had been added to the creed subsequent to the Council of Constantinople, but Charles held this teaching to be part of the ancient inheritance of Christian faith and gave voice to it in the following words:

> Our hearts are then convinc'd indeed
> That Christ is with the Father one;
> The Spirit that doth from Both proceed
> Attests the Co-eternal Son.[14]

Again he used the technical terminology of the Spirit's "proceeding" from the Father and the Son ("that doth from Both proceed") but this teaching was cast in the language of worship.

Perhaps the most surprising instance of Charles's transmission of technical trinitarian teaching is a specific reference to the doctrine of perichoresis or circumincession, the teaching that all actions of the Godhead *ad extra*, that is, to the world apart from the Godhead, are performed by all the Persons of the divine Trinity together. The teaching of perichoresis became popular in late-twentieth-century systematic theology, and when Wesleyans looked for this teaching in the corpus of works of John and Charles Wesley, the only specific reference they could find was in Charles Wesley's *Hymns on the Trinity*:

> God from hence, the God supreme
> We one and many know:
> Every act that flows from Him
> Doth from Three Persons flow.[15]

Again, a very specific historic teaching was explicated in the form of direct address to the deity.

2. The Full Divinity of Christ

The doctrine of Christ's full divinity and the related practice of the worship of Christ as God were both reflected as very frequent themes in Charles Wesley's verse. Perhaps the best-known expression of this theme comes in Charles's "Hymn for Christmas-Day" (1739) that began with the line "Hark how all the welkin rings," mercifully altered by George Whitefield to "Hark, the herald angels sing." Here Charles Wesley made explicit the worship of Christ as God incarnate:

> Veil'd in flesh, the Godhead see,
> Hail the Incarnate Deity!
> Pleased as man with men to appear
> Jesus, our Immanuel here![16]

A similar expression of wonder at the incarnation of the eternal God came in the following lines from one of Charles Wesley's *Hymns for the Nativity of Our Lord* (1745). This also provides an example of Charles Wesley's enacting or performing the belief to which he refers:

> Let earth and heaven combine,
> Angels and men agree,
> To praise in songs Divine
> The incarnate Deity,
> Our God contracted to a span,
> Incomprehensibly made man.[17]

In the following case, Charles Wesley utilized typography imitating that of English Bibles as a means of expressing Christ's divinity:

> CHRIST we praise, our GOD above;
> He is pure unspotted love.[18]

The words "CHRIST" and "GOD" in the first line of this stanza were printed (in the original printed text in *Hymns on God's Everlasting Love*, probably 1742) using small capital letters. This is the way that the word "LORD" had been formatted in English-language translations of the Bible, calling attention to the divine name (the tetragrammaton *yhwh*) and, for those who were aware of it, the substitution of "LORD" (*adonai*) for the divine name. The use of the small capitals in these cases called attention to Christ's divine nature, so that even the typography utilized by Charles Wesley became a medium through which he could communicate the piety appropriate to the acknowledgment of Christ's full divinity.

3. The Atonement and the Work of Christ

Charles Wesley's verse consistently celebrated not only Christ's divinity but also Christ's redeeming or atoning work on behalf of humankind. The terms "atone," "atonement," "atoning," and the like appear more than three hundred times in the Charles Wesley hymn corpus, as in the following lines:

> Jesus, the all-atoning lamb,
> Lover of lost mankind,
> Salvation in whose only Name
> A sinful world can find...[19]

The term "atone" was often associated in Charles Wesley's works with the blood of Christ, for example, "atoning blood," although Charles Wesley was aware that blood itself referred not only to death but to life as well, as in the following hymn on the sacrament of the Lord's Supper:

> From thy blest wounds our life we draw;
> Thy all-atoning blood
> Daily we drink with trembling awe...[20]

So references to Christ's blood in Charles Wesley's verse may be understood as referring not only to the death of Christ (and they do indeed refer to the death of Christ) but also to the life of Christ consummated in his death and represented by his blood.

Charles Wesley's verse often associated the atonement with Christ's complete sacrifice of himself, including his sufferings and his resurrection. A poem from Charles Wesley's *Hymns for Our Lord's Resurrection* (1746) illustrates this concept. It is not simply that the term "atonement" or "atoning" is used, or the term "ransom" in the following excerpt. What is important is to celebrate the full work of Christ, including Christ's life, death, and resurrection, that brings about the full redemption of God's human creatures:

Fools as we are, and slow of heart,
So backward to believe the word!
The prophets' only aim Thou art:
They sang the sufferings of their Lord,
Thy life for ours a ransom given,
Thy rising to ensure our heaven.[21]

The theme of atonement in Charles Wesley's poetic vision was often tied to the theme of Christ's full divinity, presenting the antinomy involved in thinking of the eternal and "immortal" ("undying") God who nevertheless dies on behalf of human beings:

'Tis myst'ry all! th' Immortal dies!
Who can explore His strange design?
In vain the first-born seraph tries
To sound the depths of Love Divine.
'Tis mercy all! Let earth adore;
Let angel minds inquire no more.[22]

Once again, the texts given here reveal the ability of Charles Wesley's verse to enact or perform the religious affection appropriate to the beliefs described, in this case, wonder and adoration at the thought of Christ's work on behalf of humankind.

4. The Authority of the Scriptures

Charles Wesley expressed devotion to the sacred Scriptures in two poems entitled "Before Reading the Scriptures."[23] John Wesley had written in his sermon "The Means of Grace" that the practice of "searching the Scriptures" should be accompanied by prayer before and after the reading, so these poems by Charles Wesley convey and enact the piety with respect to the Scriptures that his brother held.

For John and Charles Wesley, Christ and the message of salvation in Christ were the central concepts that gave meaning to the whole of the Scriptures. John Wesley stated this in his conception of "the analogy of faith," involving the notion that the basic Christian message is itself the key meaning of the Scriptures.[24] Charles and John Wesley expressed the same idea of the centrality of Christ for understanding the Scriptures in the following poem (or hymn) from their extensive collection of *Hymns on the Four Gospels, and the Acts of the Apostles,* a collection that was unpublished at the time of the Wesleys' deaths and was subsequently published in Osborn's edition of *The Poetical Works of John and Charles Wesley*:

> Jesus, in the sacred book
> Thou art everywhere conceal'd:
> There for Thee alone we look,
> By Thy Spirit's light reveal'd,
> Thee set forth before our eyes
> Faith in every page descries.[25]

Another poem from this collection speaks of the inspiration and infallibility of the divine Scriptures. This is a poem on John 21:25, and specifically on the word *Amen* that concludes the Fourth Gospel:

> Amen! we thus our seal set to,
> Our faith's entire assent subjoin,
> That all and every word is true,
> Inspired, infallible, Divine:
> That all doth perfectly suffice
> To' obtain the end for which 'tis given,
> Able through faith to make us wise,
> And fit us for our thrones in heaven.[26]

Although Wesleyan scholars have made the point that "infallibility" was not a typical term that Methodist doctrinal standards would use to describe the authority of the Holy Scriptures, John Wesley expressed his belief that—at least in some sense—the Scriptures do not fail.[27] Similarly, the poem given here expresses the belief "That all and every word is true/Inspired, infallible, Divine." The poem also explains the particular sense in which the Scriptures do not fail: they "perfectly suffice/To' obtain the end for which 'tis given," namely, "through faith to make us wise/And fit us for our thrones in heaven." That is to say, the Scriptures do not fail in their saving purpose, to make known the way of salvation.

The Wesleys also made clear in the following verses from the posthumously published collection of *Hymns on the Four Gospels, and the Acts of the Apostles* that the "saving benefit" of the Scriptures cannot be appropriated by a hearer or reader apart from heartfelt faith:

> Whether the word be preach'd or read,
> No saving benefit I gain
> From empty sounds, or letters dead,
> Unprofitable all and vain,
> Unless by faith Thy word I hear,
> And see its heavenly character.
>
> Unmix'd with faith, the Scripture gives
> No comfort, life, or light to me:
> But darker still the dark it leaves,
> Implunged in deeper misery
> O'erwhelm'd with nature's sorest ills;
> The spirit saves, the letter kills.[28]

This hymn makes explicit a connection between the Wesleys' belief in the authority of the Scriptures and their distinctive teaching on the role of religious experience, the belief in "perceptible inspiration" that John Wesley had called "the main doctrine of the Methodists."[29]

5. Original Righteousness and Original Sin

Charles Wesley's verse frequently expressed the doctrine that salvation was offered through Jesus Christ in response to the original guilt that human beings acquire as a result of the fall of their first parents. The expression "original sin" does not appear in Charles Wesley's verse, perhaps because it does not scan in the meters he used. But the expressions "original stain," "original guilt" (or "guilt original"), "original remains," "original wound," "original offence," "original disgrace," "original infirmity," "original filth," "original disease," "original malady," and "original depravity" all appear in *The Poetical Works of John and Charles Wesley*, and some of these expressions appear repeatedly in the collection, especially "original stain," "original guilt," and "original wound." The use of the expression "original guilt" (or "guilt original") may suggests that, despite John Wesley's qualms later in life about the notion of the inheritance of guilt from Adam and Eve, this concept did figure in Charles Wesley's thought.[30]

Charles Wesley's verse also enunciated the notion of original righteousness that typically accompanied John Wesley's teaching on original sin. He enacts or performs this belief by expressing the believer's wish to be restored to the "original, divine" state of humankind:

> For this alone I wish to live,
> That I Thy love may feel,
> Thy power a sinner to forgive,
> And all my sickness heal;
> To live, till I my strength regain
> Original, Divine,
> Thy favour forfeited obtain,
> And in Thine image shine.[31]

The heart of the doctrine of original sin was to teach the need for divine grace on the part of all human beings. The expression "Adam's helpless race" appears six times in the collected poetic works of John and Charles Wesley,[32] as in the following verse from Charles Wesley that is well known as a hymn utilized in traditional Methodist worship:

> He left His Father's throne above,
> (So free, so infinite His grace!)
> Emptied Himself of all but love,
> And bled for Adam's helpless race.[33]

Charles Wesley consistently enunciated the theme of human inability and the corresponding theme of the availability of divine grace to overcome human sin. In doing the latter, he expressed the universal availability of divine grace (what John Wesley called "preventing" grace), a distinctive emphasis of the Wesleyan movement that will be examined in more detail in the next section.

6. Justification by Faith Alone

Charles Wesley also penned hymns and poems expressing the doctrine of justification by faith. He used classical Protestant terminology, including technical theological expressions, to expound this teaching. The expression "faith alone" appears fifty times in *The Poetical Works of John and Charles Wesley*, and although Charles

Wesley also said that believers were "sanctified through faith alone,"[34] the expression usually referred to justification: the phrase "justified through faith alone" appears six times, and "justified by faith alone" appears three times in the collected poetic works,[35] as in the following poem from the 1740 collection *Hymns and Sacred Poems*:

> He would that all His truths should own,
> His Gospel all embrace,
> Be justified by faith alone,
> And freely saved by grace.[36]

This was in itself a common Protestant teaching, although it had a distinctly Methodist nuance in the claim that Christians can have an assurance of their pardon given through a unique religious experience, which will be considered in the next section on Charles Wesley's expression of distinctively Methodist teachings.

Charles Wesley's verse frequently enacted or performed the heartfelt faith that the Wesleys associated with justification, as in the following verses published in 1742 in a longer poem on Titus 2:14:

> From all iniquity, from all,
> He shall my soul redeem;
> In Jesus I believe, and shall
> Believe myself to Him.
>
> When Jesus makes my soul His home,
> My sin shall all depart;
> And, lo! He saith, "I quickly come,
> To cleanse and fill thy heart!"
>
> Be it according to Thy word!
> Redeem me from all sin;
> My heart would now receive Thee, Lord;
> Come in, my Lord, come in![37]

Such words as "In Jesus I believe" and the concluding line "Come in, my Lord, come in!" not only describe belief in justification by faith, but give the Christian words by which this faith is enacted.

7. The New Birth

Chapter 1 has shown that John Wesley identified the doctrine of the new birth or regeneration as a "fundamental" teaching in his sermon "The New Birth" (1760) and maintained that although it occurred simultaneously with justification, it marked the beginning of the new life in Christ, the start of the process of sanctification.[38] The need for the new birth was a theme frequently sounded in the verse of Charles Wesley: the expressions "born again" (forty times), "born from above" (seven times), and "regenerate" (nine times) appear consistently in the collected *Poetical Works of John and Charles Wesley*.[39]

Charles Wesley identified conversion with the new birth, as can be seen in the following couplet from a hymn on Matthew 18:3, "Except ye be converted..." (AV), in the *Hymns on the Four Gospels, and the Acts of the Apostles*:

> Ye must, ye must be born again,
> Converted by a change entire....[40]

Like his brother, Charles Wesley understood that the conversion of life associated with the new birth was the beginning of sanctification, the process that should lead to the believer's entire dedication to God. In the case of the preceding couplet, I note, Charles Wesley's enactment is not on the part of the believer but on the part of the one proclaiming "ye must be born again."

8. The Church

Charles and John Wesley inherited a doctrine of the church that defined a "visible" church as a fellowship of believers in which the Word is preached and the sacraments are administered.[41] Charles Wesley frequently expressed the idea of fellowship with the church "in earth and heaven," an idea that appears in the hymn that he composed a year after his conversion and includes the verses that his brother would redact to form the shorter hymn "O For a Thousand Tongues to Sing." The first stanza of the original hymn is as follows:

> Glory to God, and praise, and love
> Be ever, ever given,

By saints below, and saints above,
The church in earth and heaven.[42]

The same theme of Christian fellowship with those on earth and with the saints in heaven is echoed in a 1747 poem of Charles Wesley: "At the Meeting of Friends":

All praise to our redeeming Lord,
Who joins us by His grace,
And bids us, each to each restored,
Together seek His face.

. . . .

And if our fellowship below
in Jesus be so sweet,
What height of rapture shall we know
When round His throne we meet![43]

This notion of the solidarity of the church in earth and heaven was expressed in a particularly forceful way in the first hymn in Charles Wesley's second collection of *Funeral Hymns* (1769). This, like the previous example, provides an example of Charles Wesley's verse as it enacts or performs belief about the Christian community:

Come let us join our friends above
That have obtain'd the prize,
And on the eagle wings of love
To joy celestial rise;
Let all the saints terrestrial sing
With those to glory gone,
For all the servants of our King
In earth and heaven are one.

One family we dwell in Him,
One church above, beneath,
Though now divided by the stream,
The narrow stream of death:
One army of the living GOD,
To His command we bow:
Part of His host hath cross'd the flood,
And part is crossing now.[44]

102

Beyond his expression of the church as the fellowship of believers, Charles Wesley also expressed the nature of the church as proclaiming the gospel and as celebrating the sacraments. Many of Charles Wesley's hymns and entire collections of hymns were designed to complement the celebration of the liturgical year, the annual proclamation of the central narrative of the gospel. He and his brother John issued a collection of *Hymns on the Lord's Supper* (1745), and as we shall see in the following, he occasionally wrote on the sacrament of baptism.

9. Baptism

Charles Wesley's verse celebrated the same common Christian institutions that his brother John had described: the sacraments of baptism and the Lord's Supper, and what John Wesley called the "instituted" means of grace common to Christian churches, vary broadly. With respect to both of the sacraments, Charles Wesley's poems and hymns expressed the understanding that the sacraments involve an outward sign and an inward grace normatively conveyed by the outward act, but not necessarily or automatically conferred by it. Searching for words related to "baptism" in the *Poetical Works of John and Charles Wesley*, I note how often the term "baptism" and related words were used to describe the inward work of the Holy Spirit, and how few occurrences of these words referred directly to the sacrament of baptism. More common are passages like the following:

> Come, Holy Ghost, my heart inspire,
> Attest that I am born again!
> Come, and baptize me now with fire,
> Or all Thy former gifts are vain.[45]

The poem or hymn in which this stanza appeared was entitled "Groaning for the Spirit of Adoption," and in this case as in many others, "baptize" refers to the work of the Holy Spirit in granting assurance to a believer. There were, however, some hymns and poems of Charles Wesley that referred directly to the sacrament of baptism, as in the following. I note again the typography of the original version in which "JESUS CHRIST" is set in small capital letters:

> Baptiz'd into my Saviour's name,
> I of His death partake;
> Buried with JESUS CHRIST I am,
> And I with Him awake.[46]

Within the broad scope of his whole poetical work, Charles Wesley published two hymns "At the Baptism of Adults" (1742) and one hymn "At the Baptism of a Child" (1767).[47] But even in writing of the baptism of adults, Charles Wesley's prayer was that those baptized would "feel" the divinely given assurance of pardon:

> Eternal Spirit, descend from high,
> Baptizer of our spirits Thou,
> The sacramental seal apply,
> And witness with the water now.
>
> Oh! that the souls baptized herein
> May now Thy truth and mercy feel,
> May rise, and wash away their sin—
> Come, Holy Ghost, their pardon seal.[48]

The attitude of these poems (or hymns) is to pray for the new birth or regeneration of the person baptized and to pray that he or she would receive the assurance of pardon accompanying it, but Charles Wesley did not seem to take for granted that the grace of regeneration (or the inward witness) would necessarily accompany the sacrament:

> Let the promised inward grace
> Accompany the sign,
> On her new-born soul impress
> The glorious name Divine:
> Father, all Thy love reveal,
> Jesus all Thy mind impart,
> Holy Ghost, renew, and dwell
> Forever in her heart.[49]

This reveals a baptismal theology consistent with the Anglican Articles of Religion and with the main stream of the Reformed tradition including John Calvin himself, according to which the grace of regeneration was associated with baptism but was not understood as being automatically or necessarily conveyed by it, and this view of baptism was consistent with the "virtualist" and receptionist understanding of the grace associated with the sacrament of the Lord's Supper.

10. The Lord's Supper

In expressing his understanding of the work of divine grace in baptism, Charles Wesley revealed his belief that the work of justifying and regenerating grace normatively accompanied the sacrament but not necessarily so. He expressed a similar attitude toward the divine grace available in the sacrament of the Lord's Supper, and in dealing with this topic Charles Wesley's verse drew upon the very precise language of historic Christian teachings. Consider the following verse that refers to the divine presence in the Eucharist:

> Let the wisest mortal show
> How we the grace receive,
> Feeble elements bestow
> A power not theirs to give.
> Who explains the wondrous way,
> How through these the virtue came?
> These the virtue did convey,
> Yet still remain the same.[50]

The term "virtue," repeated twice in these verses, might strike a reader as being out of place unless one realizes that "virtue" was a crucial technical term in the debates over the manner of Christ's presence in the Eucharist. Steering a course between the Lutheran affirmation of bodily or corporeal presence, on the one hand, and the Zwinglian belief that the presence of Christ in the Eucharist was simply that presence "wherever two or more are gathered" (that is, a form of presence not distinctive of the eucharistic celebration), John Calvin and the main stream of the Reformed tradition had maintained that although Christ's literal body could not be present (since it had ascended to heaven), there is nevertheless a distinct spiritual "power" available to those who receive the Eucharist with true faith. This spiritual power could not be identified with the literal body and blood of Christ (and so differs from the Lutheran view), but is distinctive, that is, it is not simply the general form of Christ's presence apart from the Eucharist, and the term they used to describe this spiritual power was the Latin term *virtus* ("power" or "strength").[51] Understood in this way, the two references to "virtue" as divine power or strength in the lines quoted above from Charles Wesley's hymn make very good sense; in fact, one can see that "virtue" is used in both cases as an appositive for "power," which appears in one of the earlier lines cited. Chapter 1 has shown that the Wesleys' abridgment of Brevint's *Christian Sacrament and Sacrifice*, published in their *Hymns on the Lord's Supper*, also utilized the technical language of virtualism.

I would emphasize, however, that this view of sacramental grace was not Zwinglian because it maintained a unique sense of divine presence in the sacrament, and it did serve as the ground of a deep sacramental piety involving a reverential sense of the divine presence which Charles Wesley calls a "real presence" of Christ in the sacrament:

> We need not now go up to heaven,
> To bring the long-sought Saviour down;
> Thou art to all already given,
> Thou dost even now Thy banquet crown:
> To every faithful soul appear,
> And show Thy real presence here![52]

CHARLES WESLEY'S TRANSMISSION OF DISTINCTIVELY WESLEYAN TEACHINGS

1. Religious Experience

The previous section has shown how Charles Wesley's verse transmitted the ten common Christian teachings identified in chapter 1 as common Christian beliefs. Charles Wesley also transmitted through his poetic corpus many of the distinctively Wesleyan teachings described in chapter 2 above. Charles Wesley's verse expressed poetically a range of religious experiences commonly described by John Wesley and by early Methodist people. One need only to search for the word *feel* in the poetry of Charles Wesley to realize how consistently his verse gave voice to the affections experienced by sinners and believers in relation to almost every doctrine taught and every season of the Christian year celebrated. In addition to this, his verse expressed and enacted the inward affections associated with repentance and faith. John Wesley's sermons had insisted on the need for heartfelt repentance and faith. Charles Wesley expressed the sinner's experience of the depth of penitence in a poem entitled "Repentance" (1739) based on his reading of George Herbert,

> Have mercy, Lord! Lo, I confess,
> I feel, I mourn my foolishness.
> O, spare me, whom Thy hands have made,
> A withering leaf, a fleeting shade.[53]

Another specific religious experience described by Charles Wesley was the assurance of pardon that he and John believed to be the normative concomitant of justification. This is expressed in the poem "For the Anniversary Day of One's Conversion," written a year after Charles's own conversion experience:

> I felt my Lord's atoning blood
> Close to *my* soul applied;
> *Me, me* He loved—the Son of God
> For *me*, for *me* He died![54]

The following will show in greater detail the prominent theme of the assurance of pardon in Charles Wesley's verse. In transmitting beliefs about the "way of salvation" and religious experience, as in his expressions of common Christian beliefs, Charles Wesley crafted verse that enacts or performs the experience of the sinner or the believer.

2. The "Way of Salvation"

Charles Wesley gave voice to the distinctly Methodist beliefs about the way of salvation. The previous chapter has shown that John Wesley's expression of the most distinctive doctrines of the Wesleyan movement had strong ties to Reformed theology and practice. We may now observe a similar Reformed connection for Charles Wesley's hymns, especially as they describe the "way of salvation." The genre of the English hymn was closely tied in its development to the Reformed tradition. J. R. Watson's study of *The English Hymn* (1997) has shown the critical role played by Puritans and then by Isaac Watts in the evolution of English hymns from the Reformed tradition's use of metrical English Psalms, including their use of the image of pilgrimage to Zion and their dramatic use of the first-person singular in addressing God.[55] As the previous chapter has shown, a central focus in Puritan theology had been on the "order of salvation" (*ordo salutis*) as the out-working of salvation in such typical stages as "effectual calling," justification, sanctification, and glorification. At the same time that Charles Wesley was composing his verses, a Reformed hymn tradition was developing in the Welsh and English languages, explicating this understanding of the "order of salvation." Charles Wesley, then, found himself the immediate heir of the tradition of Reformed spirituality expressed in the earlier hymn tradition and he became a participant in the flowering of the hymn tradition that was happening in his time as he explicated the Wesleyan understanding of the way of salvation.

The web of connections between Charles and John Wesley's interpretation of the "way of salvation" and the Puritan and Reformed reading of the "order of salvation" can be seen in treatments of 1 Corinthians 1:30: "He is the source of your life in Christ Jesus, who became for us wisdom from God, and righteousness and sanctification and redemption." George Whitefield had preached on this text, and his sermon represented the Reformed understanding of this passage from 1 Corinthians as reflecting the order of salvation: "wisdom" is "the fear of the Lord" and so implies repentance, "righteousness" is justification, and "redemption" is glorification, so that the Puritan understanding of the *ordo salutis* as effectual calling, justification, sanctification, and redemption can be seen in the verse.[56] John Wesley had also preached frequently on the same text and gave it his own understanding of the "way of salvation." Charles Wesley wrote a group of four hymns, published in the 1740 collection *Hymns and Sacred Poems*, explicating this same passage. Although he did not explicitly take "wisdom" to denote the repentance of sinners in the hymn on "Christ Our Wisdom" as George Whitefield had done,[57] he did take "Christ Our Righteousness" to refer to Christ as the ground of our pardon or justification, he took "Christ Our Sanctification" to refer to Christ as the ground of the believer's sanctification, and he took "Christ Our Redemption" to refer to the promise of redemption beyond death.[58] In this respect, Charles can be understood as voicing a Wesleyan interpretation of the common Wesleyan and Reformed theme of the way of the believer's spiritual pilgrimage. As early as 1740, his brother John was at work organizing and explicating his brother's hymns as they interpreted the way of salvation.[59]

Charles Wesley's verse dealing with the "way of salvation" shows a parallel tendency to his verse explicating historic Christian doctrine, and that is in his utilization of technical vocabulary. In the case of the Methodist and Evangelical understanding of the way of salvation, the vocabulary itself was still emerging, but Charles's verse offers plenty of instances of such key terms as "repentance," "awakened," "justified," and "sanctified." Consider the following verse, which John included in the 1780 *Collection* under the heading "For Mourners Brought to the Birth":

Plenteous he is in truth and grace,
He wills that all the fallen race
Should turn, repent, and live;
His pardoning grace for all is free;
Transgression, sin, iniquity
He freely doth forgive.[60]

This verse refers explicitly both to the universal call to repentance and to the universal availability of "pardoning grace," which John Wesley would elsewhere identify with justifying grace. Printed editions of Charles Wesley's hymns often have titles utilizing more technical theological vocabulary (for example, "Gratitude for Our Conversion" or "Justified, but Not Sanctified"), although at some points it is not clear whether Charles himself entitled the poems or whether the titles were the work of John Wesley.[61] In some cases, Charles Wesley entitled whole collections of hymns utilizing the distinct language of the Wesleyan way of salvation: the title of his 1747 *Hymns for Those That Seek, and Those That Have Redemption in the Blood of Jesus Christ* has categories (seeking or "groaning for redemption") that John Wesley would later utilize in organizing the 1780 *Collection of Hymns*.[62]

John Wesley's arrangement of the Charles Wesley hymn corpus in the 1780 *Collection* did a faithful job of communicating the content of Charles's hymns as respects the teaching about the way of salvation. But even as respects the spiritual pilgrimage, the schema given by John Wesley had a tendency to reduce some of Charles Wesley's more complex hymns to one or another point in the "way of salvation," where Charles's own texts were multivalent and dealt sometimes simultaneously with different stages of the Christian journey. One suspects that John's arrangement also had the tendency not to include Charles's texts that were in fact more ambiguous as to where they might fit in the schematized "way of salvation." Perhaps most notably in this regard, "Wrestling Jacob" ("Come, O Thou Traveler Unknown") was first published by Charles Wesley in 1742 and so had been in use for thirty-eight years when John compiled the 1780 *Collection*. Why this notable omission? The reason, I suspect, is that the poem progresses from recognition of sin (repentance) through justification and the assurance of pardon:

'Tis Love, 'tis love, thou diedst for me,
I hear thy whisper in my heart.
The morning breaks, the shadows flee:
Pure UNIVERSAL LOVE thou art.[63]

It would be difficult to include it either in the schematized section of the 1780 *Collection* that includes "praying for repentance" ("Part Third" of the 1780 *Collection*) or in the section that includes "believers rejoicing" ("Part Fourth" of the 1780 *Collection*). When Methodists subsequently included the poem in their hymnals, they found it difficult to decide in which section of "The Christian Life" it should be fitted. Given John Wesley's own admission in his funeral address for Charles that this was his brother's poetic masterpiece, it would appear that John's selections for the 1780 *Collection* were grounded more in didactic considerations than in considerations of the poetic qualities or even the broader spiritual values of Charles's verse.

Perhaps it was Charles Wesley's poetic mindset that enabled him to explore the depths of Christian experience in ways that were more complex and in some ways more nuanced than his brother's analytical schemes would allow, but this was his great contribution in explicating the way of salvation, and it is in this respect that Rattenbury was justified in calling Charles "the prince of experimental theologians." Charles Wesley gave us profound words that express the depth and the complexity of the Christian pilgrimage empowered by divine grace.

Charles Wesley expressed in verse many of the precise concepts that his brother John had expressed in prose, using the technical vocabulary that John had used for describing these distinctive teachings. But rather than considering his poems by way of the headings of the "way of salvation," the following account will consider them by the most distinctive elements of these teachings, namely, universal availability of divine grace (as contrasted with the teaching of limited atonement), the assurance of pardon normally (the Wesleys believed) accompanying justification, and the teaching of entire sanctification to be expected in this life.

3. Universal Availability of Grace

Despite the connection between the Reformed tradition and hymns celebrating the way of the Christian life, however, Charles Wesley showed himself consistently the advocate of a Wesleyan and Arminian understanding of human nature and salvation, especially celebrating the free gift of salvation available to all persons. This appears frequently in Charles Wesley's addresses to sinners: "harlots," "thieves," "ruffians," and the like:

> Outcasts of men, to you I call,
> Harlots and publicans and thieves!
> He spreads his arms t'embrace you all,
> Sinners alone his grace receives:
> No need of him the righteous have,
> He came the lost to seek and save.

> Come all ye Magdalens in lust,
> Ye ruffians fell in murders old;
> Repent and live: despair and trust!
> Jesus for you to death was sold;
> Tho' hell protest and earth repine;
> He died for crimes like yours—and mine![64]

In the case of the previous verses, Charles Wesley's poetry enacts the role of the one who proclaims the message of Christ as the friend of sinners. The same image of Christ as the friend of all sinners appears in the hymn that was redacted by John Wesley and became "O For a Thousand Tongues to Sing":

> Harlots, and publicans, and thieves,
> In holy triumph join!
> Sav'd is the sinner that believes
> From crimes as great as mine!
>
> Murtherers and all ye hellish crew,
> Ye sons of lust and pride,
> Believe the Saviour died for you;
> For me the Saviour died.[65]

In other places Charles Wesley made clear the universal scope of salvation in direct opposition to claims of limited atonement, implying that the latter view impugns the goodness of God, as in the following lines from the 1740 collection, *Hymns and Sacred Poems*:

> Was there a single soul *decreed*
> Thy unrelenting hate to know,
> Then I were he—and well might dread
> The horrors of eternal woe....
>
> Whoe'er admits; my soul disowns
> the image of a tort'ring God,
> Well pleased with human shrieks and groans,
> A fiend, a Molock gorg'd with blood!
>
> Good God! That any child of thine,
> So horribly should think of thee!
> Lo, all my hopes I here resign,
> If all may not find grace with me.[66]

Charles Wesley accused his predestinarian opponents of worshiping a fiendish idol ("Molock") who intends and delights in the damnation of human beings. This strong language parallels John's sermon "Free Grace," preached in the same year as the collection *Hymns and Sacred Poems*, in which the verses of Charles Wesley quoted above appeared. In opposition to Calvinistic Evangelicals,

John described the predestinarian teachings in his 1740 sermon as an affront to God: "it represents the most holy God as worse than the devil; as both more false, more cruel, and more unjust."[67]

4. Justification, Affective Faith, and Assurance of Pardon

The previous section showed that Charles Wesley's verse proclaimed the message of justification or forgiveness of past sins through faith in Christ. Distinctive of the Evangelical movement was to teach that Christians could experience a divinely given assurance of forgiveness, and Charles Wesley's poetry also reflected this central theme of the eighteenth-century revival. The following stanzas of a poem, "The Marks of Faith" (1749), reflect the idea that there are in fact two "witnesses" or forms of assurance of pardon: one is the experiential assurance of pardon (the "witness of God's Spirit"), the other is the assurance that comes from seeing the fruits of regeneration in a believer's life (the "witness of our own spirit"):

How can a sinner know
His sins on earth forgiven?
How can my Saviour show
My name inscribed in heaven?
What we ourselves have felt, and seen,
With confidence we tell,
And publish to the sons of men
The signs infallible.—

We who in Christ believe
That He for us hath died,
His unknown peace receive,
And feel His blood applied....

The witness in ourselves we have,
And all His fruits we show.

The meek and lowly heart,
Which in our Saviour was,
He doth to us impart,
And signs us with His cross:
Our nature's course is turn'd, our mind

Transform'd in all its powers,
And both the witnesses are join'd,
The Spirit of God with ours.[68]

The last couplet epitomizes the teaching of the whole poem focused on the mutually reinforcing witnesses of the divine Spirit and of the human spirit reshaped after the image of Christ.[69]

5. Entire Sanctification

Charles Wesley also emphasized the Wesleyan teaching of entire sanctification as he explicated the way of salvation. Like John Wesley, Charles Wesley held that entire sanctification was the culmination of the process of sanctification in which the image of God was restored in human beings as fully as it can be restored.[70] This can be seen in the hymn "Christ Our Sanctification" from the sequence on 1 Corinthians 1:30 in the 1740 *Hymns and Sacred Poems*:

Reign in me, Lord, Thy foes control,
Who would not own Thy sway;
Diffuse Thy image through my soul;
Shine to the perfect day.[71]

Charles Wesley believed that the very nature of God was love, "Pure UNIVERSAL LOVE."[72] So another of Charles Wesley's characteristic ways of speaking about entire sanctification was to describe it as an infusion of love,[73] as in the following lines from what is perhaps his best-known hymn on entire sanctification which speak of the infusion of divine love into a human being:

Love Divine, all loves excelling,
Joy of heaven, to earth come down,
Fix in us Thy humble dwelling,
All Thy faithful mercies crown.[74]

This hymn weaves together a number of the images that Charles Wesley would use to describe entire sanctification. It is an infusion of the Holy Spirit ("thy loving Spirit"). It is the "second rest," which follows after the new birth (the first "rest"). It removes the power of sin, and is the "end" or goal of faith (omega) as well as

114

the beginning of faith (alpha). It is liberty to those who have been held captive by sin:

Breathe, O breathe thy loving Spirit
Into every troubled breast,
Let us all in thee inherit,
Let us find that second rest:
Take away our power of sinning,
Alpha and omega be,
End of faith as its beginning,
Set our hearts at liberty.[75]

Despite their general agreement on this doctrine, John R. Tyson has pointed out that there were some critical differences between the ways in which John and Charles Wesley thought about entire sanctification. John Wesley emphasized that entire sanctification is available "now"; Charles Wesley consistently thought of entire sanctification as the goal of the Christian life that is to be expected in the moment of death.[76] John Wesley claimed that the work of entire sanctification was instantaneous, even if believers did not "advert to the moment" when it occurred; Charles Wesley emphasized the gradual nature of sanctification.[77] John Wesley tended to speak of entire sanctification as freedom from "volitional" sins, voluntary transgressions of the law of God; Charles Wesley set a much higher bar and viewed entire sanctification as a freedom from all sin.[78] John Wesley's more restricted definition of sin may be linked to his claim that entire sanctification is available instantaneously, "now," and Charles Wesley's more inclusive definition of sin could account for his tendency to see entire sanctification as the result of a gradual process to be expected near the moment of death. Despite their differences, however, it is possible that the brothers were simply emphasizing different aspects of the teaching on sanctification: a gradual process of sanctification does not rule out the fact that complete love for God, when it occurs, occurs in a moment of time. And to some extent their differences are accounted for by the critical difference in understandings of sin: John Wesley's definition of "sin," as Tyson points out, stressed its voluntary nature, whereas Charles thought of sin in a much more inclusive way as anything that stands between humans and the divine image, whether voluntary or not.[79]

CONCLUSION

John Wesley's introduction to the 1780 *Collection of Hymns* stated that the collection "is large enough to contain all the important truths of our most holy religion."[80] This might have been true in the sense that one could delve into the 1780 *Collection* and find references to all of the most central Christian teachings. But John Wesley's organization of the *Collection* highlighted the "Evangelical" doctrines associated with the Christian experience of the "way of salvation." As John himself stated it, the hymns are "carefully ranged under proper heads, according to the experience of real Christians."[81] Thus the organization of the hymnal did not highlight Charles Wesley's work of giving voice to the broader Christian doctrinal tradition, and set in place the view of Charles Wesley consistently represented in Methodist tradition according to which he is preeminently the hymnist of religious experience.

The next two chapters will show that each of these poles of Charles Wesley's work, the ecumenical ("catholic") and the distinctively Methodist, came to be represented structurally in the organization of subsequent Methodist hymnals. The "evangelical doctrines" were enshrined in sections in Methodist hymnals entitled "The Sinner" and "The Christian," or simply, "The Christian Life," a consistent mark of Methodist hymnals from the time of the 1780 *Collection*.[82] From the time of the first Methodist hymnals subsequent to the 1780 *Collection*, Methodist hymnals consistently begin with a section of hymns in praise of the divine Trinity, with separate sections on God (typically, very seldom "The Father"), Jesus Christ, and the Holy Spirit. One could argue that explicit and sustained material on the Trinity was missing from the 1780 *Collection* only because that collection was intended for a religious society within the Church of England, and it presupposed the trinitarian devotion of the Book of Common Prayer. The appearance of the initial section in praise of the Trinity (from 1846 in Methodist hymnals in the United States) does reflect the ecumenical side of the hymn tradition inherited from Charles Wesley, although by the time Methodists began adding material on the divine Trinity to their hymnals, they had also begun to utilize a wide range of hymn writers in addition to Charles Wesley.[83]

Methodist hymnals are only the most outward and visible

expression of a core of theological and spiritual beliefs that were expressed and transmitted by John and Charles Wesley, and they have been a principal means by which Wesleyan beliefs have been transmitted to Methodist constituents. As we will see in the next chapters, hymnals were complemented by catechisms, tracts, and pamphlets, and by full-fledged works of systematic theology explicating a Wesleyan understanding of the Christian faith and, in particular, the way of the Christian life.[84]

CHAPTER 4

BELIEFS ABOUT GOD IN WESLEYAN COMMUNITIES

INTRODUCTION

The previous chapters have considered a nucleus of core beliefs of Wesleyan communities in the thought of John and Charles Wesley, considering how each of these expressed conceptions of common Christian beliefs (chapter 1 and the first part of chapter 3), and distinctly Methodist beliefs (chapter 2 and the second part of chapter 3). This and the next two chapters will consider beliefs of Wesleyan communities by examining three "core samples" that explore specific teachings through the history of Wesleyan communities and that show how the Wesleyan teachings considered in the previous chapters were taken up in Wesleyan communities beyond the eighteenth century. This chapter offers the first of these three core samples by examining beliefs about God and practices related to the worship of God, especially the worship of the divine Trinity, in Wesleyan communities. The next two chapters will take up two more core samples: chapter 5 will consider the notion of the "way of salvation" as a set of distinctly Wesleyan beliefs after the time of the Wesleys, and chapter 6 will consider the evolution of Wesleyan and Methodist beliefs about the church. These three core samples—trinitarian theology, the theology of the "way of salvation," and ecclesiology—are far from comprehensive, but they will show how Wesleyan communities have dealt with a set of common or ecumenical Christian beliefs (beliefs about God), a cluster of distinctly Wesleyan beliefs (beliefs about the "way of salvation"), and a set of beliefs that has been fraught with tension and ambiguity within Wesleyan communities (beliefs about the nature of the church).

This chapter examines understandings of God and practices related to the divine, especially the practice of divine worship, that have developed in historic Wesleyan communities, examining both formal consensus (doctrine) and the reception of formal teachings as indicated in the content of Methodist hymnals, catechisms, and liturgies. The chapter begins with a consideration of the worship of the Trinity. Chapter 1 has shown that John Wesley considered the doctrine of the Trinity to be a "necessary" or essential Christian belief. Chapter 3 showed some of the ways in which Charles Wesley transmitted this belief and practice especially as he gave voice to the praise of the divine Trinity. This chapter begins with John and Charles Wesley and then considers how the doctrine of the Trinity was expressed later in Wesleyan communities. This chapter goes on to consider how the "attributes" ascribed to God were thought of in Methodist communities as reflecting the goal toward which human life is intended.

THE WORSHIP OF THE DIVINE TRINITY IN WESLEYAN COMMUNITIES

The bishops of the African Methodist Episcopal Church offered in their Episcopal Address of 1876 the following exhortation:

> But, beloved, forget not that hymns, spiritual songs—lyrics of the most elevated poetry, breathing the noblest sentiments—avail us nothing, unless we sing with the spirit and the understanding; therefore, in the language of the Apostle, we exhort you to be filled with the Spirit, speaking to yourselves in psalms and hymns and spiritual songs, singing and making melody in your hearts to the Lord.[1]

From the very beginning the songs of Wesleyan communities have praised the Father, the Son, and the Holy Spirit. Like other churches, Methodist churches in the late twentieth century have struggled with the contemporary expression of this worship, especially with the strongly masculine language in which the worship of the Trinity has been historically couched. But the songs of Wesleyan communities remain the living thread that connects their praise to the inheritance of faith in the divine Trinity received from the ancient Christian community.[2]

In describing the Christians of Asia Minor in the early second century, the Roman official Pliny wrote to the emperor that it was the Christians' custom, *carmen . . . Christo quasi deo dicere*, "to sing a hymn to Christ, as to a god."[3] Teaching about the Trinity arose in the ancient church as a way of accounting for the Christian community's most distinctive practice, namely, the practice of offering praise to Jesus Christ. The Arian claim that Christ was a created being, not co-eternal with the Father, implied that the church's worship was an idolatrous act of praising a created being rather than the creator. Through the vicissitudes of the fourth century— the imperially assembled Council of Nicaea in 325, the ensuing opposition to Nicene teaching on the part of the imperial court, defenses of Nicene teaching by Athanasius and then the Cappadocian theologians, then the expanded creed historically associated with the Council of Constantinople in 381—the church affirmed that Christ was none other than God, "of one Being with the Father," and likewise that the Holy Spirit "with the Father and the Son is worshipped and glorified." This affirmation characterized the historic churches of the East and the West and was reaffirmed by Protestant churches at the time of the Reformation. The Nicene Creed is recognized in our time as the most universal of Christian creeds.[4]

Although reverence for the Trinity was the inheritance of John Wesley's church, it could not be taken for granted in the Wesleys' time. Ancient ideas such as Arianism had been revived by such teachers as William Whiston, whom Wesley respected. Modern ideas such as Socinianism—what is now called "Deism"—had gained ground even in traditional Christian communities such as the Church of England and among English Presbyterians and Baptists. Through the decades before John Wesley, Anglicans had earnestly defended the ancient trinitarian doctrine as part of the inheritance of Christian faith that, they believed, had been preserved or even revived in the Anglican tradition. Bishop John Pearson's *Exposition of the Creed* (1659) became an Anglican classic, illustrating a deep knowledge of ancient Christian writings and traditions in its defense of the traditional faith. Bishop George Bull's *Defensio fidei nicaenae* (1685) had defended the Nicene doctrine of the Trinity against Arianism and Socinianism, examining biblical claims about Christ and credal teachings. Other Anglicans in the seventeenth and eighteenth centuries would attempt to defend their church's trinitarian beliefs by way of philosophical arguments. Jason Vickers has shown that these attempts at philosophical defenses of trinitarian beliefs became more and more isolated from Christian communities' practices of worship of the Trinity, leaving sterile arguments detached from living piety.[5]

Samuel Wesley, the father of John and Charles Wesley, drank deeply from the wells of Anglican reverence for the Trinity. The inscription on his tomb at Epworth reads (in part) as follows:

> As he liv'd so he died,
> in the true Catholick Faith
> of the Holy Trinity in Unity,
> And that JESUS CHRIST is God
> incarnate: and the only
> Saviour of Mankind.[6]

John Wesley had read the standard Anglican defenses of the Trinity, including those of Pearson and Bull, in his Oxford days. He would later read William Jones's *The Catholic Doctrine of a Trinity* (1754), on which his brother's *Hymns on the Trinity* (1767) was based.[7] The reverence that John Wesley himself held for the Trinity can be seen in the way he used the term: most frequently when speaking in his own voice (not quoting someone else), he says "blessed Trinity" or "ever-blessed Trinity." In prayer, he addressed the "Holy, undivided Trinity."[8] Similarly, Charles Wesley's hymns offer worship to "A Trinity in Unity"[9] or "One undivided Trinity,"[10] and the trinitarian formula often concluded his hymns.

The Wesleys' commitment to historic trinitarian doctrine, then, was not merely doctrinal. Their belief in the Trinity was grounded in their devotional life and spirituality. When confronted by the contemporary revival of Arianism or contemporary "Socianianism" (Deism), John Wesley could state the difference between the two: "For whereas [Socinians] deny Christ to be any God at all, [Arians] do not; they only deny him to be *the great God*."[11] But he rejected both as inadequate: "An Arian is one who denies the Godhead of Christ; we scarce need say, the supreme, eternal Godhead; because there can be no God, but the supreme, eternal God, unless we make two Gods, a great God, and a little one."[12] As chapter 1 has shown, John Wesley's revision of the Articles of Religion for the American Methodists in 1784 left unchanged the first Article's affirmation of the Trinity, utilizing the Nicene-Constantinopolitan language of three co-eternal Persons united by one divine substance, though as we will see later, he did alter a word in this article that would leave open the question of divine impassibility.

Chapter 1 has also shown that, in the understanding of John Wesley, belief in the Trinity was a "necessary" or "essential" doctrine for Christians, not simply an "opinion" on which differences could be allowed.[13] Wesley also stated in his sermon "On the Trinity" that it is the substance of this doctrine, not its "philosophical explanation," that is necessary. He took the substance of the doctrine to be the belief that Father, Son, and Holy Spirit are one (here following the traditional reading of the "Johannine comma," 1 John 5:7), but the specific terminology of divine "substances," "Persons," and even "Trinity," were not of the essence of the doctrine itself. Wesley accepted what he believed to be Servetus's claim, that "the Father is God, the Son is God, and the Holy Ghost is God" without requiring the language of the Nicene Creed.[14] Moreover, it may be worth noting in this regard that John Wesley omitted the Nicene Creed from the Eucharistic rite in the *Sunday Service* of 1784, setting a precedent for Methodist practice that has consistently favored the Apostles' Creed.[15] John Wesley did subscribe to the language of the traditional creeds and insisted that his preachers should do so since they were charged with public explication of the faith, but he believed that it was not necessary for Christian belief or piety to utilize the language of the early creeds and councils.

Although part of John Wesley's concern was to teach the historic doctrine of the Trinity in opposition to Arianism and Socinianism, the weight of his concern was that the doctrine of the Trinity should not be "merely speculative" but should be intimately related to Christian spiritual practices. This is how he explained the contribution of his brother's *Hymns on the Trinity*:

> Mr. Jones' book on the Trinity is both more clear and more strong than any I ever saw on that subject. If anything is wanting it is the application, lest it should appear to be a mere speculative doctrine, which has no influence on our hearts and lives; but this is abundantly supplied by my brother's Hymns.[16]

There are two respects in which the doctrine of the Trinity is directly related to Christian spirituality in the thought of the Wesleys. In the first place, they understood that the goal of salvation is to restore the lost image of God, which is a trinitarian image. The full redemption for which humans are intended implies that from the beginning humans were "ordained to be / Transcripts of the Trinity."[17] Thus Charles Wesley wrote:

> And when we rise in love renewed,
>   Our souls resemble thee,
> An image of the Triune God,
>   To all eternity.[18]

In the second place, many early Methodists claimed to have vivid religious experiences in which they perceived the presence of the divine Trinity. Some described their having a "vision" of the Trinity.[19] As the Trinity expresses the perfection of God, so they believed that the culmination of human religious experience was to perceive the presence of the three divine Persons of the Trinity.

Although this particular form of religious experience seems to have been limited to the first century of Methodism when Methodism existed as a religious movement within the Church of England, Wesleyan and Methodist churches have consistently followed the historic and ecumenical insights on the doctrine of the Trinity that the Wesleys expressed. Within British Methodist churches this adherence to trinitarian doctrine did not come without a controversy that was focused around the views of the well-known Methodist biblical commentator Adam Clarke. Clarke advocated in the 1820s the idea that Christ had become "Son of God" only at the time of the Incarnation, prior to which Christ was one with the undifferentiated Godhead.[20] In fairness to Clarke's views it must be insisted upon that this was not a form of Arianism, as Cardinal Newman and others supposed. Clarke's concern was to defend on biblical grounds Christ's identity as God from eternity and he believed that this claim was necessary for the understanding of Christ's work of redemption.[21] Clarke's claim was simply that the title "Son" was not appropriate until the Incarnation. The British Conference and other Methodist leaders, including Richard Watson, responded vigorously against Clarke's claim, defending the notion of Christ's "eternal Sonship" against him. The result of this controversy, which extended into the 1860s, was a strong affirmation of historic trinitarian doctrine on the part of British and American Methodist churches.[22] A broader indication of this can be seen in the fact that Methodist churches in the nineteenth century sponsored their own editions of such classic defenses of the doctrine of the Trinity as Pearson's *Exposition of the Creed*.

Belief in the Trinity in Methodist Doctrinal Statements

The historic trinitarian teaching was also affirmed in corporate Methodist doctrinal standards. Churches of the North American episcopal Methodist pattern that utilize the Twenty-Five Articles of Religion of the Methodist Episcopal Church, affirm the language of the first Anglican Article that in turn uses the language of the Nicene-Constantinopolitan creed. British Methodist churches and those related to them affirm in their constitution their loyalty to the ancient creeds, which are taken to mean the Apostles' Creed and the Nicene Creed.[23] Although Methodists have by custom preferred the Apostles' Creed (see below on this), Methodist hymnals have included the Nicene Creed for use in public worship since the 1960s in the wake of the ecumenical movement.[24]

The Praise of the Trinity in Methodist Hymnals

Perhaps more significant than the use of creeds is the fact that Methodist hymnals since the mid-nineteenth century consistently begin with a framework of praise to the Trinity. This was not the case with the Wesleys' *Collection of Hymns for the Use of the People Called Methodists* (1780), but John Wesley's intent in organizing this hymnal was to lay out distinctive Methodist teachings about the "way of salvation," and it was not until well into the nineteenth century that Methodists produced hymnals that encompassed the breadth of Christianity. Even so, a statistical analysis of the 1780 *Collection* shows that 23 percent of its hymns include explicit references to the three Persons of the Trinity.[25]

Although a supplement was added to early nineteenth-century editions of the Wesley *Collection of Hymns* (both in British and in North American publications of it),[26] it was not until the early decades of the nineteenth century that the General Conference of The Methodist Episcopal Church in the United States offered a substantially revised Methodist hymnal.[27] From this point, Methodist hymnals were consistently organized in a creedal structure in which the praise of the divine Trinity came first among the various topics considered and celebrated. The first section of the 1848 Methodist Episcopal hymnal contains hymns in praise of God, following a recognizably trinitarian pattern even though the first Person of the Trinity was not named in the section headings as "Father." In this 1848 hymnal, the opening sections were headed "The Divine Perfections," "Jesus Christ," and "The Holy Spirit." After a brief section titled "Institutions of the Gospel," (including the ministry, the church, the Sabbath, baptism, and the Lord's Supper) there was a second characteristic section identified as "Provisions and Promises of the Gospel," which within itself has a long section on "The Sinner" (with subheadings on depravity, awakening, inviting, and penitential), and then a long section on "The Christian Life," with subheadings "Justification by Faith," "Adoption and Assurance," and "Sanctification." This 1848 hymnal was the first to utilize an organizational structure that has characterized almost every Methodist (and Wesleyan) hymnal since that time. Whatever other material may be included in the hymnal, this structure or pattern involves two consistent parts. The first is an introductory section of the hymnal in praise of the divine Trinity. The second is a lengthy section typically called "The Christian Life," and which embraces the entirety of the spiritual pilgrimage following roughly the eighteenth-century pattern of the "way of salvation," but with very significant variations on the pattern of the Christian life in each of the hymnals.

The 1848 hymnal began with sections titled "The Divine Perfections," "Jesus Christ," and "The Holy Spirit." These three sections may be compared to the beginnings of some later Methodist hymnals. The 1905 hymnal jointly produced by The Methodist Episcopal Church and The Methodist Episcopal Church, South, had sections titled "The Father," "The Son," and "The Holy Spirit." The 1935 hymnal jointly produced by The Methodist Episcopal Church, The Methodist Protestant Church, and The Methodist Episcopal Church, South, had sections on "God," "Jesus Christ," and "The Holy Spirit." The 1933 *Methodist Hymn-Book* of the British Methodist Church had sections headed "God," "The Lord Jesus Christ," and "The Holy Spirit." The 1964 *Book of Hymns* of The Methodist Church (soon to be The United Methodist Church) had "The Praise of God," "The Gospel of Jesus Christ," and "The Holy Spirit." The 1983 British Methodist hymnal *Hymns and Psalms* has as its first three sections "The Eternal Father," "The Eternal Word," and "The Eternal Spirit." The 1989 *United Methodist Hymnal* has "The Glory of the Triune God," "The Grace of Jesus Christ," and "The Power of the Holy Spirit." The Nazarene Hymnal *Sing to the Lord* (1993) has initial sections labeled "The Trinity," "God Our Father," "Jesus Our Savior," and "Holy Spirit."

This may appear to be a completely predictable and unremarkable way to begin a hymnal, but two points should be made about this pattern. First, it was not a pattern inherited from the 1780 *Collection of Hymns for the Use of the People Called Methodists.* Although that collection did have an early subsection titled "The Goodness of God," its overwhelming focus was on the "way of salvation," as John Wesley explained in the quotation from the preface given above. The addition of a complete section at the beginning of Methodist hymnals to include hymns in praise of the Trinity reflected the transition from being a religious movement focused on its distinctive apostolate to being institutions that had begun to think of themselves as churches in a fuller sense. Beginning with the praise of the Trinity is not a distinctive mark for Methodist hymnals, and the addition of this section reflects the Methodists' need in the nineteenth century to sing the faith of the broader Christian community.

The second thing that needs to be said about the expansion of Methodist hymnals to include this initial section of hymns in praise of the Trinity is that this expansion coincides with the addition of non-Wesleyan materials to the hymnals. Although "O For a Thousand Tongues to Sing" remained the first hymn in every one of these hymnals except the 1935 joint hymnal of The Methodist Episcopal, Methodist Episcopal, South, and Methodist Protestant churches (in which Reginald Heber's "Holy, Holy, Holy" was the first hymn), these sections incorporate hymns by Isaac Watts and other authors from a wide range of Christian traditions. That is to say, the transition from a religious movement with a distinct sense of mission to a church in the fuller sense of the word led

Methodists to incorporate a more ecumenical selection of hymns structured around the praise of the divine Trinity following the creedal pattern of the early church.

The Doctrine of the Trinity in Methodist Catechisms

Methodist and Wesleyan catechisms were designed to form children and young people in beliefs about the Trinity, consistently teaching them to believe in and worship God as Father, Son, and Holy Spirit. The pattern was set by John Wesley's *Instructions for Children* (1745), the first question and response of which was as follows,

> Q. How many GODS are there?

> R. One: Who is GOD the Father, GOD the Son, and GOD the Holy Ghost. These three are one.[28]

Later in the document, the following statement appeared:

> We cannot comprehend, how these three are one, GOD the Father, the Son, and the Holy Ghost.

> But tho' we do not comprehend it, yet we believe it, because God has said it.[29]

Subsequent Methodist catechisms express teaching about the Trinity in similar and typically very brief statements. *A Short Scriptural Catechism Intended for the Use of the Methodist Episcopal Church* (1793) offered a slightly expanded version of this, utilizing responses drawn from the Scriptures, but maintaining the claim that the doctrine of the Trinity is beyond human comprehension:

> *Quest. How many Gods are there?*

> *Answ.* The Lord our God is one Lord, *Deut.* vi. 4.

> *Q. How many persons are there in the Godhead?*

> A. There are three that bear record in heaven: the Father, the Son, and the Holy Ghost; and these three are one, *I John* v. 7.

Q. Can any man comprehend this mysterious union of the three persons in one God?

A. No; it is vanity, if not presumption, to think of comprehending this; yet, there is some faint similitude in ourselves, for in every man there are a body and a soul, which make one man. But, touching the Almighty, we cannot find him out, *Job* xxxvii. 23.[30]

A *Catechism for the Use of Children* from the Wesleyan Methodist Conference in Britain, published in 1817, has a question and response on the unity of God, but no explicit question or response naming the persons of the Trinity, although it acknowledges the divinity of Jesus Christ and of the Holy Spirit in separate questions and responses. This same pattern was reproduced in the first of three *Catechisms of the Wesleyan Methodists* published from 1824 by the Wesleyan Methodist Conference in the United Kingdom and also reprinted in the United States by The Methodist Episcopal Church.[31] But this first catechism was intended "For Children of Tender Years," and the second catechism in the series, intended "For Children of Seven Years of Age and Upward" has a more explicit question and response on the persons of the Trinity:

12. *Are there more Gods than one?*

There is but one God only, the living and true God.

13. *How many Persons are there in the Godhead?*

In the Godhead there are three Persons, the Father, the Son, and the Holy Ghost; and these three are one God, the same in substance, equal in power and glory.[32]

Questions very similar to these appeared in the catechism of the African Methodist Episcopal Church composed by Bishop Henry McNeal Turner and published in 1883.[33] The absence of the question on the persons of the Trinity in the 1817 and 1824 British catechisms seems to reflect the fact that these two catechisms were intended for younger children and the Wesleyan Conference deemed this question inappropriate for younger children but appropriate for older children.

The catechetical pattern of including a very brief statement on the Trinity extended into twentieth-century catechisms prepared for children by Methodist churches. A *Junior Catechism* adopted by The Methodist Episcopal Church and The Methodist Episcopal Church, South, in 1932 and still in use in the Christian Methodist Episcopal Church has a question on how God "makes himself known to us in the Bible," with the response that "God makes himself known to us in the Bible as the Father, the Son, and the Holy Spirit." A question immediately following this asks in what name Christians are baptized, and gives the formula "in the name of the Father, and of the Son, and of the Holy Spirit."[34] A *Methodist Catechism* published by the Methodist Church of Ireland in 1948 had a question about the number of persons in the Godhead, with the response:

> In the Godhead there are three Persons: the Father, the Son, and the Holy Ghost; and these Three are One God. This is the doctrine of the Holy Trinity.[35]

The *Senior Catechism of the Methodist Church*, published by the Methodist Church of Great Britain in 1952, asked, "Why do we speak of the Holy Trinity?" with the response:

> The Father is God, Jesus Christ is God, the Holy Ghost is God, yet there is one God, not three, and therefore we speak of the Holy Trinity, one God in three Persons, three Persons in one God.[36]

The most recent catechism of the British Methodist Church, *A Catechism for the Use of the People Called Methodists* (1989) has a question on the persons of the Trinity, with the response, "We believe that God, Father, Son, and Holy Spirit, truly exists as one God." This catechism also has questions on each of the three Persons of the Trinity, it teaches the triune name ("in the name of the Father and of the Son and of the Holy Spirit") in response to a question on baptism, and it teaches candidates the full texts of both the Apostles' Creed and the Nicene Creed.[37]

By their very nature, catechisms are not sophisticated theological texts, but they do reveal what churches consider to be their most important core beliefs. The fact that the doctrine of the Trinity appears consistently in the catechisms produced by Methodist churches in itself demonstrates the centrality of this teaching. The substance is not remarkable: the catechisms teach children to believe in One God who is Father, Son, and Holy Spirit. The statement in Wesley's *Instructions for Children*, "We cannot comprehend, how these three are one, GOD the Father, the Son, and the Holy Ghost. But tho' we do not comprehend it, yet we believe it, because God has said it"[38] coheres with John Wesley's general suspicion of elaborate language to describe the divine Trinity, and it is further consistent with this that Methodist catechisms do not undertake elaborate discussions of the controversies that lay behind the doctrine or the more sophisticated terminology that was developed to describe this teaching.

The Doctrine of the Trinity in Authorized Works of Systematic Theology

In a more sophisticated way, the Methodist and Wesleyan theologians whose works were prescribed for study by preachers through the early years of the twentieth century—Richard Watson, Thomas O. Summers, William Burt Pope, John Miley, and the Nazarene theologian H. Orton Wiley—consistently uphold the historic trinitarian teaching, defining this belief in the terms incorporated in the Nicene Creed and defending it with extensive scriptural citations against ancient and modern errors, especially Arianism, Sabellianism, and Socinianism. Although these theologians could write in a scholastic and philosophical manner, their various writings indicate their awareness that the issue of worship lay beneath the doctrine. Richard Watson, for example, advanced as one argument for the traditional doctrine the fact that worship was paid to Christ in the early church,[39] and William Burt Pope, commenting on the trinitarian controversies, wrote, "Nowhere is precision more necessary than in the ordering of the phraseology of worship."[40]

At least one book prescribed for preachers in the *Disciplines* of The Methodist Episcopal Church in the 1930s did spark controversy over whether it had faithfully represented historic trinitarian doctrine. This was Albert C. Knudson's *The Doctrine of God* (1930). Knudson's theology has been described as a "personalistic modalism," although this description is unfair. Knudson thought that "the heart of the Trinitarian doctrine" could be affirmed in a contemporary context by affirming "the christlikeness of God."[41] The inclusion of Knudson's book in the prescribed course of study of The Methodist Episcopal Church (1932 and 1936 *Disciplines*) and in a separate Methodist Episcopal Church list in the 1939 and 1940 *Disciplines* of The Methodist Church brought calls for General Conference action to remove the book.[42]

It is at this point that I find it rather difficult to assess what inclusion meant at this time. In the nineteenth century, it is clear that books prescribed for study had a rather strong degree of communal approbation. With the changing of theological pedagogy in the twentieth century, however, I have the impression that some works, such as Knudson's book, were included more because they were seen as positive examples of contemporary theological method, rather than as comprehensively approved assertions of church teaching.[43] It is worth stating that throughout this period Wesleyan communities continued to praise the Trinity. In fact, breaking from long-standing Wesleyan custom, the first hymn in the 1935 joint Methodist Episcopal, Methodist Episcopal, South, and Methodist Protestant hymnal was Reginald Heber's hymn to the Trinity, "Holy, Holy, Holy," set to an accompanying tune named "Nicaea."[44]

Recognizing a few important points of controversy such as those about the teachings of Adam Clarke or Alfred Knudson, it is fair to conclude that Wesleyan communities have consistently reflected not only historic beliefs about the Trinity but also the devotion and praise to the Trinity that is the underlying basis of these beliefs. The writings of John and Charles Wesley, the hymns sung by Methodists, the very arrangement of Methodist hymnals, the formal Articles of Religion of Wesleyan communities, catechisms utilized to teach children and youth, the works of systematic theologies used to train pastors, and the expressly stated ecumenical commitments of contemporary Methodist churches all concur in this.

A Minimalist and Economic Understanding of the Trinity?

If there is a qualification to make to this, it might be to note what other Christians may perceive as a minimalist understanding of the Trinity on the part of Wesleyan communities. As noted above, John

Wesley did not insist on the terms of the ancient creeds for Christian piety. Understandings of the doctrine of the Trinity that developed after the fourth century, such as the doctrine of circumincession (or *perichoresis*) or the doctrine of "appropriations" in speaking of the Persons of the Trinity, may appear in Charles Wesley's lesser known poems (see the example cited in chapter 3) but not in the 1780 *Collection of Hymns* or in other collections that could be regarded as doctrinally sanctioned by Wesleyan communities. The only exception to this might be the fact that the Wesleys and subsequent Wesleyan theologians affirmed the doctrine of the double procession of the Holy Spirit, and Methodist versions of the Nicene Creed have always included the *filioque* clause. The reason for this was the common misunderstanding inherited from the time of the Reformation that *filioque* and double procession were affirmed in the received version of the Nicene (Nicene-Constantinopolitan) Creed. In affirming *filioque* and double procession, then, John Wesley did not understand himself to be affirming a later development of trinitarian doctrine. In the light of contemporary historical understanding and ecumenical developments, Methodists should consider whether they should join other Western Christian bodies in revising the language of the Nicene Creed to reflect the received form of the creed, that is, without *filioque*.

Moreover, it is appropriate to say that the manner in which Methodists have praised the Trinity and have celebrated the work of the Trinity in the way of salvation can be described as stressing the *economic* Trinity, that is, the persons of the Trinity as revealed in the work of salvation in contrast to the mysteries of the inner relationships of the divine Persons. The "Doctrinal Statement of the Korean Methodist Church" from 1930 (also known as the "Korean Creed") has the following three points at the beginning of its doctrinal statement:

1. We believe in one God, Maker and Ruler of all things, Father of all men; the source of all goodness and beauty, all truth and love.

2. We believe in Jesus Christ, God manifest in the flesh, our Teacher, Example and Redeemer, the Savior of the world.

3. We believe in the Holy Spirit, God present with us for guidance, for comfort, and for strength.[45]

The emphasis here is on the roles of the trinitarian persons in creation, redemption, and guidance. As indicated above, the doctrine of circumincession appears in some of Charles Wesley's hymns but it does not appear as a consistent theme in Wesleyan and Methodist hymnals, catechetical reflection, or theological inquiry,[46] and the consistent stress in Wesleyan communities has been on the out-working of the Trinity in the healing of humankind. A similar "economic" structure can be seen in William Burt Pope's three-volume *Compendium of Christian Theology* (1881) that is divided into volumes organized around God and creation (volume 1), Jesus Christ and redemption (volume 2), and the Holy Spirit and sanctification (volume 3).[47]

A third trait of trinitarian belief in historic Wesleyan communities is that in the organization of Methodist hymnals, the first heading has not been "the Father," with the exception of the 1905 *Hymnal* jointly sponsored by the ME and ME South churches and the current British Methodist hymnal titled *Hymns and Psalms*, which has the heading "The Eternal Father."[48] More typical is to have a first section headed "God," "the Triune God," or "The Divine Perfections," followed by a section of hymns on Jesus Christ, and then a very brief section of hymns on the Holy Spirit. This may be due to the fact that very few hymns address only the first Person of the Trinity, but it does leave Methodists with a strong precedent for the invocation of the Trinity in a manner that lacks specific reference to the first Person. A more recent example of this would be Gilbert H. Vieira's paraphrase of the Thomas Ken doxology that has been popular in The United Methodist Church since the 1990s:

> Praise God, the source of all our gifts!
> Praise Jesus Christ, whose power uplifts!
> Praise the Spirit, Holy Spirit![49]

This tendency on the part of Methodists might be reinforced by the very commonly used "grace" from 2 Corinthians 13:14, "The grace of the Lord Jesus Christ, and the love of God, and the communion of the Holy Ghost, be with you all" (AV).

In each of these three cases—the "minimalist" doctrine of the Trinity, the "economic" emphasis of historic Wesleyan teaching on the Trinity, and the contemporary predilection for formulae like

"God, Christ, and the Holy Spirit"—it is relevant to consider for a moment the fact that Methodists have historically preferred the Apostles' Creed in worship. John Wesley, as noted above, omitted the Nicene Creed from the eucharistic rite in the *Sunday Service* (1784), and Methodist hymnals through the nineteenth century contain only the Apostles' Creed. The printed services of Methodist churches corroborate this pattern. Although the reasons why Methodists have preferred this creed are not always clear— and it is probably true that its brevity and its relative lack of technical terminology account for its popularity—it is nevertheless consistent with Wesley's stated conviction that the more technical language of the Nicene-Constantinopolitan Creed is not to be required for Christian piety. It is my impression, moreover, that this trend to use the Apostles' Creed was found to be a better fit with Methodist expressions of theological liberalism in the twentieth century. The language of the Apostles' Creed is simpler and more straightforwardly scriptural than the terms employed in the Nicene Creed, and it is also the case that the Apostles' Creed did not rule out Arianism in the way in which the Nicene Creed unequivocally did.

The implication of this is that there has been a degree of liberality allowed in Wesleyan communities with respect to the language employed in the praise of the Trinity, perhaps a larger degree of liberality in this respect than other churches have allowed. One could, I suspect, hold essentially Arian or at least semi-Arian beliefs, or modalist (Sabellian) beliefs, and worship in a Methodist congregation. One might function, in quite another mode, as the kind of Evangelical who prefers to use scriptural language only. This cannot be pressed too far: the Arian or Sabellian Methodist would have to be comfortable with singing the praise of the Father, the Son, and the Holy Spirit, or at least God, Christ, and the Holy Spirit, and would have to acknowledge that the explicitly stated doctrines of the church differed from his or her own opinions. Moreover, such beliefs would not be permissible if maintained by candidates for ordained ministry, since candidates for ordination would be asked to make a public profession and pledge to teach the explicitly stated doctrines of their church.[50] But that there is a degree of liberality allowed in the piety of Wesleyan communities would appear consistently from the practices of Methodist churches.

An expression of this liberality was experimentation in the decade of the 1980s with alternatives to the traditional trinitarian formula, "Father, Son, and Holy Spirit" in the wake of concerns that this formula is inappropriately masculine, given the historic doctrinal claim that God is "without body or parts" and thus that gender cannot be predicated literally of God.[51] An alternative ordinal adopted by The United Methodist Church in 1980 did not specify the central performative portion of the ordination prayer, traditionally performed "in the name of the Father, and of the Son, and of the Holy Spirit," suggesting instead that bishops and Annual Conference worship committee might devise local expressions.[52] In some cases, then, ordination was performed in the name of the "Creator, Redeemer, and Sustainer" and some pastors experimented with alternatives to the traditional trinitarian formula in baptism and other rites. These practices raised concerns within Methodist communities and the broader ecumenical community, and as a result the service for ordination in the 1992 United Methodist Church *Book of Worship* specified the traditional formula.[53] In 1999, a new British *Methodist Worship Book* included one version of the eucharistic prayer with the initial lines, "God our Father and our Mother, we give you thanks and praise."[54] It should be noted that this was one of eight different versions of the eucharistic prayer offered in this *Worship Book*, and although it garnered some attention from the press when first released, it has remained in place in this worship resource. Nevertheless, the conclusion I would draw is that, although Methodist liberality with respect to belief in the Trinity allows the discussion of possible communally sanctioned alternatives to the traditional trinitarian formula, these discussions to date have not succeeded in finding alternative language that has won widespread communal consensus.

DIVINE ATTRIBUTES AND THE BELIEVER'S QUEST FOR GODLINESS

Beliefs about God in Wesleyan communities are related to teachings about the "way of salvation" and especially the process of sanctification, a process in which believers become more "godly" and take on some of the characteristics of God. The language of Charles Wesley's hymns describes the perfections or "attributes" of God:

> Wisdom, and might, and love are thine;
>> Prostrate before thy face we fall,
> Confess thine attributes Divine,
>> And hail the Sovereign LORD of all.[55]

Although the divine attributes could be discussed by cataloging terms and asking how these terms could be applied to God (and some Methodist theologians proceeded in this fashion), Wesleyan piety could understand the divine attributes as giving voice to the mystery of God. They bear relevance to Christian spirituality because in the quest for sanctification some of the aspects or attributes of divinity are to be acquired through grace by the believer.

Christian devotion and doctrine have traditionally described God by a series of adjectives such as "infinite," "merciful," "omnipotent," "compassionate," and the like.[56] These, when made into abstract nouns, are said to be God's attributes ("infinity," "mercifulness," "omnipotence," "compassion," etc.). These adjectives and abstract nouns typically amount to either negations of terms that express the limitations that human beings experience (everything human beings experience is "finite" or limited, so God is said to be "infinite") or amplifications of terms that express the limitations of human experience (all human knowledge is limited, therefore God is said to have "omniscience," that is "all knowledge"). These terms, then, do not so much express what human beings *know* about God as what human beings in fact *do not know* about God. On this account, the expression of divine attributes is crucial to worship insofar as worship expresses the mystery of God that lies far beyond our comprehension. A hymn of Ernst Lange translated into English by John Wesley and included in the 1780 *Collection* sings of the attributes of God in just this way:

> O God, thou bottomless abyss,
>> Thee to perfection who can know?
> O height immense, what words suffice
>> Thy countless attributes to show?
> Unfathomable depths thou art!

> O plunge me in thy mercy's sea;
> Void of true wisdom is my heart,
> With love embrace and cover me![57]

The divine attributes become a pattern for the Christian believer in the quest of sanctification. John Wesley's "The Character of a Methodist," adapted from Clement of Alexandria's description of the true Christian "Gnostic," paints a portrait of the true believer by describing the attributes of the divine that are acquired, through grace, by the believer.[58] There is perhaps a tension between Wesleyan devotion and Wesleyan theology on this point, for such classical Wesleyan theologians as Richard Watson did suppose that they could describe the nature of God by describing the divine attributes, as revealed in Scripture and even, in a limited way, in nature.

The divine attributes appeared in John Wesley's sermons, in the Wesleyan hymns, and even in the arrangement of Methodist hymnals, which had subsections of hymns on God's "Majesty and Power" and God's "Love and Mercy."[59] They appeared in Methodist doctrinal standards, such as the first Article of Religion of The Methodist Episcopal Church and its successors. They appeared in great detail in the works of Wesleyan theologians.[60] The attributes listed are numerous and cover the span of perfections and qualities traditionally ascribed to God: William Burt Pope, to give just one example, had separate categories of absolute attributes of the divine (spirituality, infinity, immensity, eternity, self-sufficiency, immutability, and perfection), attributes related to the creation (freedom, omnipotence, omnipresence, omniscience, wisdom, and goodness), and attributes related to God's "moral government" (holiness, righteousness or justice, truth or faithfulness, love, and grace).[61]

In almost every case Methodists affirmed the attributes of God acknowledged broadly in Christian tradition. There are only a couple of instances where Methodist peculiarity or distinctiveness may be seen. The first has to do with a mysterious alteration of the first Article of Religion as it appears in the early *Disciplines* of The Methodist Episcopal Church. Although the version that John Wesley sent had the traditional Anglican wording, stating that God is "without body, parts or passions," later editions of this article omit the reference to divine impassibility, and so affirm only that

God is "without body or parts." It is not clear who was responsible for this omission[62] but it allows the possibility of speaking of divine "passions," in some sense. The reason for this may not be a deep mystery. Those who have seen William Hogarth's caricature of John Wesley titled "Credulity, Fanaticism and Superstition" will realize that "passions" were a Methodist hallmark in Wesley's day, and it may have seemed incongruous to Methodist folk that the God of their passionate devotion should be described as "without passions."

Understood in its historical context, the traditional association of impassibility with God as it appears in the first Anglican Article of Religion meant that God is not subject to the changeable passions to which human beings are subject. John Wesley could say that "God is a Spirit, not having such a body, such parts, or passions, as men have."[63] Elsewhere he could speak of "baser passions," suggesting that it is from these kinds of passions that God is free. Recognizing this distinction of passions, some Wesleyan theologians, such as Thomas O. Summers, have explicitly defended the notion of divine impassibility.[64]

But such a clarification of the meaning of divine impassibility should not prohibit us from seeing a distinctly Wesleyan tendency at this point, namely, the tendency to stress the vivid, compassionate personality of God. This appears in formal Methodist doctrine and theologies, but also in the spirituality expressed in Charles Wesley's hymns:

> Appeased by the charms of thy grace
> > We all shall in amity join,
> And kindly each other embrace,
> > And love with a passion like thine.[65]

The note of divine compassion for humanity appears even more strongly in popular Methodist devotion and hymnody after the Wesleys' time. As a single example of later Methodist piety, consider the same idea of divine compassion as it is sounded by the American Methodist hymn writer Frances Jane Crosby:

> Hear the voice that entreats you,
> > O return ye unto God!
> Hear the voice that entreats you,

O return ye unto God!
He is of great compassion
And of wondrous love;
Hear the voice that entreats you,
Hear the voice that entreats you,
O return ye unto God!
O return ye unto God![66]

The depiction of God in hymns such as this strikes a note of senti-mentality that may offend Christians of other traditions (and it may offend some Methodists), but it may also explain why many Methodists were uncomfortable saying that God is "without pas-sions." The God preached by Methodists and celebrated in their hymns is a supremely personal and compassionate God. Perhaps this is one reason why the philosophical tradition known as Personalism emerged in Methodist theological circles late in the nineteenth century.[67]

A second issue that involves a typically Wesleyan or Methodist tendency has to do with the difficult issue of describing God as simultaneously omnipotent (all-powerful) and omnibenevolent (all benevolent, or willing only good). If omnipotence means that God can accomplish whatever God wills, and God wills only good, then how can evil not only exist but so often prevail? Although piety and devotion may suggest that the only appropriate answer to this classic "problem of evil" or theodicy is to be silent and con-template the mysteries of divine omnipotence and divine good-ness, the truth is that particular Christian communities often reveal consistent tendencies to be *more* silent about one or the other of these claims. There is a tendency in Reformed communities to stress the omnipotence of God and to be much more silent about the benevolence of God—not by denial, but more typically by the claim that divine benevolence is a mystery which the human mind is incapable of probing.[68]

Wesleyan beliefs trend in the opposite direction, namely, so to defend divine goodness as to restrict, at least by implication, divine power or omnipotence. Again, this is almost never to the point of denial of omnipotence but the restriction, however subtle, tends to be in this direction for Wesleyans. This trend can be seen, for instance, in Wesley's sermon "Free Grace," which claims that the doctrine of predestination as divine predetermination of who will and will not be saved contradicts "the whole scope and tenor of Scripture" in which God's benevolence for all of humankind is expressed, and even blasphemes God and Christ by making them the authors of evil.[69] Chapter 3 has shown a correlate of this in a hymn by Charles Wesley published in the same year as his brother's sermon "Free Grace," a hymn that accused predestinarians of worshiping a fiendish deity, "a Molock gorg'd with blood!" who delights in the damnation of human beings.[70] According to the Wesleys, God's absolute power cannot be asserted at the expense of God's goodness.[71] Moreover, John Wesley consistently defended the notion of creaturely freedom as necessary for the understanding of divine goodness; for example, his treatise titled "Predestination Calmly Considered" argues that some degree of human freedom is consistent with God's wisdom, since the plan of salvation can be understood as God's manner of dealing with free creatures; with God's justice, since only a free creature can be the object of justice; and with God's love, since it would be unloving to consign creatures to hell for no fault of their own.[72]

This defense of creaturely freedom became a staple of Methodist teachings, distinguishing Methodists especially from Presbyterians and from predestinarian Congregationalists and Baptists.[73] Although later Methodists would gradually lose sight of Wesley's insistence that creaturely freedom was itself a gift of divine grace,[74] the issue of creaturely freedom was understood to be relevant not only to the question of human nature and salvation but also to the very nature of God, since it was this idea that preserved the goodness of God in making sin the result of the creaturely abuse of freedom.

In the twentieth century some Methodist theologians made even bolder claims. Edgar Sheffield Brightman's *The Problem of God* (1930) was published by Abingdon Press, which at that time was the publishing house of The Methodist Episcopal Church. It is the principal work in which he developed a distinctive idea of divine self-limitation.[75] The "problem of God," as Brightman laid it out, had not only to do with the doubts of modern people about the existence of God but also with modern concerns about the essential goodness or justice of God since these latter concerns, Brightman thought, lay behind much of the agnostic tendencies in modern cultures.[76] The problem of suffering was not an abstract one for

Brightman: his marriage to Charlotte Hülsen, whom he had met in Germany, ended tragically with Charlotte's death from cancer only three years after their wedding and a year after the birth of a son to them.

Brightman described what he called both the "expansion" and the "contraction" of the idea of God in response to modern culture. The idea of God had expanded with modern discoveries in science, astronomy, and evolution, in relation to which God had to be seen as the author of a much vaster and much more complex universe than had been imagined before.[77] On the other hand, the idea of God had "contracted" in modern culture as more and more of the universe was explained by way of scientific discovery, leaving relatively less of the universe in the category of the mysterious and unexplained that had been commonly attributed to divine intervention in premodern cultures.[78] What Brightman described as "the resultant idea of God" that emerged out of this dialogue with modern culture was a conception of God as being "infinite" and even "omnipotent" in the sense that God has, in the words of one of Brightman's interpreters, "all the power there is except that delegated to created beings."[79]

However, Brightman also argued that there is a sense in which God can be described as "limited" or "finite" and it is in this sense that Brightman posited an eternal datum or a "rational given" within God's own nature that serves as a limit to God's own power. This "Given" or datum included the immutable laws of logic and physics, especially laws of the material universe which are established in God's primordial nature and which God does not alter. As Brightman stated it by way of questions,

> Can [God] choose whether the laws of reason shall be true or not? The old questions haunt us: Can he make a round triangle, a two which multiplied by two will produce six, a time prior to his own existence? Manifestly not! Rather, his eternal nature includes reason, never-ending activity in time, and the rich realm of The Given with which his will has to cope in the task of world-building and development. His nature as a conscious being sets limits to his will; God must be finite.[80]

Brightman admitted that the idea of divine self-limitation was "abhorrent" upon its first consideration but he argued that it is a more adequate understanding of the divine character as known in human religious experience, including the Scriptures.

In opening up the possibility of divine "limitation" and thus questioning the traditional view of divine omnipotence, Brightman was not willing to sacrifice any notion of divine goodness, indeed, the defense of divine goodness seems to have been the motivation for his claims of divine limitation: "We believe that it is far more reasonable to deny the absolute omnipotence of the power manifesting itself in the world than to deny its goodness."[81] His solution to the problem of evil was framed as a response to the issues of human suffering, which is the topic of the final chapter of *The Problem of God*.[82]

Moreover, although Brightman framed his argument around the concerns of modern philosophy and broader modern cultures, he claimed a christological element in his view of a "limited God." Brightman stated:

> The conception of a God limited by The Given within his own nature, yet wresting meaning from it by the achievements of his rational will, seems to account more adequately than other ideas of God for the paradoxical assertion of religious experience that its object is both a Mighty God and a Suffering Servant. It places the Cross in the eternal nature of God.[83]

Or as he stated it elsewhere, God "is indeed love; but a suffering love that redeems through a Cross."[84] In both cases, I note, the word *Cross* is spelled with a capital letter *C*, which I take as an indication of Brightman's christological piety.

Brightman's concern for theodicy was followed by Methodist theologians John B. Cobb, Jr., and Schubert M. Ogden, who both qualify the meaning of divine omnipotence although they do not accept Brightman's conception of divine self-limitation. Instead, Ogden and Cobb make a case for divine power in a very different way than that of classical theism. Cobb pointed out that even if God were thought of as being limited in power, any degree of divine power would still need to be reconciled with the assertion of God's goodness or love.[85] Cobb's own response, following the thought of Charles Hartshone, is to qualify the meaning of divine power: divine power cannot be coercive power; rather, it must be a persuasive power:

> If we think, then, of God's power as persuasive power, we may still use the term "omnipotence" if we like, but its meaning is quite altered....It means instead that [God] exercises the optimum persuasive power in relation to whatever is. Such an optimum is a balance between urging toward the good and maximizing the power—therefore the freedom—of the one whom God seeks to persuade.[86]

Schubert Ogden also resists the notion of "limitation" or self-limitation within God and makes the case for a qualification of the notion of omnipotence. Ogden affirms a premise of process philosophy that "nothing whatever, not even God, can wholly determine the being of someone else." All beings are to some degree self-created as well as created by their interaction with other beings. This perspective allows Ogden to understand that

> even the greatest possible power over others—even the omnipotent power than which no greater power can be conceived—could not be all the power there is but only all the power that any one actual thing could be conceived to have, consistently with there being other actual things having lesser power over which its omnipotent power could alone be exercised.
>
> Put differently, for process philosophy and theology, the concept of "power," just like every other fundamental concept, is by its very meaning social, in that it necessarily presupposes relations between distinct individuals each of which does and must have some power to create both itself and others.[87]

In his own way, then, Ogden conceives of power and divine omnipotence parallel to that expressed by Cobb, according to which divine power interacts with the free agency of creatures and the classical notion of divine omnipotence is seen as a mistaken "pseudo-conception."[88] What I find fascinating in all of these twentieth-century Methodist theologians—Brightman, Cobb, and Ogden—is that all of them in one way or another need to qualify the claim of divine power and none of them seems to have any interest in qualifying the claims of divine benevolence or love.

I would stress that both the Wesleyan tendency to ascribe a kind of "passion" to God, and the tendency to emphasize God's goodness with respect to God's power should be seen as tendencies or trends within the scope of Wesleyan or Methodist communities. John Wesley and his followers *could* define divine impassibility in such a way that it might be affirmed, and they *did* affirm divine omnipotence, however this affirmation might be limited in practice by their passionate insistence on God's goodness.

In concluding this consideration of divine attributes, however, I want to emphasize their significance for Wesleyan spirituality. In the quest for sanctification, the believer is to assume progressively the attributes of divinity, especially God's holiness. The quest for sanctification, then, is indeed a kind of θέωσις, a process in which the human is not "deified" but "divinized," made godly, by God's own gift of holy love.[89]

CONCLUSION

What, then, can be said in conclusion about the teachings of Wesleyan communities about the nature of God, the Trinity, and the divine attributes? This and the preceding chapters have shown the extent of consensus in historic Wesleyan teaching expressed in the writings of John and Charles Wesley, in corporate Methodist doctrinal statements, in Methodist hymnals, liturgies, and catechisms, and in the theologies prescribed for study by Methodist preachers. These formal doctrinal sources, popular hymns, and contemporary theological reflections show how Wesleyan communities have maintained a recognizably ecumenical belief in God, but a view of God that stresses or emphasizes God's compassion (God's passion) and God's unbounded goodness or love; a classical vision of God, one might say, with a rather Evangelical personality.

Wesleyan beliefs about God teach the nature of God as Trinity formally utilizing the terms of the ancient Christian creeds, but often preferring simpler language (like that of the Apostles' Creed) and with a stress on the manner in which the Persons of the Trinity are known in the human quest of healing or salvation, sometimes identifying the Trinity under the categories of God, the Son, and the Holy Spirit. These beliefs involve a devotion that utilizes the language of traditional attributes ascribed to God, placing more stress on some attributes (divine goodness) and less stress on others (divine power) and emphasizing the compassionate, personal nature of God. Wesleyans have thus transmitted common Christian beliefs with some distinct nuances characteristic of these communities. This core sample of one particular set of Christian beliefs shows how common or ecumenical beliefs were developed in Wesleyan communities. The next chapter will consider a distinctively Wesleyan cluster of beliefs and examine how they were transmitted and reinterpreted after the time of the Wesleys.

CHAPTER 5

BELIEFS ABOUT THE "WAY OF SALVATION" AFTER THE WESLEYS

INTRODUCTION

The "way of salvation" describes a cluster of teachings embracing many of the most distinctive beliefs of Wesleyan communities. Chapter 2 examined John Wesley's construals of the "way of salvation" and the second part of chapter 3 examined Charles Wesley's expression of doctrines related to the "way of salvation." This chapter offers a core sample of distinctively Wesleyan beliefs about the "way of salvation" showing how these beliefs were reflected in hymnals, catechisms, and theologies, and then also in the ways in which Methodist people gave testimonies to their own spiritual experiences.

The scope of this chapter will differ from the previous chapter in two respects. The previous chapter considered beliefs about God as they were expressed in John and Charles Wesley and then in subsequent Wesleyan literature, but it did not deal with the testimonies of Methodist people. The subject of the "way of salvation," however, has been more extensively discussed in chapters 2 and 3, so this chapter will not return to the teachings of the Wesleys. It will focus instead on the expression of this teaching in the period after them. A second difference between the previous chapter and this one is that the previous chapter did not take up the spirituality of particular men and women except in the few examples known where Methodist people actually experienced visions of the Trinity. The "way of salvation" did become part of the regular vocabulary of Methodist people and for this reason this chapter can take up an extended account of how teachings about the "way of salvation" provided a vocabulary in which people could organize and express their own religious experiences.

THE "WAY OF SALVATION" IN FORMAL CONSENSUS

Background

Chapter 2 has shown that John Wesley, building on the understanding of the *ordo salutis* developed by Puritan authors, transmitted a set of beliefs about the "way of salvation" as the distinctive content of the Methodist movement. The second part of chapter 3 has shown how Charles Wesley, also building on the Puritan expression of the *ordo salutis* and utilizing the genre of the hymn that had been developing in the Reformed tradition, expressed distinctly Wesleyan teachings about the "way of salvation" in his hymns and other poems. I turn now to a consideration of the "way of salvation" as it is revealed in the schemata or organizational structures of Methodist hymnals, catechisms, and then in systematic theologies authorized by Methodist churches for the training of Methodist preachers. The next section will consider how this understanding of the "way of salvation" was expressed in personal testimonies of Methodist people.

The "Way of Salvation" in Methodist Hymnals

The previous chapter showed how Methodist hymnals from 1848 were organized in a creedal pattern, with hymns in praise of the divine Trinity at the beginning. Almost every one of the Methodist and Wesleyan hymnals I have studied have a lengthy section singing sinners and Christians through the "way of salvation," including repentance, faith, assurance, and the quest for sanctification or Christian holiness. In this respect the subsequent Methodist hymnals do follow the basic pattern set by John Wesley in his organization of the 1780 *Collection*. In introducing the *Methodist Hymnal* of 1964, Carlton R. Young noted this consistent organizational structure of Methodist hymnals:

A third distinctive trait of a Methodist hymnal is the prominence placed upon hymns that reflect, in Wesley's words, "the experience of real Christians." In maintaining this topical format in a hymnbook, Wesley expressed the view that the book was to be used by Methodists and must reflect the experiences of Christians within the context of the Wesley revival.[1]

Although the *Pocket Hymn Book* published by The Methodist Episcopal Church in 1793 does not clearly follow this pattern, the Wesleyan *Collection* remained in print in this early period.[2] The 1837 *Hymn Book of the Methodist Protestant Church* has a long section on the "Process of Salvation" with subheadings on repentance, faith, justification, regeneration, adoption, "witness of the Spirit," "graces of the Spirit," sanctification, "triumph in death," "glory in the resurrection," "approved in the judgment," and "immortality in heaven."[3]

Methodist hymnals after 1840 typically followed the specific pattern set by the 1780 *Collection* in dividing hymns between those appropriate to "sinners" (parts II and III of the 1780 *Collection*) and "believers" (Part IV of the 1780 *Collection*).[4] The 1848 collection entitled *Hymns for the Use of the Methodist Episcopal Church* has a section entitled "The Sinner" followed by a section entitled "The Christian Life," with subsections on "justification by faith," "adoption and assurance," and "sanctification."[5] The same general division between "The Sinner" and "The Christian" can be seen in the 1877 revision of this Methodist Episcopal hymnal.[6]

As of the 1905 hymnal jointly sponsored by The Methodist Episcopal Church and The Methodist Episcopal Church, South, these two sections are titled "The Gospel" and "The Christian Life," and a *Free Methodist Hymnal* from 1910 follows this pattern closely.[7] Both of these hymnals place entire sanctification rather early in the section on the Christian life, reflecting the prominent place of the Holiness movement in this period.[8] The British *Methodist Hymn-Book* of 1933 and The U.S. *Methodist Hymnal* of 1935 jointly produced by The Methodist Episcopal Church, The Methodist Episcopal Church, South, and The Methodist Protestant Church have a section titled "The Gospel" (1935) or "The Gospel Call" (1933) followed by a section titled "The Christian Life." But two important shifts occurred with these early twentieth-century hymnals. In the first place, the weight given to the two sections had shifted. In the 1933 *Hymn-Book*, the section titled "Gospel Call" has only 28 hymns, whereas the section titled "The Christian Life" has 300 hymns.[9] The joint American *Methodist Hymnal* of 1935 has more hymns in the section titled "The Gospel" (72 hymns in this section), but this is tempered by a second factor that appears in both of these hymnals: the first section, "The Gospel" or "The Gospel Call," is not strictly limited to "sinners" as was the pattern in earlier Methodist hymnals. Both have sections on faith in the first section titled "The Gospel," and the American hymnal even has hymns on "forgiveness" and "consecration" in this earlier section. The American hymnal of 1935 does not have a subsection explicitly labeled "sin" or "depravity," although it does have a subsection on "repentance." Moreover, in the American hymnal of 1935, the sub-section on "Christian perfection" is placed at the very end of the section titled "The Christian Life," and this probably reflects a reaction against Holiness teaching that had gone on in these denominations in the early twentieth century.[10] The same organizational division between "The Gospel" and "The Christian Life" is followed in the 1984 *Bicentennial Hymnal* of the African Methodist Episcopal Church.[11]

The weakest Methodist hymnal with respect to the sequence of hymns on the "way of salvation" was the 1964 *Hymnal* of The Methodist Church, subsequently retitled *The Book of Hymns* of The United Methodist Church. This hymnal included sections on "call" and "repentance and forgiveness," but these were structured as subheadings under "The Gospel of Jesus Christ" along with other hymns on the theme of Christology and atonement. Also, they were severed from the section on the Christian life, which begins with "faith and regeneration" and runs through "Christian perfection" to "death and life eternal." This hymnal reflected the very strong momentum of the liturgical renewal movement, which was pressing Methodists in the direction of organizing hymnals according to the seasons of the Christian year. In fact, an original proposal was to do away with the "Christian Life" section entirely until the elderly Bishop Nolan Harmon pleaded, "The Christian Life is all we have," meaning that the section titled "The Christian Life" had been the most consistent and distinctive mark of Methodist hymnals.[12]

The most recent British and American Methodist hymnals have a stronger recognition of this distinctive trait of Methodist hymnody and hymnal organization. The British Methodist hymnal *Hymns and Psalms* (1983) has a section on the Christian life (hymns 661–751), though I note that repentance is conspicuously absent from its schema. The 1989 *United Methodist Hymnal* has consecutive sections on "prevenient grace," "justifying grace," and "sanctifying and perfecting grace." This reflects the resurgence of interest in Wesleyan theology and spirituality that had been going on through the 1970s and the 1980s. The most recent hymnal of the Church of the Nazarene (1993) follows this pattern of organizing hymns on Christian experience by the categories of prevenient, justifying, and sanctifying grace.[13]

There has thus been a consistent pattern in the schemata (organizational structures) of Methodist and Wesleyan hymnals explicitly acknowledged from the time of John Wesley's arrangement of the 1780 *Collection of Hymns*. In accordance with this pattern, a substantial portion of hymns are arranged in a sequence following the Wesleyan understanding of the "way of salvation." Specific organizational schemes vary from the twofold distinction of hymns addressed to "sinners" and "believers" in earlier hymnals to the flat pattern that embraces hymns on the repentance of sinners under the category of "The Christian Life" to the more recent pattern according to which hymns are organized under the headings of prevenient, justifying, and sanctifying grace. But throughout these schemata, a sequence of moments in Christian experience appears fairly consistently: namely, the repentance of sinners, followed by justification, regeneration, assurance, sanctification, trials and difficulties, and, finally, entire sanctification.

The "Way of Salvation" in Methodist Catechisms

A similar pattern of sequential moments in Christian experience can be seen in catechisms designed for the formation of children and young people by Methodist and other Wesleyan churches. There has been a long and continuous tradition of Methodist catechisms, beginning with John Wesley's *Instructions for Children* (1745) and continuing in most branches of Methodist churches with the exception of The United Methodist Church.

The "Catechism on Faith" included in the *Disciplines* of the African Methodist Episcopal Church from 1817 is the collection of

Minutes of the earlier Wesleyan conferences known more generally as the "Doctrinal Minutes." This document discusses most of the critical points of the "way of salvation" (justification, faith, regeneration, assurance, sanctification), but because it follows the pattern of the early Methodist conferences, it does not deal with these in sequential order. The other catechisms examined here have a series of questions that follow sequentially the "way of salvation," and these can be laid out synoptically as follows:

1793 *Short Scriptural Catechism*[14]	1824 *Catechisms of the Wesleyan Methodists*[15]	1852 *Catechism of The Methodist Episcopal Church*[16]	1884 "Ten Doctrines of Grace"[17]
repentance (7)	repentance		
prayer (8)			
	faith in general		
	faith in Christ		
justification by faith (9)	justification	justification and adoption	justification (5)
	adoption		
assurance (10)			adoption (7)
			witness of the Spirit (8)
regeneration (11)	regeneration	regeneration	regeneration (6)
the divine law (12)			
sanctification, including	sanctification [begins]	sanctification	
entire sanctification (13)	entire sanctification	entire sanctification	entire sanctification (9)
possibility of falling away (14)		danger of falling from grace	final perseverance (10)

There is a consistent pattern in this material despite some distinctive nuances. The 1793 *Short Scriptural Catechism* has sections on prayer and the divine law that do not appear in the other catechisms. The 1852 *Catechism* of The Methodist Episcopal Church puts questions on justification and adoption together, and the 1884 appended list of "Ten Doctrines of Grace" has a separate section on the witness of the Spirit, and places regeneration after justification, adoption, and the witness of the Spirit. These two catechetical documents do not have separate questions on the repentance of sinners. The "Ten Doctrines of Grace" utilizes the term "final perseverance," although the content of this section describes the same content as that of the other catechisms where they discuss the possibility of falling from divine grace. Beyond these distinctive nuances, however, a common sequential pattern of moments in the "way of salvation" runs as follows:

the repentance of sinners
justification
regeneration
assurance (adoption, witness of the Spirit)
sanctification
entire sanctification
danger of falling from divine grace

These form a temporal sequence, although in Wesleyan teaching justification and regeneration and the assurance of pardon were thought of as normatively occurring at the same moment, so it is not surprising that the order of these three items is sometimes changed. Moreover, "falling away" or "falling from grace" was a danger that could present itself at any point after justification, so its location at the end of the sequence is not necessarily temporal. The sequence of these moments in Christian experience parallels the sequence in Methodist hymnals.

The "Way of Salvation" in Authorized Works of Systematic Theology

Methodist preachers and ordained clergy were trained utilizing formal works of systematic theology authorized for study by the Methodist denominations and printed by their publishing houses, beginning with Richard Watson's *Theological Institutes* (1823). Almost all of these works were published in the nineteenth century. With the exception of Thomas O. Summers's *Systematic Theology* (1888), these works of systematic theology were organized in a pattern common to theological textbooks, including prolegomena (Watson's "evidences"), doctrinal theology ("doctrines"), ethics ("morals"), and ecclesiology ("institutions").[18] Within this framework, however, they devote a great deal of attention to the defense of the Wesleyan and Arminian belief in the universal availability of grace,[19] and they devote considerable space to the explication of the "way of salvation." The exception to this is Summers, who organized his two-volume *Systematic Theology* as lectures on the Articles of Religion, and so did not have an extended discussion of the "way of salvation."[20] This could explain why Thomas N. Ralston's *Elements of Divinity* (originally published in 1847) remained in print in Southern Methodist churches for decades beyond the publication of Summers's textbook.

Richard Watson discussed moments in the way of salvation under "Doctrines of the Holy Scriptures." He dealt with justification in chapter 23 and in chapter 24 he continued with "Concomitants of Justification: Regeneration and Adoption (Assurance)."[21] Four chapters (25–28) defended the universal availability of grace; then he dealt with "benefits of redemption" in chapter 29, with an extended discussion of entire sanctification.[22] Ralston also dealt with moments in the "way of salvation" under the general topic of biblical doctrines. He offered a long sequence under the general heading of "The Remedial Scheme—Its Benefits" (Part I, Book IV), where he discussed the influence of the Holy Spirit (chapter 25), repentance (chapter 26), faith (chapter 27), justification (chapters 28–33), regeneration (chapter 34), adoption and the witness of the Spirit (chapter 35), perseverance of the saints (including the possibility of falling from grace, chapter 36) and Christian perfection (chapter 37).[23] This outline answered almost exactly to the sequence given in the 1852 Methodist Episcopal catechisms examined above.

William Burt Pope divided his material somewhat differently. His work had a trinitarian schema, indeed, one might say an "economic" trinitarian schema in which specific moments in the "way of salvation" are dealt with as aspects of Christology under the category of "The Administration of Redemption" and other moments are dealt with as aspects of pneumatology. Under Christology in the second volume of his work, Pope deals with the "preliminaries of salvation" including free will, conversion, repentance, and faith.[24] Under pneumatology in the third volume he discusses "the state of salvation," including regeneration and adoption, and then "Christian sanctification" including entire sanctification.[25]

The specific content of these nineteenth-century works of systematic theology from Watson through Pope reveals a consistent defense of the Wesleyan teachings on the "way of salvation" in a dialectic with other Christian traditions. For example, the teaching about justifying faith as heartfelt trust in Christ is contrasted with beliefs in "baptismal justification" (despite the fact that Wesley believed in a version of this) and with the notion of a merely objective faith (*fides quae creditur*) attributed to Lutheran and Reformed traditions.[26] Thomas Langford commented on the lack of originality among nineteenth-century interpreters of the Wesleyan message, finding little doctrinal development between Wesley and Pope in the 1880s. Langford faulted Pope, in particular, for his failure to deal with critical cultural issues such as the rise of Freudian thought facing the churches in his day.[27] But their lack of originality indicates a remarkable consistency in Wesleyan thought from Wesley's own time through the early twentieth century. These nineteenth-century interpreters were telling their own, internal story: the story of the "way of salvation" that had structured the distinctive spirituality of the Methodist movement.

Summary

When these officially sanctioned documents—hymnals, catechisms, and works of systematic theology—are considered together, they show a consistent and stable pattern to beliefs about the "way of salvation," according to which Christian experience was understood as embracing the following typical moments in this temporal sequence:

the *repentance* of sinners, followed by
justification by faith, occurring simultaneously with
    regeneration and
        the *assurance* of pardon (including "the witness of the Spirit"),
        followed by
the process of *sanctification,*

including trials and difficulties and the need for the
     repentance of believers
and even the possibility of falling away, but culminated
     hopefully in
entire sanctification.

I return, then, to the example of a Methodist laywoman in 1855 (I have Eliza Clark Garrett in mind) who would have regularly sung hymns laid out in the "way of salvation," who attended quarterly meetings or camp meetings where the preaching followed the sequence of the "way of salvation,"[28] keeping "a strict account" of how many souls were awakened, converted, and sanctified during the meeting, whose family might own a copy of one of the 1852 Methodist catechisms detailing the "way of salvation" in questions and answers that could be posed to children as an exercise in the evenings and on the Lord's Day, and whose circuit-riding preachers would have studied the "way of salvation" as it was explicated in a more sophisticated way in Watson's *Theological Institutes* or Ralston's *Elements of Divinity* and possibly also in Wesley's *Standard Sermons* in addition to Watson or Ralston. She would have been well familiar with the "way of salvation" as Methodists understood it.

THE "WAY OF SALVATION" IN POPULAR RECEPTION AND EXPRESSION ILLUSTRATED BY SPIRITUAL AUTOBIOGRAPHIES

How were the formal or official teachings of Methodist churches received and expressed by people in Methodist churches? Methodists produced a voluminous literature of personal conversion narratives, diaries and journals, spiritual autobiographies, and the distinctly Methodist genre of obituaries that were also used as a way of describing personal religious experience. Just as Wesley's *Sermons* and his arrangement of the 1780 hymnal set precedents for subsequent Methodist theology about the "way of salvation," so his published *Journal* set a precedent for the recording of personal religious experiences.

One way to test the level of reception of teachings about the "way of salvation" is by examining some specific spiritual autobiographies of Methodist people. Fortunately, a series of spiritual autobiographies from early American Methodist people has been published in recent decades and I will use five nineteenth-century autobiographies published in critical editions in recent decades. The first two are from a Native American, William Apess, a Pequot Indian from Massachusetts born in 1798, and his wife, Mary Apess, who was Euro-American and was born in 1788. These are published in a volume titled *On Our Own Ground: The Complete Writings of William Apess, A Pequot*.[29] William Apess had been a licensed preacher in The Methodist Episcopal Church but united with The Methodist Protestant Church at about the time of its organization in 1830.[30]

The next three autobiographies are from a volume titled *Sisters of the Spirit: Three Black Women's Autobiographies of the Nineteenth Century*, and it includes the autobiographies of three black Methodist women, Jarena Lee (1783–after 1849), Zilpha Elaw (ca. 1790–after 1845) and Julia A. J. Foote (1823–1900). Jarena Lee was associated with the African Methodist Episcopal Church in the time of its founding by Richard Allen and she was an early advocate of the right of women to preach in that denomination. Zilpha Elaw ministered as a lay preacher and evangelist in The Methodist Episcopal Church, and Julia Foote was a preacher in the AME Zion Church. Shortly before her death in 1900 she became the first woman ordained as an elder in the Zion Church. Lee, Elaw, and Foote were all free black women from northern states of the United States.[31]

In addition to these five nineteenth-century autobiographies, I will also have reference to one Methodist autobiography from the twentieth century, that of Bishop James K. Mathews whose personal narrative entitled *A Global Odyssey* offers an account of his own spiritual experience.[32] These six autobiographies illustrate the historic Methodist understanding of the "way of salvation" and show how the formal teachings of Methodist churches were received at a popular level. The fact that four of these six individuals came from minority cultures (Native American and African American) is a significant indication of how the Methodist message was received and internalized even across significant cultural frontiers.

Repentance before Conversion

William and Mary Apess, Jarena Lee, Zilpha Elaw, and Julia Foote all recount in detail the struggles of their souls leading up to conversion, including their awareness of God's impending judgment, their intense awareness of their own sinfulness, and their need for divine grace. A few excerpts will illustrate the intensity of their experiences of repentance prior to justification.

> William Apess: "My heart now became much troubled, and I felt determined to seek the salvation of my soul.... A conviction settled on my mind, more and more; and I was more serious than usual.... When I considered how great a sinner I was before God, and how often I had grieved the good Spirit of the Lord, my distress for mercy was very great."[33]

> Mary Apess: "This was the first time I had been warned to seek the salvation of my soul. [The preacher's] words sank deep on my mind; I began to weep as soon as he had left me; I went out, and for the first time I ever felt the need of praying or of a Savior; I knelt and poured out my soul to God, that he would have mercy upon me; although I had never seen anybody kneel, yet it was impressed on my mind that I must, and from that time I cried to God earnestly every day, during some months."[34]

> Jarena Lee, recounting an experience in early life after she had told a lie to the woman in whose household she worked as a domestic servant: "At this awful point, in my early history, the Spirit of God moved in power through my conscience, and told me I was a wretched sinner. On this account so great was the impression and so strong were the feelings of guilt, that I promised in my heart that I would not tell another lie."[35]

> Zilpha Elaw: "I never experienced that terrific dread of hell by which some Christians appear to have been exercised; but I felt a godly sorrow for sin in having grieved my God by a course of disobedience to His commands."[36]

> Julia Foote: "All this time conviction followed me, and there were times when I felt a faint desire to serve the Lord; but I had had a taste of the world, and thought I could not part with its idle pleasures.... [She attends a dance, and] I had taken only a few steps

when I was seized with a smothering sensation, and felt the same heavy grasp on my arm, and in my ears, a voice kept saying, 'Repent! Repent!' I immediately left the floor and sank into a seat."[37]

Mathews's account of his sense of sin prior to conversion is only a small notice embedded in the narrative of his conversion but dramatic in its own way.

James K. Mathews: "So earnestly did I seek that I wrote out all the sins I could recall having committed, filling four foolscap pages."[38]

Conversion (Justification, Regeneration, and Assurance)

Each of the six Methodist autobiographies recounts a conversion narrative, usually involving a single moment in which the narrator feels her or his sins forgiven. This moment answers to justification and the "assurance of pardon" in more formal Methodist lore and probably also includes regeneration, although the term "conversion" is more common in popular Methodist literature.[39]

William Apess: "The result was such as is always to be expected, when a lost and ruined sinner throws himself entirely on the Lord—*perfect freedom*. On the 15th day of March, in the year of our Lord 1813, I heard a voice saying unto me, in soft and soothing accents, *'Arise, thy sins that are many are all forgiven thee; go in peace and sin no more.'* There was nothing very singular, save that the Lord stooped to lift me up, in my conversion."[40]

Mary Apess: "The plan of salvation was now open to my view. The Son of God was revealed to me by faith, in all his offices as prophet, priest, and king....My load of sin and fear of hell were gone....My burden of sin now left me; my tears were dried up. I felt a sweet peace in my soul.[41]

Jarena Lee, after hearing Richard Allen preach: "That moment, though hundreds were present, I did leap to my feet, and declare that God, for Christ's sake, had pardoned the sins of my soul. Great was the ecstasy of my mind, for I felt that not only the sin of *malice* was pardoned, but that all other sins were swept away altogether. That day was the first when my heart had believed, and my tongue had made confession unto salvation."[42]

Julia Foote; "I was converted when fifteen years old. It was on a Sunday evening at a quarterly meeting [where she felt a sense of conviction].... I fell to the floor and was carried home.... In great terror I cried: 'Lord, have mercy on me, a poor sinner!' The voice which had been crying in my ears ceased at once, and a ray of light flashed across my eyes, accompanied by a sound of far distant singing; the light grew brighter and brighter, and the singing more distinct, and soon I caught the words: 'This is the new song—redeemed, redeemed!' ... Such joy and peace as filled my heart, when I felt that I was redeemed and could sing the new song. Thus was I wonderfully saved from eternal burning."[43]

In contrast to these accounts of instantaneous conversions, Elaw makes it clear that her experience of conversion was gradual rather than instantaneous, involving a growing recognition of forgiveness. Nevertheless, this culminated in an ecstatic moment in which she saw a vision of Christ that assured her of her acceptance. "After this wonderful manifestation of my condescending Saviour, the peace of God which passeth understanding was communicated to my heart, and joy in the Holy Ghost."[44]

The conversion narrative given by Mathews includes the account of his awareness of sin (given above) along with his experience of conversion:

James K. Mathews: "Then [his brother Joe] returned home and told me the story [of his conversion]. At first his excessive enthusiasm and quite dogmatic beliefs put me off, but slowly I too yielded. There were other influences also, such as a concerned and appealing college pastor and a kindly woman evangelist who helped me in my struggle and search for forgiveness. So earnestly did I seek that I wrote out all the sins I could recall having committed, filling four foolscap pages. Then she gently led me to see that God's word was what God had to say to us, that to believe the word is to believe God, that my part was to confess and God's part was to forgive. Finally, I came to see that faith is taking God at his word. Because I was a Methodist a conversion experience was part of my heritage, and I fully expected that sometime, somehow I was to be reconciled to God and incorporated into the Church. This was my conversion experience—as simple, yet as profound and far-reaching as Joe's, yet no Damascus Road event, no blinding lights, and no inner emotional upheaval."[45]

Mathews goes on to narrate how in a subsequent experience he felt the assurance of pardon:

> James K. Mathews: "Then in the summer of 1936, during our 'evangelistic foray,' it happened! As a part of our evangelistic program as I have said, we would hold Bible classes every morning, usually teaching whole books of the Bible, especially the Gospels or Acts of the Apostles. One morning after I had been teaching the Bible, I made my way, alone, back to a farmhouse where we were living. I recall that it was a beautiful summer morning. As I walked along the road, there suddenly came across me the profound awareness that I was a child of God. It was not an experience of explosive force such as Paul had along the road to Damascus. My Methodist heritage came to my mind: could this be the witness of the Spirit? Then, I didn't walk, I *ran* the rest of the way to the farmhouse. When I opened the Bible to where Paul says the Spirit himself bears witness to our spirit that we are the children of God, I was convinced that this was the witness of the Spirit. I have had this sense almost constantly ever since, however unworthy I have been at times."[46]

The Scripture passage (Romans 8:14-17) to which Mathews refers here is the one that was discussed at the Aldersgate Street meeting at which John Wesley had felt the assurance of pardon.

Sanctification and the Trials of the Soul

Each of the nineteenth-century autobiographies considered here recounts the trials of the soul after conversion, including moments of "darkness" and doubt, sometimes involving "falling away" or "backsliding" into sin. William Apess recounted that he did not have the support of a local class meeting immediately after his conversion and soon fell back into sin, from which he was later delivered in another dramatic religious experience.[47] Mary Apess continued to experience doubts and melancholy after her conversion, and as she recounts this she attributes it to the fact that she had not been willing to share with her mother and others the joy of her conversion.[48] Lee noted, "From the day on which I first went to the Methodist church," (and this was the day of her conversion) "until the hour of my deliverance," (this refers to her subsequent experience of entire sanctification) "I was strangely buffetted by that enemy of all righteousness—the devil" and she went on to recount how she eventually came to a full consciousness of her conversion (still prior to entire sanctification).[49] Elaw recounted continuing trials and persecution on account of her identification with the Methodists: "But notwithstanding this tide of divine comforts so richly replenished my soul, Satan, my great adversary, frequently assailed me with various trials and temptations, and the young folks often derided me as being a Methodist."[50] Foote offers several chapters in her autobiography recounting her spiritual struggles: some of her chapter titles following her conversion narrative epitomize the content of these struggles: "A Desire for Knowledge—Inward Foes," "Various Hopes Blasted," "Disobedience—But Happy Results."[51]

Entire Sanctification

Mary Apess, Jarena Lee, Zilpha Elaw, and Julia Foote describe how they came to understand the possibility of entire sanctification as a moment in which one can love God completely as a gift of divine grace. Mary Apess indicated that she did not believe this doctrine at first but was eventually convinced of it on the grounds that to deny it would be to deny the power of God to bring about that which God desired, namely, our complete love and dedication to God.[52] Lee was taught the doctrine of sanctification by a traveling preacher.[53] Foote had learned about sanctification but understood at first that it was only to be expected near death. Later she learned that due to the unlimited power of God, entire sanctification is immediately available.[54] This reflects the development of Holiness theology in the mid-nineteenth century that taught believers to expect entire sanctification early in a Christian's experience.

Apess, Lee, Elaw, and Foote all offer testimonies to the moments in which they experienced entire sanctification.[55]

> Mary Apess: "But before the [camp] meeting closed, God in Christ showed himself mighty to save and strong to deliver. I felt the mighty power of God again, like electric fire, go through

every part of me, cleansing me throughout soul, flesh, and spirit. I felt now that I was purified, sanctified, and justified."[56]

I would note that the use of the term "justified" is eccentric in this passage, since formal Methodist teaching would have associated justification with the earlier moment of her conversion, and this shows how language about religious experience could become fluid in popular contexts (see below).

> Jarena Lee: "But when this voice whispered in my heart, saying, 'Pray for sanctification,' I again bowed in the same place, at the same time, and said, 'Lord, *sanctify* my soul for Christ's sake?' That very instant, as if lightening had darted through me, I sprang to my feet and cried, 'The Lord has sanctified my soul!' . . . [After being tempted by Satan] But another spirit said, 'Bow down for the witness—I received it—*thou art sanctified!*" The first I knew of myself after that, I was standing in the yard with my hands spread out, and looking with my face toward heaven."[57]

> Zilpha Elaw: "It was at one of these [camp] meetings that God was pleased to separate my soul unto Himself, to sanctify me as a vessel designed for honour. . . . Whether I was in the body, or whether I was out of the body, on that auspicious day, I cannot say; but this I do know, that at the conclusion of a most powerful sermon . . . I became so overpowered with the presence of God, that I sank down upon the ground, and laid there for a considerable time. . . . I distinctly heard a voice speak unto me, which said, 'Now thou art sanctified; and I will show thee what thou must do.' "[58]

> Julia Foote: "The second day after that pilgrim's visit, while waiting on the Lord, my large desire was granted, through faith in my precious Savior. The glory of God seemed almost to prostrate me to the floor. There was, indeed, a weight of glory resting upon me. . . . I lost all fear. I went straight to my mother and told her I was sanctified."[59]

Use of Technical Language to Describe the "Way of Salvation"

Each of the persons whose narratives are considered here was keenly aware of their racial, social, and cultural backgrounds. William Apess wrote explicitly from his experience as a Pequot

Indian, and referred to Native Americans as "the children of the forest." He contrasted the native morality of American Indians with the corruptions of Euro-American culture and society; he recounted severe persecution at the hands of Euro-Americans, including stinging prejudice based on skin color, and he sometimes used native expressions, such as "the Great Spirit" as a way of referring to God.[60] Lee, Elaw, and Foote all recount the prejudicial treatment they received at the hands of white families for whom they worked, and Elaw narrated the particular dangers faced by a free black woman traveling (as an evangelist) in slave states.[61] Mary Apess recounted her own struggles growing up as a poor, orphaned white girl.[62] None of these five persons had any formal education beyond a rudimentary knowledge of the English language for reading and writing, and then the training they received at the hands of Methodist preachers and society members.

And yet each of these persons also knew and used the technical language that Methodists taught concerning the stages of the "way of salvation." They had become "bicultural" or even "tricultural" in their ability to use the language of the Methodist subculture in addition to the language of the majority Euro-American culture as well as their native ways of speaking. They speak, for example, of "the plan of salvation" (William Apess)[63] and they could recount in strikingly similar language the general scheme of the "way of salvation." Lee could write that "I have now passed through the account of my conviction, and also of my conversion to God; and shall next speak of the blessing of sanctification."[64] She recounted how a visiting black preacher, William Scott,

> inquired if the Lord had justified my soul. I answered yes. He then asked me if he had sanctified me. I answered no and that I did not know what that was. He then undertook to instruct me further in the knowledge of the Lord respecting this blessing....He told me the progress of the soul from a state of darkness, or of nature, was threefold; or consisted in three degrees, as follows:—First, conviction for sin. Second, justification from sin. Third, the entire sanctification of the soul to God.[65]

Similarly, Foote wrote, "In giving my first testimony [in Boston], I told of my thorough and happy conversion, and of my sanctification as a second, distinct work of the Holy Ghost."[66]

Reading these spiritual autobiographies, one becomes aware of the fact that in popular parlance, a number of shorthand expressions were used to describe particular moments in the "way of salvation": "conviction" was frequently used as a shorthand term for the repentance of sinners, and "sanctification" was used as a shorthand term for what would be termed "entire sanctification" in more formal Methodist doctrinal phraseology. "Conversion" was the most frequent term for the moments discretely described in formal Methodist literature as justification and assurance and regeneration, though it was natural to see these as a single moment because formal Methodist teaching from the time of John Wesley had spoken of these three events as normally occurring simultaneously. Moreover, there is some evidence of popular usages of terms that appear confused in contrast to more formal usages: in one sentence, for example, Mary Apess referred to her experience of entire sanctification as embracing "justification" as well as sanctification,[67] and although it is true that justification remains when one is sanctified, the term would be out of place in a more formal scheme of the "way of salvation."

But even noting these differences in vocabulary, one cannot help noting the strong correlation between the formal theological consensus about the "way of salvation" seen in the schemata of hymnals, catechisms, and officially sanctioned theologies, on the one hand, and the narratives of personal religious experience given by these six witnesses, on the other hand, and these six are only a small sample of the wide body of Methodist testimonial literature that bears out these correlations. The more formal theological pattern, it is true, separates justification and regeneration and the assurance of pardon, but all the while notes that these normally appear simultaneously in the experience of believers. It is to be expected, then, that these three elements of the "way of salvation" should be collapsed into the one moment of "conversion" in the actual testimonies of Methodist people.

CONCLUSION

This chapter has shown how Wesleyan communities consistently taught the "way of salvation" beyond the time of John and Charles Wesley as part of the core beliefs of their churches. There were many variations on the ways in which they described the progress of the soul, but the general pattern answers closely to John Wesley's threefold pattern described in chapter 2: a description of the divine grace that comes before justification, a description of the event of justification accompanied by regeneration (new birth) and typically by the experience of assurance, and then the process of sanctification leading to entire sanctification. The structure of Methodist hymnals, in sections typically labeled "The Sinner" and "The Christian Life," consistently taught this process, as did Methodist catechisms and systematic theologies authorized for the training of Methodist preachers.

The autobiographical narratives in the second part of the chapter have shown how ordinary Methodist people, even across the frontiers of subcultures, had "received" and internalized the teaching about the "way of salvation" that John Wesley considered to be the distinctive mark of the Methodist movement.[68] These narratives typically use the terms "conviction," "conversion," and "sanctification" or "entire sanctification" to mark out the work of grace before conversion, at the time of conversion itself, and after conversion, but the narratives also reveal a consistent period of trials and doubts following conversion. One of the marks of these testimonies is the honesty with which persons were able to recount these problematic periods in their spiritual journey.

Contemporary Methodist hymnals continue to teach the "way of salvation," and in the current Nazarene and United Methodist hymnals, this is indicated in the headings "Prevenient Grace," "Justifying Grace," and "Sanctifying Grace" (or "Sanctifying and Perfecting Grace" in *The United Methodist Hymnal*). These same terms have come to prominence in a contemporary form of spirituality drawn from the Catholic Cursillo movement but which has been given a distinctly Wesleyan expression in the "Walk to Emmaus." When Walk to Emmaus was developed, the theological lectures in the retreat were focused on central elements of the Wesleyan understanding of the "Way of Salvation," including prevenient grace, justifying grace, and sanctifying grace. A further lecture in the Emmaus series deals explicitly with the topic of means of grace.[69] In this way, the Walk to Emmaus retreat involves key elements of Wesleyan spiritual and theological beliefs, and in many cases these lectures are offered even when the Walk to Emmaus occurs in the context of other Protestant traditions such as Presbyterian churches.

CHAPTER 6

BELIEFS ABOUT THE CHURCH IN WESLEYAN COMMUNITIES

INTRODUCTION

This book began with three chapters examining a nucleus of core beliefs of Wesleyan communities as John and Charles Wesley expressed them. The two previous chapters have explored core samples of the Wesleyan beliefs as they came to expression beyond their eighteenth-century origins. Chapter 4 examined common Christian beliefs about God and teachings about divine attributes as these teachings were transmitted in Wesleyan communities. Chapter 5 examined the much more distinctive Wesleyan teaching about the "way of salvation" as this was transmitted by way of formal doctrinal sources and as it came to popular expression in the testimonies of Methodist people. This chapter takes up a third core sample, examining the way in which beliefs about the nature of the Christian church have been transmitted and received in Wesleyan communities. Wesleyan communities originated not as churches but as a religious movement within the context of an existing church. The identity of Wesleyan communities has consequently been marked by a critical tension as to whether they should think of themselves primarily as churches or as a religious movement.

In September of 1784 John Wesley made a critical decision about the future of the Methodist movement, a decision fraught with implications for subsequent Methodist understandings of what is meant by "church." It was a decision that had to be made in response to the situation of Methodists in North America who continued to ask each other in class meetings if they had observed the "ordinances of God," including the Lord's Supper. The answer to this question was inevitably "no," given the lack of Anglican clergy in North America as a result of the war. By early September 1783, Britain had acknowledged the independence of the American colonies. Wesley regarded American independence as a genuinely "strange" phenomenon, but he still had to respond to the situation of his Methodist people in North America who were without regular clergy and thus without the sacraments.[1] John Wesley faced a decision that forced him to choose between the mission of the Methodist movement and the ecclesiology he had inherited from the Church of England, from the medieval Catholic Church, and from the early Christian communities from which later churches had grown. In this case, mission trumped traditional ecclesiology albeit reluctantly, as Wesley explained it, and on 2 September John Wesley violated the canonical precedents of the Church of England ordaining two of his lay preachers to serve as "elders," with the authority to administer the sacraments among the Methodists in North America. He also consecrated (his private diary said "ordained") a priest of the Church of England, Dr. Thomas Coke, to serve as a "superintendent" among the Methodists in North America, with the authority that bishops had traditionally held to ordain other clergy. John Wesley's brother Charles was shocked at these acts, taking them as being tantamount to a schism from the church that the Wesleys had pledged themselves to serve.[2]

John Wesley's ordinations of 1784, along with his revision of the Book of Common Prayer sent with his newly ordained elders, *The Sunday Service of the Methodists in North America*, brought about a fundamentally new situation in the Wesleyan movement. Although church structures and church identity would evolve more gradually among Methodists in Britain, from 1784 Methodist lay preachers began to function as priests had historically functioned in celebrating the sacraments. Methodist "societies" came to function as local congregations. The Methodist Episcopal Church began to function as a religious denomination parallel to the Protestant Episcopal Church and Lutheran, Presbyterian, Congregational, and Baptist denominational structures. Russell Richey has shown how in this situation, Methodists had blended the distinct "languages" of popular Evangelical piety, of Anglican church traditions, and of the Wesleyan movement. In the United States, Methodists also began to utilize the democratic language of the early American Republic.³ This blending of Anglican ecclesial culture and the distinctive institutions that had grown up in the Methodist movement over the decades since the late 1730s bequeathed to Methodist communities a set of tensions noted by many interpreters of Wesleyan communities.

Colin Williams's 1960 study *John Wesley's Theology Today* included in an appendix the essay "The Unresolved Tension: Unity and Truth," but the real import of his essay is given in a heading following this title, "Wesley's Doctrine of the Church and Ministry as Seen in the History of His Relation to the Church of England." In this essay, Williams wrote, "This original organization of Methodism as a voluntary order—as ecclesiolae—has been of great moment for her subsequent life. In a true sense she has ever since been *a society in search of the Church.*"⁴ Williams's concern in this essay was to show that the Methodist concern for mission, expressed in its use of societies, classes, itinerant preaching, and other distinctive structures had consistently stood in tension with a desire for unity with the Church of England in the eighteenth century and with Anglicans as well as other Christian communities in the ensuing period, leading to "The Unresolved Tension" of which he spoke in the title of the essay, the unresolved tension of existing as *"a society in search of the Church."*⁵ Two years after Williams's work appeared, Albert C. Outler delivered an address at the second Oxford Institute of Methodist Theological Studies held at Lincoln College, Oxford, 17–27 July 1962. In this address, Outler asked, "Do Methodists Have a Doctrine of the Church?" His answer was, essentially, no—Methodists have a strong sense of the *mission* of the church, but not really a doctrine of the church beyond what Methodists inherited from Anglicanism.⁶ Both Williams's and Outler's essays on Methodist ecclesiology pointed to the same tension between Methodists' strong sense of mission, on the one hand, and their desire for unity with the Church of England and with the broader community of Christian churches, on the other hand.

It is this tension, ambiguity, and sometimes even antinomy in Wesleyan ecclesiology that I address in this chapter. John Wesley and subsequent Methodists have carried at least two distinct and sometimes conflicting understandings of what it means to be "church." This disjuncture in ecclesiology has been at points so sharp that I have described Methodists as having a "bipolar" ecclesiology, oscillating between an inherited Anglican conception of the church and a rather different understanding of the Methodist community as a "religious society" or revival movement organized for missional purposes. I will examine this ecclesiological tension in John Wesley's distinction between "instituted" and "prudential" means of grace, his distinction between "ordinary" and "extraordinary" ministries, and in his understanding of the relationship between the Methodist love feast and the ecclesial sacrament of the Lord's Supper. I will also examine this ecclesiological tension as it appears in subsequent Methodist doctrinal statements, catechisms, and systematic theologies authorized for study by Methodist preachers.

How might we examine popular expressions of this ecclesial ambiguity or equivocation on the part of Wesleyan communities? Methodists did not typically give testimonies to their ecclesial views as they did to their experiences of the "way of salvation." But they did and do build worship spaces that reveal much of their understanding of the nature of the community. Although clergy might influence the building of Methodist worship spaces, Methodist polities consistently place the responsibility for buildings in the hands of local, lay trustees. In this chapter, then, I will consider the architectures of Methodist worship spaces as they reflect ecclesial beliefs. Some Methodist worship spaces, for example, reflect the needs of a religious movement, designed primarily for preaching, teaching, singing, and missional outreach; other worship spaces reflect an understanding of "church" in a more ecumenical sense of the term with a prominent altar for the celebration of the Lord's Supper. Others, yet again, offer a "hybrid" space which itself reflects this ecclesiological tension. Reflection on church architectures will provide in this chapter some indications of the popular reception of understandings of the meaning of church on the part of local Wesleyan communities.

ECCLESIOLOGICAL TENSIONS IN FORMAL EXPRESSIONS OF DOCTRINE

Chapter 1 has shown that John Wesley considered the Christian community to be essential to Christian existence. Although he nowhere stated that a doctrine of the church is a necessary

Christian doctrine, he did include teaching about this necessary institution in the Articles of Religion that he sent to the American Methodists in 1784 and in the summary of common Christian beliefs he gave in the "Letter to a Roman Catholic." The formal doctrine that he received from the Church of England and that he passed on to the American Methodists in the Articles of Religion held the "visible church" to be a coming together (*coetus*) of believers among whom the Word is rightly preached and the sacraments are rightly administered. I have also noted in chapter 1 that the Reformed tradition had expanded this basic statement of elements of ecclesiology to include discipline (referred to as "church censures" in the Westminster Confession).[7] We may take as a general point of reference, then, four elements of church defined in these Reformation-age doctrinal statements: (1) common Christian faith, (2) the preaching of the Word, (3) the administration of the sacraments, and possibly (4) the exercise of discipline in the Christian community.

John Wesley's Ecclesiological Tensions

Although John Wesley inherited the understanding of "church" that was given in the Anglican Articles of Religion, there were consistent signs of tension or ambiguity in the ways in which he described the Wesleyan movement with regard to its identity as a "church" or part of the "church." In the first place is a tension revealed in John Wesley's understanding of the means of grace. John Wesley distinguished in the Minutes of the early Methodist conferences between "instituted" and "prudential" means of grace, where "instituted" means included prayer, "searching the Scriptures," the Lord's Supper, fasting, and "Christian conference" (carefully guarded conversation with other Christians). The "prudential" means included rules that individual Christians might make to be kept with the help of their societies, attending class and band meetings, occasions on which preachers could meet with society or class members, and even more specific items such as abstaining from meat or late meals, drinking water, and the practice of temperance in the use of wine and ale.[8]

The "instituted" means thus denoted practices instituted in Scripture from the beginning of the history of the Christian community and for this reason Wesley understood them to be binding on Christian communities in all times and places.[9] The "prudential" means, by contrast, denoted practices that were not "instituted" in Scripture but which were simply found to be prudentially helpful by Methodist people. The distinction John Wesley drew between "instituted" and "prudential" means of grace, then, suggests a pattern in his thought by which he distinguished what is commonly Christian from those things that marked the distinctive mission of the Methodist movement. Utilizing the same language, Wesley defended distinctive Methodists practices as "prudential helps" that were nevertheless "not essential, not of divine institution" in his "Plain Account of the People Called Methodists" (1748):

> That with regard to these little prudential helps we are continually changing one thing after another, is not a weakness or fault, as you imagine, but a peculiar advantage which we enjoy. By this means we declare them all to be merely prudential, not essential, not of divine institution.[10]

In other words, Wesley identified the Methodist people as part of a distinct religious movement whose "prudential" practices supplemented but did not supplant those practices common to the broader Christian community.

A parallel pattern can be seen in the distinction John Wesley drew between "ordinary" and "extraordinary" ministries in the sermon "Prophets and Priests" (sometimes entitled "The Ministerial Office").[11] In his introduction to this sermon, Outler explained that it attempted to justify Wesley's appointment of lay preachers by distinguishing "priests" (those who are ordained to celebrate the sacraments) from "prophets" (those who preach God's word).[12] In this sermon Wesley revealed his conviction that the Methodist preachers had a distinct calling: they should be considered "as *extraordinary messengers*, raised up to provoke the *ordinary* ones to jealousy."[13] Colin Williams cited this distinction between "ordinary" and "extraordinary" ministers as a prime instance of the ecclesiological tension with which he was concerned, seeing "extraordinary" ministers as an instance of the Methodist concern for mission, and "ordinary" ministers as expressing the concern for stability and unity with the existing structures of the church.[14]

What I discern in both of these cases is a pattern in John Wesley's thought according to which he distinguished that which is common to Christian communities in general from that which distinctly defined the Methodist ethos. Common to Christian communities were historic doctrines, especially those defined in the creeds, the "instituted" means of grace and the "ordinary" ministries of the churches. Distinctive of the Methodist community were the doctrines that describe the critical role of religious experience, the "way of salvation," the "prudential" means of grace that had been found experimentally helpful to the Methodists, and the "extraordinary" work of itinerant preachers, including lay preachers and (by the 1770s) women preachers. Discernment of this pattern informed my division of the material on John Wesley's transmission of Christian and Methodist beliefs between chapters 1 and 2 of this book.

A third instance of the ecclesiological tension in John Wesley's thought and practice can be seen in the relationship between the Love Feast and the Lord's Supper in the practice of the early Methodist movement. From his studies of Christian antiquity John Wesley knew that ancient Christians "broke bread" together in a common meal associated with the Eucharist, and his "Plain Account of the People Called Methodists" claimed that Methodists had taken up the practice of the Love Feast following the example of the primitive church. He did not give the Moravians any credit at this point, although he was aware of the renewed love feast as it had been practiced by Moravians.[15] The love feast became the principal sign of fellowship or communion in the Wesleyan movement, access to which was controlled by the use of tickets issued by class leaders.[16]

In addition to his belief that the love feast was related to early Christian practice of the Eucharist, John Wesley also believed that the eucharistic discipline of the early Christian church involved the use of "commendatory epistles" by which one bishop would recognize a Christian from another Christian community and on the basis of which the visitor might be received into eucharistic communion. A similar practice had been employed in the use of tokens or tickets for admission to the Lord's Supper in British Reformed churches. In the "Plain Account of the People Called Methodists," Wesley argued that the use of class tickets to identify Methodist members was consistent with the ancient practice of identifying communicants by way of commendatory letters.[17] But Wesley and the early Methodists used class tickets to control access to the love feast, whereas in ancient Christian practice it was access to the Eucharist proper that was controlled by commendatory letters. In this case, then, Wesley justified the application of an ancient eucharistic practice to the Methodist practice of love feast that he believed to have originated in the eucharistic practice of the early church. If the Church of England was defined by eucharistic communion consistent with John Wesley's definition of the Church of England cited previously, then the Wesleyan societies were defined by "communion" or fellowship in the love feast. The juxtaposition of discipline of the love feast and discipline (or lack of discipline) of the Eucharist thus supplies another instance of this twofold pattern in Wesley's ecclesiology.

Ecclesiological Tensions Revealed in Narratives of the Wesleyan Revival

As the Wesleyan movement evolved beyond the time of John Wesley these ecclesial ambiguities or tensions continued to appear. Russell E. Richey has shown how Methodists consistently used historical narratives as a way of making ecclesial claims,[18] and narratives about John Wesley, in particular, functioned in Wesleyan communities to make ecclesiological claims. The original statement of the mission of the Methodist movement recorded in the "Large Minutes" (recording actions of the Wesleyan conference from 1744) claimed that "God's design in raising up the Preachers called Methodists" was "not to form any new sect; but to reform the nation, particularly the Church; and to spread scriptural holiness over the land."[19] This statement of purpose claimed that the Methodist movement had a unique vocation within Britain and within the Church of England, but not as a church. It gave the *raison d'être* of a religious movement. Of the four formal elements constituting "church" noted above (common faith, preaching of the Word, administration of the sacraments, and the practice of discipline), the early Methodist movement focused on the preaching of the Word and the practice of discipline in small, voluntary groups, but it did not transgress the boundaries of a "church" by declaring common faith on the part of a community or by administration of the sacraments except where the latter could be done in accordance with Anglican canons and precedents.

By the 1780s and 1790s, however, Methodists in Britain and America had to deal with the ecclesial status of Methodism. John Wesley's actions in devising a Prayer Book for the American Methodists and in providing for ordained clergy had the effect of creating a Methodist church in North America, but these actions presented problems for British Methodists who remained reluctant to admit to a break with the established church. The retelling of John Wesley's life became a means of dealing with these issues of Methodism's ecclesial identity. Thomas Coke and Henry Moore's *Life* of John Wesley (1792) did not even mention the ordinations of 1784 in their continuous narrative of John Wesley's life except in a later section on Methodist expansion in America.[20] John Whitehead's *Life of Wesley* (1793 and 1796), by contrast, dealt extensively with the ordinations but represented them as a serious departure from Wesley's own stated goals for the Methodist movement.[21] Coke and Moore and Whitehead all realized that the narrative of John Wesley's actions had implications for how Methodist societies understood themselves in relation to the Church of England, and in their own ways they tried to avoid making overt claims about the ecclesial nature of the Wesleyan movement, despite the fact that British Methodists had already begun moving quietly and incrementally toward the celebration of the Lord's Supper and baptism in their own communities and with their own authorized clergy apart from the Church of England.[22]

American Methodists, by contrast, needed to tell the story of John Wesley in such a way as to legitimate their publicly acknowledged existence as a separate church. They revised the statement of the Methodist mission from the "Large Minutes" to claim that the mission of Methodism was "To reform the Continent, and to spread scripture Holiness over these Lands."[23] Missing from this statement was the earlier claim that Methodism existed to reform "the Church," since by this time in North America the Methodists had become a church and no longer functioned within the context either of the Church of England or the Protestant Episcopal Church, which was at that time being organized in the United States. Thus American Methodist *Disciplines* from 1801 added a separate section narrating the origins of The Methodist Episcopal Church as a distinct denomination following their account of the Wesleyan revival.[24] Nathan Bangs would write in 1839 that Wesley "was forced either to disobey God by relinquishing his work, or to become the leader of a distinct sect. He wisely chose the latter, for which thousands will bless God in time and eternity."[25] American Methodists had revised Wesley's own redaction of the Articles of Religion and had put into effect Wesley's plan for ordinations and celebration of the sacraments. Thus American Methodists in The Methodist Episcopal Church explicitly claimed all four of the formal elements of "church" considered here: confession of common faith in their Articles of Religion, the practice of discipline in their classes and societies, the preaching of the gospel by itinerant and local preachers, and the administration of the sacraments, which the ordinations of 1784 had authorized. The same would be true within a few decades of the African Methodist Episcopal Church and the African Methodist Episcopal Zion Church.

By the early nineteenth century American Methodists had grown comfortable with the notion of their existence as separate churches and, consistent with this, they had come to think of themselves as "church" in the conventional sense of the term. They differed among themselves, however, on issues about the leadership or governance of the church. The ME and AME churches incorporated a strongly episcopal form of church government despite John Wesley's qualms about Coke's and Asbury's use of the terms "bishop." The AME Zion Church had developed a church government with "superintendents" who could in some respects be called "bishops" (hence the term "Episcopal" in the title of the denomination), but whose authority was much more limited than the authority of bishops in the ME and AME churches.[26] Leaders of anti-episcopal Methodist reforming movements in the early nineteenth century, such as the group that formed the Methodist Protestant Church in the USA, would claim the authority of Wesley for their rejection of episcopacy in favor of limited superintendency.[27]

In the late nineteenth century, British and American Methodists revisited the narrative of the Wesleyan revival, again finding grounds for their ecclesial commitments. American Methodist historians Abel Stevens and Matthew Simpson saw in the Wesleyan revival the religious ardor and the evangelistic institutions that would enable Methodism to bring religion and civilization to the American continent.[28] AME Bishop Henry McNeal Turner wrote at length in 1885 on Wesley's ordinations of a hundred years before, rejecting Anglican insistence on an unbroken succession of bishops but also making the claim that Methodists had maintained what he called a "presbyteral" succession of ordained clergy.[29] In 1892 the historical statement in The Methodist Episcopal *Discipline* was revised, with the new statement referring to "John and Charles Wesley, of Oxford University, and Presbyters of the Church of England,"[30] indicating a degree of approbation for the Wesleys' academic and ecclesiastical credentials that American Methodists had not afforded them in the past. At about the same time, British Methodist James H. Rigg responded to Anglican R. Denny Urlin's claims about John Wesley's "high church" leanings with Rigg's own account of what "high church" meant in Georgian Britain as contrasted with the views of a "ritualising high churchman" in his own time. But Rigg also appealed to Wesley to make the case for the ecclesial proximity of Victorian Methodism to Anglicanism.[31] In each case, Methodist communities in the late nineteenth century revisited the narrative of the Wesleyan revival to justify the ways in which their churches were assuming a more traditional and ecclesial orientation than they had held in the early nineteenth century, and yet in every case Methodists maintained a highly missional and evangelistic understanding of the role of the church.

The process of recursion to the Wesleyan movement to find ecclesial models for Wesleyan communities continued in the next century. Such twentieth-century interpreters of Wesley as Herbert Brook Workman, Colin W. Williams, Frank Baker, and Albert C. Outler all found in Wesley an ecumenical figure whose theology and practices cohered with those of the wider community of Christian churches. Methodists had been involved in the ecumenical movement since its origins, and earlier phases of Faith and Order work from the 1910 Edinburgh assembly through the early 1950s have been described as dominated by "comparative ecclesiologies," that is, by the process of comparing the ecclesiological commitments of the various church traditions. This led to an intense concern with ecclesiology on the part of Williams, Baker, and Outler, as can be seen from the essay on ecclesiology and ordinations appended to Williams's *John Wesley's Theology Today*, Outler's essay on Methodist understandings of the church, and the entirety of Baker's *John Wesley and the Church of England*. Outler's argument that Wesley had no new or novel contributions to ecclesiology held a subtext of encouraging Methodists to be more open to ecumenical contributions to ecclesiology. The trend of British and American Methodist churches in the twentieth century to implement liturgical reforms grounded in ecumenical research and scholarship was another sign of the ecclesiological development of these churches in an ecumenical direction.

Ecclesiology in Methodist Doctrinal Standards

We now ask how formal Methodist doctrinal statements express the ecclesiological commitments and the ecclesiological tensions noted above. Previous chapters have noted that the British Methodist Church did not adopt a statement of faith for their church, preferring to declare their general fidelity to historic Christian creeds. Churches that have been closely related to the British Methodist Church, such as the Methodist Church Nigeria, have followed this pattern.[32] This might imply fidelity to the Anglican Articles of Religion, including the Article cited above defining the church, though this commitment has not been made explicit.

The Methodist Episcopal Church and its successors, including the AME, AME Zion, CME, and United Methodist churches, adopted Wesley's redaction of the Anglican Articles, including an Article defining the nature of the church:

> The visible Church of Christ is a congregation of faithful men, in which the pure Word of God is preached, and the Sacraments duly administered, according to Christ's ordinance, in all those things that of necessity are requisite to the same.[33]

This would commit Methodist churches with this Article of Religion to the belief that the fullness of "church" requires faith, preaching, and the administration of the sacraments as necessary elements. The United Methodist Church also inherited from The Evangelical United Brethren Church a statement on the church in the Confession of Faith that offers a somewhat different approach to the issue of defining what is meant by "church":

> We believe that the Christian Church is the community of all true believers under the Lordship of Christ. We believe it is one, holy, catholic, and apostolic. It is the redemptive fellowship in which the Word of God is preached by men divinely called, and the sacraments are duly administered according to Christ's own appointment. Under the discipline of the Holy Spirit the church exists for the maintenance of worship, the edification of believers, and the redemption of the world.[34]

This statement is generally consistent with the Anglican/ Methodist Article given above, adding a note related to church discipline (though in the context of the Holy Spirit's guidance of the church) and also adding the four "notes of the church" defined in the received text of the Nicene Creed. However, there is an important nuance in this statement that does not appear in the earlier Anglican/Methodist Article, a nuance that was also expressed in Methodist catechetical literature and in systematic theologies prepared for the use of preachers. The Confession of Faith can be read as claiming that "the community of all true believers" constitutes the church as such, and that the other elements described (preaching, administration of the sacraments, and discipline) are the normal accompaniments of this basic meaning of the church as the fellowship of believers, but perhaps not strictly essential to the nature of the church.

A consistent trend in Methodist literature from the nineteenth century emphasized the nature of the church as a fellowship of believers organized for evangelistic mission, a definition in which the sacraments were not claimed as being essential to the nature of the church. It is not surprising that the Holiness groups that emerged from Methodist churches in the late nineteenth century and the early twentieth century would take up such definitions of the church. The original *Manual* of the Church of the Nazarene (1908, at that time the denominational name was the "Pentecostal Church of the Nazarene") states in a paragraph on "The General Church" that "the Church of God is composed of and includes all spiritually regenerate persons, whose names are written in heaven."[35] Subsequently, however, the doctrinal statement was changed so that its current text is:

We believe in the Church, the community that confesses Jesus Christ as Lord, the covenant people of God made new in Christ, the Body of Christ called together by the Holy Spirit through the Word.

God calls the Church to express its life in the unity and fellowship of the Spirit; in worship through the preaching of the Word, observance of the sacraments, and ministry in His name; by obedience to Christ and mutual accountability.

The mission of the Church in the world is to continue the redemptive work of Christ in the power of the Spirit through holy living, evangelism, discipleship, and service.[36]

In this fuller definition, the church is essentially defined as "the community that confesses Jesus Christ as Lord," which is also "the covenant people" and "the Body of Christ." Preaching and the observation of the sacraments are ways of expressing its unity, and its mission is declared to involve "holy living, evangelism, discipleship, and service."

To summarize, then, an earlier definition of "church" inherited from the Anglican Article and from the Augsburg Confession before it claimed that the church is constituted by the body of faithful (believing) persons within whose fellowship the Word is preached and the sacraments are administered. Subsequent doctrinal statements, including those from The United Brethren in Christ (now The United Methodist Church's Confession of Faith) and the Church of the Nazarene place strong emphasis on the church's essential nature as being the fellowship of believers. The preaching of the Word is seen as being essential to its evangelistic task, and the sacraments are understood, according to this definition, to be important but not necessary or constitutive elements in the meaning of "church."

Ecclesiology in Methodist Catechisms

Most of the catechetical literature produced by Methodist churches would display a similar tendency to emphasize the church as the community or fellowship of believers and the missional nature of the church. This was not the case with *The Catechism of The Methodist Episcopal Church*, published originally in three graded booklets in 1852, which in the second booklet gave the full definition of the church as contained in the Article of Religion quoted above. It distinguished between the "invisible church" as "The whole body of God's true people in every period of time" and the "visible church" defined as follows:

> The visible Church of Christ is a congregation of faithful men, in which the pure word of God is preached, and the sacraments duly administered, according to Christ's ordinance.[37]

This gives the precise wording of the Article of Religion, omitting only the concluding clause "in all those things that of necessity are requisite to the same." It includes the elements of faith, preaching, and the sacraments.

However, the British *Catechisms of the Wesleyan Methodists*, first published in 1824, gives a definition of the church in which the strong emphasis was placed on the nature of the church as the fellowship of believers and on the missional nature of the church. Catechism No. I in this series, designed for children under the age of seven, did not have a question on the nature of the church. But Catechism No. II, designed for children from age seven and above, has the following series of two questions and answers:

> *7. What is the Church of Christ?*
>
> The Church of Christ is the whole body of true believers in every age and place.
>
> *8. What offices does the Holy Ghost perform for the Church of Christ?*
>
> The offices which the Holy Ghost performs for the Church of Christ are these: namely, that he calls and qualifies men from time to time, to preach the Word, and minister the Sacraments; renders their preaching effectual to the conversion of sinners, and the edification of believers; and is present in all the ordinances of public worship.[38]

The basic definition of the church given in response to question 7 identifies the church as the fellowship (or "body") of believers. The response to question 8 does refer to preaching the Word and administration of the sacraments as functions for which the Holy

Spirit prepares ministers, and the statement on preaching ("renders their preaching effectual to the conversion of sinners, and the edification of believers") places a strong stress on the evangelistic nature of the church.

The "Turner Catechism" of the AME Church (1884) has a single question on the nature of the church, "Who compose the Christian Church?" The response is "All true believers."[39] Again, the sole meaning of the church is the fellowship of believers. The *Probationer's Manual of the Methodist Episcopal Church* (1914) has a series of catechetical lessons, including one section with nine questions on the nature of the church. One question asks, "Who comprise the Church of Christ on earth?" The response is "The Church of Christ is composed of Christian believers who are banded together to worship God and to carry on Christ's work." The next question asks, "What is the special work of the church?" The response to this question is "To proclaim the gospel, to teach Christian truth, to lead men to the Saviour, and to provide for public worship and the sacraments."[40] This conforms to a pattern seen above in the *Catechisms of the Wesleyan Methodists* and in the later United Methodist Confession of Faith according to which the essential nature of the church is the fellowship of believers and the other elements (preaching, sacraments, and possibly discipline) are seen as functions that carry out the mission of the church.

This same tendency can be seen in the *Junior Catechism* jointly produced by the ME Church and the ME Church, South, in 1932 and which has continued in use in the CME Church. A question asks, "Who compose the Church of Christ?" The response is "The Church of Christ is composed of all the children of God on earth and in heaven." It is interesting that in this definition, faith or belief has disappeared from the essential nature of the church, unless it is implied in being "children of God." A further question asks, "What is the work of the church?" The catechism gives the response "The work of the church is to witness for Christ, and to carry on his work in saving the world." Thus the administration of the sacraments did not appear as an important aspect of the work of the church in this account, although the next few questions in this catechism have to do with the sacraments.[41]

The *Methodist Catechism* of the Methodist Church in Ireland (1948) was patterned after the earlier *Catechisms of the Wesleyan*

Methodists. It asked, "What is the Church of Christ?" The response was as follows:

> The Church of Christ is the Society of His disciples, consisting of those who accept Him as the Son of God and their Saviour from sin, who love one another for His sake, and unite in the worship and service of God.

The strong emphasis here was on personal faith, with the church defined as the "society" of those who have faith in Christ. Preaching and the sacraments were not specified, although they were presumably included under the phrase "the worship and service of God." The next question asked, "What is the Work of the Holy Spirit in the Church?" The response to this reflected the earlier Wesleyan *Catechisms* and gives a strong indication of what Williams and Outler described as the strong missional emphasis of Methodist ecclesiology: "The Holy Spirit calls and qualifies preachers and teachers, and makes their work effectual to the conversion of sinners and the edification of believers."[42] Similar wording was offered in *The Senior Catechism of the Methodist Church (Methodist Church* of Great Britain, 1952), which asked, "What is the Church?" The response was "The Church is the whole company of those who trust in Christ as Lord and Saviour and are united in the fellowship of the Holy Spirit." Since the early part of this catechism is set as a series of questions on the Apostles' Creed, the next question asked, "How is the Church Holy and Catholic?" But the response again revealed the missional emphasis in Methodist thought on the church: "It is holy because it belongs to God Who has set it apart to do His work, and it is catholic because it offers the whole Gospel of Christ to all men everywhere."[43] In neither the Irish (1948) nor the British (1952) catechism were sacraments explicitly mentioned in connection with the nature of the Christian church. In brief, then, Methodist catechetical literature from the nineteenth century through the middle of the twentieth century emphasized the nature of the church as a fellowship of believers and emphasized the vocation or work of the church as related to its evangelistic mission.

The British Methodist *Catechism for the Use of the People Called Methodists* (1989) reflects the influence of the ecumenical movement in its teachings on the nature of the church. It begins in a manner similar to the two previous documents discussed, but then expands on this, offering a significantly more complete understanding of the church influenced by ecumenical contact and displaying more awareness of historic Christian definitions of the church. The question is posed, "What is the Church?" To this, the *Catechism* responds:

> The church is all those on earth and in heaven who have been called by God, through Jesus Christ, to be his people, and who share the unity that the Spirit gives. The Spirit guides the Church, and equips its members with varied gifts, so that they may support one another, encourage one another and serve their neighbours with joy. The universal church takes the form of local congregations where the message of Christ received through the apostles is preached, where God is glorified in the celebration of the sacraments and other acts of worship, and Christians share the Christian life.[44]

The statement begins with a strong assertion of the nature of the church as the fellowship of believers, and expresses a missional emphasis in stating that the Holy Spirit empowers the church to "serve their neighbours with joy." In specifying the form of the church in local congregations, it makes clear the centrality of the proclamation of the Word and the administration of the sacraments, as older Protestant and Anglican definitions of the church had insisted on. In this way, it comes back around to the fuller definition of the church offered in the Anglican and Methodist Articles of Religion and which was reflected in the 1852 *Catechism of The Methodist Episcopal Church*.

Ecclesiology in Authorized Systematic Theologies

The same trends observed in ecclesiology in formal doctrinal statements and in catechetical literature on the part of Wesleyan and Methodist churches can also be seen in works of systematic theology authorized by Methodist churches for study by candidates aspiring to become preachers and ordained ministers. Richard Watson's *Theological Institutes* (originally published in 1823) offered only a brief chapter on the nature of the church. The epitome of this chapter states, "The Church of Christ, in its largest sense, consists of all who have been baptized in the name of Jesus

Christ; in a stricter sense, it consists of those who are vitally united to Christ."[45] It is an important definition in that it acknowledges a "larger" sense of the meaning of the visible church, that is, all who have been marked as Christians in baptism, then focuses on the stricter definition of the church as those who are "vitally united to Christ," which probably meant those who have had the vital or living experience of conversion and new birth. From this point, however, Watson's chapter on the church was entirely concerned with issues of church governance and it did not give a fuller definition of the church.

The American Methodist theologian Miner Raymond of Garrett Biblical Institute dealt with the doctrine of the church at some length in the third volume of his *Systematic Theology* (1881), which was to become a standard work prescribed for study by Methodist preachers. His work reveals the extent to which Methodists thought of the church as being primarily the fellowship of believers and an instrument of evangelization. He quoted the thirteenth Article of Religion in its entirety (see above), then continued,

> A Christian Church is an assembly of Christian believers, of persons who believe in Christ as the Son of God and the Savior of men. The number is not essential, agreement and association are all that is requisite; where two or three are gathered in Christ's name, there his presence is manifested and his promised blessing bestowed....
>
> The entire body of Christian believers on earth is called the church.[46]

Despite his awareness of the Article of Religion, then, Raymond seems to take only a gathering of the faithful to be strictly necessary for the existence of the church: "agreement and association are all that is requisite."

Nevertheless, although Raymond does not seem to have held preaching or the sacraments to be strictly necessary for the existence of the church, he did hold the church itself to be necessary for preaching, and preaching necessary for bringing about human salvation. He wrote in his chapter on the church:

It is not pertinent to burden this discussion with an inquiry into the methods by which pagans may attain unto eternal life; it is sufficient to speak of Gospel salvation. This is conditioned upon faith; but faith cometh by hearing, and hearing by the Word of God; how then can they hear without a preacher, and how can he preach except he be sent? An organized Church, then, is a prerequisite to the accomplishment of Gospel purposes; a Church to authorize and sustain a ministry by whom the Word may be preached; that Word which is essential to the hearing, by which faith and its conditioned salvation are made possible.[47]

This, I think, stands as a cardinal illustration of the tension in Wesleyan ecclesiology that is explored in this chapter. Raymond was not concerned to denigrate the idea of the church or of its institutions—he would go on to write about the importance of the means of grace and of the sacraments, even beginning his discussion of sacraments with the claim that "ritualistic observances are essential to a visible Church."[48] The issue was that, whether he was fully conscious of this or not, Raymond presupposed that the church existed for a higher purpose, namely, evangelization.

British Methodist theologian William Burt Pope's *Compendium of Christian Theology* (1881) organized his discussion of ecclesiology differently than Raymond, but his emphasis on the nature of the church as an instrument for evangelization paralleled that of Raymond, his near contemporary. The first paragraph of Pope's chapter on the church functions as an epitome for the whole chapter, introducing each topic in the order in which he deals with them:

The Christian Church is the sphere as well as the organ of the Spirit's administration of redemption. As a corporate body it was founded by our Lord Jesus Christ; is invested with certain attributes and notes as the representative of His agency among men; discharges its functions as an institute of worship and depository of the Faith; has definite obligations to the world as an instrument for its conversion; and, lastly, bears special relations in its temporal form to the eternal Kingdom of Christ.[49]

Pope did not deal with the issue of who constitutes the church, as other Methodist theologies and catechisms had done. His understanding of the church revolved entirely around its existence as an instrument or "organ" for "the Spirit's administration of redemption." The church's work was to serve as "an institute of worship and depository of the Faith" and as "an instrument for [the world's] conversion." In this respect, Pope gave an explicit role to the church's worship and guardianship of the faith in addition to its evangelistic task.[50]

John Miley's *Systematic Theology* (1892) includes a chapter on the church within the overall context of soteriology. His justification for this arrangement is given in the first sentence of the chapter:

> As the Church is divinely constituted for the work of evangelism and the spiritual edification of believers, and also contains the divinely instituted means for the attainment of these ends, it may be properly treated in connection with soteriology.[51]

The placement of the doctrine of the church within the category of soteriology indicates that Miley's view of the church is highly missional. He speaks of the church as an assembly that is called out (ἐκκλησία) by God for the purpose of evangelization, although it does include the means it needs for that end, the means of grace: Christian fellowship, church membership, the Word of God preached or studied privately, the preaching of the gospel, prayer, and the sacraments of baptism and the Lord's Supper. Nevertheless, Miley did give the definition of church from the Methodist Episcopal Article of Religion as the most satisfactory and specific definition of a local church or of a denomination.[52]

The works of systematic theology considered here—Watson, Raymond, Pope, and Miley—show a consistent trend in Methodist expressions of ecclesiology, and that is to place such a strong emphasis on the nature of the church as the community of believers and on its evangelistic task as to overshadow the element of sacramental worship. Watson's discussion of ecclesiology was so focused on the issue of church governance that he never dealt substantially with the definition of the church beyond the brief definition given above. Raymond stressed the church's role in evangelization, and saw preaching as an important means to this task and the sacraments as signs of the church's fellowship. Pope saw the church's worship and its keeping the faith as central, but also stressed the evangelistic task of the church. Miley acknowledged the Article of Religion, but his placement of the doctrine of the church under the category of soteriology shows his strongly missional understanding of the church.

The trend in systematic theologies, then, parallels the trends seen in shorter doctrinal statements and in catechisms to emphasize the nature of the church as a fellowship of believers and as an instrument of God for conversion, with preaching and the sacraments seen as internal functions but not defined as being strictly necessary to the definition of the church.

METHODIST ARCHITECTURES AND METHODIST ECCLESIOLOGIES

The methodology laid out in the introduction of this book insists on testing the popular reception of doctrine as well as the more formal statement of doctrine or authorized teachings on the part of Wesleyan communities. Chapter 4 considered the doctrine of the Trinity and teachings about divine attributes as they were expressed in formal doctrine and also how they have been expressed in worship practices of Wesleyan communities and as they became the subject of reflection by twentieth-century Methodist theologians. Chapter 5 considered teachings about the "way of salvation" as these teachings were expressed in formal doctrinal literature (doctrinal statements, catechisms, and works of theology authorized for study for Methodist preachers), and as these teachings were expressed in the testimonies of Methodist people to their own experience of the Christian life. Having considered Methodist understandings of the church in formal doctrinal literature, our examination now turns to ask how doctrines of the church have been "received" in Methodist culture. What could serve as a test of doctrines or teachings about the nature of the church as this was expressed by Methodist laypersons? In what follows I will try to show how some Methodist architectures, that is, the forms of buildings built by Methodists and especially structures built for worship, reflect the ecclesiological beliefs and commitments of Wesleyan and Methodist communities.

Methodist Architectures in the Wesleyan Period

The first worship spaces built as a result of the Wesleyan movement were "preaching houses" and were intended solely for the proclamation of the Word and not for sacramental worship. The first instance of this Methodist architecture was the "New Room" in Bristol, which John Wesley had built beginning in May 1739, the month after his initial open-air preaching in that city. The construction of a building only for preaching reflected Wesley's reliance on the sacraments of the Church of England and his insistence that the Methodist movement was not a church separate from the Church of England.[53] Although the Bristol preaching house had a rectangular shape, Methodists in the lifetime of John Wesley would build fourteen preaching houses in Britain with a distinctive octagonal shape. Karen B. Westerfield Tucker argues that although the octagonal shape may have been adopted for practical and aesthetic reasons, John Wesley was also aware of the octagonal shape of many early and medieval Christian baptismal fonts and may have associated this shape with the work of Christian initiation that John Wesley consistently carried on by preaching and teaching the faith.[54]

It is worth considering that the preaching house, the first distinctly Methodist architectural "space," was not a church; rather, it was a structure designed to support the particular mission that the Methodist people were undertaking at that time. In their own space, then, the Methodists were a mission-oriented society; in Anglican space, they were part of the church in the fuller sense of the word. The construction of a building for preaching and not for the celebration of the sacraments serves as a signal instance of the ecclesial tension or ambiguity that Williams, Outler, and others have pointed out in John Wesley's leadership of the Methodist movement.

Eventually John Wesley would allow for sacramental celebration in Methodist spaces. In 1749 he and Charles Wesley purchased an abandoned Huguenot place of worship on West Street in London. Since this chapel had been consecrated in the middle ages, its altar could be legitimately claimed as fulfilling canonical requirements for celebration of the Eucharist in the Church of England.[55] The "new chapel" that John Wesley built on City Road in London and which was dedicated on All Saints' Day, 1778, reflects a fuller acquiescence in the idea of sacramental celebration in a Methodist architecture. This Georgian chapel is almost exactly square and its ground floor is divided into thirds by two rows of columns. An apse situated at the front of the chapel suggests that Wesley's intention in building this chapel was to imitate the style of the Constantinian basilica, the pattern Wesley knew as the most primitive example of Christian public architecture from his study of Peter King (*Primitive Christianity*) and other authors.[56] As Frank Baker points out in *John Wesley and the Church of England*, the City Road Chapel was a space that was specifically designed for sacramental worship, with a table in front of the pulpit. But the pulpit towered over the Lord's table and it would be fair to conclude that, with the addition of a gallery to the format of the basilica, City Road Chapel had the appearance of a preaching house with only a small concession to eucharistic worship.[57]

Methodist Architectures in the Early Nineteenth Century

Wesley's Chapel on City Road in London and the early preaching houses built by Methodists were in some ways exceptional. Methodists built some chapels and small church buildings from the early 1800s in Britain and in North America, for example, the Lovely Lane Chapel in Baltimore. But early American Methodist *Disciplines* insisted that these worship spaces should be "plain and decent" spaces, that is, not ornamented.[58] British Methodist buildings in the early nineteenth century might be more ornamented than the American *Disciplines* allowed, but they studiously avoided the appearance of being traditional churches. The most common worship spaces for Methodist people in the early nineteenth century, however, were informal settings in homes, meeting halls, and in outdoor settings where Methodists prayed and preached. The common pattern of "cottage worship" led by lay stewards typically involved Scripture reading, prayers, and the singing of hymns, and was well suited to such informal worship spaces as private homes or meeting halls provided. When ordained Methodist clergy (circuit-riding preachers in North America) were present to celebrate the Lord's Supper and other traditional rites such as baptism, they most often used these informal worship spaces.

Methodists also gathered in outdoor spaces, as observed above with the example of John Wesley's outdoor preaching in Bristol. Later Methodists, especially American Methodists, exaggerated the amount of outdoor preaching that John Wesley was engaged in—sometimes the image of the American circuit-riding preacher was written back into the image of Wesley in the eighteenth century—but Methodist preachers did speak and sometimes led prayers outdoors in Britain and America in the early nineteenth century. Not only was Sunday worship carried out in such settings but preachers also hosted occasions for hearing traveling itinerants on other days of the week, and quarterly meetings with a presiding elder also were held in these informal spaces.

Although these Methodist worship spaces in the early nineteenth century were informal settings, they were not devoid of reverence nor lacking a sense of sacred presence. Accounts of Methodist worship, even of lay-led informal prayer services, often commented on the "solemnity" or reverence felt by worshipers. The sense of sacred presence was given not so much by the space itself as it was given in the manners in which prayers were said and Scriptures were read, manners that involved facial expressions, tones of voice, and other means of speaking, and in some cases trembling or other bodily expressions of reverence. Homer Thrall described such a meeting on the Texas frontier in 1838. A small company of Methodists had gathered to sing hymns in a home in Shelbyville. "After a few meetings they joined prayer with praise" and soon others joined them:

> One night there was a large company, including Messrs. Crawford, English, and Martin, local preachers. Mr. Martin gave an exhortation and, becoming unusually engaged, called for mourners. A number came forward, and were happily converted.[59]

In some cases, there was a sense that religious gatherings in homes marked a return to the primitive simplicity that characterized the earliest Christian gatherings (cf. Acts 2:46).

The Methodist use of camp meetings marked a critical development in Methodist worship spaces in North America. Although camp meetings were conventionally said to have originated with the Cane Ridge meeting in Kentucky in 1791, historical studies by Leigh Eric Schmidt and Marilyn Westerkamp in the 1980s showed that American camp meetings continued a much longer tradition of Scottish and Scots-Irish Presbyterian quarterly communion celebrations. Two things need to be said about the earlier Presbyterian pattern that Methodists were to take up. In the first place, these meetings were in fact eucharistic in their origins. Both Schmidt and Westerkamp point out that Scottish and Scots-Irish quarterly communions often involved worship in outdoor spaces, due to the size of congregations that would attend.[60] Second, Marilyn Westerkamp points out that these "sacramental seasons" dramatized the understanding of the "order of salvation" (*ordo salutis*) that had developed in the Reformed tradition, with a pattern of preaching that began with repentance, continued with preaching on justification, then concluded with preaching on sanctification and glorification. The celebration of the Lord's Supper was the culmination of this cycle of preaching and represented the fellowship with Christ restored in the believer's sanctification and glorification.[61]

As Methodists took over the format of camp meetings from the early nineteenth century, both Eucharist and love feast were celebrated, but Methodist camp meetings came to be focused consistently on preaching the "way of salvation," and the physical layout of the camp meeting assembly area was regarded as a sacred space representing the stages of the way of salvation. The camp meeting was typically laid out around a central meeting area that could be an open-air "brush arbor," a large tent, or a more permanent frame tabernacle with a roof but sides open to the air. Around the meeting space were tents or cabins for individual families. At the front of the central meeting space itself was a raised platform from which speakers would preach or exhort. An altar rail just beneath the speaker's platform, originally designated for receiving the Lord's Supper, came to represent the surrender of oneself in conversion and in entire sanctification. The "mourner's bench" (or "anxious bench," as it was decried by the theologians of the Mercersburg movement) was situated in front of the altar rail and represented the experience of spiritual "awakening" that typically preceded conversion in the understanding of the "way of salvation."[62] In a weekend camp meeting event one might expect a sermon on sin, awakening, and repentance on Friday, sermons on conversion and assurance on Saturday, and preaching on sanctification (including entire sanctification) on Sunday. Within the camp meeting space the older pattern of cottage worship could be carried on in the form of small groups that met on the camp meeting grounds. In these prayer groups women and men were typically separated for prayer, as had been the case in earlier Methodist band meetings.

Early Methodist buildings (with the possible exception of City Road Chapel), the informal settings in which Methodists conducted worship and quarterly meetings in the early nineteenth century, and camp meeting grounds were mission-oriented architectures. Sacramental celebration could be accommodated by simply placing a table at the front of the space, but the space itself did not give the appearance of traditional churches and was designed (when it was designed at all) for speaking and hearing the proclamation of the Word.

The Flourishing of Methodist Architectures in the Late Nineteenth Century and the Early Twentieth Century

The later nineteenth century saw the flourishing of Methodism in the United States, Britain, and elsewhere in the world as Methodists attracted large numbers of members and adherents and also advanced socially and economically. In this period, Methodists began to adopt a variety of architectural forms, and the variety of forms itself displays the ecclesiological tensions examined previously in this chapter. Some particular forms bore the ecclesiological ambiguity within themselves. This section will consider both the late nineteenth century and the early twentieth century because Methodist architectures followed some consistent trends and made use of specific forms in this extended period.

One form that Methodists began to embrace in the later nineteenth century was that of the public auditorium, a building that looked more like a theater or music hall than a sacred space and in fact was intended to attract persons who might feel uncomfortable in more traditional church architectures. As evangelism moved into cities in the late nineteenth century in the United States, older camp meetings gave way to urban revivals and the camp meeting assembly space came to be institutionalized as the evangelical auditorium. Examples of this architecture in the United States outside of Methodist circles are the Ryman Auditorium in Nashville, Tennessee, which was originally built as the Union Gospel Tabernacle (1892; it subsequently housed the *Grand Ole Opry*), and the Moody Memorial Church in Chicago (1925). Both of these show that auditoriums could embrace other architectural styles at least in their facades: the Ryman Auditorium has a red-brick Victorian Gothic facade, and the Moody Memorial Church was built in the Romanesque style. The auditorium became so popular among Methodists that by the end of the nineteenth century many had come to use the term "auditorium" to refer to their worship space.[63]

The auditoriums provided space not only for Sunday morning worship but also for a variety of events that could be held within them. They often used theater seating, that is, individual cushioned seats that would have been found in music halls and other performance venues in this period. The auditorium format was a natural setting for musical presentations in an age when Methodists had begun to favor gospel music, itself patterned after the music hall entertainment of the Victorian era. Gospel songbooks from this period often reveal that these new songs were not intended for Sunday morning use but were employed in such settings as revivals, Sunday school assemblies, "Sunday evening congregations," and "young peoples meetings."[64] The auditorium, then, can be described as a space where Methodists hoped to reach out to those who were unfamiliar with traditional church culture. Again, a strong sense of evangelistic mission motivated the choice of architectural space.

A British counterpart to this American use of auditoriums was the development of large urban "Central Halls" in the period between 1885 and 1934. The Welsh Methodist leader Hugh Price Hughes was known for his work among the urban poor of the late nineteenth century in Britain, and he led the "Forward Movement" that began in 1885 and sought to build new ministries aimed at the urban poor.[65] The Central Halls that resulted from this work are architecturally imposing structures that included not only auditorium space but also space for church ministries for outreach to the urban poor. They were made available for public (civic) gatherings, and this too was seen as a form of outreach. Perhaps the best-known example of the Central Hall is Westminster Central Hall on Parliament Square opposite Westminster Abbey. Westminster Central Hall was built as a result of a Methodist fund-raising campaign that began shortly after the 1891 centennial of the death of John Wesley, the "Wesleyan Methodist Twentieth Century Fund," which came to be known as the "Million Guinea Fund" because its goal was to raise a guinea each from a million supporters for a variety of ministries including the Hall. The request for architectural proposals for this structure stated explicitly that the structure was not to be Gothic, and the resulting building, which opened in 1912, was built in a French Renaissance style with a large domed auditorium. In 1946 it served as the venue for the first meeting of the United Nations General Assembly. In the case of the British Central Halls as well as the auditoriums built by American Methodists in the late nineteenth century and the early twentieth century, architectural decisions were guided by missional, especially evangelistic, priorities, and these structures, like the Wesleyan "preaching houses" of the eighteenth century, stand as monuments to the mission-oriented ecclesiology that was one pole of the Methodist tension in ecclesiology.

Representing the other pole, in contrast to auditoriums and Central Halls, British and America Methodists began to build worship spaces in the Gothic style in the late nineteenth century. The Gothic revival in church architecture began in the early nineteenth century in Britain[66] but it did not come to prominence until after the Civil War in the United States. In Britain it was associated with Tractarianism and in the United States it was associated early on with Episcopal Tractarianism and also with the Mercersburg theology movement among Presbyterian and German Reformed churches. It represented an affirmation of medieval Catholic architecture and, especially for the Mercersburg school, a reaction against revivalistic religion in the United States. Despite these associations, versions of Gothic church architecture were being widely adopted by the 1870s in the United States, where new white-frame rural churches sported windows with pointed arches, and many older and simpler church buildings were retrofit with Gothic-style windows. In the United States, Gothic came to represent a traditional view of church that was not particularly associated with a Catholic or Anglo-Catholic ethos. An early example of Gothic architecture among American Methodists is the Asbury Methodist Episcopal Church (now Asbury Crestwood United Methodist Church) in Crestwood, New York, opened in 1867 in commemoration of the hundredth anniversary of the coming of the first Methodist missionaries to North America. Gothic architecture was not common in British Methodist churches in the nineteenth century because, as noted above, British Methodists had worked hard to keep their chapels from looking like Anglican churches. But British Methodists from the Victorian age did erect a few Gothic structures, especially in urban centers of university settings: prominent examples are the Wesley Memorial Church in Oxford, opened in October 1878, and the Wesley Methodist Church, Cambridge, opened in 1913 "to attract and retain, and not repel, the young Methodists who come to this University."[67]

The significance of Gothic for Methodists was that it represented an unequivocal attempt to claim the identity of "church" in the fullest sense of the word. Gothic had come to be seen as the traditional Christian space for worship. The development of Gothic coincided with Methodists' growing prominence in urban areas and Methodists' growing sense of identification with Western culture and learning.[68] Thus the main building for Garrett Biblical Institute in Evanston, Illinois, built in 1924 and celebrated in a whole issue of *Western Architect* magazine in 1925 as the "pride of the North Shore," is completely Gothic and complete with rich and elaborately documented medieval symbolism, such as the seal of Lincoln College, Oxford, over one of its doors. Similarly, the architecture of Duke University's West Campus is built in the Gothic style, in this case representing both churchly and academic space. Methodists in the United States even vied to "out-Gothic" each other in this period: the Italian Renaissance architecture of the Lovely Lane Methodist Church in Baltimore, designed by architect Edward White and completed in 1884, represents just such an attempt to display sophistication in an age when Gothic was becoming commonplace.

I would interpret the importance of Methodist Gothic as representing a high point of a more churchly or traditional ecclesiology in Methodist church life. In the twentieth century it represented Methodists' growing involvement in the ecumenical movement and, closely related to this, in the movement for liturgical renewal. By the 1950s many Methodist churches were built with "split chancels," that is, with separate pulpit and lectern, reflecting a growing emphasis on the use of the lectionary in Sunday worship. In this period many Methodist churches were built with altars at the very back of the church, reflecting Catholic traditions from the

Middle Ages, and ironically within a decade of Catholics' decision to bring the altars out toward the congregation as a result of the Second Vatican Council.

Between Evangelical auditoriums (or Central Halls) and traditional Gothic church structures that flourished from the late nineteenth century was a third and distinctly Methodist example of a hybrid church architecture, a form of church building that combines elements of the different architectural styles noted above. In some cases these hybridizations amounted to simple alterations of earlier church structures: the Lovely Lane Methodist Episcopal Church in Baltimore (1884) was built on an Italian Renaissance pattern, as noted above, but also sported theater-style seats and an astronomically correct representation of the night sky in the ceiling of the dome. Much more thoroughgoing as an example of hybrid space is the so-called "Akron Plan" of church architecture, following the pattern of First Methodist Church in Akron, Ohio, built in 1872.[69] The Akron Plan combined elements of Gothic style (pointed arches) with fixtures from the urban Evangelical auditorium. It is a basically square building often oriented toward one corner where there is a chancel platform. Around the opposite two sides is a wraparound gallery, and behind the seats in the main floor, underneath the gallery, are rooms that could be enclosed as Sunday school meeting spaces or could be opened up to the main sanctuary for additional seating for worship.

The Akron Plan and other Methodist examples of hybrid spaces allow for the tension or ambiguity inherent in Methodist ecclesiologies. They combine elements of an auditorium architecture characteristic of a revival movement with elements of more traditional worship space characteristic of a more sacramental understanding of the meaning of "church." They could even be reconfigured to serve the needs of different uses and these reconfigurations also reflect the ambiguities inherent in Methodist ecclesiologies. The problem inherent in the use of such a hybrid space involves the disjarring movement between different forms of sacred space: think of ushers busily reconfiguring Sunday school rooms into worship space in an Akron Plan church on a Sunday morning between Sunday school and worship. It would be difficult to think of a better concrete illustration of the longstanding tension in Methodist ecclesiologies.

Contemporary Methodist Architectures

A variety of architectural styles have been embraced by Wesleyan communities since the middle of the twentieth century. The postmodern turn in architecture has encouraged the rediscovery of some traditional architectural forms and has also allowed for the creation of new spaces that echo or match traditional spaces nearby. Thus the interior of the 1878 Wesley Memorial Church in Oxford was completely reconfigured in 1978 in a modular way that allows the interior of this Gothic structure to be utilized in a variety of different configurations. The Orange United Methodist Church in Chapel Hill, North Carolina, added a new mixed-use fellowship hall and worship facility alongside its traditional white-frame Gothic sanctuary in 1987, and the new addition carried through the architectural design of the older sanctuary building.[70] In both cases, traditional structures were reconfigured or expanded to allow for new forms of missional outreach.

Another contemporary example in The United Methodist Church affords a graphic example of how the characteristically Wesleyan tensions in ecclesiology continue to be expressed in church architectures. The Woodlands United Methodist Church, north of Houston, Texas, is now one of the largest congregations in The United Methodist Church. This congregation built an expansive and entirely new facility in the 1990s. From the exterior, one might think that it was an Eastern Orthodox church, judging from its domed, Mediterranean-style central sanctuary. But inside, the sanctuary space has much more the format of contemporary performance space, more like the format of a camp meeting assembly or an Evangelical auditorium, updated to accommodate contemporary video and audio technologies. This reflects the rising prominence of "Contemporary Christian" worship styles among Methodists in the last two decades.

But The Woodlands United Methodist Church also has a smaller worship space, the Robb Chapel, in a contemporary version of the Romanesque style, and at the very back of the Robb Chapel is a small prayer chapel named in honor of St. John Chrysostom, complete with Byzantine-style lamps and icons. Between the Robb Chapel and the main sanctuary are spaces for Sunday school classes, meeting rooms, administrative offices, and halls for fellowship and common meals. The Woodlands United Methodist Church facility thus can represent the consistent tensions in Methodist ecclesiology: the sanctuary, even with the appearance of a traditional church from the outside, reflects a strongly missional understanding of the church. The Robb Chapel and the Chrysostom Chapel reflect a much more traditional ecclesiology, representing the depth of Christian faith into which seekers and believers are to be drawn through the missional outreach of the congregation. Thus the architecture of The Woodlands United Methodist Church may also be a sign that the tension in Wesleyan ecclesiology can also be a creative tension when the poles of this ecclesiological tension are deliberately held together.

CONCLUSION

Wesleyan communities originated as a religious movement that presupposed existing church structures, and only later added elements necessary to configure these communities as churches. This process differed between Britain and America because British Methodists only incrementally separated from the Church of England, whereas American Methodists made a clean break in 1784. Some of the more creative proposals for Methodists as related to the ecumenical movement involve rediscovering our identity as a religious movement within the broader Christian community.[71]

The earliest Methodist doctrinal standards, the Methodist Articles of Religion, formally teach that the church is constituted as a community of believers in which the Word is preached and the sacraments are administered. However, subsequent doctrinal statements, catechisms, and systematic theologies designed for the training of preachers showed a strong tendency to define the church primarily as (a) a community of believers, and (b) a community constituted by its evangelistic mission. These statements give a less definitive role to worship, including the sacraments, in the understanding of the church. The older doctrinal statement reflects the ecclesiology inherited from Anglicanism and emphasizes stability and continuity; the newer view reflects the consistent stress on new missional outreach that has been crucial to Wesleyan communities.

These same trends can be seen in Methodist worship spaces as they evolved from the "cottage" and other informal worship spaces of early Methodist gatherings to the camp meeting assemblies of the nineteenth century to the Methodist Gothic architectures of the late nineteenth and early twentieth centuries. Wesleyan communities have continued to evolve new forms of worship spaces as Methodist churches, for example, adopting postmodern forms of church architecture. This evolution of sacred spaces reveals some spaces that reflect the nature of a religious movement structured for evangelistic outreach (like the Evangelical auditoriums of the late nineteenth century) and others that reflect the fuller sense of church (represented in Gothic and other traditional forms of church architecture). The use of "hybrid" spaces uniquely reveals both sides of Methodist ecclesiologies.

John Wesley's ordinations of 1784 reflected his desire, on the one hand, to allow the American Methodists to be a church according to the full definition of church given in his church's Articles of Religion and in the Articles he sent to America with Thomas Coke. On the other hand, they also reflected his belief that presbyters or elders had "an inherent right to ordain" and they reflect his missional concern that the American Methodists needed urgently to celebrate baptisms and the Lord's Supper. Contemporary conversations between The United Methodist Church and the Episcopal Church in the USA have reexamined this history and have explored ways in which both of these churches had to adapt to the new situation in North America for missional reasons. In fact, both churches began with a consideration of whether the office of episcopacy might be reshaped in the new American context. A study guide for United Methodist–Episcopal dialogue has expressed it in this manner:

> William White was a prominent Anglican and one of the first consecrated as bishop for the new [Episcopal] church. In his pamphlet, *A Case for the Episcopal Churches, Considered*, he argued for a different kind of episcopate than in the Church of England: he spoke of the restoration of an apostolic episcopacy, where bishops would be pastors, teachers, and leaders, not prelates. Likewise, in John Wesley's ordination of superintendents for the American Methodist societies, and in the implementation of episcopacy in the Methodist Episcopal Church, the goal was for the

restoration of apostolic models of episcopacy to suit the needs of the new American society. Both churches retained the threefold office of deacon, elder/presbyter, and bishop, though adapted in different ways.[72]

It is important for Methodists to realize that the tension that often arises between a formal definition of the church that stresses its stability and continuity over time, on the one hand, and the needs of the church for its evangelistic mission, on the other hand, is not unique to Wesleyan communities. It has a specific form in Wesleyan communities because these communities did not originate as separate churches and only later, in the crucible of their evangelistic work, had to develop institutions that marked them as churches.

The World Council of Churches Faith and Order Commission's *The Nature and Mission of the Church: A Stage on the Way to a Common Statement* (in its most recent draft, 2005) has a twofold consideration of "The Nature of the Church" (¶¶ 9–33) that includes the elements of a fellowship of believers, proclamation, and sacramental celebration, including eucharistic communion (¶ 32), and then "The Mission of the Church" (¶¶ 34–42) which speaks of the goal of calling all of humanity to God by the proclamation of Jesus Christ.[73] This document does not envision a tension between these aspects of the life of the church, though in presenting different views of the church it becomes apparent that some Christian traditions have placed more emphasis on the elements of continuity and stability, and others have placed more emphasis on the need for missional outreach. The Methodist tension in ecclesiology, then, may reflect a larger spectrum of views of the church that converge in the distinct experience of Wesleyan communities.

CHAPTER 7

FOURTEEN CORE BELIEFS OF WESLEYAN COMMUNITIES

The preceding chapters have explored core beliefs of Wesleyan communities. Chapters 1 through 3 examined the nucleus of Wesleyan beliefs as they were expressed in the works of John and Charles Wesley. Chapters 4 through 6 have examined three core samples of Wesleyan beliefs from the time of the Wesleys to the present time, considering in more depth beliefs about God (chapter 4), beliefs about the "way of salvation" (chapter 5), and beliefs about the nature of the Christian church (chapter 6).

Up to this point I have taken as a basic, organizational key to the content of Wesleyan beliefs two sets of claims that Wesley and subsequent Methodists made: first, their claims that many if not most of their beliefs and practices were consistent with the common content of the Christian faith; and second, their claims that there were distinct emphases and institutions associated with the Methodist movement and which enabled this movement to pursue its distinctive mission or calling within the catholic church. In what follows, I shall organize a single list of core beliefs that were expressed by the Wesleys and subsequent Wesleyan communities. Both distinctive and common beliefs will be integrated into this list, but I will indicate which beliefs are relatively "common" (ecumenical) and which ones are relatively distinctive of Wesleyan communities. In both cases, however, these are relative claims, since many common teachings have a distinctly Wesleyan nuance and many distinctive teachings bear strong resemblances and connections to teachings of other Christian traditions.

Chapter 1 has quoted John Wesley's claim that "Methodism, so-called, is the old religion, the religion of the Bible, the religion of the primitive Church, the religion of the Church of England."[1] According to Wesley, Methodism was nothing less than the

Christian faith. This sense of the fundamental identity of Wesley's movement was not missed by his immediate followers, who inscribed on his tombstone:

> This Great Light Arose
> by the Singular Providence of God
> To Revive, Enforce and Defend
> The Pure Apostolical Doctrines and Practices
> of the Primitive Church[2]

Nineteenth-century Methodists loved to quote the Scots Presbyterian Thomas Chalmers's saying that Methodism was "Christianity in earnest."[3] Historian Abel Stevens described Methodism as offering "a catholic, living, working Church of the common people," and James M. Buckley could claim that "the *doctrines* taught by Wesley and his itinerant and lay preachers included the fundamental principles of Christianity as held by the Reformed churches generally."[4]

Today the Methodist Church of Great Britain, the Methodist Church Nigeria, and other churches that follow the pattern set by the British Methodist church proclaim at the beginning of their constitutions their loyalty to the faith of the universal church and to the beliefs they have inherited from the Reformation (here quoting the constitution of the Methodist Church of Great Britain):

> The Methodist Church claims and cherishes its place in the Holy Catholic Church which is the Body of Christ. It rejoices in the inheritance of Apostolic Faith and loyally accepts the fundamental principles of the historic Creeds and the Protestant Reformation.[5]

Similarly, the World Methodist Council's "Wesleyan Essentials of Christian Faith" claims on behalf of the community of churches represented in the WMC, "We claim and cherish our true place in the one holy, catholic and apostolic church."[6] The United Methodist Church today declares its solidarity with the apostolic faith shared by Christians:

> United Methodists share a common heritage with Christians of every age and nation. This heritage is grounded in the apostolic witness to Jesus Christ as Savior and Lord, which is the source and measure of all valid Christian teaching.[7]

Methodist churches have consistently claimed their fundamental identity as Christian bodies. Thus, Wesleyan beliefs are first and foremost Christian beliefs.

Methodists have been known since Wesley's time for their liberality; indeed, Wesley's expression "catholic spirit" might be paraphrased as an "open-minded" or even a "liberal spirit." Methodists have sometimes defined themselves over against Fundamentalist Christian groups by appealing to this sense of liberality, and there is more than a grain of truth in this claim. Methodist churches have consistently claimed a relatively small list of essential or fundamental teachings as definitive of Christian faith and have often been content to leave matters of "opinion" or "modes of worship" to be freely discussed.[8]

But the chapters preceding have shown that Methodist liberality was not a vague and general sense of unity but a specific sense of which teachings and practices lie at the heart of the Christian faith. Chapter 1 has examined John Wesley's own sense of "essential" or "necessary" or even "fundamental" teachings and practices, and chapter 3 has examined these doctrines as expressed in the verse of Charles Wesley. Chapters 4 and 6 have examined two of these common teachings in some depth as they have been expressed through the history of Wesleyan communities.

At the same time that Wesleyan communities claim their place within the broader Christian community, "the holy catholic church," they also claim a distinctive calling and this has given Wesleyan communities certain distinctive or distinctively expressed beliefs. In the account following of core beliefs of Wesleyan communities I will give some of the claims that Methodists have made about their most distinctive teachings. I have not dealt directly with Wesleyan practices except for the practice of baptism and the Lord's Supper in this section in the hopes that a future volume can be dedicated to Wesleyan practices.

In what follows I offer a statement of fourteen core beliefs that the Wesleys and subsequent Wesleyan communities have claimed as common to the Christian faith as well as distinctive teachings of these communities. These are not precisely the same as the items given in chapters 1 through 3 because Wesleyan communities have in some cases expanded on or added to the teachings identified by the Wesleys. Moreover, I have tried to state the following teachings in more contemporary and ecumenical terminology as reflecting the living teachings of Wesleyan communities.

Three of the most distinctive teachings given below as core teachings have to do with the "way of salvation" examined in chapters 2 (with reference to John Wesley), 3 (with reference to Charles Wesley), and 5 (with reference to Methodist teachings and testimonies subsequent to the Wesleys). These distinctive teachings are stated well in the *Senior Catechism of the Methodist Church* (Methodist Church of Great Britain, 1952). This catechism poses the question, "What is the Methodist Church?" In response to this question, the following answer is given:

> Within the one, holy, catholic, and apostolic Church, the Methodist Church is the communion which was brought into being by the Holy Spirit, chiefly through the work of John Wesley, and continues as a witness to the universal grace of God, to the gift of assurance by the Holy Spirit, and to the power of the Holy Spirit to make us perfect in love.[9]

Three things are claimed here as constituting the continuing witness of the British Methodist Church. The "universal grace of God" refers to the belief that divine grace is available to all persons, in opposition to the doctrine of limited atonement. The "gift of assurance by the Holy Spirit" refers to the belief in the assurance of pardon associated with justification and regeneration. The "power of the Holy Spirit to make us perfect in love" refers to the belief in entire sanctification. These three matters of continuing witness are easily related to the threefold structure of the "way of salvation" that appeared consistently in John Wesley's thought.

Because the source material for each of the listed teachings has been spread out in the notes to the preceding chapters, it may be helpful to organize them together in a single location, so in association with each of the following items I will give a paragraph in a smaller font with some basic references to the specific doctrine in John Wesley's writings, in Methodist creedal and other doctrinal statements, in standard works (secondary sources) interpreting Methodist or Wesleyan teachings, in common Anglican and Protestant doctrinal sources (since some Methodist churches profess a general loyalty to the creeds and confessions of the Reformation), and in contemporary ecumenical sources to which

Methodist bodies have given some degree of assent. Where readers can refer to material referenced in the sources' paragraphs I have not given extensive notes in the text.

1. Common Belief in and Worship of the Divine Trinity

Ancient and Ecumenical sources: the Apostles' Creed (in Pelikan and Hotchkiss, 1:669; in Leith, ed., *Creeds of the Churches*, 24–25); the original Nicene Creed and the Nicene-Constantinopolitan Creed (A.D. fourth century; in Pelikan and Hotchkiss, 1:162–63; in Leith, ed., *Creeds of the Churches*, 28–33); WCC Faith and Order text, *Confessing the One Faith*, passim. **Anglican and Reformation sources:** Augsburg Confession 1 (in Pelikan and Hotchkiss, 2:58–59; in Leith, *Creeds of the Churches*, 67–68); Anglican Articles of Religion 1 and 8 (the latter affirmed the Nicene, Apostles', and Athanasian creeds (in Pelikan and Hotchkiss, 2:528, 530–31; in Leith, *Creeds of the Churches*, 266 and 269); Westminster Confession of Faith 2 (in Pelikan and Hotchkiss, 2:608–9; in Leith, *Creeds of the Churches*, 197); cf. Calvin, *Institutes*, I:13 (in Battles and McNeill, 1:120–50). **Wesleyan sources:** John Wesley explicitly claimed the doctrine of the Trinity as a necessary Christian teaching in "On the Trinity" (1775) ¶ 2 (in Outler, ed., *Sermons*, 3:376; and in Jackson, ed., *Works*, 6:200); cf. his "Letter to a Roman Catholic" ¶¶ 6–8 (in Jackson, ed., *Works*, 10:81–82); *Instructions for Children*, 5. **Doctrinal sources:** Methodist Articles of Religion 1 (in Pelikan and Hotchkiss, 3:202; in Leith, ed., *Creeds of the Churches*, 354); United Methodist Confession of Faith, Article 1 (UMC *Discipline* 2008, ¶ 103, pp. 66–67); Church of the Nazarene Articles of Faith,[10] article 1 (cf. Pelikan and Hotchkiss, 3:410); World Methodist Council, "Wesleyan Essentials of Christian Faith," sections on "The People Called Methodists" and "Our Worship" (in WMC *Handbook of Information 2007–2011*, 95 and 96). **Catechetical sources:** *Short Scriptural Catechism Intended for the Use of The Methodist Episcopal Church*, (unnumbered) page facing p. iv; *Catechism for the Use of Children*, chapter 2, p. 2 (on the unity of God); chapter 3, p. 3 (on Jesus Christ); chapter 1, p. 1 (on the Holy Spirit); *Catechisms of the Wesleyan Methodists*, no. I (New York 1829, 3–9); *Catechisms of the Wesleyan Methodists*, no. II, section 1, "Of God," questions 12 and 13 (Toronto 1867, 4 and 5); *The Catechism (Formerly "The Turner Catechism") of the A.M.E. Church*, lesson II, "The Persons of the Godhead"; *Junior Catechism of The Methodist Episcopal Church and the Methodist Episcopal Church*,

South (1932 printing, p. 3); *Junior Catechism* (Memphis: C.M.E. Church, p. 7); *Methodist Catechism* (Methodist Church in Ireland), qu. 8, (1948, p. 3); *Senior Catechism of The Methodist Church* (Methodist Church of Great Britain, 1952), qu. 18 (p. 6); *Catechism for the Use of the People Called Methodists* (1989), qu. 48 (on baptism, 22 and 24), qu. 54 (the Apostles' Creed, p. 26), qu. 55 (the Nicene Creed, p. 28), qu. 56, 57, 58, and 62 (on the Trinity, God the Father, Jesus Christ, and the Holy Spirit, 30 and 32). **Methodist theologians:** Watson, *Theological Institutes*, II:8–17 (in 1854 edition; 1:447–642); Summers, *Systematic Theology* (I–II:1–2; in 1888 printing, 1:147–57); Pope, *Compendium of Christian Theology*, chapter on "God," subsection on "The Triune Name" (1880 printing, 1:255–86); Raymond, *Systematic Theology*, book II, chs. III–IV, and VI (1:374–479, 491–94); Miley, *Systematic Theology*, II:5–8 (1892 printing, 1:223–75); Wiley, *Christian Theology*, ch. 15 (1940 printing, 1:393–439). **Secondary sources:** Williams, *John Wesley's Theology Today*, 93–97; Maddox, *Responsible Grace*, specifically 136–40, but more generally 48–64, 94–118, 119–40; Campbell, *Methodist Doctrine*, 41–47; Jones, *United Methodist Doctrine*, 99–125; Collins, *Theology of John Wesley*, specifically 143–49, but more generally 19–48, 87–120, and 121–53.

Three of the preceding chapters have considered the doctrine and worship of the Trinity. Chapter 1 considered this teaching as one of John Wesley's "essential" Christian doctrines. Chapter 3 considered Charles Wesley's doxological expressions of the doctrine of the Trinity. Chapter 4 took a deeper look at the doctrine of the Trinity and teaching about divine attributes as a central part of Wesleyan theology, piety, and spirituality. That chapter noted that Methodist hymnals after the 1780 *Collection of Hymns* have an opening section of hymns in praise of God, of Jesus Christ, and of the Holy Spirit, so Methodists know the common trinitarian pattern even when lacking specific reference to the first Person of the Trinity and most are accustomed to singing the *Gloria Patri* and doxologies (like that of Thomas Ken) that conclude with an ascription of praise to the persons of the Trinity. Reginald Heber's hymn to the Trinity, "Holy, Holy, Holy" displaced "O For a Thousand Tongues to Sing" as the first hymn in the jointly produced American *Methodist Hymnal* of 1935, and in fact, this hymn even appeared in a Methodist-sponsored collection of popular gospel songs, the *Cokesbury Worship Hymnal*, that came out in 1938.[11]

The doctrine of the Trinity, then, is more than simply a nod to orthodox doctrine on the part of Wesleyan communities: it reflects the consistent worship practice of Methodist people and this is consistent with the fact that, as chapter 4 has shown, the doctrine of the Trinity emerged in the first place as an explication of the church's practice of worshiping Jesus Christ. That chapter has also shown that the doctrine of the Trinity and the related teaching about divine attributes were bound together for Wesleyan communities with the issue of sanctification, since in the process of sanctification the believer becomes "godly," that is, takes upon herself or himself some of the attributes of divinity, and so Christian believers are called to be "Transcripts of the Trinity" in their godly character and in their unity with God and with each other.[12]

There are some nuances to the Wesleyan way of transmitting the doctrine of the Trinity. John Wesley himself demurred from insisting on any "philosophical" explanation of the doctrine, naming the so-called "Athanasian Creed" as an example of a "philosophical" explanation of it. Wesleyan communities have historically used the Apostles' Creed much more frequently than the Nicene Creed, and the Apostles' Creed presents Christian faith in the three divine Persons in a simpler and more primitive form than the Nicene Creed. Methodist reflection on the doctrine of the Trinity has tended to stress the "economic" Trinity, that is, the role of the divine Persons in creation and redemption rather than their internal relationships. As noted above, the organization of Methodist hymnals has seldom named the first Person of the Trinity, perhaps because few traditional hymns are addressed to God the Father alone, and Methodists seem to be comfortable with the threefold formula involving God, the Son Jesus Christ, and the Holy Spirit that appears in "the grace" (2 Corinthians 13:14) and in the contemporary version of the Thomas Ken doxology by Gilbert H. Vieira.[13]

2. Common Belief in the Divine and Human Work of Christ

Ancient and Ecumenical sources: The original Nicene Creed and the Nicene-Constantinopolitan Creed (A.D. fourth century; in Pelikan and Hotchkiss, 1:158–59, 162–63; in Leith, ed., *Creeds of the Churches*, 28–33); Definition of Faith of the Council of Chalcedon (A.D. 451; in Pelikan and Hotchkiss, 1:174–81; in Leith, ed., *Creeds* *of the Churches*, 34–36); WCC Faith and Order text, *Confessing the One Faith*, 43–72. **Anglican and Reformation sources:** Augsburg Confession 3 (in Pelikan and Hotchkiss, 2:60; in Leith, *Creeds of the Churches*, 68–69); Anglican Articles of Religion 2 and 31 (in Pelikan and Hotchkiss, 2:528, 536; in Leith, *Creeds of the Churches*, 267, 277); Westminster Confession of Faith, 8:1–8 (in Pelikan and Hotchkiss, 2:616–18; in Leith, *Creeds of the Churches*, 203–5). **Wesleyan sources:** John Wesley maintained that the doctrine of the full divinity of Christ is a necessary Christian doctrine in "The Character of a Methodist" ¶ 1 (in Jackson, ed., *Works*, 8:340); he claimed the doctrine of the atonement to be a necessary Christian doctrine in a letter to Mary Bishop, dated 7 February 1778 (in Telford, ed., *Letters*, 6:297–98); cf. also "Letter to a Roman Catholic" ¶ 7 (in Jackson, ed., *Works*, 10:81–82). **Doctrinal sources:** Methodist Articles of Religion 1, 2, and 20 (in Pelikan and Hotchkiss, 3:202, 206; in Leith, ed., *Creeds of the Churches*, 354, 359); United Methodist Confession of Faith, Article 2 (UMC *Discipline* 2008, ¶ 103, p. 67); Church of the Nazarene Articles of Faith, articles 2 and 6 (cf. Pelikan and Hotchkiss, 3:410, 411); World Methodist Council, "Wesleyan Essentials of Christian Faith," section on "Our Beliefs" (in WMC *Handbook of Information 2007–2011*, 95–96). **Methodist theologians:** Watson, *Theological Institutes*, II:11–16, 20–22 (1857 edition, 274–353, 416–75); Summers, *Systematic Theology*, II:1–3 (1:162–298); Raymond, *Systematic Theology*, book II, ch. IV, which is titled "Bible Proofs of Trinity" but is consistently on the human and divine natures of Jesus Christ (1:395–479) and book IV, ch. II, entitled "Theories of Salvation" (2:211–307); Pope, *Compendium of Christian Theology*, "The Mediatorial Ministry" (1880 printing, 2:106–316); Miley, *Systematic Theology*, II:6 (1:232–56), IV and V (2:3–240). **Secondary sources:** Deschner, *Wesley's Christology*, 14–44 (on the human and divine natures of Christ), 45–190 (on the work of Christ); Williams, *John Wesley's Theology Today*, 74–93; Maddox, *Responsible Grace*, 94–118; Campbell, *Methodist Doctrine*, 41–44; Jones, *United Methodist Doctrine*, 112–15; Collins, *John Wesley's Theology*, 87–120.

John Wesley identified both the doctrine of the full divinity of Jesus Christ and the doctrine of the atonement as necessary Christian doctrines, but in subsequent Methodist doctrinal statements and theological reflection these two doctrines have often been subsumed under the larger category of the divine and human work of Christ on behalf of humankind, including Christ's incarnation as well as the atonement. For example, the second Methodist Article of Religion (following the second Anglican Article of Religion) deals with the divine and human natures of Christ, then the Incarnation, crucifixion, death, and burial of Christ as part of his work of reconciliation.[14] Similarly, The United Methodist Church's Confession of Faith, inherited from the Evangelical United Brethren Church and from its doctrinal tradition that reached back to the German Reformed Church, deals with the divinity and humanity of Jesus Christ and then whole work of Christ on behalf of humankind in its second article.[15]

These christological teachings were expressed in the rich hymnody of Charles Wesley that has been explored in chapter 3 and which continues to be a foundational core of Methodist hymnals throughout the world. It is also expressed in traditional spirituals, gospel songs from the late nineteenth century and the early twentieth century, and in a variety of contemporary songs and worship resources. These beliefs have been consistently taught in Methodist catechisms for children and in the systematic theologies that Methodist churches approved for the training of preachers. As a result of the ecumenical movement and the movement for liturgical renewal in the twentieth century, Methodist churches began to celebrate the cycle of the Christian year as a regular part of their church life, and this has provided another means for expressing the church's praise for the work of Jesus Christ.

3. Common Belief in the Authority of the Holy Scriptures

Anglican and Reformation sources: Augsburg Confession, the preface and the preface to the second part of the Confession on disputed matters (in Pelikan and Hotchkiss, 2:53–58, 77–78; in Leith, *Creeds of the Churches*, 64–67, 79); Anglican Articles of Religion 6–7 (in Pelikan and Hotchkiss, 2:529–30; in Leith, *Creeds of the Churches*, 267–69); Westminster Confession of Faith 1 (in Pelikan and Hotchkiss, 2:604–8; in Leith, *Creeds of the Churches*, 193–96). **Wesleyan sources:** John Wesley maintained that the doctrine of biblical authority is a constitutive Christian doctrine in "The Character of a Methodist" ¶ 1 (in Jackson, ed., *Works*, 8:340). **Doctrinal sources:** Methodist Articles of Religion 5–6 (in Pelikan and Hotchkiss, 3:202–3; in Leith, *Creeds of the Churches*, 355); United Methodist Confession of Faith, Article 4 (UMC *Discipline*

2008, ¶ 103, p. 67); United Methodist Church, "Our Theological Task" (UMC *Discipline* 2008, ¶ 104, pp. 74–86); Church of the Nazarene Articles of Faith, article 4 (cf. Pelikan and Hotchkiss, 3:411); World Methodist Council, "Wesleyan Essentials of Christian Faith," section on "Our Beliefs" (in WMC *Handbook of Information 2007–2011*, 95–96). **Methodist theologians:** Watson, *Theological Institutes*, I (1857 edition, 9–149); Summers, *Systematic Theology* V (1:417–552); Raymond, *Systematic Theology*, book I in its entirety, which demonstrates the inspiration and authority of the Holy Scriptures (1:19–243); Pope, *Compendium of Christian Theology*, "The Divine Rule of Faith" (1880 printing, 1:36–230); Miley, *Systematic Theology* introduction II:2 (1:11) and appendix, "The Inspiration of the Scriptures" (2:479–89). **Secondary sources:** Williams, *John Wesley's Theology Today*, 23–38; Jones, *John Wesley's Conception and Use of Scripture*, passim; Maddox, *Responsible Grace*, 28–32, 36–47; Campbell, *Methodist Doctrine*, 35–40; Jones, *United Methodist Doctrine*, 127–43.

John Wesley asserted that the doctrine of biblical authority was a constitutive doctrine of the Christian faith, a doctrine that distinguishes Christians from non-Christians. Scott J. Jones's study of John Wesley's understanding and use of the Scriptures has shown that John Wesley consistently maintained that the central meaning of the Bible as a whole, what he and a tradition of theologians before him called the "analogy of faith," lay in its teaching about Jesus Christ and the way of human salvation that has been made possible through Jesus Christ. However, I note that Wesley's own statement about the "analogy of faith" in his comment on Romans 12:6 in the *Explanatory Notes upon the New Testament* seems to equate the "analogy of faith" with his understanding of the "way of salvation" whereas in the theological tradition before him, the "analogy of faith" was understood as referring preeminently to the work of Christ, not specifically the "way of salvation" as apprehended by humans, as the focus of the Scriptures.[16]

The doctrine of biblical authority has been asserted in traditional Methodist doctrinal statements, including the Articles of Religion held by the AME, AME Zion, CME, and UM churches, and the Confession of Faith of The United Methodist Church, which assert the "sufficiency" of the Scriptures, that is, they assert that the Scriptures contain everything that is necessary for knowledge about salvation, so that nothing that is not taught in them can be thought of as being necessary to human salvation. Similarly, the 1930 "Doctrinal Statement" of the Korean Methodist Church (also known as the "Korean Creed") asserted the church's belief in "the word of God contained in the Old and New Testaments as the sufficient rule both of faith and of practice."[17] Methodist doctrinal statements have traditionally not utilized the language of biblical inerrancy or infallibility, although an article of the Church of the Nazarene refers to the authority of the Scriptures "given by divine inspiration, inerrantly revealing the will of God concerning us in all things necessary to our salvation."[18] I note, however, that the scope of this claim of inerrancy is "the will of God concerning us in all things necessary to our salvation" and it does not explicitly claim biblical inerrancy in matters of scientific facts or historical claims.

Methodist theologians in the nineteenth century whose works were prescribed for study by preachers were intensely concerned to demonstrate the inspiration of the Holy Scriptures as the prolegomenon to any systematic understanding of the Christian faith, that is, once the authority of the Scriptures had been established then other doctrines could be established on the basis of the authority of the Scriptures. This pattern was set by Richard Watson's *Theological Institutes* (1823) and was followed by Summers (1875–76), Pope (1876–77), and Raymond (1877). John Miley's *Systematic Theology* (1892) broke the pattern, giving only a brief justification for biblical authority in his main text and then an extended consideration of biblical inspiration in an appendix.[19] Miley stressed that faith is itself a prerequisite for understanding the Scriptures, so he may not have been quite convinced by the elaborate apologetic writings of earlier Methodist theologians who had labored to prove the inspiration of the Holy Scriptures.

In 1972 The United Methodist Church adopted a statement of "Our Theological Task," which included four guidelines for United Methodist theological and ethical reflection: Scripture, tradition, experience, and reason. Although the statement did not ascribe these guidelines to John Wesley, they came to be known in popular Methodist circles as the "Wesleyan Quadrilateral." In them "tradition" was taken in a positive sense in contrast to the way in which the term had been treated by John Wesley and nineteenth-century Methodist theologians. This new and positive sense of "tradition" associated it with the work of God through the history of the Christian community, and reflected growing ecumenical understandings of the relationship between Scripture and tradition.[20] The use of reason and experience allowed for the role of critical reflection and reflection on human experience as criteria in the interpretation of the Scriptures. Objections to the perception that the criteria of tradition, experience, and reason could somehow override the authority of Scripture were addressed in a 1988 revision of the statement, which clarified the primacy of Scripture in relation to other authorities.

Although the statement of the Quadrilateral was made by The United Methodist Church, a similar though briefer statement, including a reference to the role of tradition, experience, and reason in the interpretation of Scripture, was adopted by the Methodist Church in India.[21] The basic idea is also expressed in the statement of "Wesleyan Essentials of Christian Faith" adopted by the World Methodist Council: "Methodists acknowledge that scriptural reflection is influenced by the processes of reason, tradition and experience, while aware that Scripture is the primary source and criteria of Christian doctrine."[22] The idea of the Quadrilateral has had broad influence in Wesleyan churches, for example in a proposal by Donald Thorsen on the role of biblical authority in Evangelical churches of the Wesleyan tradition as an alternative to Fundamentalist understandings of the authority of Scripture.[23]

Thorsen's volume indicates that the United Methodist discussion of the Quadrilateral is part of a larger discussion in Wesleyan churches over the nature of biblical authority in the light of modern biblical criticism and subsequent reflections on the nature of biblical authority. The doctrinal standards of Wesleyan communities have seldom described biblical authority utilizing the language of "inerrancy" or "infallibility" characteristic of Fundamentalist Christian communities,[24] preferring the language of "sufficiency" inherited from the Anglican Articles and Reformation statements of scriptural authority. It may be important for Wesleyans to recognize the christological principle that Wesley employed in the understanding of the Sriptures, a principle that has been explored in the work of Scott J. Jones. The reading of the Holy Scriptures in Wesleyan churches following the pattern of the Christian liturgical year allows for a renewed focus on the narrative of the work of Jesus Christ as the key to the meaning of the Bible as a whole.

4. Distinctive Belief in the Role of Religious Experience and the Religious Affections

Reformation Sources: Calvin, *Institutes* 1.7.5 (in McNeill, ed., *Calvin: Institutes* 1:80–81). **Wesleyan Sources:** "Earnest Appeal to Men of Reason and Religion" ¶¶ 6–10 (Cragg, ed., *Appeals,* 46–48); *Journal* for 22 May 1749 (Curnock, 3:401; Ward and Heitzenrater, 3:274); "Justification by Faith" IV:2 (in Outler, ed., *Sermons,* 1:194); "The Great Privilege of Those That Are Born of God" I:2–10 (in Outler, ed., *Sermons,* 1:432–35); "The Scripture Way of Salvation," II:1 (in Outler, ed., *Sermons,* 2:160–62); "On the Discoveries of Faith" passim (in Outler, ed., *Sermons,* 4:28–38); Sermon "On the Difference between Walking by Sight, and Walking by Faith" passim (in Outler, ed., *Sermons,* 4:49–59); "On Faith" passim (in Outler, ed., *Sermons,* 4:188–200); *Explanatory Notes upon the New Testament on Hebrews 11:1* (1948 edition, note on p. 841); "The End of Christ's Coming," III:1 (Jackson, 6:274–75; in Outler, ed., **Sermons,** 2:481). **Doctrinal Sources:** United Methodist Church statement on "Our Theological Task" (UMC *Discipline* 2008, ¶ 104, pp. 81–82). **Methodist Theologians:** Watson, *Theological Institutes,* II:B:II, chapter 24 on effects of justification including adoption (1857 edition, 269–81); Summers, *Systematic Theology,* book IV, chapter IV (1:406–14); Raymond, *Systematic Theology,* I:VI on the "Argument from Experience" (1:208–16); Pope, *Compendium of Christian Theology,* "Revelation or the Faith" (1880 printing, 1:36–155), "The Administration of Redemption," section on "Calling and Election" (1880 printing, 2:345–46), "Christian Sonship," section on "Adoption" (1880 printing, 3:13–20), "Tenure of Covenant Blessings," section on "Assurance" (1880 printing, 3:113–30); Miley, *Systematic Theology* introduction (1:16–22). **Secondary Sources:** Herbert Brook Workman, *The Place of Methodism in the Catholic Church* (London: Epworth Press, 1921); Umphrey Lee, "The Historical Backgrounds of Early Methodist Enthusiasm" (PhD dissertation, Columbia University, 1931); and *John Wesley and Modern Religion* (Nashville: Cokesbury Press, 1936); Frederick Dreyer, "Faith and Experience in the Thought of John Wesley," *American Historical Review* 88 (1983): 12–30; Richard E. Brantley, *Locke, Wesley, and the Method of English Romanticism* (1984); Gregory S. Clapper, *John Wesley on Religious Affections: His Views on Experience and Emotion and Their Role in the Christian Life and Theology* (Metuchen, N.J.: Scarecrow Press, 1989); Williams, *John Wesley's Theology Today,* 32–38; Maddox, *Responsible Grace,* 44–46, 48–49; Runyon, *New*

Creation, 146–67; Campbell, *Methodist Doctrine*, 39; Jones, *United Methodist Doctrine*, 139; Collins, *Theology of John Wesley*, 2.

One of the elements of the Quadrilateral discussed in the previous section is experience, but the notion of religious experience, in particular, has been so consistently important in Methodist culture as to warrant the claim that a particular understanding of religious experience and of the religious affections arising from such experience constitute a consistent and distinctive teaching of Wesleyan communities. Chapter 2 has discussed the influence of Calvin's notion of the "inward witness of the Holy Spirit" and its subsequent influence on Puritan authors and, through them, on John Wesley. The Methodist movement arose in tandem with the Pietist movement among the Lutheran and Reformed churches of the European continent, and it was paralleled by developments in Baroque Catholic spirituality, for example, the rise of devotion to the Sacred Heart of Jesus. These religious movements had a common focus on the human experience of the divine and personal affection for the humanity of Jesus Christ.[25] Chapter 2 above took note of John Wesley's claim that the immediate experience of the divine, "perceptible inspiration," was "the main doctrine of the Methodists."[26] John Wesley developed a fairly elaborate account of the importance of religious experience, consistently defining "faith" in a general sense as "the evidence of things not seen" (Hebrews 11:1 AV), that is, the knowledge of the divine that parallels the bodily senses and their corresponding evidence of "things seen" (material realities). John Wesley's elaboration of this epistemology of religious experience has been shown by contemporary interpreters to have roots in Platonic thought and the Cambridge Platonists of the seventeenth century,[27] and in Aristotelian thought.[28] Wesley, moreover, employed some of the terminology of Enlightenment epistemologies, including the empirical terminology utilized by John Locke, in expressing this belief.[29] Chapter 3 above has shown how the poetry and hymnody of Charles Wesley utilized an elaborate vocabulary for the expression of human experiences of the divine and the religious affections associated with such experiences.

The experiences of Methodist people described in chapter 5 above show how central religious experience was to the popular spirituality of Methodism in the nineteenth century, and such contemporary historians as David Hempton, John Wigger, and Ann Taves have all emphasized this aspect of Methodist popular culture.[30] Thomas A. Langford, describing a different range of Methodist culture, made the case that reflection on the "vital experience of God" was one of the consistent hallmarks of the more sophisticated Methodist theologians he studied from the nineteenth as well as twentieth centuries.[31] Theological textbooks utilized for the training of Methodist preachers in the late nineteenth century including those of Miner Raymond (1872) and John Miley (1893) placed the discussion of religious experience early on among their discussions of the sources of Christian theology.[32]

The emphasis on personal religious experience has had a deep effect on other aspects of Wesleyan cultures. Why should Wesleyan communities have proceeded to recognize women as exhorters, preachers, and then as ordained clergy in advance of other Protestant groups? One reason is that Wesleyans from the time of John Wesley himself, and including the most conservative Wesleyan groups, found women's testimonies to their experience of a divine calling to preach and to serve as ministers of the sacraments compelling in a way that other Christian communities did not.

Sophisticated Methodists in the late nineteenth century and in the early twentieth century may not have spoken as freely or confidently about personal religious experiences as Methodists had in the past. The work of Methodist theologian Borden Parker Bowne of Boston University prompted Harvard philosopher William James to comment in a footnote to his Gifford Lectures on *The Varieties of Religious Experience*, "See how the ancient spirit of Methodism evaporates under those wonderfully able rationalistic booklets (which every one should read) of a philosopher like Professor Bowne."[33] In the context of James's *Varieties of Religious Experience*, this means that James considered "the ancient spirit of Methodism" to be characterized by an emphasis on religious experience. But as Thomas Langford has pointed out, religious experience was a central conception in Bowne's own philosophy![34] And despite any declension in Methodists' willingness to speak directly of their religious experiences, Methodist literature in the early twentieth century, for example, works by British Methodist

Herbert Brook Workman (1921)[35] and American Methodist Umphrey Lee (1931 and 1936),[36] maintained an emphasis on personal religious experience as a consistent hallmark of Methodist life.

From the time of Colin W. Williams's *John Wesley's Theology Today* (1960), many Methodist interpreters emphasized the elements of the "way of salvation" as the most distinctive elements of the Wesleyan doctrinal and spiritual inheritance, and consequently deemphasized the role of religious experience. In Williams's own work, this seems grounded in a neo-orthodox concern that, in his words, "experience is not the test of truth, but truth the test of experience."[37] The contemporary texts on Wesleyan theology and Methodist doctrine cited above by Maddox, Campbell, Jones, and Collins devote little attention to this topic.

However, one particular contemporary line of the interpretation of John Wesley has continued to emphasize the central importance of religious experience and the religious affections that flow from religious experience as cardinal elements of Wesleyan culture, a line of interpretation represented by Theodore Runyon of Candler School of Theology, Emory University, and his student Gregory S. Clapper. Clapper's *John Wesley on Religious Affections* (1989) explores John Wesley's elaborate vocabulary for describing religious affections and the relevance of this for the contemporary reappropriation of the Wesleyan theological inheritance.[38] Runyon's *The New Creation* (1998) devotes an entire chapter to religious experience and the religious affections.[39] Both Runyon and Clapper make the case that alongside Christian orthodoxy (right belief and worship) and orthopraxy (right practice), the Wesleyan inheritance calls us to recognize the importance of what they call *orthokardia* (Clapper) or *orthopathy* (Runyon), that is, right affections in regard to God and one's neighbor.

Clapper and Runyon and other interpreters recognize the problem inherent in seeing religious experience and religious affections as sources or criteria for theology. They are not in disagreement with Colin Williams's concern that "experience is not the test of truth, but truth the test of experience." They clarify that individual experience needs to be balanced by the experience of communities.[40] But the case they make is that our religious experience and the range of our affective or emotional life are very important parts of what it means to be human, and Christian faith should be as concerned with these elements of human experience as with such other elements as intellectual and moral life.

The current Archbishop of Canterbury writes,

> Theology is primarily speaking about God; but since God is by definition not available for inspection as an object in the laboratory, this entails speaking about the imprint of God on human lives—and thus about what humanity looks like when exposed to an active, intelligent transcendent reality.[41]

In speaking of "the imprint of God on human lives," I do not suppose that the archbishop has reference primarily to particular religious experiences. Knowing his scholarship, I suspect that he thinks of saintliness as the principal divine imprint on humanity. But here Methodists might want to say that saintliness does entail the cultivation of the religious affections, and preeminently the human embodiment of divine love, perfect love, the "LOVE" that Wesleyan hymnody holds to be the secret name that most fully reveals the divine nature. Saintliness entails the complete or entire sanctification of our love for God and, concomitant with our love for God, love for our neighbors (see section 10 below). Saintliness entails the sanctification of the affections among our other human capacities.

5. Common Beliefs about Original Righteousness and Original Sin

Anglican and Reformation sources: Augsburg Confession 2 (in Pelikan and Hotchkiss, 2:59; in Leith, *Creeds of the Churches*, 68); Anglican Articles of Religion 9–10 (in Pelikan and Hotchkiss, 2:531; in Leith, *Creeds of the Churches,* 269–70); Westminster Confession of Faith 6 (in Pelikan and Hotchkiss, 2:614; in Leith, *Creeds of the Churches,* 201–2); Anglican Article 9 (given in Leith, ed., 269–70). **Wesleyan sources:** John Wesley claimed the doctrine of original sin as a necessary Christian doctrine in "The Doctrine of Original Sin, according to Scripture, Reason and Experience" ¶ VI:VI (in Jackson, ed., *Works,* 9:429). **Doctrinal sources:** Methodist Articles of Religion 7 (in Pelikan and Hotchkiss, 3:203; in Leith, *Creeds of the Churches,* 356); United Methodist Confession of Faith, Article 7 (UMC *Discipline* 2004, ¶ 103, p. 68); Church of the

Nazarene Articles of Faith, article 5 (cf. Pelikan and Hotchkiss, 3:411). **Methodist theologians:** Watson, *Theological Institutes*, II:18 (1857 edition, 361–408); Summers, *Systematic Theology*, VI:I–II (2:17–90); Raymond, *Systematic Theology*, book III, chs. I–III (2:2–172), and especially ch. III (2:64–172); Pope, *Compendium of Christian Theology*, "Sin" (1880 printing, 2:17–90); Miley, *Systematic Theology*, III (1:351–533). **Secondary sources:** Williams, *John Wesley's Theology Today*, 47–56; Outler, *Theology in the Wesleyan Spirit*, 23–43; Maddox, *Responsible Grace*, 65–83; Runyon, *New Creation*, 13–24; Campbell, *Methodist Doctrine*, 48–50; Jones, *United Methodist Doctrine*, 145–56; Collins, *John Wesley's Theology*, 49–73.

Chapter 1 has shown that from the middle of the 1750s, when confronted with contemporary works dismissing the traditional understanding of original sin, John Wesley began to claim that the doctrine of original sin was a necessary Christian doctrine. He understood the doctrine of original sin as teaching that all human beings stand in need of divine grace, and thus that human beings cannot do good or avoid evil apart from divine grace. This teaching called for repentance as a response to divine grace, which often took the form of a dramatic experience of "awakening" on the part of early Methodist people, an experience in which they came to recognize their own need for divine help. The doctrine of original sin is affirmed in Methodist doctrinal standards, and in associating themselves with the "Joint Declaration on the Doctrine of Justification" originally agreed on by the Catholic Church and the Lutheran World Federation, the World Methodist Council declared in 2006, "According to John Wesley the doctrine of original sin is an essential Christian doctrine. The corruption of human nature cannot be cured by ourselves."[42]

Chapter 1 has shown that John Wesley coupled discussion of original sin with his belief in original righteousness, and this is related to his sense of the goodness that God intended for the whole creation. That chapter also discussed John Wesley's private doubts about whether humans would be liable to damnation on the basis of original sin alone, and an important fact in Methodist doctrine is that the Methodist Article of Religion on original sin omits a critical phrase in the Anglican Article, leaving open the question of whether humans inherit guilt as a result of original sin.

Leaving this question open may seem to open the door to a Pelagian claim of human self-reliance, and some Methodist theologians and preachers have been tempted in this direction,[43] but this has not been the case with communally sanctioned doctrine that makes it clear that whether or not human beings inherit guilt from their parents, they are nevertheless liable to sin and are not capable apart from divine help or grace to be forgiven or overcome sin. The doctrines of original righteousness and original sin, then, are not only affirmations of common Christian teachings but they are also a critical presupposition of the Wesleyan understanding of the "way of salvation."

6. Distinctive Belief in Universally Available Prevenient Grace

Wesleyan sources: John Wesley gives a definition of "preventing grace," which includes the claim that this grace is available to every person in "The Scripture Way of Salvation," I:2 (in Outler, ed., *Sermons*, 2:156–57; in Jackson, ed., *Works*, 6:44). **Doctrinal sources:** Church of the Nazarene Articles of Faith, articles 7 and 8 (cf. Pelikan and Hotchkiss, 3:411, 412); World Methodist Council, "Wesleyan Essentials of Christian Faith," section on "Our Witness": "We seek the realization of God's will for the salvation of humankind" (in WMC *Handbook of Information 2007–2011*, 96–97). **Methodist theologians:** Summers, *Systematic Theology* VI (2:31–90). **Secondary sources:** Williams, *John Wesley's Theology Today*, 41–46; Maddox, *Responsible Grace*, 83–93; Runyon, *New Creation*, 26–42; Campbell, *Methodist Doctrine*, 50–52, 53–56; Jones, *United Methodist Doctrine*, 156–73, 180–82; Collins, *Theology of John Wesley*, 73–82.

The British Methodist *Senior Catechism* (1952) claimed that the Methodist Church "continues as a witness to the universal grace of God." John Wesley and nineteenth-century Methodist theologians called this grace *preventing* grace. Due to the shifting connotations of the word *prevent*, contemporary Wesleyans have preferred to call it "prevenient grace," the grace that "prevenes" or comes before justification and makes possible our turning to God. The distinctive claim that Wesleyan communities have consistently made, against proponents of limited atonement, is that this grace is available to all human beings. Christ is "the true light, which enlightens everyone" (John 1:9) and "this is right and is acceptable in the sight of God our Savior, who desires everyone to be saved" (1 Tim. 2:3-4a), so John Wesley claimed that "preventing" grace "works in every child of man,"[44] and his brother Charles expounded the universal invitation in this manner:

> Come, sinners, to the gospel feast,
> Let every soul be JESUS' guest;
> You need not one be left behind,
> For GOD hath bidden all mankind.[45]

The evangelistic mission of Wesleyan communities is grounded in this claim of universal prevenient grace and its implication, that all persons can come to Christian faith. Charles Wesley drew this implication in graphic terms:

> Harlots, and publicans, and thieves
> In holy triumph join;
> Saved is the sinner that believes
> From crimes as great as mine.
>
> Murderers, and all ye hellish crew,
> Ye sons of lust and pride,
> Believe the Saviour died for you;
> For me the Saviour died.[46]

Wesleyan evangelistic outreach has also been grounded in a post-millennial eschatological vision, according to which the sanctification of the world leading to the second advent of Christ involves evangelistic outreach to the whole world (see section 14 below).[47]

In an ecumenical perspective, the teaching of universally available prevenient grace has placed Wesleyan communities at odds with versions of the doctrine of predestination taught by some Catholics (late medieval Augustinians, and Dominicans in the controversy *De Auxiliis* of the late sixteenth century), and by Lutheran as well as Reformed churches. The Wesleyan perspective contrasts particularly sharply with Reformed understandings of limited atonement, and much of Methodist polemic literature, from the time of John Wesley and forward, was directed against the doctrine of limited atonement. In North American Methodist circles, this issue was of special concern given the strong Puritan cultural core that had been established in New England from the seventeenth century.[48] The Wesleyan perspective has affinities with ancient Christian writers prior to the time of Augustine (for example, Irenaeus, Clement of Alexandria, and Origen), with a long tradition of Eastern Christian thought and spirituality that grew from these patristic sources, with specific Catholic theological traditions (such as that of the Jesuits in the sixteenth-century controversy *De Auxiliis*), with Protestant Remonstrants (Arminians), and with those in the Church of England in the seventeenth century who identified themselves as Arminians (for example, the party associated with Archbishop William Laud).[49]

It has been important in ecumenical discussions to make the point that the Wesleyan understanding of prevenient grace rules out Pelagianism and insists that any possibility of human turning to God is the result of God's prior gift of grace. This is stated explicitly in the World Methodist Council's "Statement of Methodist Association" (2006) with the "Joint Declaration on the Doctrine of Justification." After stating that the doctrine of original sin has been held as a necessary or essential Christian teaching in Wesleyan communities, the statement makes the following claim:

> The destructive effects of the Fall are countered by the universal availability of prevenient grace (Sermon 85, On Working Out Our Own Salvation, III.4). That people are able to respond to God's call is due only to God's prior work. According to Wesley, the grace of God "assists" but does not "force" the human response (Sermon 63, The General Spread of the Gospel, 11). By God's grace believers are commissioned and empowered to tell people that God has reconciled the world to himself and to entreat them on behalf of Jesus Christ to be reconciled to God (2 Corinthians 5:20).[50]

Another way to put this is to say that for salvation to be the result of God's grace, there must be some divine work that goes before (pre-) our believing in Christ, our justification. Predestination was one way of accounting for this, although in many of its forms it raised the problem of limited atonement. Prevenient grace is an alternative that maintains the prior (pre-) work of divine grace but rejects belief in limited atonement.

7. Common Belief in Justification by Faith Alone

Ecumenical sources: "Joint Declaration on the Doctrine of Justification," to which the World Methodist Council became a signatory on 23 July 2006.[51] Anglican and Reformation sources: Augsburg Confession 4 (in Pelikan and Hotchkiss, 2:60–61; in Leith, *Creeds of the Churches*, 69); Anglican Articles of Religion 11 (in Pelikan and Hotchkiss, 2:531; in Leith, *Creeds of the Churches*, 271); Westminster Confession of Faith 11–12, 14 (in Pelikan and Hotchkiss, 2:620–22, 623; in Leith, *Creeds of the Churches*, 207–8, 209). Wesleyan sources: John Wesley, "The New Birth," introduction, ¶ 1 (in Outler, ed., *Sermons*, 2:187; and in Sugden, ed., *Sermons*, 2:226–27) claimed that the doctrine of justification by faith alone is a necessary Christian doctrine; cf. his sermon "Justification by Faith," introduction, ¶ 1 (in Outler, ed., *Sermons*, 1:182). Doctrinal sources: Methodist Articles of Religion 9 (in Pelikan and Hotchkiss, 3:203; in Leith, ed., *Creeds of the Churches*, 356); United Methodist Confession of Faith, Article 9 (UMC *Discipline* 2008, ¶ 103, p. 69); Church of the Nazarene Articles of Faith, article 9 (cf. Pelikan and Hotchkiss, 3:412); World Methodist Council, "Wesleyan Essentials of Christian Faith," section on "Our Beliefs": "Methodists believe in the centrality of grace; prevenient, justifying, and sanctifying" (in WMC *Handbook of Information 2007–2011*, 96). Methodist theologians: Watson, *Theological Institutes*, II:23 (1857 edition, 475–508); Summers, *Systematic Theology*, VI:III (2:91–127); Raymond, *Systematic Theology*, IV:III (2:319–44); Pope, *Compendium of Christian Theology*, chapter on "The Administration of Redemption" (1880 printing, 2:371–451); Miley, *Systematic Theology*, V:[2]:5 (2:308–26). Secondary sources: William R. Cannon, *The Theology of John Wesley with Special Reference to the Doctrine of Justification* (New York: Abingdon-Cokesbury Press, 1946); Williams, *John Wesley's Theology Today*, 57–73; Outler, *Theology in the Wesleyan Spirit*, 45–64; Maddox, *Responsible Grace*, 141–76; Campbell, *Methodist Doctrine*, 56–58; Jones, *United Methodist Doctrine*, 175–80, 182–93; Collins, *Theology of John Wesley*, 155–89.

Interpretations of Wesleyan theology up to the present time have stated that the doctrine of justification by faith is one of the cardinal doctrines of the Protestant Reformation that John and Charles Wesley and Wesleyan communities after them inherited. This remains true, but this doctrine has become a point of critical ecumenical convergence in the last decade with the signing of the

"Joint Declaration on the Doctrine of Justification," originally between churches of the Lutheran World Federation and the Catholic Church (31 October 1999). The World Methodist Council became a signatory to this declaration on 23 July 2006. In affirming John Wesley's sermons and in their own doctrinal statements, and now with the signing of the "Joint Declaration," Wesleyan churches have affirmed in company with the broader Christian community that the forgiveness of our sins, justification, comes about by faith in Christ through the work of God's grace.

John Wesley's sermons on faith and justification as well as his brother's hymns on these subjects insist that Christian faith cannot be a matter of the understanding only; true Christian faith, like true repentance, must be a matter of the heart and the affections. The faith through which human beings are saved, John Wesley wrote, "is not a barely speculative, rational thing, a cold, lifeless assent, a train of ideas in the head; but also a disposition of the heart. For thus saith the Scripture, 'With the heart man believeth unto righteousness.' "[52] That is to say, true Christian faith engages the whole of a person's being, including their affections, and this links the Wesleyan understanding of justifying faith with the Wesleyan emphasis on religious experience ("perceptible inspiration") discussed in chapter 2 and in section 4 above. This teaching was historically the ground of Methodist preachers' insistence on the conversion of the heart, and the hymns of Charles Wesley as well as later spirituals and gospel songs performed or enacted this understanding of Christian faith as the turning of the heart to Jesus Christ.

The emphasis on the role of the heart in justifying faith has sometimes left Methodists vulnerable to the charge that justifying faith is (for them) *merely* or *simply* or *only* a matter of the heart or emotions. This was not what Wesley claimed nor what Methodist doctrinal statements assert, since they all claim that trust in Christ as the source of our salvation is a component of justifying faith as well as the conversion of the heart. Perhaps, however, this suspicion of the Methodist tendency to emphasize the role of the heart and the affections in justifying faith is the reason why the World Methodist Council's "Statement of Association" with the "Joint Declaration on the Doctrine of Justification" does not specifically name this aspect of Wesleyan understanding of the nature of justifying faith in its account of Methodist teachings on justification. I would note, however, that the Methodist "Statement of Association" does explicitly name the doctrine of assurance of pardon (see the next section) as a distinctive Wesleyan accompaniment to the doctrine of justification by faith alone.

8. Distinctive Beliefs in Affective Faith and the Assurance of Pardon

Wesleyan sources: "The Witness of the Spirit," discourses I and II (in Outler, ed., *Sermons*, 1:267–98; in Jackson, ed., *Works*, 5:111–34) and "The Witness of Our Own Spirit" (in Outler, ed., *Sermons*, 1:299–313; in Jackson, ed., *Works*, 5:134–44). **Doctrinal sources:** Church of the Nazarene Articles of Faith, article 9 (cf. Pelikan and Hotchkiss, 3:412): "that to this work and state of grace the Holy Spirit bears witness." **Catechetical sources:** the *Methodist Catechism* of the Methodist Church in Ireland (1946), qu. 64 (p. 23); *Senior Catechism of the Methodist Church* (Methodist Church of Great Britain, 1952), qu. 42 (p. 12); *Catechism for the Use of the People Called Methodists*, qu. 68 (p. 36). **Secondary sources:** Williams, *John Wesley's Theology Today*, 102–14; Maddox, *Responsible Grace*, 124–28; Runyon, *New Creation*, 58–70; Campbell, *Methodist Doctrine*, 56–58; Jones, *United Methodist Doctrine*, 205–6; Collins, *Theology of John Wesley*, 129–42.

Section 4 above, on the distinctive emphasis on religious experience and religious affections in Wesleyan cultures, has emphasized how important "the heart" and affections have been for Methodist life. Chapters 2 (on John Wesley) and 3 (on Charles Wesley) have shown that Christian faith involved for the Wesleys a combination of two elements. One element was the insistence that Christian faith must involve the heart and the affections: "it is not barely a speculative, rational thing, a cold, lifeless assent, a train of ideas in the head; but also a disposition of the heart."[53] The other element was the notion that Christian faith normatively bears with it a supernaturally given assurance of pardon. At points in his career, especially in the 1730s and 1740s, John Wesley could define Christian faith as involving the heartfelt belief that Christ has forgiven one's sins, and in this way that faith itself was defined as necessarily involving the assurance of pardon.

The *Senior Catechism of the Methodist Church* (Methodist Church of Great Britain, 1952) claimed that a second distinctive mark of the

Methodist Church beyond its claim of universally available grace is "a witness...to the gift of assurance by the Holy Spirit."[54] Wesleyan communities from the time of John and Charles Wesley have consistently claimed that it is possible for a believer to know of the forgiveness of their sins in two ways: one is through the direct witness of the Holy Spirit, a supernatural, inwardly given assurance of the forgiveness of sins; the other is through "the witness of our own spirit," which means the evidence of a change of life by which one can see that divine grace has brought about a decisive change. Chapter 5 above has shown how Methodists in the nineteenth and twentieth centuries testified to the experience of assurance (typically accompanying conversion, but in the narrative given by James K. Mathews, a few years after his conversion).

The claim of a direct witness of the Spirit was not unique to the Wesleyan movement. Pietistic Puritan authors such as William Perkins and William Ames and Calvinistic Evangelicals such as George Whitefield had claimed such a witness, which in their understanding was an assurance that one was among God's elect.[55] But the claim was controversial and has remained so through the history of Wesleyan communities, especially as these communities have interpreted John Wesley's Aldersgate Street experience of 24 May 1738. The controversy over the interpretation of this experience can be seen in two biographies produced immediately after John Wesley's death. The biography of Wesley by Thomas Coke and Henry Moore (1792) represented the Aldersgate Street experience straightforwardly as Wesley's conversion and regeneration, allocating Wesley's later corrections to his account to footnotes and playing down subsequent references to Wesley's remaining struggles and doubts.[56] John Whitehead's biography (1793 and 1796), by contrast, gave considerable attention to Wesley's later corrections to the account of Aldersgate and the period preceding it, and also to Wesley's continuing struggles and doubts after the event.[57] The controversies continued, as can be seen in the papers given to celebrate the 200th anniversary of Aldersgate in 1938 and in interpretations given in celebration of the 250th anniversary of Aldersgate in 1988.[58]

As I see it, the controversy is not over the *possibility* of a supernatural assurance of pardon; it is, rather, over the claim that John Wesley often made that there is no true Christian faith apart from such an assurance, that is, that the very definition of justifying faith implies such an assurance. It is true that John Wesley allowed "exempt cases" or exceptions to this,[59] but his insistence on the normative nature of this experience landed him more than once in semantic as well as theological quagmires, for example, when, in opposition to particular Moravian views, he stated that a person may have "*a degree* of justifying faith" before that person is "wholly free from all doubt and fear; and before he has, in the full, proper sense, a new, a clean heart."[60] I understand that what Wesley meant here is that one could actually have justifying faith apart from the experience of assurance, as an exception to what he took to be the general rule, namely, that such an assurance accompanied justifying faith. But from an ecumenical perspective, the notion of having "a degree of justifying faith" is a very problematic conception because it is difficult to imagine that justification or justifying faith could have "degrees." Either one's sins are pardoned or they are not. Contemporary Methodist expressions of this teaching in ecumenical contexts have typically stated only the possibility of such an experience, not its normative nature.[61]

Here I venture a more intuitive perception, which is that Wesleyan communities have in fact found it very difficult to maintain the specific claim that Wesley made in regard to the necessity or normative nature of the experience of assurance. Although Methodist communities today insist that justifying faith must be a matter of the heart, that is, must represent a heartfelt turning to Jesus Christ, they do not, to my knowledge, insist that this affective conversion will necessarily involve a specific supernatural assurance that one's sins have been forgiven. It could hardly be expected that a person should experience conversion primarily as an assurance of pardon from sin when that person has not been inculturated in such a way that he or she is conscious both of his or her own sinfulness and of the dire consequences of it. Such a vivid consciousness of sin is rare even in the most traditional of Evangelical communities today.[62]

Consequently, my judgment is that Methodists have been correct since the time of John and Charles Wesley in insisting that true Christian faith must engage the heart and the affections (see the discussion of justifying faith in the previous section and the discussion of religious experience and affections in section 4 above). However one describes the wholeness of human personality, our most basic religious commitment must engage the wholeness of humanity, and this, I would maintain, is a gem of wisdom in historic Wesleyan teachings on the nature of justifying faith. The assertion at the head of this item stands, then, because Wesleyan communities do continue to claim that a person can know the forgiveness of sins, but it might be an agendum for any future revision of Methodist doctrinal standards to consider if the experience of Methodist communities since the time of the Wesleys might help their heirs discern and state more carefully the wisdom that they can offer on the matter of justification and assurance.

9. Common Beliefs about Regeneration and Sanctification

Anglican and Reformation sources: Anglican Articles of Religion 27 (in Pelikan and Hotchkiss, 2:535; in Leith, *Creeds of the Churches*, 275–76); Westminster Confession of Faith 13:1 (in Pelikan and Hotchkiss, 2:622; in Leith, *Creeds of the Churches*, 208). **Wesleyan sources:** John Wesley insisted that the doctrine of regeneration is a necessary Christian doctrine in "The New Birth," Introduction, ¶ 1 (in Outler, ed., *Sermons*, 2:187; and in Sugden, ed., *Sermons*, 2:226–27); "Letter to a Roman Catholic," ¶ 6 (in Jackson, ed., *Works*, 10:81). **Doctrinal sources:** United Methodist Confession of Faith, Articles 9–11 (UMC *Discipline* 2008, ¶ 103, pp. 69–70); Church of the Nazarene Articles of Faith, article 9 (cf. Pelikan and Hotchkiss, 3:412); World Methodist Council, "Wesleyan Essentials of Christian Faith," section on "Our Beliefs": "Methodists believe in the centrality of grace; prevenient, justifying, and sanctifying" (in WMC *Handbook of Information 2007–2011*, 96). **Methodist theologians:** Watson, *Theological Institutes*, II:24, 29 (1857 edition, 509–19, 611–15); Raymond, *Systematic Theology*, IV:III (2:344–406); Pope, *Compendium of Christian Theology*, "The Administration of Redemption (continued)" (1880 printing, 3:1–100); Miley, *Systematic Theology*, V:[2]:6–8 (2:327–84). **Secondary sources:** Williams, *John Wesley's Theology Today*, 98–140, 167–90; Outler, *Theology in the Wesleyan Spirit*, 73–74; Maddox, *Responsible Grace*, 159–60, 170, 176–77; Runyon, *New Creation*, 71–91; Campbell, *Methodist Doctrine*, 58–61; Jones, *United Methodist Doctrine*, 195–210; Collins, *Theology of John Wesley*, 195–235.

John Wesley claimed that regeneration, as well as justification, is a necessary teaching, and he maintained that these two events usually occur simultaneously. However, it was important to make a distinction between them, because justification denotes pardon or the forgiveness of past sins, while regeneration marks the beginning of the new life in Christ and the process of sanctification. We can paraphrase this by saying that at the same moment as a person is forgiven of her or his sin (justification), that person is born again to a new life in Christ (regeneration). In John Wesley's own formulation, "there is a *real* as well as a *relative* change. We are inwardly renewed by the power of God."[63] Insofar as regeneration is understood as the beginning of sanctification, I will deal with these topics together as they relate to Methodist affirmation of common Christian teachings. It is a distinctly Wesleyan nuance to claim that the doctrines of regeneration and sanctification are essential or necessary Christian doctrines; other Christian communities may affirm a process of sanctification following conversion (for example, Baptists often speak of "the Lordship of Jesus Christ") but do not state this as an essential or core belief alongside the teaching about justification by faith.

The World Methodist Council's "Statement of Association" with the "Joint Declaration on the Doctrine of Justification" makes the point that Methodist understandings of regeneration and sanctification are linked to Methodist understandings of justification:

> The deep connection between forgiveness of sins and making righteous, between justification and sanctification, has always been crucial for the Methodist understanding of the biblical doctrine of justification. John Wesley saw in salvation a twofold action of God's grace: "By justification we are saved from the guilt of sin and restored to the favor of God; by sanctification we are saved from the power and root of sin, restored to the image of God" (Sermon 85, II.1). The redemptive acceptance into communion with God and the creative renewal of our lives are entirely the work of God's grace.[64]

There is of course a very specific Wesleyan emphasis in the doctrine of sanctification, namely, the teaching that Christians may expect to be entirely sanctified in this life (see the next item). But this teaching also links the Wesleyan emphasis on regeneration and sanctification with the broader church's understanding of the Christian quest for holiness, godliness, sanctity, and saintliness. It links Wesleyan communities with "the communion of saints," the fellowship of those whose lives have been marked by the holiness that is the gift of divine grace to Christians in every age. Chapter 3 has shown this belief to have been a prominent theme in Charles Wesley's hymnody.

10. Distinctive Belief in Entire Sanctification

Wesleyan sources: John Wesley, "Christian Perfection" (in Outler, ed., *Sermons*, 2:97–121; in Jackson, ed., *Works*, 6:1–19). **Doctrinal sources:** United Methodist Confession of Faith, Article 11 (in UMC *Discipline* 2008, ¶ 103, pp. 69–70); Church of the Nazarene Articles of Faith, article 10 (cf. Pelikan and Hotchkiss, 3:412). **Secondary sources:** Williams, *John Wesley's Theology Today*, 167–90; Outler, *Theology in the Wesleyan Spirit*, 65–88; Maddox, *Responsible Grace*, 179–90; Runyon, *New Creation*, 91–101, 222–33; Campbell, *Methodist Doctrine*, 61–63; Jones, *United Methodist Doctrine*, 210–16; Collins, *Theology of John Wesley*, 279–312.

Wesleyan communities have often defined their distinctive mission as related to the cultivation of holiness and specifically, to the cultivation of "entire sanctification" or "Christian perfection," which John Wesley called "the grand depositum which God has lodged with the people called Methodists."[65] The doctrinal grounds for this belief lie in Wesley's sermon corpus, not only the sermon entitled "Christian Perfection" but in many of the Standard Sermons that urge believers to pursue the goal of entire sanctification or Christian perfection. The teaching is also grounded in Charles Wesley's hymns, for example, the well-known and much-used hymn "Love Divine, All Loves Excelling," which specifically describes entire sanctification. The United Methodist Church has a nonbinding doctrinal article, "Of Sanctification," inherited from The Methodist Protestant Church, and its constitutionally binding Confession of Faith has an article, "Sanctification and Christian Perfection." Chapter 5 above has shown how three Methodist women in the nineteenth century described their experiences of entire sanctification.

Candidates for the orders of deacon and elder in many Methodist denominations, including The United Methodist Church, are asked a series of questions publicly before they can be ordained. The first four of these questions are as follows:

(1) Have you faith in Christ?
(2) Are you going on to perfection?
(3) Do you expect to be made perfect in love in this life?
(4) Are you earnestly striving after it?[66]

The third question is perhaps the most difficult for candidates, especially if "expect to be made perfect in love" is understood to mean "predict that you will be made perfect in love." This may be a misreading, since in eighteenth-century parlance, "expect" could carry the sense "look forward to," thus the question might be paraphrased, "Are you looking forward to being made perfect in love in this life?" But the point here is that all candidates for ordained ministry under this discipline must make a solemn and public vow that they are "going on to perfection," that they "expect" or look forward to it, and that they are "earnestly striving" for it.

The doctrine of entire sanctification has at some points proved an embarrassment to Methodists, perhaps especially to those involved in ecumenical dialogue with other Protestant churches for which any talk of "Christian perfection" may be seen as an arrogant claim to an attribute (perfection) that should be predicated only of God.[67] In ecumenical discussions, Wesleyans have been concerned to explain that Christian perfection "is not the absolute perfection which belongs to God alone; and," quoting Wesley at this point, "it 'does not imply an exemption either from ignorance, or mistake, or infirmities, or temptations.' "[68]

The doctrine of entire sanctification is a great gift at the heart of historic Wesleyan communities, a gift that, I am inclined to say, Wesleyan Christians could neglect only at the peril of losing what has been the heart of their distinctive beliefs. It is grounded in the consistent biblical mandate that the end ($\tau \acute{\epsilon} \lambda o \varsigma$) or goal of human existence is complete love for God, and love for our neighbors as the natural concomitant and sign of love for God. The command that follows the $Sh^{e}ma$ $Yisrael$ (Deuteronomy 6:4–5) is the command that Jesus held to be "the greatest commandment." I find John Wesley's twofold rationale for the doctrine of entire sanctification unassailable:

1. God intends that we should love God completely.
2. God can accomplish what God intends.[69]

232

Once these two points are understood, the doctrine of entire sanctification can be understood as the heart of biblical religion.

The focus of Wesleyan communities on the doctrine of entire sanctification gives this doctrine a unique position within the ecumenical community, for holiness or sanctity has often been the province of adepts and ascetics, of monastic communities separated from the world living under a rule. The Methodist societies made it possible to cultivate holiness and live in a world in which modernity was rapidly encroaching. The Wesleyan emphasis on entire sanctification is unique among Evangelical communities and rare among Protestant communities. It creates a space where ancient saintliness can meet modern life and thus it is a gift of grace for the contemporary world.[70]

11. Common Belief about the Church

Ecumenical sources: World Council of Churches Faith and Order study of *The Nature and Mission of the Church: A Stage on the Way to a Common Statement* (Faith and Order paper no. 198; Geneva: World Council of Churches, 2005). **Anglican and Reformation sources:** Augsburg Confession 3 (in Pelikan and Hotchkiss, 2:62–63; in Leith, *Creeds of the Churches*, 68–69); Anglican Articles of Religion 19–21 (in Pelikan and Hotchkiss, 2:533–34; also in Leith, *Creeds of the Churches*, 273); Westminster Confession of Faith 25 (in Pelikan and Hotchkiss, 2:638–39; in Leith, *Creeds of the Churches*, 203–5). **Wesleyan sources:** John Wesley, manuscript giving his definition of the Church of England (cited in Frank Baker, *John Wesley and the Church of England*, 327). Wesley's letter "To Dr. Coke, Mr. Asbury, and Our Brethren in North America" (10 September 1784) is also an important source for his ecclesiology (in Jackson, ed., *Works*, 13:251–52). **Doctrinal sources:** Methodist Articles 16, 17 (in Pelikan and Hotchkiss, 3:205); United Methodist Confession of Faith, Article 5 (in UMC *Discipline* 2008, ¶ 103, pp. 67–68); Church of the Nazarene Articles of Faith, article 11 (cf. Pelikan and Hotchkiss, 3:413); World Methodist Council, "Wesleyan Essentials of Christian Faith," sections on "The People Called Methodists" and "Our Common Life" (in WMC *Handbook of Information 2007–2011*, 95, 98). **Catechetical sources:** *Catechism of The Methodist Episcopal Church* (1852), catechism II, section V, § 1, questions 65 and 64 (in *Pictorial Catechism of The Methodist Episcopal Church*, 20; *Catechisms of the Wesleyan Methodists*, Catechism no. II, section 5, "Of the Holy Ghost," questions 7 and 8, 22–23; *The Catechism (formerly "the Turner Catechism") of the A.M.E. Church,* 19; *Probationer's Manual of The Methodist Episcopal Church* (1914), questions 94 and 95 on p. 38; *Junior Catechism of The Methodist Episcopal Church and the Methodist Episcopal Church, South,* questions 84 and 86, p. 17; cf. *Junior Catechism* published by the CME Church, 19; *Methodist Catechism* (Methodist Church in Ireland, 1948), questions 59 and 60, 21–22; *Senior Catechism of the Methodist Church* (Methodist Church of Great Britain, 1952), questions 19 and 20, p. 6; *Catechism for the Use of the People Called Methodists* (Methodist Church of Great Britain, 1989), question 43, p. 20. **Methodist theologians:** Watson, *Theological Institutes,* IV:1 (1857 edition, 680–99); Summers, *Systematic Theology,* VII:I (2:213–44); Raymond, *Systematic Theology,* book 7, chapter 1 (3:233–42); Pope, *Compendium of Christian Theology,* "The Administration of Redemption (continued)," subsection on "The Church" (1880 printing, 3:259–364); Miley, *Systematic Theology,* V:[2]:9 (2:385–95). **Secondary sources:** Williams, *John Wesley's Theology Today,* 141–66, 207–42; Frank Baker, *John Wesley and the Church of England* passim; Runyon, *New Creation,* 102–7; Campbell, *Methodist Doctrine,* 64–71; Jones, *United Methodist Doctrine,* 246–56; Collins, *Theology of John Wesley,* 237–46.

Chapter 1 above includes the doctrine of the church among John Wesley's understanding of core, common doctrines because although there was no clear assertion on Wesley's part that the doctrine of the church was a necessary Christian doctrine, he did consider the church itself to be necessary to Christian existence. Moreover, he included teaching about the church in his account of common Christian doctrines in the "Letter to a Roman Catholic," and he included an Article of Religion defining the church, derived from that of the Church of England, among the Articles he sent to North America with Thomas Coke in 1784. The first point of his fourth sermon in a series on the Sermon on the Mount was that "Christianity is essentially a social religion; and that to turn it into a solitary religion is indeed to destroy it," and he went on to claim that Christianity "cannot subsist at all, without society,—without living and conversing with other men."[71] This was directed, in the first place, against the practice of anchoritism, but the point he made here is that although a *doctrine* of the church might not be strictly necessary, the *church* as a "society" of believers is necessary for the Christian life. As chapter 6 has shown, Methodist doctrinal statements, catechisms, and works of systematic theology designed for preachers have consistently dealt with the nature of the Christian church.

That chapter has also shown that a critical ambiguity or tension has remained within Wesleyan communities between a model of the church, on the one hand, that emphasizes its missional nature, and a more traditional model of the church emphasizing stability and continuity, according to which the church is constituted as the fellowship of believers in which the Word is preached and the sacraments are administered. Thus the most traditional Methodist doctrinal standards affirm that the church in its fullness or catholicity requires not only a fellowship of believers but also the preaching of the Word and the due administration of the sacraments. Later doctrinal statements, catechisms, and systematic theologies placed strong emphasis on the church as a fellowship of believers that exists primarily to serve its missional objectives. These elements of ecclesiology do not need to be in conflict with each other (see the WCC Faith and Order document on *The Nature and Mission of the Church* discussed at the end of chapter 6), but Methodists have sometimes been forced to make decisions in which one or the other of these understandings of church will be given priority in practice.

Ecumenical engagement through the twentieth century has called on Wesleyan Christians to clarify their understandings of the meaning of church in relation to other bodies of Christians. This motivated Colin W. Williams, Frank Baker, and Albert C. Outler to consider the doctrine of the church, and they noted the tensions I have discussed here and in chapter 6. But on the other hand, the notion of Methodism as a society with a distinctive purpose within the catholic church has also proved fruitful as a way of envisioning future relationships between Methodists and other Christian communities.[72]

12. Common Practice of and Belief about Christian Baptism

Ecumenical sources: World Council of Churches Faith and Order Commission, *Baptism, Eucharist, and Ministry* (1982), section on Baptism. **Anglican and Reformation sources:** Augsburg Confession 9 (in Pelikan and Hotchkiss, 2:63; in Leith, *Creeds of the Churches*, 70–71); Anglican Articles of Religion 27 (in Pelikan and

Hotchkiss, 2:535; also in Leith, *Creeds of the Churches,* 275–76; Westminster Confession of Faith 28 (in Pelikan and Hotchkiss, 2:641–42; in Leith, *Creeds of the Churches,* 224–25). **Wesleyan sources: Doctrinal sources:** Methodist Articles of Religion 17 (in Pelikan and Hotchkiss, 3:205; in Leith, *Creeds of the Churches,* 358); United Methodist Confession of Faith, Article 6 (UMC *Discipline* 2008, ¶ 103, p. 68). United Methodist Statement "By Water and the Spirit," adopted by the 1996 General Conference; Church of the Nazarene Articles of Faith, article 12 (cf. article 13 in the 1952 version in Pelikan and Hotchkiss, 3:413); World Methodist Council, "Wesleyan Essentials of Christian Faith," section on "Our Worship" (in WMC *Handbook of Information 2007–2011,* 96). **Methodist theologians:** Watson, *Theological Institutes,* IV:3 (1857 edition, 703–29); Summers, *Systematic Theology,* VII:V (2:351–404); Raymond, *Systematic Theology,* VII:IV–VI (3:275–342); Pope, *Compendium of Christian Theology,* "The Church" (1880 printing, 3:310–24); Miley, *Systematic Theology,* V:[2]:9 (2:395–410). **Secondary sources:** Williams, *John Wesley's Theology Today,* 115–22; Bernard G. Holland, *Baptism in Early Methodism* (1970); Laurence H. Stookey, *Baptism: Christ's Act in the Church* (1982); Gayle Carlton Felton, *This Gift of Water: The Practice and Theology of Baptism among Methodists in America* (1993); Maddox, *Responsible Grace,* 221–28; Runyon, *New Creation,* 140–45; Campbell, *Methodist Doctrine,* 71–74; Jones, *United Methodist Doctrine,* 256–62; Collins, *Theology of John Wesley,* 262–65.

One of the reasons why baptism has sometimes presented a problem to Methodist churches is that it was so little practiced or discussed in early Methodist circles. For the first decades of Methodism's existence, baptism was practiced within the context of the Church of England, and only after the crisis of the American Revolution and the independent existence of Methodist churches (from 1784) did it come to be practiced within Wesleyan communities by their own clergy. Much of baptismal doctrine and practice was presupposed in this critical transition from religious societies to churches.

As seen in the previous item and in chapter 6, the Methodist Articles of Religion affirmed by the AME, AME Zion, CME, and UM churches assert that the church is constituted by a body of the faithful where the Word is preached and the sacraments are administered, and the Articles go on to define the sacraments as including baptism and the Lord's Supper. To the extent that the British Methodist Church (and churches that follow the British pattern) "loyally accepts the fundamental principles of the historic creeds and the Protestant Reformation," they would be committed to a similar definition, since it was not only stated in the Anglican Article of Religion but also in the Augsburg Confession before it and Methodist churches of the British pattern also practice baptism in the same ways as other Methodist churches.[73] Thus baptism is understood to be an essential or constitutive practice for Christian churches according to Methodist doctrinal sources.

The status of Methodist doctrinal statements on the relationship between baptism and the new birth (regeneration) has been disputed. Chapter 1 has shown that John Wesley believed that infants are born again when baptized, although he has been accused of inconsistency in believing this and also claiming that adults stand in need of new birth by an affective conversion experience. An article published in 1824 in the *Wesleyan-Methodist Magazine* by "T.J." (almost certainly Thomas Jackson) offered the following summary of Wesley's views, and it remains the most accurate summary I am aware of:

[Wesley] not only acknowledged that a gracious communication is made to the minds of children in baptism, but to the effect of that communication he gave the name of the New Birth....Mr. Wesley, nevertheless, denied that the same effect is invariably produced in cases of adult baptism; and believed that those children who receive that blessing in their infancy, generally lose it as they grow in years, and mix with the world. He also believed that when they are brought under the power of sinful affections and habits, the renewal of their minds in righteousness and true holiness, after the image of God, becomes a matter of indispensable necessity; and to that renewal, whenever it is effected, and how often soever it may be repeated, he used to give the name of REGENERATION, or of the NEW BIRTH.[74]

Charles R. Hohenstein has pointed out that the belief that infants—but not necessarily adults—are regenerate as a result of baptism is consistent with the long-standing Catholic tradition that maintained that the grace of the sacrament was effective so long as a person did not disbelieve or otherwise reject the faith into which he or she had been baptized.[75] On the other hand, it might also reflect the Reformed understanding that regeneration is normatively associated with baptism, but which maintains that the moment of application of water might not coincide with the divine gift of the new birth.[76]

The Methodist Articles of Religion utilized in the AME, AME Zion, CME, and UM churches, reflecting the revision of the Articles of Religion that accompanied the *Sunday Service* of 1784, omitted a key phrase from the Anglican Article on baptism that asserted that

> as by an instrument, they that receive Baptism rightly are grafted into the Church; the promises of forgiveness of sin, and our adoption to be the sons of God by the Holy Ghost, are visibly signed and sealed; Faith is confirmed, and Grace increased by virtue of prayer unto God.[77]

This critical omission makes the Methodist Article of Religion on baptism much less clear on the matter of whether regeneration is conveyed in the sacrament, and in fact the Confession of Faith of The United Methodist Church, derived from The Evangelical United Brethren Church, speaks of baptism only as "a symbol of repentance and inner cleansing from sin, a representation of the new birth in Christ Jesus and a mark of discipleship."[78] Similarly, a 1996 United Methodist statement on baptism, "By Water and the Spirit," asserts that "new birth may not always coincide with the moment of the administration of water or the laying on of hands."[79]

It is a matter of doctrine and of consistent liturgical practice in Wesleyan churches that infants are incorporated into the Christian community through baptism. In recent decades Methodist churches have been influenced by ecumenical work on baptism and by the liturgical renewal movement, both of which have stressed the normative nature of adult baptism accompanied by profession of the faith. This is represented, for example, in the 1982 World Council of Churches Faith and Order Commission consensus statement, *Baptism, Eucharist and Ministry*, which states that "baptism upon personal profession of faith is the most clearly attested pattern in the New Testament documents."[80] This does not mean a rejection of infant baptism but it does mean that adult baptism should be seen as a theologically normative practice, and the fact that the *United Methodist Hymnal* of 1989 places the rite of Christian baptism for those who are able to make a public profession of their faith *before* the rite of baptism for infants and other persons unable to answer for themselves (reversing the positions in previous Methodist hymnals) shows the influence of this ecumenical trend on Wesleyan communities today. The form for adult baptism in this hymnal also includes an interrogative form for the profession of faith utilizing the words of the Apostles' Creed, following the ancient pattern attested in such documents as the Latin recension of *The Apostolic Tradition*.[81]

13. Common Practice of and Belief about the Lord's Supper

Ecumenical sources: World Council of Churches Faith and Order Commission, *Baptism, Eucharist and Ministry* (1982), section on Eucharist. **Anglican and Reformation sources:** Augsburg Confession 3 (in Pelikan and Hotchkiss, 2:64; in Leith, *Creeds of the Churches*, 71); Anglican Articles of Religion 28–30 (in Pelikan and Hotchkiss, 2:535–36; also in Leith, *Creeds of the Churches*, 276–77); Westminster Confession of Faith 24 (in Pelikan and Hotchkiss, 2:642–44; in Leith, *Creeds of the Churches*, 225–27). **Wesleyan sources:** John Wesley, "The Duty of Constant Communion" (in Outler, ed., *Sermons*, 3:427–39); John and Charles Wesley, *Hymns on the Lord's Supper* (1745), including their abridgment of Brevint's *Christian Sacrament and Sacrifice*. Both of these sources are given in Rattenbury's edition of the *Eucharistic Hymns of John and Charles Wesley*. **Doctrinal sources:** Methodist Articles of Religion 18–20 (in Pelikan and Hotchkiss, 3:205–6; in Leith, *Creeds of the Churches*, 358–59); United Methodist Confession of Faith, Article 6 (UMC *Discipline* 2008, ¶ 103, p. 68); United Methodist Church statement "This Holy Mystery" approved by the 2004 General Conference; Church of the Nazarene Articles of Faith, article 14 (cf. article 13 in the 1952 version in Pelikan and Hotchkiss, 3:413); World Methodist Council, "Wesleyan Essentials of Christian Faith," section on "Our Worship" (in WMC *Handbook of Information 2007–2011*, 96). **Methodist theologians:** Watson, *Theological Institutes*, IV:4 (1857 edition, 729–35); Summers, *Systematic Theology* VII:VI (2:405–70); Raymond, *Systematic Theology*, VII:VII (3:343–71); Pope, *Compendium of Christian Theology*, "The Church" (1880 printing, 3:325–34); Miley, *Systematic Theology* V:[2]:9 (2:411–15). **Secondary sources:** Laurence H. Stookey, *Eucharist: Christ's Feast with the Church*

(1993); Mark Stamm, *Let Every Soul Be Jesus' Guest: A Theology of the Open Table* (2005); Williams, *John Wesley's Theology Today*, 158–66; Maddox, *Responsible Grace*, 202–5; Runyon, *New Creation*, 128–40; Campbell, *Methodist Doctrine*, 74–78; Jones, *United Methodist Doctrine*, 262–66; Collins, *Theology of John Wesley*, 259–62.

John Wesley included the Lord's Supper in every list of the "means of grace" or "ordinances of God" that he gave out as normative practices for the Christian community. Methodist hymnals, doctrinal standards, catechisms, systematic theologies prepared for the training of preachers, and consistent liturgical practice all reinforce the priority of the sacrament of the Lord's Supper in Wesleyan communities. Moreover, from the time when John and Charles Wesley purchased the West Street Chapel in London (1749), Methodists had celebrated the Lord's Supper within their own communities with increasing frequency, so that by the 1780s and 1790s when Methodists became independent churches in North America and Britain, the celebration of the sacrament was a common practice. In this respect, the sacrament of the Lord's Supper differed from the sacrament of baptism, for which there had been no such consistent precedent for celebration within Wesleyan communities.

Methodist people have inherited a sacramental piety that expects to find divine grace in the sacrament, though the precise mode of Christ's presence has not been spelled out with great clarity. One cannot read the Wesleys' *Hymns on the Lord's Supper* without recognizing the depth of reverential piety with which they are endued. These hymns sometimes utilize the precise Reformed language of receptionism and virtualism, that is, the teachings that those who receive the sacrament with faith (receptionism) experience a distinctive form of divine power (the Latin term was *virtus*, thus virtualism) as if they were encountering Jesus Christ directly:

> Let the wisest mortal show
> How we the grace receive,
> Feeble elements bestow
> A power not theirs to give.
> Who explains the wondrous way,
> How through these the virtue came?
> These the virtue did convey,
> Yet still remain the same.[82]

As shown in chapters 1 and 3, the term "virtue" in this instance does not denote moral virtue but rather represents the distinct "power" available in the sacrament ("a power not theirs to give"), and it is precisely the term that Calvin had used to describe the manner of Christ's presence in the Supper.[83] One could utilize the term "real presence" to describe the Wesleys' view of the presence of Christ (the Wesleys themselves used this expression twice in the *Hymns on the Lord's Supper*),[84] but one could not be sure that this term meant anything different from virtualism (see the comments on this in chapter 1). In any case, the Wesleys' piety here, parallel to what John Wesley wrote about "philosophical explanations" of the doctrine of the Trinity, ends not in a precise explanation but in adoration and mystery. Speaking again of Christ's presence, they write of the mystery of Christ's presence and power in the sacrament:

> Angels round our altars bow
> To search it out in vain.[85]

From some point in the nineteenth century, it became the custom of Methodists to invite other Christians to participate in the sacrament of the Lord's Supper. Although this practice was not grounded in doctrinal sources—and it may be important to state that it is not ruled out in doctrinal sources—the practice of open communion has become nearly universal in Methodist churches and stands as an instance of doctrine that has come into existence as a communal consensus arrived at without formal means of consent.[86] Prospective Methodist communicants are bound, as Scott J. Jones points out, to the terms expressed in the invitation to holy communion in historic and contemporary liturgies, which, quoting a summary of these invitations by Jones, "basically invite those who are Christians to come and participate in the sacrament."[87]

As in other areas of church life, Wesleyan communities have been influenced from the twentieth century by the ecumenical and liturgical movements, and the liturgies for the celebration of the Lord's Supper in British, American, and many international Methodist churches have evolved in ways that now show very close similarities to eucharistic liturgies in Catholic, Anglican, Lutheran, and Reformed churches. Ecumenical reflection on the meaning of the Lord's Supper, such as the section on the Eucharist in the 1982 WCC Faith and Order study of *Baptism, Eucharist and Ministry*, have emphasized a variety of meanings of the Supper beyond the traditional debates about the mode of Christ's presence. This document, for example, asks Christian communities to think of the Lord's Supper as thanksgiving to the Father, the *anamnesis* or remembrance of Christ, the invocation of the Holy Spirit, the fellowship or communion of the faithful, and the feast of the Kingdom.[88] Many of these meanings are present in traditional as well as contemporary liturgies for the Lord's Supper.

14. Common Christian Hope

Anglican and Reformation sources: Augsburg Confession 17 (in Pelikan and Hotchkiss, 2:68; in Leith, *Creeds of the Churches*, 73); Anglican Articles of Religion 4 (in Pelikan and Hotchkiss, 2:528; in Leith, *Creeds of the Churches*, 267; Westminster Confession of Faith 32–33 (in Pelikan and Hotchkiss, 2:646–47; in Leith, *Creeds of the Churches*, 228–30). **Wesleyan sources:** "Letter to a Roman Catholic," ¶ 10 (in Jackson, ed., *Works*, 10:82); *Explanatory Notes upon the New Testament*, on Revelation and other eschatological loci. **Doctrinal sources:** Methodist Articles of Religion 14 (in Pelikan and Hotchkiss, 3:204; in Leith, *Creeds of the Churches*, 357); United Methodist Confession of Faith, Article 12 (UMC *Discipline* 2008, ¶ 103, p. 70); Church of the Nazarene Articles of Faith, articles 15–16 (not in the 1952 version given in Pelikan and Hotchkiss); World Methodist Council, "Wesleyan Essentials of Christian Faith," section on "Our Witness": "We witness to God's reign among us now, as proclaimed by Jesus, and look forward to the full realization of the coming Kingdom when every form of evil will be destroyed" (in WMC *Handbook of Information 2007–2011*, 97). **Methodist theologians:** Watson, *Theological Institutes*, II:29 (1857 edition, 615–21); Summers, *Systematic Theology* VII:II:1, refuting the doctrine of purgatory (2:245–71); Raymond, *Systematic Theology*, book V (2:427–524); Pope, *Compendium of Christian Theology*, "Eschatology, or The Last Things" (1880 printing, 3:365–454); Miley, *Systematic Theology* VI (2:421–75). **Secondary sources:** Williams, *John Wesley's Theology Today*, 191–200; Maddox, *Responsible Grace*, 230–53; Runyon, *New Creation*, 7–12; Campbell, *Methodist Doctrine*, 80–83; Jones, *United Methodist Doctrine*, 216–18; Collins, *Theology of John Wesley*, 313–31.

It is perhaps most difficult to make a case for a doctrine of

Christian hope as a necessary or constitutive Christian doctrine for Wesleyan communities, but I have also found it difficult to avoid this claim entirely. The doctrinal passage in Wesley's "Letter to a Roman Catholic" concluded with the hope of eternal happiness for those who are in Christ.[89] To my knowledge, however, John Wesley never made any claims that eschatological views were necessary Christian doctrines, and his sermons that deal explicitly with eschatological issues, such as his 1785 sermon "The New Creation," fall outside the range of the "Standard" sermons that are formally affirmed as doctrine in Methodist churches. Methodist doctrinal standards have little to say about eschatology beyond their affirmation of the eschatological content of historic creeds and their rejection of late medieval Catholic views of purgatory. Nevertheless, in the Lord's Prayer Wesleyan Christians pray "thy kingdom come," in the Apostles' Creed they affirm their belief in "the resurrection of the body and the life everlasting." In the Nicene Creed Wesleyan Christians affirm that Christ "will come again in glory to judge the living and the dead, and his kingdom will have no end," and they further affirm in the Nicene Creed, "We look for the resurrection of the dead, and the life of the world to come."[90]

One reason why I believe that it is important to include a doctrine about Christian hope is my growing recognition of the extent to which Methodist views of the second coming of Jesus influenced their progressive vision of social change, especially in the nineteenth century. Nineteenth-century and early twentieth-century Methodists consistently espoused a postmillennial eschatology according to which Jesus would come to reign on the earth: God's will was to be done "on earth" and God's kingdom would also come "on earth." The implication was that the world had to be sanctified in preparation for Christ's coming. Taking this postmillennial view, Methodists were not terribly worried about exactly when Jesus would return. In fact, the postmillennial outlook had the effect of "postponing" the second coming of Jesus: in the words of Princeton historian James H. Moorhead, the postmillennial outlook "postponed history's cataclysmic end until after the millennium and thereby allowed the temporal interval necessary for the gradual evangelical conquest of the world and the triumph of secular progress."[91] This postmillennial vision conflicted sharply with the premillennial eschatology that came to prominence in Evangelical communities in the United States from the 1890s. The premillennial theology maintained that Jesus would come immediately and "rapture" the church up to heaven. As a consequence, souls were to be saved for heaven but the world could be left to its own devices. Wesleyan communities would consistently resist the premillennial outlook.

Both conservative and liberal Wesleyan theologians in the United States expressed this common postmillennial teaching at the beginning of the twentieth century. Dr. Solomon Jacob Gamertsfelder was the president of the Evangelical Theological Seminary in Naperville, Illinois, in the early twentieth century. Evangelical Theological Seminary was the principal theological institution of The Evangelical Church, a denomination constituted largely of German American people, influenced by the Wesleyan movement in its origin, and which would later (1946) enter into a union with The United Brethren in Christ. Gamertsfelder wrote a textbook, *Systematic Theology*, that was to be the standard theological text in the Evangelical Church for decades to come. It was originally published in 1913 but it was subsequently revised at the request of the Evangelical bishops, who felt that the book as it stood was too liberal to accommodate a more conservative and Holiness-oriented group that had divided from the denomination in the 1890s and with whom the bishops were negotiating for reunion. But despite the Evangelical bishops' concern, the 1913 version of his *Systematic Theology* was hardly liberal by wider standards: it staunchly defended biblical inerrancy in matters of scientific and historical fact as well as Christian doctrine, and this could easily mark Gamertsfelder as a Fundamentalist.[92] But on the other hand Gamertsfelder rejected the premillennial outlook that was so definitive of the Fundamentalist movement in his age, laying out a classic and socially progressive postmillennial vision.[93]

At about the same time that Gamertsfelder was revising his *Systematic Theology*, a progressive young clergyman who had grown up in the Evangelical Church, Harris Franklin Rall, left that denomination to join The Methodist Episcopal Church because he felt that The Evangelical Church had in fact capitulated to Fundamentalism. Rall became one of the best-known of liberal Methodist theologians of the early twentieth century, but Rall pas-

sionately defended Methodist postmillennialism against premillennial views, even writing (in 1920 and 1921) a detailed, critical
account of the millennial views that John Wesley had inherited
from Johann Albrecht Bengel.[94]

The postmillennial outlook was a prominent ground for
Methodist social activism in the late nineteenth century and the
early twentieth century. An example is offered by Lucy Rider
Meyer, who founded the Chicago Training School for City, Home,
and Foreign Missions in 1885 and went on to develop an order of
deaconesses within The Methodist Episcopal Church. Her personal
motto expressed the postmillennial vision she advocated: "I do
believe the world is swinging toward the light."[95] Her biographer
Isabelle Horton wrote of her development of the Chicago Training
School:

> So as she marked out the policy for the infant institution she had
> in mind not only a comprehensive study of the Bible but studies
> in hygiene, in citizenship, in social and family relations, in every-
> thing that could help or hinder in the establishment of the
> Kingdom of Heaven on earth.[96]

Meyer had at one point worked with Chicago Evangelist D. L.
Moody, but her sense of calling to active social work in the inner
city of Chicago differed markedly from Moody's premillennial
eschatology and his concomitant goal of spiritual evangelization. [97]

But despite the fact that Wesleyan communities once had a
definable view of Christian hope involving this progressive, postmillennial vision of the last things, there appears to have been a
major break of continuity in this teaching from around the 1930s.
Despite the fact that Wesleyan conservatives and liberals alike
(Gamertsfelder and Rall) defended the postmillennial ethos in the
early twentieth century, Methodist postmillennialism all but disappeared from the 1930s. This could reflect a general reaction
against Fundamentalism, a general reaction in which all forms of
millennialism came to be identified with premillennialism and
with resistance to efforts at progressive social change from this
period. For American Methodists, it could also be related to what
they almost universally understood as the tragedy of 5 December
1933, the congressional repeal of Prohibition that dealt a severe
blow to American Methodist confidence that the world was

steadily improving and that the larger world was amenable to Methodist influence. Whatever the reason, Wesleyan communities from the 1930s ceased to transmit a distinctive approach to Christian eschatology.

Wesleyan theologians returned to eschatological interests in the wake of Jürgen Moltmann's influential work *A Theology of Hope* (1964). One contemporary interpretation of John Wesley's work, that of Theodore Runyon, has taken its cue from John Wesley's 1785 sermon "The New Creation." Runyon specifically names the relevance of Wesley's vision of the new creation to contemporary concerns for justice and human rights.[98] The topic of "The New Creation" was also the focus of the 2002 Oxford Institute of Methodist Theological Studies, which resulted in a collection of essays exploring the topic.[99] Runyon's work and the essays in this collection were largely grounded in the eschatological views expressed in John Wesley's sermon by that title and they did not make the connection between Wesley's millennial views and the postmillennial outlook that I have come to see as a consistent mark of Methodist culture in the nineteenth century through the early twentieth century.

But although these connections have been little explored in Wesleyan circles, I have the intuition that there was more consistency and abiding significance to Methodist eschatological views than has been perceived in the past, and I do intuit the strong link between this eschatological outlook and Methodist social progressivism that Runyon posited. The topic may have to await further elaboration, but I have invoked the views of Gamertsfelder, Rall, Runyon, and other Wesleyan theologians here as a way of explaining why I believe it is important to include a doctrine of Christian hope as one of the items of common Christian faith that Methodists have affirmed with the broader Christian community.

This chapter has offered a sketch of how Wesleyan communities have thought of the core beliefs of the Christian faith, the faith they share with other Christians, as well as the distinctive elements of Christian faith that they have maintained. I am as liable to myopia as any other interpreter, if not more so, and it may well be that future historians will recognize other areas of Christian faith that have been consistently prized in Wesleyan communities, but based on my study of Wesleyan and Methodist literature, these fourteen items are the ones that I most consistently see Wesleyan communities claiming as core teachings. Many of the common Christian beliefs described here are strongly tinged with particularly or peculiarly Methodist perspectives at a number of points. In the view of many other church bodies, this will be seen as an incomplete list, altogether too brief for defining the central meaning of the Christian faith. But this in itself reflects the fundamental idea of a "catholic spirit" that maintains that only a core group of beliefs and practices is necessary to define unity in the Christian faith, and other matters ("opinions" and "modes of worship," *adiaphora*) can be left to the discretion of local communities or of individual interpreters.

CONCLUSION

Contemporary Wesleyan communities offer a way of being Christian that sings praise to the divine Trinity, celebrates the work of God in Christ, searches the Scriptures, cultivates religious experience and the religious affections, proclaims grace universally available, teaches seekers to mourn their sins and find pardon and peace and new life in Christ, calls believers to the great goal of sanctity, empowers them to live together as a church that welcomes new members in baptism, celebrates Christ's grace-filled presence in the Lord's Supper, and works for the transformation of the world into the reign of God and the gracious new creation that God intends. These are consistent, core beliefs that have characterized Wesleyan communities through their history in formal as well as popular expressions.

This book has focused on the consistently expressed beliefs of Wesleyan communities, examining both formal and popular expressions of these beliefs. Subsequent works will take up Wesleyan narratives and Wesleyan practices. I am keenly aware of the limitations of this book. Chapters 1 through 3 focus on John and Charles Wesley's explication of central beliefs common among Christian communities as well as beliefs distinctive of the Wesleyan movement. These chapters have not explored the depths of the Wesleys' theologies that other authors have explicated. Chapters 4 through 6 offer three core samples of Wesleyan beliefs as expressed in formal and popular sources, focusing on beliefs about God (chapter 4), beliefs about the "way of salvation" (chapter 5), and beliefs about the Christian church (chapter 6). The book does not offer this level of depth with respect to other teachings such as sacramental beliefs or beliefs about scriptural authority. Consequently, the description of fourteen core beliefs of Wesleyan communities in chapter 7 builds upon the material in the previous six chapters, but inconsistently so, because some beliefs described in chapter 7 do not have the depth of background material as those beliefs that have stronger grounding in the three core samples offered in chapters 4, 5, and 6. My only plea is that I am trying to do something a little different with this material so that this is an initial foray and I hope to return to do it more justice in the future.

THE INTERPLAY OF FORMAL AND POPULAR EXPRESSIONS OF BELIEFS IN WESLEYAN COMMUNITIES

The Wesleyan movement began as a popular religious movement in the eighteenth century and, despite the fact that it developed more formal ecclesiastical and theological structures over the last two centuries, it has continued to spawn popular literature and popular expressions of beliefs, practices, and the narratives of its origins. In the course of my own life I have witnessed the popular Methodist spirituality expressed in *The Upper Room,* a devotional manual largely written by lay Methodists, in Gospel hymns sung from *The Cokesbury Worship Hymnal,* in traditional revivals, in Lay Witness Missions, in the movement for Covenant Discipleship, and in Emmaus Walk, a Methodist expression of the Catholic Cursillo movement.

Chapter 1 has suggested that there has been a long interplay between popular and formal expressions of beliefs in Wesleyan communities. The Wesleys' literary works originally appeared as products of a popular religious movement and only later were accorded the status of formally authorized theological or doctrinal texts. Similarly, the hymns of Frances Jane Crosby in the late nineteenth century originally appeared in cheaply printed collections of Gospel songs intended for use in Sunday school assemblies, evening services, prayer meetings, and revivals. Only with the passage of decades were some of her hymns utilized for Sunday morning worship, and eventually a very small sample of them was printed in Methodist hymnals. Moreover, some of the source material utilized in this book lies in the boundaries between formal and popular expressions of religious beliefs. Catechisms and tracts, for example, were sometimes authorized by denominations, but sometimes they were simply published by denominational publishing houses without formal approbation.

The preceding chapters have pointed to significant correlations between formal and popular expressions of the beliefs of Wesleyan communities. A positive correlation between formal and popular expressions of beliefs was a working hypothesis with which I began and which has found strong confirmation in the historical evidence presented in this work. Wesleyan people have continued to sing hymns and utilize liturgies that reflect the more formal doctrinal commitments of their churches. They learned to give their testimonies in a way that reflected the "way of salvation" taught by the Wesleys as the distinctly Wesleyan vision of the Christian life. As we have seen, the popular expression of the "way of salvation" given in Methodists' personal testimonies tended to use such terms as "conviction" for the repentance of sinners, "conversion" as a single event embracing justification and regeneration, and "sanctification" as a shorthand expression for what was more formally described as entire sanctification. Methodist church architectures reflect the tensions inherent in Methodist ecclesiologies between a formal understanding of "church" as described in the Articles of Religion and in the Methodist use of Gothic architecture, and a more popular understanding of the church as a primarily missional body reflected in Wesleyan chapels, cottage settings for worship, auditoriums, and settings designed for contemporary Christian worship.

Despite these correlations, there certainly have been popular expressions of beliefs at variance with the formally enunciated beliefs of Wesleyan communities. The divergence of Holiness and Methodist visions in the late nineteenth century provides one example of significant variance, though I would caution two things in interpreting it. In the first place, it happened later than some imagine. Within the decade of the 1890s the bishops of both The Methodist Episcopal Church and The Methodist Episcopal Church, South, proclaimed their fidelity to the immediate availability of the experience of entire sanctification and encouraged believers to testify to this experience.[1] In the second place, Methodists who continue to feel a divinely given assurance that their view is the true Wesleyan view of sanctification and that the Holiness understanding of entire sanctification is a strange perversion should be cautioned against the possibility of excessive enthusiasm. The Holiness movement continued to maintain John Wesley's claim of the instantaneous nature of entire sanctification, even though Wesley also claimed that believers might not "advert to the particular moment" when this occurred.[2] The divergence with the Holiness movement eventually became an irreparable breach to the impoverishment (I believe) of both Methodist and Holiness communities. The Holiness movement led within a few decades to the origins of the Pentecostal movement, at yet another remove from Wesleyan communities but following a theological trajectory that had roots in the Wesleyan movement. I am sure there are other ways in which popular expressions of beliefs diverged from the formally stated beliefs of Wesleyan communities. This book has demonstrated, however, that popular beliefs could and often did complement formal expressions of belief in Wesleyan communities, and in some cases popular expressions of beliefs influenced the formally stated beliefs of Wesleyan communities.

WESLEYAN BELIEFS AND A "WESLEYAN TRADITION"

When I began this project I conceived of it as a way of explicating the characteristic beliefs of what many contemporary scholars since the decade of the 1970s have called "the Wesleyan tradition." Reactions to earlier versions of this material alerted me to the fact that the conception of the "Wesleyan tradition" is something like a minefield loaded with a host of contemporary issues, a minefield that a scholar must enter warily if at all. I decided, then, to focus this work on the characteristic core beliefs of Wesleyan communities as expressed in formal and popular sources: "Wesleyan communities" are much more easily defined than the more ethereal "Wesleyan tradition." For Wesleyan communities one can start with the list of member churches of the World Methodist Council, work backward to their predecessor organizations, and have a fairly concrete list of communities for research focus. But in this conclusion I want to return to the notion of a Wesleyan Christian subculture or "Wesleyan tradition" in relation to the beliefs described here.

The first thing I would observe about this is that the notion of a "Wesleyan tradition" is a construction from the 1970s and the term has been construed in a variety of ways since then, none of which can claim anything like magisterial authority. It is a construct created and used at first by scholars and now in popular church life as a way of accounting for the culture of Wesleyan and Methodist churches beyond the boundaries of existing Wesleyan and Methodist denominations. Scholars need to be clear about what they mean in using such constructs, and they need to be able to assess the relative advantages and disadvantages of particular definitions.

The etymology of the word *tradition* reveals a basic meaning of that which is "handed on" from one generation and "received" by another.[3] "Tradition" is not coterminous with "history" in the larger sense where the latter denotes everything that happened in the past whether valued positively or negatively or indifferently by its narrators. "Tradition" implies a positive valuing of the past. These senses of "tradition" are mutually reinforcing: that which is handed on from one generation and received by another generation in the process of transmission is that which has been selected *because* it is valued positively by a community. This process of selection and transmission means that a tradition may have consistent content over time and yet this content is subject to reinterpretation as new generations re-evaluate the content of the tradition and decide what should be transmitted or what should be emphasized in the process of transmission.[4]

The expression "a tradition" or "a Christian tradition," as in "the Wesleyan tradition," denotes a cluster of narratives and beliefs and practices that particular communities have transmitted through successive generations. The expression thus designates a small-scale culture or subculture, a nexus of beliefs, practices, and narratives that have been associated with the communities that transmit them. In an ecumenical perspective, "a tradition" can denote what the ecumenical movement has sometimes called a "confessional tradition," as in the 1963 World Council of Churches Faith and Order report "Scripture, Tradition, and traditions" that identified "Tradition" (with an uppercase "T") as the gospel itself as it has been transmitted in Christian communities, and identified "traditions" either as particular cultural traditions or as confessional traditions, for example, the Lutheran or Reformed traditions.[5]

Following these senses of the term "tradition," I would claim that the previous chapters of this book have demonstrated that a certain body of teachings or beliefs has been consistently transmitted through several generations of constituents of Wesleyan communities. That is to say, these chapters have demonstrated the existence of a "tradition" as the term denotes that which is handed on from one generation and received by another generation in the process of transmission, and the content of the "tradition" demonstrated here is that which has been selected because it has been consistently, positively valued by Wesleyan communities.

But this understanding of "Wesleyan tradition" will differ from understandings of the "Wesleyan tradition" employed by other interpreters. The introduction to this book has noted Thomas Langford's *Practical Divinity: Theology in the Wesleyan Tradition* and it has noted that Langford took "theology in the Wesleyan tradition" to denote the work of systematic theologians, mostly professional theologians, who were members of Methodist or Wesleyan churches. The understanding of beliefs characteristic of a Wesleyan tradition shown in this book, by contrast, involves both formal doctrinal material, popular spirituality, and some material (such as catechisms) that falls into the interstices between formal and popular expressions of Wesleyan beliefs. Langford's conclusions about the content of the Wesleyan theological tradition are commensurate with his definition of this tradition and the literature he studied, and they show very general areas of agreement between Wesleyan theologians, in come cases, as he points out, agreement only in the typical questions that have been asked by Wesleyan theologians.[6] The conclusions about consistently transmitted beliefs shown in this book (especially in chapter 7) are much more specific than Langford's conclusions and are commensurate with the definition of Wesleyan communities and the types of literature examined here. Neither offers a definitive account of "the Wesleyan tradition"; both define Wesleyan traditions in certain ways and reach certain conclusions commensurate with their definitions.

I have made a case for the utilization of both formal and popular expressions of beliefs as a way of understanding what a Wesleyan Christian subculture or a Wesleyan "tradition" might mean. I hope to explore the transmission of narratives about the founding of the Wesleyan movement and the transmission of specific Wesleyan practices in future volumes. I hope that through three studies of Wesleyan beliefs, Wesleyan narratives, and Wesleyan practices I can show with some particularity how Wesleyan communities have transmitted a distinct body of narratives and practices as well as beliefs that can be fairly described as a distinctively Wesleyan Christian subculture or tradition.

A CATHOLIC SPIRIT

John Wesley's 1749 sermon "Catholic Spirit" advocated what we might call an open-minded spirit, perhaps even a liberal spirit toward other Christians and toward humanity. It was not an open-ended liberality, as has been shown in chapter 1: "A man of a truly catholic spirit, has not now his religion to seek. He is fixed as the sun in his judgment concerning the main branches of Christian doctrine."[7] A catholic spirit meant, as he explained it, a spirit that, while fixed squarely in certain principles, is nevertheless willing to extend "strong and cordial affection" to "neighbours and strangers, friends and enemies," in fact "toward all mankind, those he knows and those he knows not." He offered this definition of "catholic love" and the "catholic spirit" that flows from it: "This is catholic or universal love. And he that has this is of a catholic spirit. For love alone gives the title to this character: Catholic love is a catholic spirit."[8]

Six years after writing this, responding to calls within the body of Methodist preachers to separate from the Church of England and also responding to ongoing divisions with the Calvinist wing of the revival and at the very point where he and his brother Charles Wesley were dividing over the matter of itinerant preaching, John Wesley republished his sermon as a separate tract and included with it a poem written by his brother entitled "Catholic Love," the first stanza of which is as follows:

Weary of all this wordy strife,
These notions, forms and modes, and names,
To thee, the way, the truth, the life,
Whose love my simple heart inflames,
Divinely taught, at last I fly
With thee, and thine, to live, and die.[9]

It is typically Wesleyan to pray that beyond "wordy strife" is the spirit of catholic love, the spirit in which Wesleyan communities have sought to define and to proclaim their most central teachings: a spirit of openness grounded in a confident sense of the core teachings that a community shares. This solemn prayer seems especially appropriate at the conclusion of such a work as this.

The term "catholic" is appropriately translated "universal," since it comes from the expression καθ' ὅλος, "throughout" or "through the whole," as in the very similar expression in Acts 9:31, ἐκκλησία καθ' ὅλης τῆς Ἰουδαίας, "the church throughout Judea." The "catholic" church, as Wesleyan communities use the term in the Apostles' Creed and as Charles Wesley had used it in his poem "Catholic Love," means the universal church, the church throughout the world. Affirming the catholic church in this sense anathematizes any notions that the church can be limited to one race or nationality.

Moreover, the term "catholic" as it has been interpreted in the historic creeds also denotes the fullness of Christian teaching. An example of this appears in the quaint inscription on the tomb of Samuel Wesley that asserts that Samuel lived and died "in the true Catholick Faith."[10] The inscription names his belief in the divine Trinity and in the full divinity of Jesus Christ as evidence of this "Catholick" faith. With respect to his son's sense of a "catholic spirit," though, the term raises the issue of *how much* doctrine needs to be defined by a community to claim the fullness of catholic teaching. As chapter 1 has shown, the answer was that it did require some key or core Christian affirmations, but not at all the level of doctrinal affirmation that had come to characterize European Protestant churches and the Catholic Church in the Baroque flourishing of confessionalism that grew out of the Reformation age and accompanied the inter-Christian warfare of the seventeenth century.

The Wesleyan vision of Christian faith embraces such a "catholic spirit" or what I have termed an "adiaphorist" approach to Christian faith, an approach that insists on a few key doctrines or teachings as matters of strong consensus and leaves other matters, "opinions" and "modes of worship" as *adiaphora* left to the discretion of local communities or individual believers. This approach has the advantage of an open-minded attitude toward other Christians and indeed toward communities and people outside of the Christian faith.

But the "catholic spirit" also bears some challenges with it. On the one hand, the evolution of a religious movement often involves a trajectory toward increasing liberality with respect to the teachings and practices that characterized the movement in its infancy. But when a movement starts out, as the Wesleyan movement did, with a relatively small list of essential or core teachings and practices, further reduction of the core can leave very little defined or transmitted as core teachings and practices. This has been a problem for Methodists and other Wesleyan communities when the adiaphorist vision has been taken as a general license to teach or practice whatever one wishes to teach and practice rather than what communities have agreed to teach and practice. This I would interpret as the appropriate kernel of concern that conservative constituents of Wesleyan churches have consistently expressed in the last century or more.

But on the other hand, it is also genuinely problematic to take an eighteenth-century definition of essential or core teachings and practices as binding for communities into the future. Just as the Wesleys had genuine insights into the nature of Christian faith in their age, so Wesleyan communities and Wesleyan constituents have had genuine and new insights since the time of the Wesleys. I have noted above the problems inherent in claiming an "assurance of pardon" as a normative teaching. In a different way, chapter 7 identifies the practice of "open communion" as a practice that has found nearly universal *de facto* approval in Wesleyan communities since the time of the Wesleys, yet in most of these communities it has not been formally defined as a central or core practice and belief. Ecumenical insights, moreover, have shown that many items defined as doctrine inherited from the era of the Reformation in Wesleyan communities were either grounded upon misunderstandings (for example, the claim that Catholics "worship" saints) or were directed against Late Medieval Catholic teachings or practices that no longer characterized the Catholic Church (for example, the practice of withholding the cup or chalice from the laity). Cultural changes raise issues that were not considered in the past, for example, the question of whether Wesleyan communities could allow remarriage after divorce. New technologies raise new issues for Christian believers that were not addressed in historic definitions of core teachings.

The conclusion I reach, then, is that a catholic spirit and an adiaphorist definition of central teachings need to be nurtured by consistent engagement on the part of Wesleyan communities. The Twenty-Five Articles of Religion defined by The Methodist Episcopal Church in 1784 have remained unchanged since that time. The "General Rules" promulgated by the Wesleys in 1743 have remained unchanged since the eighteenth century in most Wesleyan communities, with the enormous exception of treatments of the restriction against slave trade. They are frozen in eighteenth-century parlance ("spirituous liquors," "exhorting all we have any intercourse with") with references to eighteenth-century notions ("that enthusiastic doctrine that 'we are not to do good unless *our hearts be free to do it'*") entirely unfamiliar to modern readers. Not surprisingly, the "General Rules" have largely fallen out of use despite their protected status in the constitutions of Wesleyan communities.

I admit that I would fear such a broad dialogue as I envision here and its possible results, but I cannot avoid the conclusion that the definition of central or core teachings needs to be taken up and reexamined in every generation, including the present generation in Wesleyan communities. I would hope that this might involve a broad-based dialogue in Wesleyan communities, not one in which individual Wesleyan and Methodist denominations simply adopt their own doctrinal statements without consultation of other Wesleyan communities and without consultation of other ecumenical partners. I would hope that such a dialogue would be undertaken with Bibles and hymnals in hand, and with the habitual attitude of "catholic love" guiding our deliberations.

CONCLUSION

To believe and to live as Wesleyan communities today is not to replicate the Wesleyan communities of the past. It is to know the foundational narratives, the core beliefs, and the consistent practices that have shaped Wesleyan communities as keys to their contemporary mission as Christian communities today. Wesleyan communities today face a variety of challenges in finding and expressing consensus about core beliefs in the face of internal and external threats, "Fightings within and fears without."[11] The World

Methodist Council has called Wesleyan communities to unity in the midst of these challenges:

> Knowing that the love we share in Christ is stronger than our conflicts, broader than our opinions, and deeper than the wounds we inflict on one another, we commit ourselves to participation in our congregations, denominations and the whole Christian family for the purpose of nurture, outreach and witness.[12]

This is a call today to the "catholic spirit" that John Wesley envisioned in his time and to the "catholic love" that Charles Wesley had advocated. It is not an easy task, but the self-knowledge that comes from knowing deeply who we are as Wesleyan communities can be a source of strength and confidence today. Wesleyan communities not only teach but sing of their belief in the grace that calls them into this particular way of being Christian:

> Didst thou not make us one,
> That we might one remain,
> Together travel on,
> And share our joy and pain,
> Till all thine utmost goodness prove,
> And rise renew'd in perfect love?[13]

ABBREVIATIONS

AME	African Methodist Episcopal
AME Zion	African Methodist Episcopal Zion
AV	Authorized (or King James) Version of the Bible
CME	Christian Methodist Episcopal
ME	Methodist Episcopal
MEC	Methodist Episcopal Church
MECS	Methodist Episcopal Church, South
MP	Methodist Protestant
UM	United Methodist
UMC	United Methodist Church
WCC	World Council of Churches
WMC	World Methodist Council

NOTES

PREFACE

1. Maximin Piette, *John Wesley in the Evolution of Protestantism*, trans. J. B. Howard (New York: Sheed and Ward, 1937); Bernard Semmel, *The Methodist Revolution* (New York: Basic Books, 1973).

2. Henry C. Vedder, review of *History of Methodists in the United States* (1899 edition), by J. M. Buckley in *American Journal of Theology* (1900), 200–3; quotation is on p. 201.

3. *Bulletin of the John Rylands University Library of Manchester* 85, nos. 2–3: 405–20.

4. *Asbury Theological Journal* 59, nos. 1–2 (Spring and Fall 2004): 27–48.

5. Kenneth J. Collins and John H. Tyson, eds., *Conversion in the Wesleyan Tradition* (Nashville: Abingdon Press, 2001), 160–74.

6. Kenneth G. C. Newport and Ted A. Campbell, eds., *Charles Wesley: Life, Literature, and Legacy* (Peterborough: Epworth Press, 2007), 264–77.

7. M. Douglas Meeks, ed., *Trinity, Community and Power: Mapping Trajectories in Wesleyan Theology* (Nashville: Kingswood Books, 2000), 85–109.

8. *Asbury Theological Journal* 63, no. 1 (Spring 2008): 5–31.

9. S T Kimbrough Jr., ed., *Orthodox and Wesleyan Ecclesiology* (Crestwood, N.Y.: St. Vladimir's Theological Seminary Press, 2007), 215–25.

INTRODUCTION

1. Nathan Hatch, *The Democratization of American Christianity* (New Haven: Yale University Press, 1989), 81–93.

2. John H. Wigger, *Taking Heaven by Storm: Methodism and the Rise of Popular Christianity in America* (Urbana: University of Illinois Press, 1998); Ann Taves, *Fits, Trances, and Visions: Experiencing Religion and Explaining Experience from Wesley to James* (Princeton: Princeton University Press, 1999), chapter 3, "Shouting Methodists," 76–117; David Hempton, *Methodism: Empire of the Spirit* (New Haven: Yale University Press, 2005).

3. For example, Frederick A. Norwood, *The Story of American Methodism* (Nashville: Abingdon Press, 1974), whose work begins with the Wesleys (23–41), and then focuses largely on the institutional development of American Methodism, with relatively little attention paid to doctrine, theology, or spirituality.

4. Wigger's subtitle indicates his primary interest in popular spirituality: "Methodism and

the Rise of Popular Christianity in America," and his book carries this through. Hempton's introduction makes clear his desire to focus on popular spirituality, concluding with his hope that he will make a substantial contribution to historiography "by examining the rise of Methodism as a transnational movement of ordinary people not easily confined to particular times, places, and institutions" (10).

5. Hempton, 7, summarizing chapter 3.

6. Ibid., 56–60 (Wesley's theology), 60–68 (popular spirituality expressed in personal narratives), 68–74 (hymns), 74–79 (sermons), and 84 (development of formal systematic theologies). Wigger also discusses John Wesley's theology briefly, then deals with more popular expressions of Methodist piety: Wigger, 15–20 (John Wesley's theology), and (e.g.) 104–24 ("Boiling Hot Religion").

7. Hempton, 60, and following in chapter 3.

8. In chapter 5 "Beliefs about the 'Way of Salvation' after the Wesleys."

9. Thomas A. Langford, *Practical Divinity: Theology in the Wesleyan Tradition*, rev. ed., 2 vol. (Nashville: Abingdon Press, 1998); hereafter cited as "Langford, *Practical Divinity* (1998)."

10. Ibid., 1:249–58.

11. "Boiling Hot Religion" is the title of chapter 5 of Wigger, 104–24.

12. I will describe in what follows many of the same phenomena that Hempton and Wigger and Taves have described, but I will be concerned to show how the popular spirituality of the "way of salvation" was related to the more formal teachings expressed in Methodist theological literature, hymnals, and catechisms, and thus how these formal documents and Methodist preaching based on them came to structure the spiritual autobiographies of Methodist people. Russell E. Richey argues that there were four distinct "languages" in early American Methodism: the language of popular evangelicalism, Wesleyan language, episcopal or Anglican language, and republican language (*Early American Methodism* [Bloomington: Indiana University Press, 1991], chapter 6, 82–97). With respect to his categories, I would see formal consensus as reflecting Wesleyan language (although consistently revised and restated by American Methodist churches) and popular narratives as reflecting the language or culture of popular evangelicalism, but I will argue for a strong correlation between these "languages."

13. I have in mind in this paragraph Eliza Clark Garrett, who founded Garrett Biblical Institute in Evanston, Illinois. Russell E. Richey's *The Methodist Conference in America: A History* (Nashville: Kingswood Books, 1996) makes the point that early Methodist conferences (quarterly as well as annual conferences) were primarily occasions for preaching, worship, hymn-singing, and generally matters related to spirituality rather than business meetings (chapter 6, 51–61).

14. Chapter 5 below will show how the vocabulary employed by Methodist people reflected a common language about the "way of salvation" developed from Wesleyan and Methodist sources.

15. In the earlier category of Methodist theologians whose works were prescribed for study by Methodist churches, I have in mind Richard Watson, Thomas N. Ralston, Thomas O. Summers, Miner Raymond, William Burt Pope, John Miley, and H. Orton Wiley. From the middle of the twentieth century, Methodist churches began to expect clergy to study in theological colleges or theological seminaries and no longer prescribed a church-administered course of study that would identify specific theologians to be read by all candidates for ordained ministry. But we can identify some theologians, such as Colin W. Williams, Albert C. Outler, and others whose works have been hugely influential and regularly studied by Methodist candidates for ordained ministry, even if not prescribed by a formal course of study.

16. Randy L. Maddox, *Responsible Grace: John Wesley's Practical Theology* (Nashville: Kingswood Books, 1994), 15–18. The expression "practical divinity" came from a letter from Susanna Wesley to John Wesley at the time of John Wesley's decision to seek Anglican orders in 1725, and by this term she denoted the literature of the Anglican "Holy Living" tradition and of Late Medieval works of the *Devotio Moderna* tradition (such as Thomas à Kempis), which had been favored by advocates of the "Holy Living" tradition. The term, then, did denote what Maddox calls "first-order" theological activities (Susanna Wesley, letter to John Wesley, 23 February 1724/25; in Charles Wallace Jr., ed., *Susanna Wesley: The*

Complete Writings [New York: Oxford University Press, 1997], 106–7). John Wesley also used the term "practical divinity" in the preface to the 1780 *Collection of Hymns for Use of the People Called Methodists* (see the quotation in chapter 5 below), and used it to refer to the *Collection* itself, another instance suggesting that "practical divinity" ought to extend to such first-order theological work.

17. Colin W. Williams, *John Wesley's Theology Today* (Nashville: Abingdon Press, 1960).

18. Albert C. Outler, *Theology in the Wesleyan Spirit* (Nashville: Discipleship Resources, 1975), based on his Fondren Lectures at Perkins School of Theology, Southern Methodist University, 1973.

19. Maddox, *Responsible Grace*; Theodore Runyon, *The New Creation: John Wesley's Theology Today* (Nashville: Abingdon Press, 1998); Kenneth J. Collins, *The Theology of John Wesley: Holy Love and the Shape of Grace* (Nashville: Abingdon Press, 2007).

20. Scott J. Jones, *United Methodist Doctrine: The Extreme Center* (Nashville: Abingdon Press, 2002).

21. Ted A. Campbell, *Methodist Doctrine: The Essentials* (Nashville: Abingdon Press, 1999).

22. Josef V. Polišenský, *War and Society in Europe, 1618–1648* (Cambridge: Cambridge University Press, 1978); Lawrence Stone, *The Causes of the English Revolution, 1529–1642* (New York: Harper and Row, 1972). Neither Polišenský nor Stone offered a purely economic interpretation of the Thirty Years' War or the causes of the English Revolution, respectively, though economic factors weighed heavily in their interpretations.

23. Albert C. Outler, "The Reformation and the Vitality of Classical Protestantism," in *Albert C. Outler as Historian and Interpreter of the Christian Tradition*, ed. Ted A. Campbell (Anderson, Ind.: Bristol Books, 2003), 223–28.

24. Ted A. Campbell, *John Wesley and Christian Antiquity: Religious Vision and Cultural Change* (Nashville: Kingwood Books, 1991), 11–15.

25. John Wesley, "Catholic Spirit," III:1 (in Albert C. Outler, *Sermons*. 4 vols.; *Bicentennial Edition of the Works of John Wesley* [Nashville: Abingdon Press, 1984], 197; hereafter referred to as "Outler, ed., *Sermons*"), 2:93; in Thomas Jackson, ed., *The Works of the Reverend John Wesley, AM*. 14 vols. (London: Wesleyan Conference Office, 1873; hereafter referred to as "Jackson, ed., *Works*"), 5:502.

26. This will be taken up in the section below: "Some Principles and Criteria."

27. Gareth Lloyd, *John Wesley and the Struggle for Methodist Identity* (Oxford: Oxford University Press, 2007), 147–61, 180–212, 219–33.

28. *The Book of Discipline of The United Methodist Church 2008* (Nashville: United Methodist Publishing House, 2008), 9–20.

29. This "adiaphorist" approach was adumbrated in John Wesley's sermon "Catholic Spirit," where Wesley distinguished between "the main branches of Christian doctrine" on which unity is essential and those "opinions" or "modes of worship" on which disagreement could be allowed. See John Wesley, "Catholic Spirit," ¶ III:1 (in Outler, ed., *Sermons*, 2:93; and in Edward H. Sugden, ed., *Wesley's Standard Sermons* ["Standard Edition" of the *Works of John Wesley*. 3rd ed.; 2 vols. (London: Epworth Press, third edition, 1951); hereafter referred to as "Sugden, ed., *Sermons*"], 2:143).

30. Ted A. Campbell, *Christian Confessions* (Louisville: Westminster John Knox Press, 1996), 2–5; Campbell, *Methodist Doctrine*, 17–20; cf. Jones, *United Methodist Doctrine*, 22–29. Jones has made the case that formal Methodist doctrine does not itself acknowledge an authoritative role for reception, and although this may be the case, I argue nevertheless that the study of reception conjoined with the study of formal consensus offers a strong historical methodology for studying the core beliefs of the Wesleyan tradition.

31. See the constitution of the Methodist Church of Great Britain, given in Rupert E. Davies, *Methodism* (Harmondsworth: Penguin Books, 1963), 209–11.

32. There are two different printings of the *Plan of Union*. An earlier printing dated 1966 represents the proposals sent to the General Conferences of The Methodist Church and The Evangelical United Brethren Church meeting in Chicago in that year, and it does not have this reference to the "Wesleyan standards": Joint Commissions on Church Union between The Methodist Church and The Evangelical United Brethren Church, *Plan of Union: Report to the General Conferences, November 1966 of The Methodist Church and The Evangelical United Brethren Church* (n.p., 1966), 20. The reference to the Wesleyan standards appears in an

italicized preface to the doctrinal standards in the second printed edition of 1967, which represented the legislation adopted by the 1966 General Conferences and sent to annual conferences in 1967 and then to the Uniting Conference of 1968: The Ad Hoc Committee on E.U.B. Union of The Methodist Church and The Commission on Union of The Evangelical United Brethren Church, *The United Methodist Church: The Plan of Union as Adopted by the General Conferences, November 1966, and the Annual Conferences, 1967, of The Methodist Church and The Evangelical United Brethren Church* (n.p., 1967), 22. This statement appears as the preface to the doctrinal standards in *The Book of Discipline of The United Methodist Church 1968* (Nashville: The Methodist Publishing House [sic], 1968), preface to ¶ 90, pp. 35–37.

33. A reference to the "Wesleyan standards" in the *Plan of Union* has appeared in United Methodist *Disciplines* since 1988: cf. *Book of Discipline of The United Methodist Church 2008*, ¶ 102, p. 58, and the Wesleyan writings are also mentioned among the doctrinal standards in ¶ 103, p. 71. There was a debate throughout the 1980s within United Methodist circles on the legal status of the Wesleyan standards; cf. Richard P. Heitzenrater, "'At Full Liberty': Doctrinal Standards in Early American Methodism" in *Mirror and Memory: Reflections on Early Methodism* (Nashville: Kingswood Books, 1989), 189–204; and Thomas C. Oden, *Doctrinal Standards in the Wesleyan Tradition*, 2nd rev. ed. (Nashville: Abingdon Press, 2008).

34. *Book of Discipline of The United Methodist Church 2008*, ¶ 102, p. 53.

35. My own questions about the status of Wesley's *Explanatory Notes upon the New Testament* are more related to the issue of reception mentioned in the text following. Wesley's *Notes* were quickly supplanted in the nineteenth century by Adam Clarke's *Commentary*, and have not been used (or appealed to) nearly as frequently as Wesley's *Standard Sermons*. Thus, although they may have had (and may still have) some degree of formal authority, they lack the authority of a doctrinal source to which Methodists have had consistent recourse.

36. *Book of Discipline of The United Methodist Church 2008*, ¶ 102, p. 54.

37. See the constitution of The Methodist Church of Great Britain, given in Davies, *Methodism*, 209–11, and especially the statement about loyalty to "the fundamental principles of the historic creeds and the Protestant Reformation" at the beginning of the constitution, on p. 209; *Constitutional Practice and Discipline of the Methodist Church*, vol. 2 (Peterborough: Methodist Publishing, 2009, PDF version), 213–14.

38. William G. Rusch, *Reception: An Ecumenical Problem* (Philadelphia: Fortress Press in cooperation with the Lutheran World Federation, 1988) discusses historical and contemporary issues surrounding ecumenical reception. He stresses that although ecumenical work on reception in the 1960s focused on the reception of conciliar teachings (at the time of and following the Second Vatican Council), ecumenical reception must be considered in a broader sense as the dynamic work of the Holy Spirit enabling Christian communities to discern the gospel in, and thus "receive," ecumenical teachings and actions. See also Jaroslav Pelikan's chapter "The Orthodoxy of the Body of the Faithful" (chapter 12 in Pelikan, *Credo: Historical and Theological Guide to Creeds and Confessions of Faith in the Christian Tradition* [New Haven: Yale University Press, 2003], 336–64 and especially 336–52).

1. JOHN WESLEY AND COMMON CHRISTIAN BELIEFS

1. John Wesley, "On Laying the Foundation of the New Chapel, Near the City-Road, London," II:1 (in Outler, ed., *Sermons*, 3:585; in Jackson, ed., *Works*, 7:423).

2. Transcribed from photograph.

3. Maddox, *Responsible Grace*, 15–25; Runyon, *The New Creation*, 7–12; Collins, *John Wesley's Theology*, 5–16.

4. John Wesley, "Catholic Spirit," ¶ III:1 (in Outler, ed., *Sermons*, 2:93; and in Sugden, ed., *Sermons*, 2:143).

5. In his sermon "On the Trinity" (1775), John Wesley acknowledged that he did not prefer the term "fundamental," because the term was ambiguous and there were "so many warm disputes about the number of *fundamentals*" (¶ 2; in Outler, ed., *Sermons*, 2:376), but at

this point he offered no other term except to say that "there are some truths more important than others" (ibid.). In the sermon "The New Birth" he did use the term "fundamental" to describe the doctrines of justification and regeneration (introduction, ¶ 1; in Outler, ed., *Sermons*, 2:187 and in Sugden, ed., *Sermons*, 2:425–26).

6. John Lenton, *John Wesley's Preachers: A Social and Statistical Analysis of the British and Irish Preachers Who Entered the Methodist Itinerancy before 1791* (Milton Keynes: Paternoster Press, 2009), 21–26.

7. Carter Lindberg, *The European Reformations* (Oxford: Basil Blackwell, 1996), 244–45; cf. Owen Chadwick, *The Reformation*, vol. 3 of the Pelican History of the Church (Harmondsworth: Penguin Books, 1972), 31–39.

8. The dispute over *adiaphora* took on a new meaning late in the seventeenth century when Pietists (including August Hermann Francke) argued that worldly pleasures were strictly forbidden by the gospel, in contrast to so-called Orthodox Lutherans, who maintained that worldly pleasures might be indifferent matters (*adiaphora*) and thus perhaps allowable to Christians.

9. The distinction between essential or fundamental "doctrines" and "opinions" is drawn at length in John Wesley's sermon "Catholic Spirit" (1749), where Wesley insisted that although we may not share the same opinions or ways of worship as others, our hearts should nevertheless be right with God and with all our neighbors, and our "hands" should be extended to them (¶¶ I–II; in Outler, ed., *Sermons*, 2:82–92). Wesley maintained, however, that a "catholic spirit" is not to be confused with a "speculative Latitudinarianism," an "indifference to all opinions," nor with an "indifference to all congregations" (¶ III:1–3; in Outler, ed., *Sermons*, 2:92–94). Wesley's sermon titled "A Caution against Bigotry" (1750) maintains that we should not forbid the efforts of persons who do not have an outward connection with us, who are not of our "party," with whose opinions we differ, with whose practices we differ, who belong to a church we consider to be beset with error, or who hold bitter affections toward us, so long as their ministries bring forth good fruits (¶¶ II–III; in Outler, ed., *Sermons*, 2:69–76). On the general distinction between doctrine and opinion, cf. Williams, *John Wesley's Theology Today*, 13–22.

10. Lawrence Meredith lays out a number of loci where Wesley maintains the distinction between "essential" doctrines and "opinions" (Lawrence Meredith, "Essential Doctrine in the Theology of John Wesley with Special Attention to the Methodist Standards of Doctrine" [PhD diss., Harvard University, 1962], 2–6). These include the following: (a) John Wesley's letter to John Newton, 14 May 1765 (in John Telford, ed., *Letters of the Rev. John Wesley, A.M.* [standard edition of the *Works of John Wesley*; 8 vols.; London: Epworth Press, 1931; hereafter referred to as "Telford, ed., *Letters*"], 4:297); (b) sermon "On the Death of the Rev. Mr. George Whitefield," ¶ III:1 (in Outler, ed., *Sermons*, 2:341; and in Sugden, ed., *Sermons*, 2:522); (c) sermon "Self Denial," ¶ 2 (in Outler, ed., *Sermons*, 2:238–39; and in Sugden, ed., *Sermons*, 2:281–82), although this passage does not appear to define a doctrine as "necessary"—rather, it asserts that self-denial itself (not necessarily the doctrine of self-denial) is necessary to Christian existence; (d) sermon "Of Former Times," ¶ 11 (1787; in Outler, ed., *Sermons*, 3:448; and in Jackson, ed., *Works*, 7:162); (e) sermon "On Laying the Foundation of City Road Chapel," ¶ II:10 (1 November 1778; in Outler, ed., *Sermons*, 3:588; and in Jackson, ed., *Works*, 7:427); (f) "Farther Appeal to Men of Reason and Religion, Part II," ¶ I:1 (18 December 1745; in Gerald R. Cragg, ed., *The Appeals to Men of Reason and Religion and Certain Related Open Letters* [Oxford/Bicentennial Edition of the *Works of John Wesley*, 11; Oxford: Oxford University Press, 1975; hereafter cited as "Cragg, ed., *Appeals*"], 203; and in Jackson, ed., *Works*, 8:206–7). (g) sermon "On Obedience to Pastors," ¶ I:4 (in Outler, ed., *Sermons*, 3:376; and in Jackson, ed., *Works*, 7:110); (h) "A Farther Appeal to Men of Reason and Religion, Part III," ¶ IV:9 (in Cragg, ed., *Appeals*, 320–21; and in Jackson, ed., *Works*, 8:243); (i) *Journal* for 6 May 1760 (in W. Reginald Ward and Richard P. Heitzenrater, eds., *Journal and Diaries* [Bicentennial edition of the *Works of John Wesley*; Nashville: Abingdon Press, 1988–; hereafter referred to as "Ward and Heitzenrater, eds., *Journal and Diaries*"], 21:259; and in Nehemiah Curnock, ed., *The Journal of the Rev. John Wesley, A.M., Sometime Fellow of Lincoln College, Oxford* ["Standard Edition" of the *Works of John Wesley*; 8 vols.; London: Epworth Press, 1906–19; hereafter referred to as "Curnock, ed., *Journal*"], 4:388); (j) letter "To the Rev. Dr. Conyers Middleton," ¶ VI:1:15 (4 January 1749; in Telford, ed., *Letters*, 2:380;

and in Jackson, ed., *Works*, 10:71); and (k) sermon "Christian Perfection," ¶ I:4 (in Outler, ed., *Sermons*, 2:101–2; and in Sugden, ed., *Sermons*, 2:153).

11. Lenton, 21–26.

12. Williams, *John Wesley's Theology Today*, 16–17.

13. Williams cites Wesley's doctrinal treatise "The Doctrine of Original Sin, according to Scripture, Reason, and Experience," ¶ VI:VI (in Jackson, ed., *Works*, 9:429), although at this point, it should be noted, Wesley was apparently quoting (with approval) a treatise of Dr. Isaac Watts on the doctrine of original sin.

14. Williams cites the introductory paragraph of John Wesley's tract "The Character of a Methodist," ¶ 1 (in Jackson, ed., *Works*, 8:340); similarly, the 1765 sermon "The Lord Our Righteousness" begins with the assertion that, although Christians might disagree over many issues, they should be united in their teaching about Christ, which is fundamental (introduction, ¶¶ 4–6; in Outler, ed., *Sermons*, 1:450–52; and in Sugden, ed., *Sermons*, 2:425–26).

15. Williams cites a letter from John Wesley to Mary Bishop, dated 7 February 1778 (in Telford, ed., *Letters*, 6:297–98).

16. Williams cites John Wesley's sermon "The New Birth," introduction, ¶ 1 (in Outler, ed., *Sermons*, 2:187; and in Sugden, ed., *Sermons*, 2:226–27), although it is interesting that in this passage John Wesley asserted that both the doctrine of justification and the doctrine of the new birth are fundamental, and Williams lists only justification as an essential or fundamental doctrine based on this passage. Williams also cites John Wesley's sermon "The Lord Our Righteousness," introduction, ¶¶ 4–6 (in Outler, ed., *Sermons*, 1:450–52; and in Sugden, ed., *Sermons*, 2:425–26), apparently taking the reference to Luther's *articulus stantis vel cadentis ecclesiae* as a reference to the doctrine of justification by faith alone, although it seems likely to me that in this instance Wesley was claiming that doctrine about Christ is "the article [or doctrine] on which the church stands or falls."

17. Williams cites a letter of John Wesley to his nephew Samuel Wesley dated 19 August 1784 (in Telford, ed., *Letters*, 7:231) and "The Character of a Methodist," ¶ 5 (in Jackson, ed., *Works*, 8:341); although I do not read either of these references as clearly defining a necessary doctrine; rather, they seem to say that the work of the Holy Spirit itself (not necessarily a *doctrine* or teaching about the Holy Spirit) is necessary for Christian existence.

18. Williams cites John Wesley's sermon "On the Trinity" (1775), ¶ 2 (in Outler, ed., *Sermons*, 3:376; and in Jackson, ed., *Works*, 6:200).

19. In a letter to the anonymous and yet unidentified "John Smith," John Wesley states that "perceptible inspiration" is "the main doctrine of the Methodists" (letter of 30 December 1745, ¶ 13; in Frank Baker, ed., *Letters*. 2 vols. to date; Bicentennial Edition of the *Works of John Wesley* [Nashville: Abingdon Press, 1980 and 1982]; hereafter referred to as "Baker, ed., *Letters*," 26:181–82; and in Jackson, ed., *Works*, 12:70; cf. a letter to Smith dated 22 March 1748, ¶ 7, in Baker, ed., *Letters*, 26:289, and in Jackson, ed., *Works*, 12:100), and this is consistent with his introduction to the *Earnest Appeal to Men of Reason and Religion*, which argues that the teaching of a distinct spiritual sensation characterizes the Methodist movement that Wesley defended in this tract (¶ 12; in Cragg, ed., *Appeals*, 11:49; and in Albert C. Outler, ed., *John Wesley: A Representative Collection of His Writings*. A Library of Protestant Thought [New York: Oxford University Press, 1964], 3–4; and in Telford, ed., *Letters*, 2:64, 2:135). The issue of "perceptible inspiration" as a distinctively Wesleyan teaching is taken up in chapter 2 below.

20. Cited above.

21. "The Principles of a Methodist Farther Explained" (1746), ¶ VI:4–6 (in Rupert E. Davies, ed., *The Methodist Societies: History, Nature and Design*. Bicentennial Edition of the *Works of John Wesley*, 9 [Nashville: Abingdon Press, 1989]; hereafter cited as "Davies, ed., *Societies*," 195; in Jackson, ed., *Works*, 8:472–75; and in Telford, ed. *Letters*, 2:267–70).

22. A telephone conversation with Lawrence Meredith, 3 October 2002.

23. Cf. Jones, *United Methodist Doctrine*, 90–103, where Jones, like Meredith, focuses on the doctrines most distinctive of the Methodist movement.

24. John Wesley, "Upon Our Lord's Sermon on the Mount, Discourse 4," I:1 (in Outler, ed., *Sermons*, 1:533–34; in Jackson, ed., *Works*, 5:296).

25. John Wesley, "Catholic Spirit," ¶ I:1 (in Outler, ed., *Sermons*, 2:81).

26. Ibid., ¶ I:1–11 (in Outler, ed., *Sermons*, 2:81–87).

27. Ibid., ¶ I:12–13 (in Outler, ed., *Sermons*, 2:87).

28. John Wesley, "Letter to a Roman Catholic," ¶¶ 2 and 13 (in Jackson, ed., *Works*, 10:80, 83); in the latter paragraph "opinions" are linked to "outward manner of worship" as in the sermon "Catholic Spirit." On the general context of the "Letter to a Roman Catholic," cf. Richard P. Heitzenrater, *Wesley and the People Called Methodists* (Nashville: Abingdon Press, 1995), 172–74.

29. The quotation is in ¶ 5 (in Jackson, ed., *Works*, 10:81); the summary of creedal teachings comprises ¶¶ 6–10 (in Jackson, ed., *Works*, 10:81–82).

30. Ibid., ¶ 11 (in Jackson, ed., *Works*, 10:82).

31. This reading is supported by Outler's introduction to the sermon "Catholic Spirit," where Outler refers to this passage from the "Letter to a Roman Catholic" as John Wesley's "fullest summary" of his understanding of essential teachings, although Outler warns in this passage that Wesley "never ever tried to formulate them in an unrevisable statement" (in Outler, ed., *Sermons*, 2:79). Similarly, Henry Rack observes that the "Letter to a Roman Catholic" expresses John Wesley's sense of "common basic Christianity" (Henry Rack, *Reasonable Enthusiast: John Wesley and the Rise of Methodism* [Philadelphia: Trinity Press International, 1989], 310).

32. John Pearson, *An Exposition of the Creed* (New York: D. Appleton and Co., 1851); cf. Wallace, ed., *Susanna Wesley*, 377–407.

33. Wesley, "Letter to a Roman Catholic," ¶ 6 (in Jackson, ed., *Works*, 10:81).

34. Ibid., ¶ 7 (in Jackson, ed., *Works*, 10:81–82).

35. Ted A. Campbell, *The Gospel in Christian Traditions* (New York: Oxford University Press, 2009), 14–18.

36. Wesley, "Letter to a Roman Catholic," ¶ 8 (in Jackson, ed., *Works*, 10:82).

37. Ibid., ¶ 9.

38. Ibid., ¶ 10.

39. Ibid.

40. Ibid., ¶ 6.

41. Ibid., ¶ 10.

42. Ibid., ¶ 8.

43. Ibid., ¶ 6 (in Jackson, ed., *Works*, 10:81).

44. Although it has been generally presumed that John Wesley edited the Articles of Religion, it is possible, as mentioned in the text, that Thomas Coke or another of Wesley's associates revised the Articles. I have written this section on the presumption that Wesley was the editor, although it would make little difference to the argument here, since the work was received and applied by American Methodists as a doctrinal standard, and it does serve to confirm the beliefs about essential doctrines maintained by John Wesley or the circle of his close associates.

45. Anglican Article 1 (in Jaroslav Pelikan and Valerie Hotchkiss, eds., *Creeds and Confessions of Faith in the Christian Tradition*. 3 vols. (with a collection of source material in original languages on CD-ROM [New Haven: Yale University Press, 2003]; hereafter referred to as "Pelikan and Hotchkiss"), 2:528; Methodist Article 1 (in Pelikan and Hotchkiss 3:202).

46. John Wesley, "The Means of Grace" (from ca. 1739–41), I:1 and II:1 (in Outler, ed., *Sermons*, 1:378, 381).

47. It is very important to note that the views of this particular group of Moravians have been regarded by subsequent Moravians as highly eccentric, and in fact it came at the beginning of a very problematic period in the development of the renewed Unity of Brethren that Moravians call "the sifting time." Wesleyan and Methodist scholars, then, should not report the views of this group as representing (in Outler's phrase) "the Moravian position": see Outler's comment including this phrase in his introduction to John Wesley's "The Means of Grace" (in Outler, ed., *Sermons*), 1:376.

48. Wesley, "The Means of Grace," III:1–12 (in Outler, ed., *Sermons*, 1:384–90).

49. "General Rules," ¶ 6 (in Davies, ed., *Societies*, 9:73; and in Jackson, ed., *Works*, 8:269–71).

50. John Wesley, *Instructions for Children* (London: M. Cooper, 1745), 7.

51. "Large Minutes," qu. 48 (in Jackson, ed., *Works*, 8:322–24).

52. Cf., for example, Wesley's argument about these practices in the sermon "The Means of Grace" (in Outler, ed., *Sermons*, 1:379–80).

53. John Wesley, "A Plain Account of the People Called Methodists," II:9 (in Davies, ed., *Societies*, 9:262–63).

54. Anglican Articles of Religion 25 and 27 (in Pelikan and Hotchkiss, 2:534–35); Methodist Articles 16 and 17 (in Pelikan and Hotchkiss, 3:205).

55. Cf. Outler's introduction to "The Means of Grace" (in Outler, ed., *Sermons*, 1:376) and Heitzenrater, *John Wesley and the People Called Methodists*, 106.

56. We should note that baptism for John Wesley was essential or definitive for a full definition of Christian community (church), even if it was not strictly essential to salvation. Wesley allowed, for example, that Quakers might be saved even apart from baptism: Wesley, a letter to Gilbert Boyce dated 22 May 1750 (in Baker, ed., *Letters*, 2:425; cf. Williams, *John Wesley's Theology Today*, 117).

57. Wesley's *Sunday Service of the Methodists in North America* (London: [Strahan], 1784), ii.

58. *The Book of Common Prayer: 1662 Version*. Everyman's Library, no. 241 (London: David Campbell Publishers, 1999), 189; John Wesley, "The Means of Grace," II:1 (in Outler, ed., *Sermons*, 1:381).

59. John Wesley, "The New Birth," introduction, ¶ 1 (in Outler, ed., *Sermons*, 2:187; and in Sugden, ed., *Sermons*, 2:226–27).

60. In the passage from ¶ 1 of "The Character of a Methodist," cited above and below.

61. John Wesley, "On the Trinity" (1775), ¶ 2 (in Outler, ed., *Sermons*, 3:376; and in Jackson, ed., *Works*, 6:200); cf. Williams, 17 and n. 15.

62. Reading for this the whole of ¶¶ 1–2 (in Outler, ed., *Sermons*, 3:374–76).

63. See the notice affixed to the beginning of the sermon, where Wesley indicated that he did not have his books available at Cork when he wrote the sermon. This could explain why the sermon is lacking in specific reference to historic Trinitarian texts, with the exception of his concern about the anathemas in the so-called Athanasian Creed. Surprisingly, Outler does not note the Catholic context in which the sermon was written, although he may have presupposed that readers would glean this from the affixed note (cf. Outler, ed., *Sermons*, 3:373–74 and the affixed note at 3:374).

64. John Wesley, "Letter to a Roman Catholic," ¶¶ 6–8 (in Jackson, ed., *Works*, 10:81–82).

65. Methodist Articles of Religion 1 (in Pelikan and Hotchkiss, 3:202; in John Leith, ed., *Creeds of the Churches*, 3rd rev. ed. [Atlanta: John Knox Press, 1982], 354).

66. John Wesley, "On the Trinity," ¶ 17 (in Outler, ed., *Sermons*, 2:384–85).

67. Cf. M. Douglas Meeks, "Trinity, Community, and Power" (in Meeks, ed., *Trinity, Community, and Power*, 17); and cf. my own essay in the same collection, " 'Pure, Unbounded Love': Doctrine about God in Historic Wesleyan Communities" (in Meeks, ed., *Trinity, Community, and Power*, 95).

68. Jason E. Vickers, *Invocation and Assent: The Making and Remaking of Trinitarian Theology* (Grand Rapids: William B. Eerdmans Publishing Co., 2008), *passim*; his discussion of "The Wesleys' Hymns and Prayers" is on 169–89.

69. John Wesley, "The Character of a Methodist," ¶ 1 (in Jackson, ed., *Works*, 8:340); cf. Williams, *John Wesley's Theology Today*, 16 and n. 11.

70. "Character of a Methodist," ¶ 1 (in Jackson, ed., *Works*, 8:340). The understatement or *meiosis* is revealed in the last paragraphs, where Wesley stated,

> These are the principles and practices of our sect; these are the marks of a true Methodist.... If any man say, "Why, these are only the common, fundamental principles of Christianity!" thou hast said; so I mean; this is the very truth; I know they are no other; and I would to God both thou and all men knew that I, and all who follow my judgment, do vehemently refuse to be distinguished from other men, by any but the common principles of Christianity. (¶ 17; in Jackson, ed., *Works*, 8:346)

But we should note that on other occasions, Wesley would in fact indicate beliefs or teachings that distinguish the Methodists (see the next chapter).

71. Ibid.

72. John Wesley, "Letter to a Roman Catholic," ¶ 7 (in Jackson, ed., *Works*, 10:81–82).

73. Methodist Articles of Religion 1 and 2 (in Pelikan and Hotchkiss, 3:202; in Leith, ed., *Creeds of the Churches*, 354).

74. Campbell, *John Wesley and Christian Antiquity*, 17, 79–80; on the challenge of Deists influenced by Locke, cf. Vickers, *Invocation and Assent*, 135–67.

75. John Wesley, "The Question, 'What Is an Arminian?' Answered," ¶ 4 (in Jackson, ed., *Works*, 10:358–59).

76. See, for example, "Salvation by Faith," introduction ¶ 3 and ¶ I:4 (1738; in Outler, ed., *Sermons*, 1:118, 120).

77. Letter from John Wesley to Mary Bishop, dated 7 February 1778 (in Telford, ed., *Letters* 6:297–98); cf. Williams, *John Wesley's Theology Today*, 16.

78. Ibid. (in Telford, ed., *Letters* 6:297–98).

79. John Wesley, "Letter to a Roman Catholic," ¶ 7 (in Jackson, ed., *Works*, 10:81–82); Methodist Articles of Religion 2 and 30 (in Pelikan and Hotchkiss, 3:202, 206; in Leith, ed., *Creeds of the Churches*, 354, 359).

80. Collins, *John Wesley's Theology*, 99–103 and especially 101 on the Anselmian theory of the atonement.

81. John Deschner, *Wesley's Christology: An Interpretation* (Dallas: Southern Methodist University Press, 1960), 165–69.

82. John Wesley, "The Character of a Methodist," ¶ 1 (in Jackson, ed., *Works*, 8:340).

83. Methodist Articles of Religion 5–6 (in Pelikan and Hotchkiss, 3:202–3; in Leith, ed., *Creeds of the Churches*, 355).

84. John Wesley, "A Roman Catechism, with a Reply Thereunto," qqu. 5–13 (in Jackson, ed., *Works*, 10:90–94).

85. For further elaboration of the doctrine of John Wesley's understanding of biblical authority, cf. Scott J. Jones, *John Wesley's Conception and Use of Scripture* (Nashville: Kingswood Books, 1998), *passim*.

86. John Wesley, "The Doctrine of Original Sin, according to Scripture, Reason and Experience," ¶ VI:VI (in Jackson, ed., *Works*, 9:429). As noted above, Wesley was quoting in this passage (with approval) a treatise of Dr. Isaac Watts on the doctrine of original sin; cf. John Wesley, "Original Sin," ¶ III:1–2 (in Outler, ed., *Sermons*, 2:182–84), where John Wesley made the point that the doctrine of original sin distinguishes Christianity from heathenism. On original sin as a necessary doctrine, cf. also Runyon, *New Creation*, 25.

87. Methodist Articles of Religion 7 (in Pelikan and Hotchkiss, 3:203).

88. John Wesley, "Justification by Faith," I:1–4 (on original righteousness; in Outler, ed., *Sermons*, 1:184–85), I:5–6 (on original sin; in Outler, ed., *Sermons*, 1:186); "The New Birth," I:1 (on original righteousness; in Outler, ed., *Sermons*, 2:188–89), I:2 (on original sin; in Outler, ed., *Sermons*, 2:189).

89. John Wesley, "God's Approbation of His Works," II:2 (in Outler, ed., *Sermons*, 2:399).

90. Ibid. On the perfection of the original creation, see this sermon in its entirety, and cf. Runyon, *New Creation*, 7–12.

91. Anglican Article 9 (given in Leith, ed., *Creeds of the Churches*, 269–70); cf. Methodist Article 7 (in Leith, ed., *Creeds of the Churches*, 356).

92. John Wesley, letter to John Mason, 21 November 1776 (in Telford, ed., *Letters* 6:239–40).

93. Cf. Maddox, *Responsible Grace*, 78–83; and Collins, *John Wesley's Theology*, 64.

94. As distinguished from "the repentance of believers"; the distinction is drawn very clearly in John Wesley's "The Repentance of Believers," introduction ¶ 1–3 (in Outler, ed., *Sermons*, 1:335–36). Cf. Collins, *John Wesley's Theology*, 156–57.

95. The list with original sin in the first position is given in a letter from John Wesley to George Downing, 6 April 1761 (in Telford, ed., *Letters*, 4:161; cf. Heitzenrater, *Wesley and the People Called Methodists*, 156, 204, 215); the list with repentance in the first place is given in "The Principles of a Methodist Farther Explained" (1746), ¶ VI:4–6 (in Davies, ed., *Societies*, 9:195; in Jackson, ed., *Works*, 8:472–75; and in Telford, ed., *Letters*, 2:267–70).

96. Although some Wesleyan scholars have attempted to distinguish "regeneration" and "new birth," (cf. Randy Maddox, *Responsible Grace*, 159–60, 176–77), it must be noted that *generatio* in Latin denotes "birth," and thus *regeneratio* denotes "new birth" or "rebirth." That Wesley identified the terms "regeneration" and "new birth" is very clear from ¶ IV:1 of the sermon "The New Birth," where he quotes the Westminster Catechism, which uses the term

"regeneration" (John Wesley, "The New Birth," ¶ IV:1 [in Outler, ed., *Sermons*, 2:196; and in Sugden, ed., *Sermons*, 2:237]); cf. also John Wesley's sermon "On God's Vineyard" (1787), which takes "born again," "born from above," and "born of the Spirit" to be synonyms for regeneration (¶ I:6, in Outler, ed., *Sermons*, 3:506).

97. John Wesley, "The New Birth," introduction, ¶ 1 (in Outler, ed., *Sermons*, 2:187; and in Sugden, ed., *Sermons*, 2:226–27).

98. John Wesley, "The Lord Our Righteousness," introduction, ¶¶ 4–6 (in Outler, ed., *Sermons*, 1:450–52; and in Sugden, ed., *Sermons*, 2:425–26).

99. For example, the introduction to his sermon "Justification by Faith," where John Wesley asserted that the doctrine of justification by faith is "the foundation of our hope" (introduction ¶ 1; in Outler, ed., *Sermons*, 1:182).

100. Methodist Articles of Religion 9 (in Pelikan and Hotchkiss, 3:203–4; in Leith, ed., *Creeds of the Churches*, 356).

101. The two lists are given in a letter from John Wesley to George Downing, 6 April 1761 (in Telford, ed., *Letters*, 4:161; cf. Heitzenrater, *Wesley and the People Called Methodists*, 156, 204, 215); and in "The Principles of a Methodist Farther Explained" (1746), ¶ VI:4–6 (in Davies, ed., *Societies*, 9:195; in Jackson, ed., *Works*, 8:472–75; and in Telford, ed., *Letters*, 2:267–70).

102. John Wesley, "The New Birth," introduction, ¶ 1 (in Outler, ed., *Sermons*, 2:187; and in Sugden, ed., *Sermons*, 2:226–27).

103. John Wesley, "Letter to a Roman Catholic," ¶ 6 (in Jackson, ed., *Works*, 10:81).

104. Methodist Articles of Religion 17 (in Pelikan and Hotchkiss, 3:202; in Leith, ed., *Creeds of the Churches*, 358).

105. For example, in the "Letter to a Roman Catholic," ¶ 8 (in Jackson, ed., *Works*, 10:82).

106. Campbell, "Conversion and Baptism in Wesleyan Spirituality," 169–70.

107. Ted A. Campbell, *The Religion of the Heart: A Study of European Religious Life in the Seventeenth and Eighteenth Centuries* (Columbia: University of South Carolina Press, 1991), 90.

108. John Wesley, "Upon Our Lord's Sermon on the Mount, Discourse 4," I:1 (in Outler, ed., *Sermons*, 1:533–34; in Jackson, ed., *Works*, 5:296).

109. Anglican Articles of Religion 19 (in Pelikan and Hotchkiss, 2:533; in Leith, ed., *Creeds of the Churches*, 273); cf. Methodist Articles of Religion 13 (in Pelikan and Hotchkiss, 3:204); cf. Augsburg Confession, item 7 among "Chief Articles of Faith" (in Pelikan and Hotchkiss, 2:62). The Anglican Article has the word *be* noted in square brackets in the text given above; the Methodist Articles does not include it.

110. John Wesley, "Letter to a Roman Catholic," ¶ 9 (in Jackson, ed., *Works*, 10:82).

111. Cited in Frank Baker, *John Wesley and the Church of England* (Nashville: Abingdon Press, 1970), 327.

112. Westminster Confession of Faith, chapters 25 and 30 (in Pelikan and Hotchkiss, 2:638–39, 644; in Leith, ed., *Creeds of the Churches*, 222, 227). In his "Thoughts upon Necessity," I:7, and in his treatise "Predestination Calmly Considered," ¶ 7, John Wesley cited the Westminster Confession of Faith (in Jackson, ed., *Works*, 10:459, 206), although in his treatise "Original Sin," he observed a passage in which a polemical opponent cited the Westminster Catechism and responded, "To this I never subscribed; but I think it is in the main a very excellent composition, which I shall therefore cheerfully endeavor to defend, so far as I conceive it is grounded on clear Scripture" (in Jackson, ed., *Works*, 9:261).

113. Methodist Articles of Religion 16 (in Pelikan and Hotchkiss, 3:205).

114. John Wesley, *Journal* for 24 May 1738, ¶ 1 (in Ward and Heitzenrater, eds., *Journal and Diaries*, 1:242–43). I acknowledge the controversy over whether or not Wesley's Aldersgate-Street experience described here should be described as a "conversion" experience, but Wesley's own language in the conclusion to the previous fascicle of the *Journal*, which acknowledges that at the time of the writing of the first and second fascicles he did not consider himself to have been "converted unto God" (*Journal* for 1 February 1738; in Ward and Heitzenrater, 1:214), makes it natural to see the account of Aldersgate as the account of a "conversion" experience, however Wesley may have altered his views as to whether or not he then received the "assurance of pardon" at that time.

115. John Wesley, "The New Birth," IV:2 (in Outler, ed., *Sermons*, 2:197).

116. Cf. Bernard G. Holland, *Baptism in Early Methodism* (London: Epworth Press, 1970),

53–71; Williams, *John Wesley's Theology Today*, 116–19; Kenneth J. Collins, *The Scripture Way of Salvation: The Heart of John Wesley's Theology* (Nashville: Abingdon Press, 2001), 126–27.

117. Wesley, "The New Birth," IV:1–2 (in Outler, 2:196, 197).

118. Ibid., IV:1 (in Outler, 2:196–97), where Wesley cites the catechism.

119. John Wesley, "On the Great Privilege of Those That Are Born of God," *passim* (in Outler, 1:431–43); Wesley mentions that the new birth is "not barely the being baptized" at I:1 (in Outler, ed., *Sermons*, 1:432).

120. John Wesley, "The Original, Nature, Properties, and Use of the Law," IV:2 (in Outler, ed., *Sermons*, 2:16).

121. John Wesley, "The Marks of the New Birth," *passim* (in Outler, ed., *Sermons*, 1:417–30) and "The First Fruits of the Spirit," *passim* (in Outler, ed., *Sermons*, 1:234–47); in the former sermon Wesley notes that regeneration is "ordinarily annexed to baptism" (the introduction, ¶ 1; in Outler, ed., *Sermons*, 1:417).

122. A letter to the editor of the *Wesleyan-Methodist Magazine*, 1824, 238ff.; cited in Holland, 4–5.

123. Charles R. Hohenstein, "New Birth through Water and the Spirit: A Reply to Ted A. Campbell," *Quarterly Review* 11, no. 2 (Summer 1991): 105.

124. On the influence of Reformed theology and spirituality in eighteenth-century Anglicanism, see John Walsh and Stephen Taylor, "Introduction: The Church and Anglicanism in the 'Long' Eighteenth Century," in *The Church of England, c. 1689–c. 1833: From Toleration to Tractarianism,* ed. John Walsh, Colin Haydon, and Stephen Taylor (Cambridge: Cambridge University Press, 1993), 29–45.

125. Ole Borgen, *John Wesley on the Sacraments: A Definitive Study of John Wesley's Theology of Worship* (Grand Rapids: Francis Asbury Press, 1985), 49–57.

126. Westminster Confession 28 (in Leith, 224–25).

127. On Wesley's revision of the Prayer Book service for infant baptism, cf. Charles R. Hohenstein's "The Revisions of the Rites of Baptism in The Methodist Episcopal Church, 1784–1939" (PhD diss, Notre Dame University, 1990), 52, and appendix 1, 248–53; the prayer in question is given on p. 253.

128. Anglican Articles of Religion 27 (in Pelikan and Hotchkiss, 3:535; in Leith, ed., *Creeds of the Churches*, 275–76).

129. Even the expression "they that receive Baptism rightly" in the Anglican Article may indicate an acknowledgment of the "receptionist" tendency of Reformed sacramental theology (seen explicitly in Article 29, which had been added to the original 38 Articles in 1571). There is a long-standing question of whether John Wesley himself was responsible for all the alterations of the Articles of Religion (and the same issue applies to the revisions of the Prayer Book) in the *Sunday Service* book that accompanied Whatcoat and Vasey to America in 1784. This question itself will probably not be easily (if ever) resolved, but the case I advocate here is that the Reformed understanding of baptism illuminates trends reflected in the revisions in the 1784 *Sunday Service* on the part of the Methodist movement in Wesley's day, if not by Wesley himself.

130. John Wesley, "The Duty of Constant Communion," I:5 (in Outler, ed., *Sermons*, 3:430).

131. John Wesley, "The Means of Grace," III:11 (in Outler, ed., *Sermons*, 1:389).

132. Methodist Articles of Religion 18 (in Pelikan and Hotchkiss, 3:205).

133. John Wesley, "The Duty of Constant Communion," I:2–3 (in Outler, ed., *Sermons,* 3:429).

134. Methodist Articles of Religion 18 (in Pelikan and Hotchkiss, 3:205–6).

135. John Wesley, "The Duty of Constant Communion," II:19 (in Outler, ed., *Sermons,* 3:438).

136. For example, in the Wesleys' abridgment of Brevint's *Christian Sacrament and Sacrifice,* in section IV, "Concerning the Sacrament, as It Is a Means of Grace," the Wesleys' text asserts that the Scriptures "allow it [the sacrament] a far greater virtue than that so representing only" (IV:1; in J. Ernest Rattenbury, ed., *The Eucharistic Hymns of John and Charles Wesley* [London: Epworth Press, 1948], 182). Cf. also in section II, "Concerning the Sacrament as It Is a Memorial of the Sufferings and Death of Christ," "Blessed Jesu, strengthen my faith, prepare my heart, and then bless Thine Ordinance. If I but *touch* as I ought *the hem of thy*

garment—the garment of Thy Passion—virtue will proceed out of Thee" (II:9; in Rattenbury, ed., *Eucharistic Hymns*, 179).

137. John Calvin, *Institutes,* IV.17.10–12, in John T. McNeill, ed., *Calvin: Institutes of the Christian Religion*, 2 vols. Library of Christian Classics series (Philadelphia: Westminster Press, 1960), 2:1370–73. McNeill used the term "virtualism" to describe Calvin's sacramental views in this edition of Calvin's *Institutes* (2:1370, n. 27).

138. Eric Richard Griffin, "Daniel Brevint and the Eucharistic Calvinism of the Caroline Church of England, 1603–1674" (ThD thesis, University of Toronto, 2000), 252.

139. On John Wesley's understanding of eucharistic presence of Christ and its Reformed moorings, cf. Borgen, 58–69.

140. William Nicholson, *A Plain, but Full Exposition of the Catechism of the Church of England* (Oxford: John Henry Parker, 1842), 179.

141. Borgen, 58–69.

142. On the consistency of eighteenth-century Anglicanism in defining itself as a Reformed church, cf. William Gibson, *The Church of England 1688–1832: Unity and Accord* (London and New York: Routledge, 2001), 182–210.

143. Methodist Articles of Religion 1–2 (in Pelikan and Hotchkiss, 3:202; in Leith, ed., *Creeds of the Churches*, 354).

144. On the issue of consistency through his career, we note that these three doctrines (the Trinity, the divinity of Christ, and the atonement) were all affirmed in his 1749 "Letter to a Roman Catholic" (see the text above), in the 1784 revision of the Articles of Religion, and at a number of intervening points along the way: 1775 for his sermon "The Trinity," 1742 for his tract "The Character of a Methodist" affirming the divinity of Christ, and 1778 for his letter to Mary Bishop affirming the doctrine of atonement as a necessary Christian doctrine.

145. Matthew Simpson, *A Hundred Years of Methodism* (New York: Nelson and Phillips; Cincinnati: Hitchcock and Walden, 1876), 352.

146. Abel Stevens, *A Compendious History of American Methodism* (New York: Phillips and Hunt; Cincinnati: Walden and Stowe, 1867, although a preface printed in the book carries the date 1868), 584.

147. James M. Buckley, *A History of the Methodists in the United States* (New York: Christian Literature Co., 1896), 90–91.

148. Hughes, "'Robert Elsmere' and Mr. Gladstone's Criticism of the Book," in *Social Christianity: Sermons Delivered in St. James Hall, London* (London: Hodder and Stoughton, 1890), 99–100.

2. JOHN WESLEY'S CLAIMS ABOUT DISTINCTIVELY METHODIST BELIEFS

1. Noting, as in the previous chapter, that we can speak of distinct Wesleyan movements led by John and Charles Wesley after 1755–56.

2. For example, the denomination that has the name "Presbyterian Church of Wales" (*Eglwys Bresbyteraidd Cymru*) also uses the more historic name "Calvinistic Methodist Church of Wales" (*Eglwys Fethodistaidd Galfinaidd*). Cf. Lenton, 21–26.

3. The term "way of salvation" appears in the title of John Wesley's sermon "The Scripture Way of Salvation" (in Outler, ed., *Sermons*, 2:153–69, and see Outler's note on the title, 2:154). The expression "way to heaven" is used in the preface to the *Sermons on Several Occasions*, ¶¶ 5, 6; in Outler, ed., *Sermons*, 1:105, 106. Cf. also Collins, *The Scripture Way of Salvation*, 13, on the expression "scripture way of salvation." On the use of the *ordo salutis* in the Reformed tradition, see the next section on the background of John Wesley's views.

4. Cited above.

5. "The Principles of a Methodist Farther Explained" (1746), ¶ VI:4–6 (in Davies, ed., *The Methodist Societies*, 195; in Jackson, ed., *Works*, 8:472–75; and in Telford, ed., *Letters*, 2:267–70).

6. A telephone conversation with Lawrence Meredith, 3 October 2002.

7. Williams's book has "The Order of Salvation: Prevenient Grace" (chapter 3), "The Order of Salvation: Repentance and Justification" (chapter 5), "The Order of Salvation: The Work of the Holy Spirit in New Birth and Assurance" (chapter 7), "The Order of Salvation: Repentance in Believers" (chapter 8), "The Order of Salvation: Christian Perfection" (chapter 10), and "The Order of Salvation: Eschatology" (chapter 11).

8. Albert C. Outler, *Theology in the Wesleyan Spirit* (Nashville: Tidings, 1975), chapter 2 (23–43), chapter 3 (45–64), and chapter 4 (65–88).

9. Maddox, *Responsible Grace*, chapter 7, 157–91.

10. Runyon, *New Creation*, chapters 2, "Grace in the New Creation," and 3, "Transforming Grace," 26–101.

11. Especially in chapters 5–6 and 8 of *The Theology of John Wesley* (155–235, 279–312).

12. Herbert Brook Workman, *The Place of Methodism in the Catholic Church*, rev. and enl. ed. (London: Epworth Press, 1921; 1st edition was 1909), 16 and *passim*. Umphrey Lee, *John Wesley and Modern Religion* (Nashville: Cokesbury Press, 1936).

13. Horton Davies, *The English Free Churches* (London: Oxford University Press, 1952), 141; cited in Robert C. Monk, *John Wesley: His Puritan Heritage: A Study of the Christian Life*, 2nd rev. ed. (Lanham, Md.; and London: Scarecrow Press, 1999), 51.

14. Monk, *John Wesley*.

15. Calvin, *Institutes*, 1.7.5 (in McNeill and Battles, eds., 1:80–81).

16. Calvin, *Institutes*, 3.1.1 (in McNeill and Battles, eds., 1:537–38).

17. In a letter to "John Smith" dated 22 March 1748, ¶ 6; in Baker, ed., *Letters*, 2:289. These words are sometimes represented as Samuel Wesley's last words, but the letter goes on to state other things that Samuel Wesley said near the time of his death, and the letter does not make it clear that this quotation was from the day of Samuel Wesley's death.

18. The four "degrees" are specifically outlined in William Perkins, A *Golden Chaine, or The Description of Theologie, Containing the Order of the Causes of Salvation and Damnation, according to God's Word*, 2nd ed. (Cambridge: John Legate, 1597), on pp. 138, 145, 149 (mislabeled as "145"), and 168; cf. William Haller, *The Rise of Puritanism, Or, The Way to the New Jerusalem as Set Forth in Pulpit and Press from Thomas Cartwright to John Lilburne and John Milton, 1570–1643* (New York: Columbia University Press, 1938), 86–92.

19. The five stages are given in William Ames, *The Marrow of Theology*, trans. John Dykstra Eusden (Cleveland: United Church Press, 1968; reprint ed. Durham, N.C.: Labyrinth Press, 1983), 157–74.

20. Westminster Confession of Faith, chapters 10–13 (in Pelikan and Hotchkiss, *Creeds and Confessions of Faith in the Christian Tradition*, 2:619–23).

21. Perkins, 138–45; Ames, 157–60.

22. Perkins, 145; Ames, 162.

23. Perkins, 149–67; Ames, 167–71.

24. Perkins, 168ff.; Ames, 171–74.

25. Perkins, 144; italics as in text.

26. Ibid., 210. On the intent of Perkins's *Golden Chaine* in dealing with the question of knowledge of election, cf. Richard A. Muller, "Perkins' A *Golden Chaine*: Predestinarian System or Schematized *Ordo Salutis?*" (*Sixteenth Century Journal* 9, no. 1 [1978]): 69–81. The theme was obviously central to Perkins: another of his works bears the title "A Treatise Tending unto a Declaration, Whether a Man be in the Estate of Damnation, or in the Estate of Grace" (London: John Porter, 1597).

27. Perkins, *Golden Chaine*, 148.

28. Ames, 164–67.

29. Ibid., 167.

30. John Wesley, letter to George Downing, 6 April 1761 (in Telford, ed., *Letters*, 4:161); cf. Heitzenrater, *Wesley and the People Called Methodists*, 156, 204, 215.

31. John Wesley, "The Character of a Methodist," ¶ 1 (in Jackson, ed., *Works*, 8:340) and ¶ 17 (in Jackson, ed., *Works*, 8:346).

32. Letter to "John Smith" [anonymous] 30 December 1745, ¶ 13 (in Baker, ed., *Letters*, 26:181–82; and in Jackson, ed., *Works*, 12:70; cf. a letter to Smith dated 22 March 1748, ¶ 7, in Baker, ed., *Letters*, 26:289, and in Jackson, ed., *Works*, 12:100).

33. John Wesley, introduction to the *Earnest Appeal to Men of Reason and Religion*, ¶ 12 (in

Cragg, ed., *Appeals*, 11:49; in Outler, ed., *John Wesley*, 3–4; and in Telford, ed., *Letters*, 2:64, 135). The same definition of faith as involving religious experience is given in the sermon "The Scripture Way of Salvation," ¶ II:1 (in Outler, ed., *Sermons*, 2:160–61).

34. Frederick Dreyer, "Faith and Experience in the Thought of John Wesley" (*American Historical Review* 88 [1983]: 12–30); Gregory S. Clapper, *John Wesley on Religious Affections: His Views on Experience and Emotion and Their Role in the Christian Life and Theology* (Metuchen, N.J.: Scarecrow Press, 1989), 55–58; Richard E. Brantley, *Locke, Wesley, and the Method of English Romanticism* (Gainesville: University Press of Florida, 1984), 27–47, 96–102; Rex Dale Matthews, "'Religion and Reason Joined': A Study in the Theology of John Wesley" (PhD diss., Harvard University, 1986), esp. chapter 4, 247–312; Henry Rack, *Reasonable Enthusiast*, 384–87, and I note Rack's word of caution in comparing Wesley and Locke, 386–87.

35. "Christian faith," in this case, is a distinct subspecies of "faith" in general or "in its broadest extent" (Wesley's terms), where it implies any spiritual sensation; Christian faith specifically involves trust in Christ; cf. Wesley's sermon "The Scripture Way of Salvation," II:2, in Outler, ed., *Sermons*, 2:161.

36. Collins, the subtitle of his work on *The Scripture Way of Salvation: The Heart of John Wesley's Theology*, and see his comment on this subtitle, 13.

37. John Wesley, "Salvation by Faith" (1738), the outline given at the end of the introduction (Outler, ed., *Sermons*, 1:118).

38. John Wesley, "The Scripture Way of Salvation" (1765), the outline given at the end of the introduction (Outler, ed., *Sermons*, 2:156).

39. "Salvation by Faith" (1738), II:1 (in Outler, ed., *Sermons*, 1:121); "The Scripture Way of Salvation," I:1 (in Outler, ed., *Sermons*, 2:156).

40. "Salvation by Faith" (1738), II:2–7 (in Outler, ed., *Sermons*, 1:121–25).

41. "Salvation by Faith" (1738), III:9 (in Outler, ed., *Sermons*, 1:129).

42. Cf. Outler's note on this: Outler, ed., *Sermons*, 1:129, n. 119.

43. "The Scripture Way of Salvation," I:2–9 (in Outler, ed., *Sermons*, 2:156–60).

44. "The Principles of a Methodist Farther Explained" (1746), ¶ VI:4–6 (in Davies, ed., *Societies*, 195; in Jackson, ed., *Works*, 8:472–75, and in Telford, ed., *Letters*, 2:267–70).

45. Cf. Heitzenrater, *Wesley and the People Called Methodists*, 156.

46. John Wesley, letter to George Downing, 6 April 1761 (in Telford, ed., *Letters*, 4:146); cf. Heitzenrater, *Wesley and the People Called Methodists*, 156, 204, 215.

47. John Wesley, "The Means of Grace" (from ca. 1739–41), I:1 and II:1; in Outler, ed., *Sermons*, 1:378, 381.

48. John Wesley, "The Way to the Kingdom," II:1–7 (on the repentance of sinners), and II:8–12; in Outler, ed., *Sermons*, 1:225–29.

49. Timothy Smith dated this sermon to 1739; Albert C. Outler tentatively suggested the date of 1746; cf. the index to his edition of the *Sermons*, 1:720.

50. John Wesley, "The Spirit of Bondage and of Adoption," I (on the natural state), II (on the legal state), and III (on the evangelical state); in Outler, ed., *Sermons*, 1:251–55, 255–60, 260–63.

51. John Wesley, "On Working Out Our Own Salvation," II:1, in Outler, ed., *Sermons*, 3:203–4.

52. Ibid.

53. Albert C. Outler, *Theology in the Wesleyan Spirit*, 13.

54. John Wesley, note on 1 Corinthians 1:30 in *Explanatory Notes upon the New Testament* (Naperville, Ill.: Alec R. Allenson; and London: Epworth Press, 1950), 589.

55. George Whitefield, "Christ the Believer's Wisdom, Righteousness, Sanctification, and Redemption," in *Select Sermons of George Whitefield* (London: Banner of Truth Trust, 1959), 61–71.

56. John Wesley, introduction to the *Collection of Hymns for the Use of the People Called Methodists*, ¶ 4 (in Franz Hildebrandt and Oliver Beckerlegge, eds., *A Collection of Hymns for the Use of the People Called Methodists*, Bicentennial Edition of the Works of John Wesley, 7 [Nashville: Abingdon Press, 1983; hereafter cited as "Hildebrandt and Beckerlegge, eds., *Collection*"], 73–74).

57. Ibid., section II comprises hymns 88–95 (in Hildebrandt and Beckerlegge, eds., *Collection*, 188–200); section III comprises hymns 96–181 (in Hildebrandt and Beckerlegge, eds., *Collection*, 201–307).

58. Ibid., section IV comprises hymns 182–465 (in Hildebrandt and Beckerlegge, eds., *Collection*, 308–648).

59. John Wesley, "On God's Vineyard," I:5; in Outler, ed., *Sermons*, 3:505–6.

60. "Large Minutes," questions 3 and 4 (in Jackson, ed., *Works*, 8:299–300).

61. John Wesley, "On God's Vineyard," I:5; in Outler, ed., *Sermons*, 3:506.

62. Letter to Robert Carr Brackenbury, 15 September 1790 (in Telford, ed., *Letters*, 8:238; in Jackson, ed., *Works*, 13:9).

3. *Charles Wesley and the Transmission of Wesleyan Beliefs*

1. Lloyd, *Charles Wesley and the Struggle for Methodist Identity*, 147–61, 180–212, 219–33.

2. J. Ernest Rattenbury, *The Evangelical Doctrines of Charles Wesley's Hymns*, 3rd ed. (London: Epworth Press, 1954), 85.

3. Cf. the introduction that Franz Hildebrandt wrote for the critical edition of the 1780 *Hymnal* that he edited with Oliver Beckerlegge, 3–4.

4. Campbell, *John Wesley and Christian Antiquity*, 9–21.

5. In Wallace, ed., *Susanna Wesley*, 377–407.

6. Quoted in Adam Clarke, *Memoirs of the Wesley Family*, 2nd ed. (New York: Lane and Tippett, 1848), 281; a longer excerpt of this inscription is given in the text of chapter 4 below.

7. Charles Wesley, *Hymns on the Trinity* (Bristol: Felix Farley, 1767; repr. ed., Madison, N.J.: The Charles Wesley Society, 1998).

8. John R. Tyson, "The Lord of Life Is Risen: Theological Reflections on *Hymns for Our Lord's Resurrection* (1746)" Proceedings of the Charles Wesley Society 7 (Madison, N.J.: The Charles Wesley Society, 2001), 81–99.

9. Charles Yrigoyen Jr., *Praising the God of Grace: The Theology of Charles Wesley's Hymns* (Nashville: Abingdon Press, 2005), xi.

10. In the *Collection of Hymns for the Use of the People Called Methodists*, hymns 22–38 (in Hildebrandt and Beckerlegge, eds., 107–28).

11. Wilma Quantrille, introduction to the *Hymns on the Trinity* in the reprint edition of the Charles Wesley Society (1998), cited above, vii–ix.

12. Charles Wesley, *Hymns on the Trinity*, no. 19 in the separate sequence of "Hymns and Prayers to the Trinity" (102).

13. Ibid., no. 87 in the initial sequence (58), this is the initial verse of the first hymn in the section "The Plurality and Trinity of Persons."

14. Ibid., no. 63 in the initial sequence (42); cf. Quantrille's introductory comments on this, x–xi.

15. Ibid., no. 99 in the initial sequence (64); cf. Wilma J. Quantrille, "The Triune God in the Hymns of Charles Wesley" (PhD diss., Drew University, 1989), 119.

16. Charles Wesley, "Hymn for Christmas-Day," in Charles and John Wesley, *Hymns and Sacred Poems* (London: William Strahan, 1739), 206; in George Osborn, ed., *The Poetical Works of John and Charles Wesley* (London: Wesleyan Conference Office, 1868), 1:183; orthography as in Osborn.

17. Charles Wesley, hymn V in *Hymns for the Nativity of Our Lord* (n.d. [believed to be 1745], n.p.), 7; in Osborn, 4:110.

18. Charles Wesley, "Gloria Patri," section X, in *Hymns on God's Everlasting Love* (London: W. Strahan, n.d. [believed to be 1742]), 59; in Osborn, 3:104. Although I have normally followed Osborn's orthography, in this case I have retained the small capitals in the words *Christ* and *God* in the first line, as they appear in the original printing, since Charles Wesley often uses the small capitals reminiscent of the way in which the divine name was printed in English-language Bibles.

19. Charles Wesley, "An Evening Hymn," in Charles and John Wesley, *Hymns and Sacred Poems* (London: W. Strahan, 1740), 26; in Osborn, 1:226.

20. Charles Wesley, "Prayer to Christ before the Sacrament," in *Hymns and Sacred Poems* (1739), 190; in Osborn, 1:169.

21. Charles Wesley, hymn V, in *Hymns for Our Lord's Resurrection* (London: William Strahan, 1746), 8; in Osborn, 4:135; orthography as in Osborn.

22. Charles Wesley, "Free Grace" in *Hymns and Sacred Poems* (1739), 118; in Osborn, 1:105; orthography as in Osborn, except that I have restored the elided vowels in "myst'ry" and "th'" as the original printing had them, indicating Charles Wesley's syllabification.

23. Charles Wesley, "Before Reading the Scriptures," in *Hymns and Sacred Poems* (1740), 41; and in Osborn, 1:237–38; "Before Reading the Scriptures," in *Hymns for Children* (Bristol: Felix Farley, 1763), 27–28, and in Osborn, 6:398–99.

24. John Wesley, comment on Romans 12:6, in *Explanatory Notes upon the New Testament* (1950), 569–70; cf. Jones, *John Wesley's Conception and Use of Scripture*, 43–53.

25. John and/or Charles Wesley, a hymn on Acts 8:35, in the *Hymns on the Four Gospels, and the Acts of the Apostles*, in Osborn, 12:229.

26. John and/or Charles Wesley, a hymn on John 21:25, in the *Hymns on the Four Gospels, and the Acts of the Apostles*, in Osborn, 12:133.

27. Jones, *John Wesley's Conception and Use of Scripture*, 23–31.

28. Hymn on Hebrews 4:2, "For indeed the good news came to us just as to them; but the message they heard did not benefit them, because they were not united by faith with those who listened" in the *Hymns on the Four Gospels, and the Acts of the Apostles*, in Osborn, *Poetical Works*, 13:123–24.

29. John Wesley, letter to "John Smith" [anonymous] 30 December 1745, ¶ 13 (in Baker, ed., *Letters*, 26:181–82; and in Jackson, ed., *Works*, 12:70). See the discussion of "perceptible inspiration" in chapter 2.

30. Campbell, *Methodist Doctrine*, 49–50. John Wesley expressed doubts about whether God would condemn a person on the basis of original sin alone in a letter to John Mason, 21 November 1776 (in Telford, ed., *Letters*, 6:239–40). Cf. also Randy Maddox, *Responsible Grace*, 74–83.

31. Charles Wesley, poem LXXXIX from *Hymns for the Use of Families and On Various Occasions* (Bristol: William Pine, 1767), 95; in Osborn, 7:106; orthography as in Osborn.

32. Based on a scan of the electronic text of Osborn, ed., *Poetical Works of John and Charles Wesley*.

33. Charles Wesley, hymn on "Free Grace," in *Hymns and Sacred Poems* (1739), 118; in Osborn 1:105.

34. The expression "sanctified through faith alone" appears in a "Hymn on the Sixty-First chapter of Isaiah" in Charles and John Wesley, *Hymns and Sacred Poems in Two Volumes*. 2 vols. (Bristol: Felix Farley, 1749), 1:29; in Osborn, 4:311.

35. My counts of occurrences of "faith alone" and the phrases "justified through faith alone" and "justified by faith alone" are based on a scan of the electronic edition of Osborn, ed., *Poetical Works of John and Charles Wesley*.

36. Charles Wesley, "Another" hymn on the subject of "Universal Redemption," in *Hymns and Sacred Poems* (1740), 138; in Osborn, 1:312.

37. Charles Wesley, poem on Titus 2:14, in Charles and John Wesley, *Hymns and Sacred Poems* (Bristol: Felix Farley, 1742), 247; in Osborn, 2:305.

38. John Wesley, "The New Birth," introduction, ¶ 1 (in Outler, ed., *Sermons*, 2:187; and in Sugden, ed., *Sermons*, 2:226–27).

39. Counts of occurrences of these expressions are based on a scan of the electronic edition of Osborn's *Poetical Works of John and Charles Wesley*.

40. John and/or Charles Wesley, a hymn on St. Matthew 18:3, in *Hymns on the Four Gospels, and the Acts of the Apostles*, in Osborn, 10:313.

41. The Nineteenth Anglican Article of Religion, echoing the wording of the Augsburg Confession in defining "church": in Pelikan and Hotchkiss, 3:205; cf. 2:62–63 (definition of the church in the Augsburg Confession) and 2:533–34 (definition of the church in the Anglican Articles of Religion).

42. Charles Wesley, "For the Anniversary Day of One's Conversion," in *Hymns and Sacred Poems* (1740), 120; in Osborn, 1:299.

43. Charles Wesley, "At the Meeting of Friends," in *Hymns for Those That Seek and Those*

That Have Redemption in the Blood of Jesus Christ (Bristol: Felix Farley, 1747), 45; in Osborn, 4:252–53.

44. Charles Wesley, hymn in *Funeral Hymns* (Bristol: William Pine, 1769), 3; in Osborn, 6:215.

45. Charles Wesley, "Groaning for the Spirit of Adoption," in *Hymns and Sacred Poems* (1740), 132; in Osborn, 1:308.

46. Charles Wesley, hymn on Romans 6, in *Hymns and Sacred Poems* (1742), 185; in Osborn, 2:246; orthography as in Osborn except that I have retained the elision in "Baptiz'd" and the small capitals used for "JESUS CHRIST" as in the original 1742 printing.

47. Charles Wesley, two sequential hymns "At the Baptism of Adults," in *Hymns and Sacred Poems* (1749), 2:245–46; in Osborn, 5:388–90. Charles Wesley, "At the Baptism of a Child," in *Hymns for the Use of Families and on Various Occasions* (Bristol: William Pine, 1767), 63–64; in Osborn, 7:71.

48. Charles Wesley, "At the Baptism of Adults," in *Hymns and Sacred Poems* (1749), 2:245; in Osborn, 5:389.

49. Ibid., the second hymn or poem in the sequence "At the Baptism of Adults," 2:246; in Osborn, 5:389; orthography as in Osborn, although I have restored the spelling "forever" (as opposed to Osborn's division into "for ever") and removed a comma to conform to the original publication. On Reformed views of baptism, cf. Campbell, *Christian Confessions*, 177–78; cf. Campbell, "Conversion and Baptism in Wesleyan Spirituality," 160–74.

50. Charles Wesley, hymn from *Hymns on the Lord's Supper* (1745), no. 57; in Rattenbury, ed., *Eucharistic Hymns*, 213.

51. Cf. Calvin, *Institutes*, IV.17.10–12 (in McNeill and Battles, eds., *Calvin: Institutes*, 2:1370–73). McNeill used the term "virtualism" to describe Calvin's sacramental views in this edition of *Calvin's Institutes* (2:1370, note 27); cf. Campbell, *Christian Confessions*, 181–83.

52. This is from the first hymn (beginning with the words "Victim Divine") in the section "The Holy Eucharist as It Implies a Sacrifice" in *Hymns on the Lord's Supper* (1745); in Rattenbury, ed., *Eucharistic Hymns*, page numbered as "H–38"; in Osborn, 3:301.

53. Charles Wesley, "Repentance," in *Hymns and Sacred Poems* (1739), 68; in Osborn, 1:62.

54. Charles Wesley, "For the Anniversary Day of One's Conversion," in *Hymns and Sacred Poems* (1740), 120; in Osborn, 1:300; italics as in original printing.

55. J. R. Watson, *The English Hymn: A Critical and Historical Study* (Oxford: Oxford University Press, 1997), 110–32 (the emphasis on Christian experience in earlier Puritan hymns), 136–37 (Watt's use of the image of the pilgrimage to Zion), and 160–70 (the dramatic use of the first-person singular in Watt's "When I Survey the Wondrous Cross").

56. George Whitefield, "Christ the Believer's Wisdom, Righteousness, Sanctification, and Redemption," in *Sermons on Important Subjects: With a Memoir of the Author*, by Samuel Drew, and a Dissertation on His Character, Preaching, &c., by the Rev. Joseph Smith (London: H. Fisher, Son, and Jackson, 1828), 500–518.

57. In this respect, Charles's explication of the hymn very closely parallels John's treatment of the passage in his *Explanatory Notes upon the New Testament*.

58. Charles Wesley, hymns on "Christ Our Wisdom," "Christ Our Righteousness," "Christ Our Sanctification," and "Christ Our Redemption," in *Hymns and Sacred Poems* (1740), 94–99.

59. See the introduction to *Hymns and Sacred Poems* (1740), presumably by John Wesley, which explicates the "way of salvation" in serial order (iii–xi).

60. In the *Collection of Hymns for the Use of the People Called Methodists*, hymn 138 (in Hildebrandt and Beckerlegge, eds., 255).

61. The titles quoted in parentheses are from *Hymns and Sacred Poems* (1739), 150, 198.

62. See the bibliographical reference above for *Hymns for Those That Seek, and Those That Have Redemption in the Blood of Jesus Christ* (1747).

63. Charles Wesley, "Wrestling Jacob," in *Hymns and Sacred Poems* (1742), 117; in Osborn, 2:175.

64. Charles Wesley, "Christ, the Friend of Sinners," in *Hymns and Sacred Poems* (1739), 102.

65. "For the Anniversary Day of One's Conversion," in *Hymns and Sacred Poems* (1740), 122. The hymn appears in the 1780 *Collection* as hymn number 1 (in Hildebrandt and Beckerlegge, eds., 79–80), although these verses were not included.

66. Charles Wesley, "Another" (following a hymn on "Universal Redemption"), stanzas 5,

7, and 8; in *Hymns and Sacred Poems* (1740), 134, 135; in Osborn, 1:309. This is part of a series of three hymns on "Universal Redemption" in this collection, 132–42.

67. John Wesley, "Free Grace," ¶ 25 (in Outler, ed., *Sermons*, 3:555; in Jackson, ed., *Works*, 7:382).

68. Charles Wesley, "The Marks of Faith," in *Hymns and Sacred Poems* (1749), 2:220–22; in Osborn, 1:363–64; orthography and spelling as in Osborn (the original "shew" is replaced by "show").

69. See John R. Tyson, *Charles Wesley on Sanctification: A Biographical and Theological Study* (Grand Rapids: Francis Asbury Press, 1986), 42–45.

70. Tyson, *Charles Wesley on Sanctification*, 181–225.

71. Charles Wesley, "Christ Our Sanctification," in *Hymns and Sacred Poems* (1740), 97, 98 (in Osborn, 1:284), orthography as in Osborn.

72. Charles Wesley, "Wrestling Jacob," in *Hymns and Sacred Poems* (1742), 117; in Osborn, 2:175.

73. Cf. Tyson, *Charles Wesley on Sanctification*, 157–79.

74. Charles Wesley, hymn IX, "To–Jesus, shew us thy Salvation," in Charles Wesley, *Hymns for Those That Seek, and Those That Have Redemption in the Blood of Jesus Christ* (1747), 13 (in Osborn, 4:219).

75. Ibid.

76. On John Wesley's belief that entire sanctification is available "now," cf. his sermon "The Scripture Way of Salvation," III:16 (in Outler, ed., *Sermons*, 2:168; in Jackson, ed., *Works*, 6:52–53). On Charles Wesley's consistent tendency to see entire sanctification at the end of life, cf. Tyson, *Charles Wesley on Sanctification*, 237–48.

77. On John Wesley's belief that entire sanctification occurs instantaneously, cf. his sermon "The Scripture Way of Salvation," III:18 (in Outler, ed., *Sermons*, 2:168–69; in Jackson, ed., *Works*, 6:53). On Charles Wesley's tendency to emphasize the gradual work of sanctification, cf. Tyson, *Charles Wesley on Sanctification*, 248–52.

78. Tyson, *Charles Wesley on Sanctification*, 252–61.

79. Ibid., 297–301.

80. John Wesley, introduction to the *Collection of Hymns for the Use of the People Called Methodists*, ¶ 4 (in Hildebrandt and Beckerlegge, eds., *Collection of Hymns*, 73–74).

81. Ibid.

82. Cf. Carlton R. Young, *An Introduction to the New Methodist Hymnal* (Nashville: Methodist Publishing House/Graded Press, 1966), 7. In the current British Methodist hymnal, *Hymns and Psalms: A Methodist and Ecumenical Hymn Book*, rev.ed. (London: Methodist Publishing House, 1984), this is represented in the hymnal section "The Christian Life," comprising hymns 661–751. In the current *United Methodist Hymnal: Book of United Methodist Worship* (Nashville: United Methodist Publishing House, 1989), this is represented in the sections on "Prevenient Grace" (hymns 337–60), "Justifying Grace" (hymns 361–81), and "Sanctifying and Perfecting Grace" (hymns 382–536).

83. In the current British Methodist hymnal, *Hymns and Psalms* (1983), this is represented in the hymnal sections "The Eternal Father" (hymns 21–73), "The Eternal Word" (hymns 74–278), and "The Eternal Spirit" (hymns 279–328). In the current *United Methodist Hymnal* (1989), this is represented in the sections "The Glory of the Triune God" (hymns 57–152), "The Grace of Jesus Christ" (hymns 153–327), and "The Power of the Holy Spirit" (hymns 328–36).

84. Cf. Campbell, "John Wesley and the Legacy of Methodist Theology," 405–20.

4. BELIEFS ABOUT GOD IN WESLEYAN COMMUNITIES

1. Cited in the preface to the *African Methodist Episcopal Church Hymnal* (also known as the "AMEC Bicentennial Hymnal") (Nashville: African Methodist Episcopal Church, 1984; hereafter cited as "AME *Hymnal* 1984"), ix.

2. So far as possible, I have tried to utilize the organization of Methodist hymnals as pro-

viding the basic organizational framework for this chapter. Systematic theologies, including those by Wesleyan and Methodist authors included in this study, typically begin with a consideration of the existence and attributes of God (the locus *de Deo Uno*) and then consider the Triune nature of God (the locus *de Deo Trino*). This order is reversed in this chapter in deference to the consistent pattern of Methodist hymnals (see the note below), which begin with the praise of the Trinity and then typically celebrate the attributes of God under the heading of God the Father.

3. Pliny the Younger, letter to the emperor Trajan; in R. A. B. Mynors, ed., *C. Plini Caecili: Epistularum Libri Decem* (Oxford: Clarendon Press, 1963), 339; my translation. Cf. Robert L. Wilken, "The Christians as the Romans (and Greeks) Saw Them," *Jewish and Christian Self-Definition*, ed. E. P. Sanders. 3 vols. (Philadelphia: Fortress, 1980), 1:111–13. Wilken points to Lucian's *Peregrinus* and to the *Martyrdom of Polycarp* as parallels to the passage in Pliny and as further instances of the practice of the worship of Christ as a central element in early Christian self-definition.

4. On contemporary ecumenical appropriation, see the report of the Joint Commission between the Roman Catholic Church and the World Methodist Council, 1991, on *The Apostolic Tradition*, ¶ 38 (21–22), jointly affirming the Nicene-Constantinopolitan Creed; and the World Council of Churches Faith and Order Commission document, *Confessing the One Faith: An Ecumenical Explication of the Apostolic Faith as It Is Confessed in the Nicene-Constantinopolitan Creed (381)* (Faith and Order Paper no. 153; Geneva: World Council of Churches, 1991), *passim*. Cf. Campbell, *Christian Confessions*, ¶ 1.2.1, 2.2.1–2, 3.2.1, 4.2.1.a–b. The first Article of Religion of the Church of England affirmed the doctrine of the Trinity in terms drawn from the Nicene-Constantinopolitan Creed. The eighth Article affirmed the Nicene, Apostles', and Athanasian creeds, and these were all utilized in public worship according to the Anglican BCP (1662). Cf. Calvin, *Institutes*, I:13 (in McNeill, ed., *Calvin: Institutes*, 1:120–50).

5. Vickers, *Invocation and Assent*, chapters 1–5, pp. 1–167.

6. Adam Clarke, *Memoirs of the Wesley Family*, 281.

7. This, it might be noted, was Charles Wesley's second volume of hymns on the Trinity; the first one had borne the title *Gloria Patri, etc....Hymns on the Trinity* (1746). Cf. Barry E. Bryant, "Trinity and Hymnody: The Doctrine of the Trinity in the Hymns of Charles Wesley" (*Wesleyan Theological Journal* 25, no. 2 [Fall 1990]: 64–65).

8. Passages that show the devotional nature of Wesley's references to the Trinity: "blessed Trinity" (Jackson, ed., *Works*, 3:434, 10:408); "ever-blessed Trinity" (Jackson, 5:78, 8:49); "Holy, Undivided Trinity" (in Jackson, ed., *Works*, 11:203, cf. 11:230).

9. Wesley, 1780 *Collection of Hymns*, no. 249, verse 4 (in Hildebrandt and Beckerlegge, eds., 390).

10. Wesley, 1780 *Collection of Hymns*, no. 251, verse 2 (in Hildebrandt and Beckerlegge, eds., 392).

11. "On Knowing Christ after the Flesh," ¶ 5 (in Outler, ed., *Sermons*, 4:100; in Jackson, ed., *Works*, 7:292), italics as in original.

12. "The Question, 'What Is an Arminian?' Answered," ¶ 4 (in Jackson, ed., *Works*, 10:359). Cf. other passages refuting Arianism or Socianianism: "The Lord Our Righteousness," II:4 (in Jackson, ed., *Works*, 5:242; in Sugden, ed., *Sermons*, 2:435; in Outler, ed., *Sermons*, 1:459–60); "On Knowing Christ after the Flesh," ¶ 5 (in Outler, ed., *Sermons*, 4:100; in Jackson, ed., *Works*, 7:292); *Journal* 14 January 1756 (in Jackson, ed., *Works*, 2:352–53; in Curnock, ed., *Journal*, 4:145–46); *Letters* 3 July 1756 (to the Rev. Mr. Clarke; in Jackson, ed., *Works*, 13:211; and in Telford, ed., *Letters*, 3:182); *Letters* 5 October 1756 ("to the Monthly Reviewers"; in Jackson, ed., *Works*, 13:386); *Letters* 24 April 1765 (to Dr. Erskine; in Telford, ed., *Letters*, 4:296); *Letters* 16 September 1774 ("to a Member of the Society"; in Jackson, ed., *Works*, 12:296; in Telford, ed., *Letters*, 6:113); *Letters* 8 June 1780 (to Charles Wesley; in Jackson, ed., *Works*, 12:147; in Telford, ed., *Letters*, 7:21–22); *Letters* 17 September 1788 (to Joseph Benson; in Telford, ed., *Letters*, 8:89–90).

13. "On the Trinity," ¶ 2 (1775; in Outler, *Sermons*, 2:376; in Jackson, ed., *Works*, 6:200).

14. "On the Trinity," ¶ 4 (in Outler, *Sermons*, 2:377–78; in Jackson, ed, *Works*, 6:201); but Wesley had not remembered the quotation from Servetus correctly, and the original quotation

is much more questionable, affirming only that the Father is God and Christ is the "Son of God"; cf. Outler, ed., *Sermons*, 2:378, n. 11.

15. Cf. Nolan B. Harmon, "The Creeds in American Methodism" (in *Encyclopedia of World Methodism*, s.v. "Confession of Faith," 1:563).

16. John Wesley, letter to Mary Bishop, 17 April 1776 (in Telford, ed., *Letters*, 6:213).

17. Wesley, 1780 *Hymnal*, no. 7, verse 3 (in Hildebrandt and Beckerlegge, eds., 88).

18. Wesley, 1780 *Hymnal*, no. 248, verse 6 (in Hildebrandt and Beckerlegge, eds., 390).

19. Henry D. Rack, "Early Methodist Visions of the Trinity" (*Proceedings of the Wesley Historical Society*, 45:38–44, 46:57–69).

20. Adam Clarke, *Commentary* on Luke 1:35 (*The Holy Bible, Containing the Old and New Testaments, the Text Carefully Printed from the Most Correct Copies of the Present Authorised Translation, including the Marginal Readings and Parallel Texts, with a Commentary and Critical Notes* [London: Thomas Tegg and Son, 1836; four Old Testament vols. and two New Testament vols.]; New Testament 1:375–76).

21. Langford, *Practical Divinity* (1998), 1:49–50; cf. David Tripp, "Methodism's Trinitarian Hymnody: A Sampling, 1780 and 1989, and Some Questions," *Quarterly Review* 14:4 (1994): note 6, 384–85. The most extensive study of Clarke's views and the response to them is given in E. Dale Dunlap's unpublished doctoral dissertation, "Methodist Theology in Great Britain in the Nineteenth Century: With Special Reference to the Theology of Adam Clarke, Richard Watson, and William Burt Pope" (PhD diss., Yale University, 1956; repr. ed.: Ann Arbor, Mich.: University Microfilms International), 104–8.

22. Langford, *Practical Divinity* (1998), 1:50; and Dunlap (see the preceding note). There is a reference to this controversy in Thomas O. Summers's *Systematic Theology*, I:1 (in 1888 printing, 1:165), which indicates that American Methodists were aware of the British controversy.

23. Constitution of the Methodist Church in the United Kingdom and of other churches related to it such as the Methodist Church of Southern Africa and Methodist Church Nigeria, based on the 1932 Deed of Union (*Constitutional Practice and Discipline of the Methodist Church*, volume 2 [2009], 213–14); on the interpretation of the constitution of the Methodist Church in the United Kingdom, cf. A. Raymond George, "Foundational Documents of the Faith: IX. Methodist Statements" (*Expository Times* 91 [June 1980]: 260). The first Article of Religion of The Methodist Episcopal Church and its successors, including The United Methodist Church, and the AME, AME Zion, and CME Churches (*Discipline of The United Methodist Church 2008*, ¶ 62, section 3, Article 1 of the Articles of Religion, p. 59). Cf. also the Confession of Faith that The United Methodist Church inherited from The Evangelical United Brethren Church (*Book of Discipline of The United Methodist Church 2008*, ¶ 62, section 3, Article 1 of the Confession of Faith, p. 66); and the first Article of Faith of the Church of the Nazarene (in Pelikan and Hotchkiss, 3:401).

24. American Methodist hymnals include the use of the Apostles' Creed (in the 1935 *Methodist Hymnal*, p. 512; in the 1964 *Methodist Hymnal (Book of Hymns)*, no. 738, and in the 1989 *United Methodist Hymnal*, nos. 881, 882); the two most recent hymnals have also the Nicene Creed (1964, no. 739; 1989, no. 880, where it appears in the first position before the Apostles' Creed). Both the *United Methodist Hymnal* of 1989 and the *African Methodist Episcopal Church Hymnal* of 1984 give the Apostles' Creed in the communion service and both utilize it as the means by which candidates for baptism affirm their faith (UMC 1989, 7, 35; AME 1984, nos. 799 [p. 10] and 802). The AME declaration on Apostolic Succession and Religious Formalism (1884) states that "we grant that the orderly repetition of the…Apostles' Creed…may conduce to the attainment" of spiritual worship (cited in the *Doctrines and Discipline of the African Methodist Episcopal Church*, 47th ed. [Nashville: AMEC Publishing House, 2005], 22).

25. Tripp, "Methodism's Trinitarian Hymnody," 363–70.

26. For example, the *Collection of Hymns for the Use of The Methodist Episcopal Church, Principally from the Collection of the Rev. John Wesley* (New York: Bangs and Emory, 1825).

27. *Hymns for the Use of The Methodist Episcopal Church* (New York: Carlton and Porter, 1849).

28. Wesley, *Instructions for Children*, 5; small capital letters in the word GOD as in the original printing.

29. Ibid., 23.

30. *A Short Scriptural Catechism Intended for the Use of The Methodist Episcopal Church* (Philadelphia: Henry Tuckniss, 1795), on the (unnumbered) page facing p. iv.

31. *A Catechism for the Use of Children* (London: T. Cordeux, 1817), chapter 2, p. 2 (on the unity of God); chapter 3, p. 3 (on Jesus Christ); chapter 1, p. 1 (on the Holy Spirit). *Catechisms of the Wesleyan Methodists,* no. I, "For Children of Tender Years" (New York: J. Emory and B. Waugh, 1829), 3–9.

32. *The Catechisms of the Wesleyan Methodists: Compiled and Published by Order of the Conference,* no. II, "For Children of Seven Years of Age and Upward" (Toronto: Samuel Rose, 1867), section 1, "Of God," questions 12 and 13, 4 and 5; I have omitted the Scripture verses following each of the responses.

33. *The Catechism (Formerly "The Turner Catechism") of the A.M.E. Church,* repr. ed. (Nashville: A.M.E.C. Sunday School Union, 2000), lesson II, "The Persons of the Godhead."

34. *The Junior Catechism of The Methodist Episcopal Church and The Methodist Episcopal Church, South* (New York: The Methodist Book Concern, [1932]), 3. Cf. *The Junior Catechism* (Memphis: C.M.E. Church Publishing House, n.d.; I purchased this volume new at a Chicago CME congregation in June 2005), 3.

35. *A Methodist Catechism: Compiled by Order of the Conference of the Methodist Church in Ireland* (London: Epworth Press, [1948]), qu. 8, p. 3.

36. *The Senior Catechism of the Methodist Church* (London: Methodist Publishing House, 1952), qu. 18, p. 6.

37. *A Catechism for the Use of the People Called Methodists* (Peterborough: Methodist Publishing House, [1989]), qu. 48 (on baptism, 22 and 24), qu. 54 (the Apostles' Creed, 26), qu. 55 (the Nicene Creed, 28), qqu. 56, 57, 58, and 62 (on the Trinity, God the Father, Jesus Christ, and the Holy Spirit, 30 and 32).

38. Ibid., 23.

39. Richard Watson, *Theological Institutes; Or, A View of the Evidences, Doctrines, Morals, and Institutions of Christianity,* ed. John McClintock, II:15, "Divine Worship Paid to Christ" (New York: Carlton and Phillips, 1854, 1:596–616).

40. William Burt Pope, *A Compendium of Christian Theology: Being Analytical Outlines of Theological Study; Biblical, Dogmatic, and Historical.* 3 vols. (New York: Phillips and Hunt; Cincinnati: Walden and Stowe, 1881), 1:282. More complete references to the doctrine of the Trinity in the works of Wesleyan theologians studied by preachers are as follows: (1) Richard Watson, *Theological Institutes,* 1:8–17 (in 1854 edition; 1:447–642). (2) Thomas O. Summers, *Systematic Theology: A Complete Body of Wesleyan Arminian Divinity Consisting of Lectures on the Twenty-Five Articles of Religion,* I:II:1–2 (Nashville: Publishing House of The Methodist Episcopal Church, South, 1888), 1:147–57). (3) Pope, *Compendium of Christian Theology,* unnumbered chapter "God," subsection "The Triune Name" (in 1880 printing, 1:255–86). (4) John Miley, *Systematic Theology,* II:5–8. 2 vols. (New York: Hunt and Eaton, 1892–94, 1:228–75). (5) H. Orton Wiley, *Christian Theology,* ch. 15 (Kansas City, Mo.: Beacon Hill Press, 1962–63; 1:393–439). Studies of the doctrine of the Trinity in nineteenth-century Methodist circles are given in the following: E. Dale Dunlap, "Methodist Theology in Great Britain in the Nineteenth Century" (see above); and Sam Powell, "The Doctrine of the Trinity in Nineteenth Century American Wesleyanism, 1850–1900" (*Wesleyan Theological Journal* 18:2 [Fall 1983]: 33–46). I would have to register a dissent on Powell's initial comment that the doctrine of the Trinity had the status of "a vulgar joke in polite company" among nineteenth-century Methodists. Although the case could be made that Wesleyans in general took the doctrine of the Trinity for granted and so did not make an original contribution to it, it is also the case that the doctrine of the Trinity was centrally taught in all nineteenth-century Wesleyan communities of which I am aware. Treatments of the doctrine of the Trinity by more recent Wesleyan systematic theologians are as follows: Colin Williams, *John Wesley's Theology Today,* 93–97; Lycurgus M. Starkey Jr., "The Holy Trinity" (in *Encyclopedia of World Methodism,* s.v. "Trinity," 2:2366–77); Geoffrey Wainwright, "Methodism and Apostolic Faith" (in M. Douglas Meeks, ed., *What Should Methodists Teach? Wesleyan Tradition and Modern Diversity* [Nashville: Kingswood Books, 1990], 101–17); Bryant, "Trinity and Hymnody," 64–73; and Maddox, *Responsible Grace,* 136–40.

41. Albert C. Knudson, *The Doctrine of God* (Nashville: Cokesbury Press, 1930), cf. the conclusion to the book, 422–28; quotation given is on p. 427.

42. Cf. Langford, *Practical Divinity* (1998), 1:166–70, although Langford stresses Knudson's belief that his views affirmed the "central intention of the doctrine of the Trinity" (180). Cf. also Knudson's essay "Henry Clay Sheldon—Theologian" in Langford, ed., *Practical Divinity* (1998), 2:125–36, and especially Knudson's comments on Sheldon's Trinitarian theology, 2:133–34.

43. In fact, the method of Knudson's book was to give an account of traditional doctrinal teachings and then to offer contemporary ways of thinking about them, not prescribing his own views or insisting that they were the church's teachings, but opening students up to think critically and creatively for themselves.

44. *Methodist Hymnal* (1935), no. 1.

45. "Doctrinal Statement" of the Korean Methodist Church (1930; in Pelikan and Hotchkiss, 3:486).

46. See the previous note.

47. Pope, *Compendium, passim*.

48. *Hymns and Psalms* (1984), hymns 21–73.

49. Adaptation of the Thomas Ken doxology by Gilbert H. Vieira, in *The United Methodist Hymnal* (1989), no. 94.

50. Candidates for ordination as elders in The United Methodist Church (USA and global) are asked if they have studied the doctrines of the denomination, if they believe these doctrines to be consistent with the Scriptures, and if they will "preach and maintain them" (*Book of Discipline of The United Methodist Church 2008*, ¶ 336, questions 8–10, p. 246). Candidates for ordination in the Methodist Church of Great Britain are historically asked, "Do you believe the doctrines of the Christian faith as this Church has received them?" and of ministers it is annually asked, "Does he believe and preach our doctrines?" (A. Raymond George, 261; citing the *Constitutional Practice and Discipline* for 1977 [310] and 1979 [400] and the *Methodist Service Book* [1975], p. G9).

51. Methodist Articles of Religion 1 (in Pelikan and Hotchkiss, 3:202; in Leith, *Creeds of the Churches*, 354).

52. *An Ordinal: The United Methodist Church: Adopted for Official Alternative Use by the 1980 General Conference* (Nashville: United Methodist Publishing House, 1980), cf. 47–48 for one example of the ordination prayer without specified wording.

53. *The United Methodist Book of Worship* (Nashville: United Methodist Publishing House, 1992), 677.

54. *Methodist Worship Book* (Peterborough: Methodist Publishing House, 1999), 204.

55. "The Lord's Prayer Paraphrased," first published in *Hymns and Sacred Poems* (1742), 276; in Osborn, 2:336. This was subsequently published in the hymnal of 1780, no. 225 (in Hildebrandt and Beckerlegge, eds., 363).

56. The first Article of Religion of the Church of England asserts that God is one and eternal, "without body, parts, or passions" (Lat. *incorporealis, impartibilis, impassibilis*). Cf. Calvin, *Institutes*, I:10.2 (in McNeill, ed., *Calvin: Institutes*, 1:97–99), I:14.3 (in McNeill, ed., *Calvin: Institutes*, 1:162–63), III:25.4 (in McNeill, ed., *Calvin: Institutes*, 2:993–94).

57. Hymn of Ernst Lange translated into English by John Wesley, first published in *A Collection of Psalms and Hymns* (Charleston, S.C.: Lewis Timothy, 1737), 15–18, and then in *Hymns and Sacred Poems* (1739), 161; in Osborn, 1:143. The hymn was subsequently published in the 1780 *Collection of Hymns*, no. 231, part I (in Hildebrandt and Beckerlegge, eds., 370).

58. John Wesley, "The Character of a Methodist" (1742; in Jackson, ed., *Works*, 8:339–47). Wesley indicated in a letter to the editor of *Lloyd's Evening Post* twenty-five years later (5 March 1767), that the "Character of a Methodist" had been inspired by "the character of a perfect Christian drawn by Clemens Alexandrinus" (in Jackson, ed., *Works*, 3:273; in Curnock, ed., *Journal*, 5:197; in Telford, ed., *Letters*, 5:43). Cf. Campbell, *John Wesley and Christian Antiquity*, 57. Cf. Clement of Alexandria, *Stromateis*, book 7 (in Alexander Roberts and James Donaldson, eds., *The Ante-Nicene Fathers* [Buffalo: Christian Literature Publishing Co., 1885; repr. ed.: Grand Rapids: William B. Eerdmans Publishing Co., 1971], 2:523–56). Charles Wesley had written a poem "On Clemens Alexandrinus's Description of a Perfect Christian" (in *Hymns and Sacred Poems* [1739], 37–38; cf. Osborn, 1:34–36).

59. "Upon Our Lord's Sermon on the Mount, Discourse VI" (1748; III:7; in Outler, ed., *Sermons*, 1:580–81; in Sugden, ed., *Sermons*, 1:435–36; also in Robert W. Burtner and Robert E. Chiles, eds., *A Compend of Wesley's Theology* [New York and Nashville: Abingdon Press, 1954], 2:A:6); "On Eternity" (28 June 1786; ¶ 20; in Outler, ed., *Sermons*, 2:371–72; in Jackson, ed., *Works*, 6:198; in Burtner and Chiles, 2:A:5); "On the Omnipresence of God" (12 August 1788; I:2–3; in Outler, ed., *Sermons*, 4:42; in Jackson, ed., *Works*, 7:239–40; Burtner and Chiles, 2:A:4); "The Unity of the Divine Being" (9 April 1789; ¶¶ 2–8; in Outler, ed., *Sermons*, 4:61–63; in Jackson, ed., *Works*, 7:265–66; in Burtner and Chiles, 2:A:3). On Wesley's appropriation of the Alexandrian tradition of the pursuit of divine virtues or attributes in the sanctification of the believer, see David Bundy, "Christian Virtue: John Wesley and the Alexandrian Tradition" (*Wesleyan Theological Journal* 26, no. 1 [Spring 1991]: 139–63); and Maddox, *Responsible Grace*, 50–55. Hymns no. 231–32 in the 1780 *Collection of Hymns* are titled "The Attributes of God," and describe God's immortality, perfection, wisdom, power, infinity, eternity, greatness, unchangeableness, omniscience, benevolence, love, holiness, and omnipotence. These appear in the section "For Believers Rejoicing," and the implication is that believers rejoice in the attributes of God. The Methodist Episcopal Church, Methodist Episcopal Church, South, and Methodist Protestant *Methodist Hymnal* of 1935 has subsections on God's "Majesty and Power" (nos. 59–67) and God's "Love and Mercy" (nos. 75–82). Similarly, the AME *Hymnal* of 1984 has subsections on God's "Majesty and Power" (nos. 52–74) and God's "Love and Mercy" (nos. 75–85). The Methodist Church (UK) *Hymns and Psalms* of 1983 has subsections on "God's Creating and Sustaining Power" (nos. 21–29), "God's Revealing and Transforming Power" (nos. 30–48), "God's Justice and Perfection" (nos. 49–61), and "God's Patience and Guidance" (nos. 62–73).

60. Discussion of divine attributes among Wesleyan theologians prescribed for study by preachers: (1) Watson, *Theological Institutes*, II:8–17 (1854 edition; 1:447–642). (2) Summers, *Systematic Theology* (I:I:2, in 1888 printing, 1:70–109). (3) Pope, *Compendium of Christian Theology* (unnumbered chapter on "God," subsection "The Attributes of God"; in 1880 printing, 1:287–358). (4) Miley, *Systematic Theology* (II:3–4; in 1892 printing, 1:174–222). (5) Wiley, *Christian Theology*, II:15 (in 1940 printing, 1:320–92) and II:13 (1:290–319). Some commentary on these is offered in Dunlap, "Methodist Theology in Great Britain in the Nineteenth Century," 144–48, 287–92.

61. Pope, *Compendium* (in 1880 printing, 1:287–358).

62. Ted A. Campbell, "The Mystery of the First Article of Religion, and the Mystery of Divine Passibility" (*OXFORDnotes*, 4:1 [24 May 1996], 5).

63. "On the Unity of the Divine Being," ¶ 8 (in Outler, ed., *Sermons*, 4:63; in Jackson, ed., *Works*, 7:266).

64. Summers, *Systematic Theology*, I:1:2:3, §3 (in 1888 printing, 1:80–82). Cf. also contemporary Methodist authors David Bundy, in the work cited in the bibliographical notes above, 147, and Roberta C. Bondi, *To Love as God Loves: Conversations with the Early Church* (Philadelphia: Fortress Press, 1987), 57–77, both of whom explain the appropriateness of speaking of passionlessness, in a carefully defined sense, as one aspect of the Christian's endeavor.

65. 1780 *Collection of Hymns*, no. 211 (in Hildebrandt and Beckerlegge, eds., 345).

66. Hymn of Frances Jane Crosby, in AME *Hymnal* 1984, no. 279.

67. Langford, *Practical Divinity* (1998), 1:105–10, 164–66.

68. Campbell, *Christian Confessions*, 3.2.1 (esp. 146); cf. John Macquarrie, *Principles of Christian Theology*, 2nd ed. (New York: Charles Scribner's Sons, 1977), 163.

69. Wesley, "Free Grace," ¶¶ 20–27 (in Outler, ed., *Sermons*, 3:542–63; in Jackson, ed., *Works*, 8:379–84).

70. Charles Wesley, "Another" (following a hymn on "Universal Redemption"), stanza 7; in *Hymns and Sacred Poems* (1740), 135; in Osborn, 1:309.

71. Wesley's "Thoughts upon God's Sovereignty" (in Jackson, ed., *Works*, 10:361–63) makes a sharp distinction between God's role as Creator and God's role as Governor, and maintains that in the former role God requires full justice, but in the latter role God allows the grace of divine mercy. Again, Wesley will not allow that divine goodness can be undermined by divine sovereignty or power.

72. Wesley, "Predestination Calmly Considered," ¶¶ 50–54 (in Jackson, ed., *Works*, 10:232–36; in Burtner and Chiles, 2:B:1).

73. Cf. the article by Sam Powell, cited above.

74. Robert E. Chiles, *Theological Transition in American Methodism, 1790–1935* (New York: Abingdon Press, 1965), chapter 5, "From Free Grace to Free Will," 144–83.

75. Edgar Sheffield Brightman, *The Problem of God* (New York: Abingdon Press, 1930). Brightman also dealt with these issues in *The Finding of God* (New York: Abingdon Press, 1931), esp. 94–122.

76. Brightman, *The Problem of God*, 13–34.

77. Ibid., 60–85.

78. Ibid., 86–106.

79. John H. Lavely, describing Brightman's view, in "Edgar Sheffield Brightman: Good-and-Evil and the Finite-Infinite God," in Paul Deats and Carol Robb, eds., *The Boston Personalist Tradition* (Macon, Ga.: Mercer University Press, 1986), 136.

80. Ibid., 133.

81. Ibid., 137.

82. Ibid., 166–93.

83. Ibid., 189.

84. Ibid., 137.

85. John B. Cobb Jr., *God and the World* (Philadelphia: Westminster Press, 1969), 88. Cobb does not explicitly name Brightman at this point but his account seems clearly enough oriented toward Brightman's idea of "the theory of [God's] limited power."

86. Cobb, *God and the World*, 87–102 generally; the quotation is on p. 90.

87. Schubert M. Ogden, "Evil and Belief in God: The Distinctive Relevance of a 'Process Theology,'" *Perkins School of Theology Journal* 31 (1978): 29–34; quotations on 32, 32–33.

88. Ibid., 34, where the phrase "pseudo-conception" is applied repeatedly to classical understandings of divine omnipotence.

89. Cf. Kelley Steve McCormick's extensively documented study "Theosis in Chrysostom and Wesley: An Eastern Paradigm on Faith and Love," *Wesleyan Theological Journal* 26, no. 1 (Spring 1991): 38–103; and Michael Christensen, "John Wesley: Christian Perfection as Faith Filled with the Energy of Love," in Michael Christensen, ed., *Partakes of the Divine Nature: The History and Development of Deification in Christian Traditions* (Madison, N.J.: Farleigh Dickinson University Press, 2007), 219–29.

5. BELIEFS ABOUT THE "WAY OF SALVATION" AFTER THE WESLEYS

1. Young, *Introduction to the New Methodist Hymnal*, 7. The quotation from John Wesley is from the preface to the 1780 *Collection of Hymns*, given above in the text. Young describes the topical layout of the 1780 *Collection* as a precedent for the organization of subsequent Methodist hymnals. However, in using the term "real Christians" Wesley seems to have denoted his sense of an ideal, that is, what a "real" Christian ought to be, where Young takes this expression as referring to the actual or lived experiences of Christians.

2. *A Pocket Hymn Book: Designed as a Constant Companion for the Pious, Collected from Various Authors* (Philadelphia: Henry Tuckniss, 1800; original printing was 1793). This hymnal, designed as an inexpensive alternative to the Wesleyan *Collection*, follows some of the categories of the 1780 *Collection* but is quite jumbled, with (for example) three different sections marked "penitential."

3. *Hymn Book of The Methodist Protestant Church: Compiled by the Authority of the General Conference*, 14th ed. (Baltimore: Book Concern, Methodist Protestant Church, 1852; original printing was 1837).

4. The version cited here is *Hymns for the Use of The Methodist Episcopal Church with Tunes for Congregational Worship* (New York: Carlton and Porter, 1857), hymns 187–260.

5. Ibid., hymns 261–330.

6. *Hymnal of The Methodist Episcopal Church* (Cincinnati: Cranston and Stowe, 1878). The

section "The Sinner" comprises hymns 302–417, and the section "The Christian" comprises hymns 418–762.

7. In *The Methodist Hymnal: Official Hymnal of The Methodist Episcopal Church and the Methodist Episcopal Church, South* (New York: Methodist Book Concern, 1905), the section "The Gospel" comprises hymns 241–97, and the section "The Christian Life" comprises hymns 298–567. In the *Free Methodist Hymnal: Published by Authority of the General Conference of the Free Methodist Church in North America* (Chicago: The Free Methodist Publishing House, 1910), the section "The Gospel" comprises hymns 177–255 and the section "The Christian Life" comprises hymns 256–560.

8. In the 1905 Methodist Episcopal Church and Methodist Episcopal Church, South, hymnal, the subsection on entire sanctification is titled "entire consecration and perfect love" and comprises hymns 353–81. In the 1910 *Free Methodist Hymnal* this subsection is titled "entire sanctification" and comprises hymns 333–86.

9. *The Methodist Hymn-Book* (London: Wesleyan Conference Office, 1933), hymns 311–38 (on "The Gospel Call") and 339–638 (on "The Christian Life").

10. The subsection "Christian Perfection" in the 1935 joint Methodist Episcopal Church, Methodist Episcopal Church, South, and Methodist Protestant Church hymnal comprises hymns 371–78.

11. *African Methodist Episcopal Church Hymnal* (1984): the section "The Gospel" comprises hymns 210–25, and the section "The Christian Life" comprises hymns 226–514.

12. The quotation from Bishop Harmon is from the recollection of Professor James Logan of Wesley Theological Seminary, who was part of the process leading up to the 1964 hymnal.

13. *Sing to the Lord: Hymnal* (Kansas City: Lillenas Publishing Company, 1993).

14. *Short Scriptural Catechism* (1793), lessons 7–14 (11–26).

15. *Catechisms of the Wesleyan Methodists* (1824), 17–20.

16. *Catechism of The Methodist Episcopal Church* (1852), 37–40.

17. "Ten Doctrines of Grace" (1884), 30–31.

18. But note that Ralston places the doctrinal section ahead of the "evidences" (what we would think of as prolegomena).

19. Cf. Langford, *Practical Divinity* (1998), 1:55–56 (on Watson), 1:90–94 (on Bledsoe and Whedon).

20. Summers does have discussions of regeneration (2:73ff.), "preventing" grace (2:77ff.), justifying faith (2:102ff. and 2:125ff.), and the amissibility of grace (2:173ff.).

21. Watson, 242–452 (chapter 23) and 453–61 (chapter 24).

22. Ibid., 544–53 (chapter 29); the discussion of entire sanctification is on 544–48.

23. Thomas N. Ralston, *Elements of Divinity; Or, A Concise and Comprehensive View of Bible Theology, Comprising the Doctrines, Evidences, Morals, and Institutions of Christianity, with Appropriate Questions Appended to Each Chapter*, ed. Thomas O. Summers (Nashville: Cokesbury Press, 1928), 329–472.

24. Pope, 2:358–85.

25. Ibid., 3:1–27 (on regeneration and adoption) and 27–61 (on sanctification, including entire sanctification).

26. Watson distinguishes the Wesleyan conception of heartfelt faith from other options, 424–53; Ralston devotes six chapters to this topic, 367–416; Pope makes a similar distinction between living faith and "dead faith" in his discussion of the "preliminaries of salvation," 2:358–85; Summers elaborates a similar argument about justifying faith in 2:102ff. and 2:125ff.

27. Langford, *Practical Divinity* (1998), 1:62–63 (on Pope), 1:95 (on Ralston and Bascom), and 1:96 (on Summers).

28. Russell E. Richey's *The Methodist Conference in America* makes the point that early Methodist conferences (quarterly as well as annual conferences) were primarily occasions for preaching, worship, hymn-singing, and generally matters related to spirituality rather than business meetings (chapter 6, 51–61).

29. William Apess, *On Our Own Ground: The Complete Writings of William Apess, a Pequot*, ed. Barry O'Connell (Amherst: University of Massachusetts Press, 1992).

30. He actually gives the date of his joining The Methodist Protestant Church as 11 April 1829, and this was during the period when the Methodist Protestant denomination was

becoming separate from The Methodist Episcopal Church, but prior to its formal organization (133).

31. William Andrews, ed., *Sisters of the Spirit: Three Black Women's Autobiographies of the Nineteenth Century* (Bloomington: Indiana University Press, 1986). In addition to these five complete autobiographies, we have some excerpts published in a volume recently edited by Lester Ruth titled *Early Methodist Life and Spirituality: A Reader* (Nashville: Kingswood Books, 2005).

32. James K. Mathews, *A Global Odyssey: The Autobiography of James K. Mathews* (Nashville: Abingdon Press, 2000).

33. Apess, 126, 127; the entire section from 121 through 127 recounts the period of mourning over sin leading up to William Apess's conversion.

34. Ibid., 134; the entire section from 133 through 139 recounts the period of mourning over sin leading up to Mary Apess's conversion.

35. Lee, in *Sisters of the Spirit*, 27.

36. Elaw, in *Sisters of the Spirit*, 55.

37. Julia Foote, in *Sisters of the Spirit*, 178.

38. Mathews, *A Global Odyssey*, 76.

39. Lester Ruth's collection of materials titled *Early Methodist Life and Spirituality: A Reader* (Nashville: Kingswood Books, 1990) includes a number of testimonies to conversion experiences in language similar to these, 72–82.

40. Apess, 129.

41. Ibid., 139–40.

42. Lee, in *Sisters of the Spirit*, 29.

43. Foote, in *Sisters of the Spirit*, 180 (the conversion narrative continues through the next page).

44. Elaw, in *Sisters of the Spirit*, 55–57; the quotation is on 57.

45. Mathews, *A Global Odyssey*, 76.

46. Ibid., 86–87.

47. Apess, 130–32.

48. Ibid., 140–42.

49. Lee, in *Sisters of the Spirit*, 27–32.

50. Elaw, in *Sisters of the Spirit*, 58.

51. Foote, in *Sisters of the Spirit*, chapter titles on 182 (chapter 8), 184 (chapter 9), and 186 (chapter 10).

52. Apess, 142.

53. Lee, in *Sisters of the Spirit*, 33.

54. Foote, in *Sisters of the Spirit*, 186: "They told me that sanctification was for the young believer, as well as the old."

55. Lester Ruth's collection of materials exhibiting early Methodist life includes a number of testimonies to entire sanctification, 115–30.

56. Apess, 143.

57. Lee, in *Sisters of the Spirit*, 34.

58. Elaw, in *Sisters of the Spirit*, 66.

59. Foote, in *Sisters of the Spirit*, 186–87.

60. Apess, 119–21. He refers to God as "the Great Spirit" on 121.

61. Elaw in *Sisters of the Spirit*, 98–99.

62. Apess, 133–35.

63. Ibid., 122.

64. Lee, in *Sisters of the Spirit*, 32–33.

65. Ibid., 33.

66. Foote, in *Sisters of the Spirit*, 192.

67. Apess, 143.

68. This is consistent with Russell Richey's argument that Methodist conferences and other institutional structures in the nineteenth century were primarily concerned with spirituality rather than business matters; see his conclusions in *The Methodist Conference in America*, 199–204.

69. Robert Wood, *The Early History of the Walk to Emmaus* (Nashville: Upper Room Books, 2001), 22–29.

6. BELIEFS ABOUT THE CHURCH IN WESLEYAN COMMUNITIES

1. In John Wesley's letter "To Dr. Coke, Mr. Asbury, and Our Brethren in North America" (10 September 1784), he stated, "By a very uncommon train of providences, many of the provinces of North America are totally disjoined from their mother-country, and erected into independent States" and at the conclusion he refers to "that liberty wherewith God has so strangely made [the American Methodists] free" (in Jackson, ed., *Works*, 13:251–52).
2. Baker, *John Wesley and the Church of England*, 272–78.
3. Russell E. Richey, "Four Languages of Methodist Self-Understanding," in *Doctrine in Experience: A Methodist Theology of Church and Ministry* (Nashville: Kingswood Books, 2009), 3–20.
4. Williams, *John Wesley's Theology Today*, 215–16.
5. Ibid., 207–42.
6. Albert C. Outler, "Do Methodists Have a Doctrine of the Church?" in *The Doctrine of the Church*, ed. Dow Kirkpatrick (Nashville: Abingdon Press, 1964), 11–28.
7. See the discussion of John Wesley's understanding of ecclesiology in chapter 1. The discussion of church discipline in the Westminster Confession of Faith comes in chapters 25 and 30 (in Pelikan and Hotchkiss, 2:638–39, 644; in Leith, *Creeds of the Churches*, 222, 227).
8. "Large Minutes," qu. 48 (in Jackson, ed., *Works*, 8:322–24).
9. John Wesley also spoke of the means of grace in this way in "The Means of Grace," ¶ 3–6 (in Outler, ed., *Sermons*, 1:379–80).
10. John Wesley, "A Plain Account of the People Called Methodists," II:9 (in Jackson, ed., *Works*, 8:323–24; in Davies, ed., *Methodist Societies*, 262–63).
11. "Prophets and Priests" (in Outler, ed., *Sermons*, 4:75–84). Earlier printed editions of this sermon carried the title "The Ministerial Office."
12. Outler's introduction (in Outler, ed., *Sermons*, 4:73–74).
13. ¶ 11 (in Outler, ed., *Sermons*, 4:79, here recollecting [not quite accurately] the minutes of the annual conference of 14 May 1746); cf. Campbell, *John Wesley and Christian Antiquity*, 82.
14. Williams, *John Wesley's Theology Today*, 228–29.
15. John Wesley, "Plain Account of the People Called Methodists," VI:5–8 (in Davies, ed., *Methodist Societies*, 267–68; in Jackson, ed., *Works*, 8:258–59); cf. Campbell, *John Wesley and Christian Antiquity*, 97–98.
16. Ibid., IV:1–3 (in Davies, ed., *Methodist Societies*, 266–67; in Jackson, ed., *Works*, 8:256–57).
17. Ibid., IV:3 (in Jackson, ed., *Works*, 8:257); cf. Campbell, *John Wesley and Christian Antiquity*, 86–87.
18. Richey, *Doctrine in Experience*, 21–41.
19. "Large Minutes," question 3 (in Jackson, ed., *Works*, 8:299–300).
20. Thomas Coke and Henry Moore, *The Life of the Rev. John Wesley, A.M.: Including an Account of the Great Revival of Religion, in Europe and America, of Which He Was the First and Chief Instrument* (London: G. Paramore, 1792), 458–62.
21. John Whitehead, *The Life of the Rev. John Wesley, M.A., Sometime Fellows of Lincoln College, Oxford.* 2 vols. (London: Stephen Couchman, 1793 and 1796), vol. 2, book 3, chapter 5, 418–39.
22. Baker, *John Wesley and the Church of England*, 283–303.
23. *A Form of Discipline for the Ministers, Preachers, and Members of The Methodist Episcopal Church in America* (1787), 4.

24. Methodist Episcopal *Disciplines* from 1801 and ff. have a statement "Of the Origins of The Methodist Episcopal Church" in chapter 1, Section 1 of the *Discipline*.

25. Nathan Bangs, *A History of the Methodist Episcopal Church*. 4 vols. (New York: T. Mason and G. Lane, 1839), 1:45.

26. I am grateful to Reginald Broadnax for information concerning the use of the term "Episcopal" in the name of the African Methodist Episcopal Zion Church.

27. Alexander McCaine, *The History and Mystery of Methodist Episcopacy; Or, A Glance at "The Institutions of the Church as We Received Them from Our Fathers"* (Baltimore: Richard J. Matchett, 1827), and his later *Letters on the Organization and Early History of The Methodist Episcopal Church* (Boston: Thomas F. Norris, Olive Branch Office, 1850).

28. Stevens, *A Compendious History of American Methodism*, 18–19, 31; and Simpson, *A Hundred Years of Methodism*, 28.

29. Henry McNeal Turner, *The Genius and Theory of Methodist Polity; Or, The Machinery of Methodism* (1885; repr. ed.; Nashville: AMEC Sunday School Union, 1986), chapter 2, 8–29.

30. *The Doctrines and Discipline of The Methodist Episcopal Church* (New York: Eaton and Mains, 1892), 13.

31. James H. Rigg, *Was John Wesley a High Churchman? A Dialogue for the Times* (London: The Wesleyan Methodist Book Room, 1882). Rigg was responding to the work of Richard Denny Urlin, *John Wesley's Place in Church History: Determined with the Aid of Facts and Documents Unknown to, or Unnoticed by, His Biographers* (London: Rivingtons, 1870).

32. *Constitutional Practice and Discipline of the Methodist Church*, vol. 2 (2009), 213–14. On the interpretation of the constitution of the Methodist Church of Great Britain, cf. A. Raymond George, "Foundational Documents of the Faith: IX. Methodist Statements," 260. Cf. the *Methodist Church Nigeria Constitution 1990* (a typescript document with no further bibliographical data consulted at the archives of the World Methodist Council in Lake Junaluska, North Carolina), which states, "The Methodist Church claims and cherishes its place in the Holy Catholic Church which is the Body of Christ. It rejoices in the inheritance of the Apostolic Faith and loyally accepts the fundamental principles of the historic creeds and of the Protestant Reformation" (1). Nearly the same wording appears in the *Manual of the Laws and Discipline of the Methodist Church in Southern Africa*, 6th ed. (n.p.: Methodist Church of Southern Africa Publishing House and Book Depot, 1981), 1.

33. Methodist Articles of Religion 13 (in Pelikan and Hotchkiss, 3:204; in Leith, ed., *Creeds of the Churches*, 357). This article also appears in *The Book of Discipline of the Methodist Church in India*, 2nd ed. (Bombay: Methodist Church in India, n.d., but after 1982), 50–51.

34. *The Book of Discipline of The United Methodist Church* 2008, ¶ 103, article V of the Confession of Faith, pp. 67–68.

35. *Manual of the Pentecostal Church of the Nazarene: Published by Authority of the General Assembly Held at Pilot Point, Texas, 1908* (Los Angeles: Nazarene Publishing Company, 1908), 27.

36. Church of the Nazarene Articles of Faith, article 11, as it appears on the Web site of the Church of the Nazarene: http://www.nazarene.org.

37. *The Catechism of The Methodist Episcopal Church* (1852), Catechism II, section V, § 1, questions 65 and 64; the edition cited is *The Pictorial Catechism of the Methodist Episcopal Church* (New York: Carlton and Phillips, 1855), 20.

38. *The Catechisms of the Wesleyan Methodists: Compiled and Published by Order of the Conference*, Catechism No. II, section 5, "Of the Holy Ghost," questions 7, 8, pp. 22–23.

39. *The Catechism (formerly "the Turner Catechism")* of the A.M.E. Church, 19.

40. *Probationer's Manual of The Methodist Episcopal Church: Prepared under the Authorization of the General Conference* (New York: Methodist Book Concern, 1914), questions 94 and 95 on p. 38.

41. *The Junior Catechism of The Methodist Episcopal Church and The Methodist Episcopal Church, South*, questions 84 and 86, p. 17. Cf. *The Junior Catechism* as published by the CME Church, 19.

42. *Methodist Catechism* (Methodist Church in Ireland, [1948]), questions 59 and 60, pp. 21–22.

43. *The Senior Catechism of the Methodist Church* (Methodist Church of Great Britain, 1952), questions 19 and 20, p. 6.

44. *A Catechism for the Use of the People Called Methodists* (Methodist Church of Great Britain, 1989), question 43, p. 20.

45. Watson, *Theological Institutes*, IV:1 (1870 edition), 680.

46. Miner Raymond, *Systematic Theology* (Cincinnati: Hitchcock and Walden; and New York: Phillips and Hunt, 1879), book 7, chapter 1, 3:234.

47. Raymond, *Systematic Theology*, book 7, chapter 1, 3:240.

48. Ibid., 3:256.

49. Pope, *Compendium of Christian Theology*, "The Church," 3:259.

50. Ibid., 3:259–87.

51. Miley, *Systematic Theology*, 2:385.

52. Ibid., 2:385–87; the reference to the Article of Religion is on 387.

53. Baker, *John Wesley and the Church of England*, 75–80.

54. Karen B. Westerfield Tucker, "'Plain and Decent': Octagonal Space and Methodist Worship," *Studia Liturgica* 24 (1994): 136–41.

55. Baker, *John Wesley and the Church of England*, 85–87.

56. Campbell, *John Wesley and Christian Antiquity*, 120.

57. The original pulpit was considerably higher than it presently is; Baker, *John Wesley and the Church of England*, 212–14.

58. Cf. Karen B. Westerfield Tucker, *American Methodist Worship* (Oxford: Oxford University Press, 2001), 239–43.

59. Homer S. Thrall, *History of Methodism in Texas* (Houston: E. H. Cushing, 1872), 27–28.

60. Marilyn J. Westerkamp, *The Triumph of the Laity: Scots-Irish Piety and the Great Awakening, 1625–1760* (New York: Oxford University Press, 1988); Leigh Eric Schmidt, *Holy Fairs: Scottish Communions and American Revivals in the Early Modern Period* (Princeton, N.J.: Princeton University Press, 1989).

61. Westerkamp, 29.

62. Ruth, ed., *Early Methodist Life and Spirituality*, 195, 200–1.

63. On the development of the auditorium style of architecture among Methodists, cf. Tucker, *American Methodist Worship*, 243–51 and 248 in particular.

64. See, for example, the subtitles of *Songs of the Soul, No. 2: For Use in Sunday Evening Congregations, Revivals, Camp Meetings, Social Services, and Young People's Meetings*, ed. James M. Black (Cincinnati: Curts and Jennings; and New York: Eaton and Mains, 1896); *The Voice of Praise: A Compilation of the Very Best Sacred Songs for Use in Sunday Schools and Praise Services* (Philadelphia and New York: Hall-Mack Company, 1904). Both of these volumes came out from publishing houses associated with The Methodist Episcopal Church. Later collections (from the early twentieth century) reveal that these songs were beginning to be used in regular worship: *Praise Evangel: For Sunday-Schools, Revivals, Singing Schools, Conventions, and General Use in Christian Work and Worship* (Lawrenceburg, Tenn.: James D. Vaughn, 1919).

65. Kenneth Cracknell and Susan J. White, *An Introduction to World Methodism* (Cambridge: Cambridge University Press, 2005), 43.

66. Spiro Kostof, *A History of Architecture: Settings and Rituals* (New York: Oxford University Press, 1995), 583–94.

67. The quotation is from the president of the Methodist Conference in 1913, as it appears on the church's Web site: http://www.wesleycam.org.uk/building.htm. This site was accessed in August 2008.

68. Cf. Tucker, *American Methodist Worship*, 252–56.

69. Jesse A. Earle and Dorothea Derrig, "Akron, Ohio," in *Encyclopedia of World Methodism*, ed. Nolan B. Harmon (Nashville: United Methodist Publishing House, 1974), 1:73.

70. See the photos and explanation of this project on the Web site of the architectural firm of McClure Hopkins: http://www.mcharch.com/newsite-1.2.swf.

71. Geoffrey Wainwright, "Ecclesial Location and Ecumenical Vocation," in *The Future of the Methodist Theological Traditions*, ed. M. Douglas Meeks (Nashville: Abingdon Press, 1985), 93–129.

72. Episcopal-United Methodist Dialogue Team, *Make Us One with Christ: The Study Guide Version* (n.p.: Office of Ecumenical and Interfaith Relations of the Episcopal Church in the USA and the General Commission on Christian Unity and Interreligious Concerns of The United Methodist Church, 2006), 19.

73. World Council of Churches Faith and Order Commission, *The Nature and Mission of the Church: A Stage on the Way to a Common Statement.* Faith and Order Paper no. 198 (Geneva: World Council of Churches, 2005).

7. FOURTEEN CORE BELIEFS OF WESLEYAN COMMUNITIES

1. John Wesley, "On Laying the Foundation of the New Chapel, Near the City-Road, London," II:1 (in Outler, ed., *Sermons*, 3:585; in Jackson, ed., *Works*, 7:423).
2. Transcribed from photograph.
3. See the quotation from Matthew Simpson in chapter 2 above: Simpson, *A Hundred Years of Methodism*, 28; cf. Thomas Chalmers, *Sermons and Discourses.* 2 vols. (New York: Robert Carter, 1844), 1:345.
4. Stevens, *Compendious History of American Methodism*, 584; Buckley, *History of the Methodists in the United States* (1896), 90–91.
5. Constitution of the Methodist Church of Great Britain; in Davies, *Methodism*, 209. Cf. the *Manual of the Laws and Discipline of the Methodist Church in Southern Africa*, 1; and the *Methodist Church Nigeria Constitution* (1990), 1.
6. World Methodist Council, "Wesleyan Essentials of Christian Faith," section on "The People Called Methodists," in *World Methodist Council Handbook of Information 2007–2011* (Lake Junaluska, N.C.: World Methodist Council, 2007), 95.
7. *The Book of Discipline of The United Methodist Church 2008*, ¶ 101, pp. 41–42.
8. John Wesley, "Catholic Spirit," II:1–2 and III:1–4 (in Outler, ed., *Sermons*, 2:89–90; in Jackson, ed., *Works*, 5:499, 501–3).
9. *Senior Catechism of the Methodist Church* (Methodist Church of Great Britain, 1952), qu. 42 (p. 12); cf. the *Methodist Catechism* of the Methodist Church in Ireland (1946), qu. 64 (p. 23) and the *Catechism for the Use of the People Called Methodists*, qu. 68 (p. 36).
10. References to the Articles of Faith of the Church of the Nazarene are to the current version available on the denomination's Web site, http://www.nazarene.org. I will also refer in the parentheses to the 1952 version as given in Pelikan and Hotchkiss, 3:409–14.
11. *Cokesbury Worship Hymnal* (Nashville: Abingdon Press, 1966 [reprint of 1938 edition]), no. 6.
12. The line quoted is from a hymn in the 1780 *Collection of Hymns*, no. 7, verse 3 (in Hildebrandt and Beckerlegge, eds., 88).
13. The Vieira version of the Doxology is in *The United Methodist Hymnal* (1989), no. 94.
14. Methodist Articles of Religion 2 (in Pelikan and Hotchkiss, 3:202; in Leith, ed., *Creeds of the Churches*, 354); cf. the Anglican Articles of Religion 2 (in Pelikan and Hotchkiss, 2:528; in Leith, ed., *Creeds of the Churches*, 267). The resurrection of Christ is dealt with in separate articles.
15. UMC Confession of Faith, article 2 (in *The Book of Discipline of The United Methodist Church 2008*, ¶ 103, p. 67).
16. John Wesley, *Explanatory Notes upon the New Testament*, comment on Romans 12:6 (in 1950 printing, 569–70). Reformed theologian Guillaume du Buc (Bucanus) of Lausanne asserted that the analogy of faith meant "the constant and unchanging sense of Scripture expounded in open [or "clear," *apertis*] passages of Scripture and agreeing with the Apostles' Creed, the Decalogue, and the Lord's Prayer." In Guillaume du Buc (Bucanus), *Institutiones Theologicae seu Locorum Communium Christianae Religionis ex Dei Verbo et Praestantissimorum Theologorum Orthodoxo Consensu Expositorum Analysis* (Geneva, 1609), 4:21–24; cited in Heinrich Heppe, *Reformierte Dogmatik* (Kreis Moers: Buchhandlung des Erziehungsvereins, 1935), 30 (in footnote); English translation as given in Ernst Bizer, ed., and G. T. Thompson, trans., *Reformed Dogmatics: Set Out and Illustrated from the Sources* (London: Allen and Unwin, 1950), 35. In the English translation the material from du Buc has been moved to the main text. Cf. Jones, *John Wesley's Conception and Use of Scripture*, 45–46.
17. "Doctrinal Statement" of the Korean Methodist Church (1930), item 5 (in Pelikan and

Hotchkiss, 3:486). The Web site of the Korean Methodist Church has a 1997 revision of this doctrinal statement in which the statement on the Holy Scriptures is item 4: "We believe in the Holy Scripture as the Word of God, written by the inspiration of the Holy Spirit, which leads the way to the true salvation and the sufficient standards of our life of faith" (http://www.kmc.or.kr/new_eng/about/about02.html).

18. Church of the Nazarene Articles of Faith, article 4 (current on the denomination's Web site; cf. Pelikan and Hotchkiss, 3:411).

19. Miley, *Systematic Theology*, 1:22–47 (on the "scientific basis of theology") and 2:479–89 (appendix on the inspiration of the Holy Scriptures).

20. Some of the wording in the 1972 section on "tradition" in this United Methodist statement was taken directly from the World Council of Churches Faith and Order document on "Scripture, Tradition, and traditions" adopted at the 1963 Montreal World Conference on Faith and Order: Fourth World Conference on Faith and Order (Montreal 1963), report on "Scripture, Tradition, and traditions," in Günther Gassmann, ed., *A Documentary History of Faith and Order, 1963–1993* (Faith and Order Paper no. 159; Geneva: World Council of Churches, 1993), 10–18. This reflected the involvement of Dr. Albert C. Outler, who had been present at Montreal and had led earlier ecumenical work on Scripture and tradition, and who had also chaired the Theological Study Commission of The United Methodist Church that met between 1968 and 1972 and developed the statement of "Our Theological Task."

21. *Book of Discipline of the Methodist Church in India* (second edition, after 1982), ¶ 192, p. 60.

22. World Methodist Council, "Wesleyan Essentials of Christian Faith," section "Our Beliefs" (in WMC *Handbook of Information 2007–2011*, 95).

23. Methodist Church in India, *Book of Discipline of the Methodist Church in India*, 2nd ed., ¶ 192, pp. 59–60. Donald Thorsen, *The Wesleyan Quadrilateral: Scripture, Tradition, Reason and Experience as a Model of Evangelical Theology* (Grand Rapids: Zondervan Publishing House, 1990). Cf. also W. Stephen Gunter, Scott J. Jones, Ted A. Campbell, Rebekah Miles, and Randy L. Maddox, *Wesley and the Quadrilateral: Renewing the Conversation* (Nashville: Abingdon Press, 1997).

24. See the discussion above of the Nazarene Article of Faith on biblical authority and the restricted scope of its claim that the Scriptures teach "inerrantly" what is necessary for salvation.

25. The subject of my study of *The Religion of the Heart, passim*.

26. John Wesley, letter to "John Smith" [anonymous] 30 December 1745, ¶ 13 (in Baker, ed., *Letters*, 26:181–82; and in Jackson, ed., *Works*, 12:70). See the discussion of "perceptible inspiration" in chapter 2.

27. D. Stephen Long demonstrates the importance of Platonism for Wesley, showing that Wesley "presents us with a 'spiritual sensorium' that uncritically mixes an Augustinian theory of illumination (mediated through Cambridge Platonism) with the sensibility of knowledge plundered from Locke"; in *John Wesley's Moral Theology: The Quest for God and Goodness* (Nashville: Kingswood Books, 2005), quotation on p. 13.

28. Rex Dale Matthews, "'Religion and Reason Joined': A Study in the Theology of John Wesley" (PhD diss., Harvard University, 1986).

29. Frederick Dreyer, "Faith and Experience in the Thought of John Wesley," *American Historical Review* 88 (1983): 12–30. Cf. also Richard E. Brantley, *Locke, Wesley, and the Method of English Romanticism* (Gainesville: University Press of Florida, 1984); and Gregory Clapper, *John Wesley on Religious Affections* (Metuchen, N.J.: Scarecrow Press, 1989).

30. See the works of Wigger, Taves, and Hempton discussed in the introduction.

31. Langford, *Practical Theology* (1998), 1:252–54.

32. Raymond, *Systematic Theology*, I:VI, on the "Argument from Experience" (1:208–16); Miley, *Systematic Theology* introduction (1:16–22).

33. William James, *The Varieties of Religious Experience: A Study in Human Nature* (New York: The Modern Library, 1902), 492.

34. Langford, *Practical Theology* (rev. and enl. ed. 1998), 1:105–10, 253.

35. Workman's *The Place of Methodism in the Catholic Church*, rev. and enl. ed. (London: Epworth Press, 1921; first edition was 1909) saw Methodism's distinctive contribution to modern Christianity as its stress on religious experience.

36. Umphrey Lee's Columbia dissertation, "The Historical Backgrounds of Early Methodist Enthusiasm" (1931) and a published study based on it titled *John Wesley and Modern Religion* (1936) argued that Methodism is distinctively "modern" in its stress on religious experience, pointing to parallels with Schleiermacher.

37. Williams, *John Wesley's Theology Today*, 34.

38. Clapper, *John Wesley on Religious Affections, passim.*

39. Runyon, *New Creation,* 146–67.

40. Ibid., 163–64.

41. A letter of commendation from Archbishop Rowan Williams in the first issue of *The Oxford Theologian* 1 (Spring 2010): 6.

42. The "Methodist Statement of Association with the Joint Declaration on the Doctrine of Justification," approved by the World Methodist Council on 23 July 2006, ¶ 4.1; the text is available on the Web site of the World Methodist Council: http://worldmethodist council.org/index.php?option=com_docman&task=doc_download&gid=45.

43. The tendency toward a Pelagian understanding of "freedom of the will" and the need for good works on the part of Methodist theologians was explored by Chiles in *Theological Transition in American Methodism, 1790–1935, passim.*

44. John Wesley, "The Scripture Way of Salvation," I:2 (in Outler, ed., *Sermons,* 2:156–57; in Jackson, ed., *Works,* 6:44).

45. Charles Wesley, "The Great Feast," hymn 50 in *Hymns for Those That Seek and Those That Have Redemption in the Blood of Jesus Christ,* 65; in Osborn, 4:274; orthography as in Osborn, except that I have restored the small capital letters in "Jesus" and "God" as in the original printing.

46. Charles Wesley, "For the Anniversary Day of One's Conversion," in *Hymns and Sacred Poems* (1740), 122 (in Osborn, 1:301).

47. John Wesley expressed a vision of contiguous evangelization according to which that is, a revival beginning in one place and spreading from thence to contiguous areas until the world was saturated. It was the model suggested, in general, by the Acts of the Apostles: "You will be my witnesses in Jerusalem, in all Judea and Samaria, and to the ends of the earth" (Acts 1:8b); and that is, roughly, the outline of the missionary evangelism described in the Acts; cf. "The General Spread of the Gospel," ¶¶ 13–26 (in Outler, ed., *Sermons,* 2:490–99; in Jackson, ed., *Works,* 6:281–87). Cf. also Ted A. Campbell, "John Wesley on the Mission of the Church" (in Alan G. Padgett, ed., *The Mission of the Church in Methodist Perspective.* Studies in the History of Missions 10 (Lewiston: Edwin Mellen Press, 1992), 45–62.

48. Langford, *Practical Divinity* (1998), 73–77.

49. Some of these connections and affinities have been explored by interpreters of the Wesleyan tradition: cf. Maddox, *Responsible Grace,* 89–90; Collins, *John Wesley's Theology,* 70–76.

50. "Methodist Statement of Association with the Joint Declaration on the Doctrine of Justification," ¶ 4.1. The references in the quotation are from John Wesley's sermon "On Working Out Our Own Salvation," III:4 (in Outler, ed., *Sermons,* 3:207; in Jackson, ed., *Works,* 6:512) and his sermon "The General Spread of the Gospel," ¶ 11 (in Outler, ed., *Sermons,* 2:489; in Jackson, ed., *Works,* 6:280).

51. The World Methodist Council action, including its response to the Joint Declaration, is available on the Web site of the World Methodist Council, http://worldmethodistcoun cil.org.

52. John Wesley, "Salvation by Faith," I:4 (in Outler, ed., *Sermons,* 1:120; in Jackson, ed., *Works,* 5:9).

53. John Wesley, "Salvation by Faith," I:4 (in Outler, ed., *Sermons,* 1:120).

54. *Senior Catechism of the Methodist Church* (Methodist Church in Great Britain, 1952), qu. 42 (p. 12); cf. the *Methodist Catechism* of the Methodist Church in Ireland (1946), qu. 64 (p. 23) and the *Catechism for the Use of the People Called Methodists,* qu. 68 (p. 36).

55. See chapter 5 above for an extended discussion of the *ordo salutis* in Ames and Perkins (and in the Westminster Confession), including their understanding of the place of assurance in this *ordo.*

56. Coke and Moore, *Life of the Rev. John Wesley,* refers to Aldersgate as "his Conversion" in the title of book 1, chapter 4, on p. 130. The account of Aldersgate is given on 148–60, and

the expression quoted here is on 148 ("He was now *brought to the birth*"). Similarly, they wrote of the Aldersgate-Street experience, "Now that he was a child of God ..." (159). Jean Miller Schmidt has shown that Moore's later biography of Wesley, though it borrowed heavily from Whitehead, nevertheless displayed this Evangelical tendency in strongly representing Aldersgate as Wesley's experience of the new birth: Schmidt, "'Strangely Warmed': The Place of Aldersgate in the Methodist Canon," in Randy L. Maddox, ed. *Aldersgate Reconsidered* (Nashville: Kingswood Books, 1990), 111.

57. Whitehead, *Life of the Rev. John Wesley*, book 2, chapter 4, 80–81. Schmidt also notes the moderating tendencies in Whitehead's account of the Aldersgate-Street experience: Schmidt, "'Strangely Warmed': The Place of Aldersgate in the Methodist Canon," 110–11.

58. See the collection of essays on the Aldersgate bicentennial edited by Elmer T. Clark, *What Happened at Aldersgate* (Nashville: Methodist Publishing Corporation, 1938), and the collection of essays on the 250th anniversary of Aldersgate edited by Randy L. Maddox, *Aldersgate Reconsidered* (Nashville: Kingswood Books, 1990).

59. For example, in the Minutes of the annual conference of 1745 (in Jackson, ed., *Works*, 8:282).

60. John Wesley, preface to the second published fascicle of the *Journal* (in Ward and Heitzenrater, eds., *Journals and Diaries*, 1:220; in Jackson, ed., *Works*, 1:82), italics as in original.

61. See, for example, the "Methodist Statement of Association with the Joint Declaration on the Doctrine of Justification," ¶ 4.6.

62. One sign of this in the architecture of Evangelical worship spaces is the loss of the mourner's bench or its reconfiguration as a place for prayer for specific needs rather than a sign of mourning over one's sins. Twentieth-century evangelism, as represented in the Billy Graham Crusades, has typically not insisted on a vivid experience of "awakening" or conviction prior to conversion.

63. John Wesley, "The Scripture Way of Salvation," I:4 (in Outler, ed., *Sermons*, 1:158; in Jackson, ed., *Works*, 6:45), italics as in original.

64. "Methodist Statement of Association with the Joint Declaration on the Doctrine of Justification," ¶ 4.2. The reference in the quotation is from John Wesley's sermon "On Working Out Our Own Salvation," II:1 (in Outler, ed., *Sermons*, 3:204; in Jackson, ed., *Works*, 6:508).

65. John Wesley, letter to Robert Carr Brackenbury, 15 September 1790 (in Telford, ed., *Letters*, 8:238; in Jackson, ed., *Works*, 13:9).

66. *The Book of Discipline of The United Methodist Church 2008*, ¶¶ 330, 336, pp. 235, 246. The questions for deacons (¶ 330, p. 235) expand the last question to "Are you earnestly striving after perfection in love?"

67. Colin Williams wrote in 1960 in a footnote to his *John Wesley's Theology Today* that "Modern Methodism has found the doctrine [of Christian perfection] an embarrassment, but is still officially bound to it" (167, n. 2).

68. The "Methodist Statement of Association with the Joint Declaration on the Doctrine of Justification," ¶ 4.4(b). The quotation is from John Wesley's "Christian Perfection," I:9 (in Outler, ed., *Sermons*, 2:104; in Jackson, ed., *Works*, 6:5). The entire section ¶ 4.4 is concerned with explaining the idea of Christian perfection, and it amounts to the largest single topic covered in the "Statement of Association."

69. John Wesley, "The Scripture Way of Salvation," III:14–15, where Wesley makes the points that "God hath promised it [the gift of entire sanctification] in the Holy Scripture" (¶ 14) and "what God hath promised he is able to perform" (¶ 15).

70. An international conference in Rome in 1994 explored the theme of "Sanctification in the Benedictine and Wesleyan Traditions." Papers from this conference were published in the *Asbury Theological Journal* 50:2 and 51:1 (together in a single issue for Fall 1995 and Spring 1996). Methodist theologian Roberta Bondi has explored issues of ascetic spirituality in relation to Wesleyan spirituality: *To Love as God Loves* (referred to in chapter 7), and *To Pray and to Love: Conversations on Prayer with the Early Church* (Minneapolis: Fortress Press, 1991) and her articles "The Meeting of Oriental Orthodoxy and United Methodism," in *Christ in East and West*, ed. Paul Fries and Tiran Nersoyan (Macon, Ga.: Mercer University Press, 1987), 171–84 and "The Role of the Holy Spirit from a United Methodist Perspective," *Greek Orthodox Theological Review* 31:3–4 (1986): 351–60.

71. John Wesley, "Upon Our Lord's Sermon on the Mount, Discourse 4," I:1 (in Outler, ed., *Sermons*, 1:533–34; in Jackson, ed., *Works*, 5:296).

72. Wainwright, "Ecclesial Location and Ecumenical Vocation" (in Meeks, ed., *The Future of the Methodist Theological Traditions*, 93–129).

73. The quotation is from the constitution of the Methodist Church of Great Britain, as given in Davies, *Methodism*, 209.

74. A letter to the editor of the *Wesleyan-Methodist Magazine*, 1824, 238, cited in Holland, *Baptism in Early Methodism*, 4–5.

75. Hohenstein, "New Birth through Water and the Spirit: A Reply to Ted A. Campbell," 103–12.

76. Cf. Westminster Confession 28 (in Pelikan and Hotchkiss, 2:641–42; in Leith, ed., *Creeds of the Churches*, 224–25).

77. Anglican Articles of Religion 27 (in Pelikan and Hotchkiss, 2:535; in Leith, *Creeds of the Churches*, 275–76); cf. the Methodist Articles of Religion 17 (in Pelikan and Hotchkiss, 3:205; in Leith, *Creeds of the Churches*, 358).

78. United Methodist Confession of Faith, Article 6 (*The Book of Discipline of The United Methodist Church 2008*, ¶ 103, p. 68).

79. "By Water and the Spirit: A United Methodist Understanding of Baptism" (Nashville, Tenn.: General Board of Discipleship of The United Methodist Church, 1996), section on "Baptism as New Life" (15).

80. World Council of Churches Faith and Order Commission, *Baptism, Eucharist and Ministry* (Faith and Order Paper no. 111; Geneva: World Council of Churches, 1982), 4.

81. Latin recension of the Apostolic Tradition; in Bernard Botte, ed., *Hippolyte de Rome: La Tradition Apostolique d'après les anciennes Versions*. Sources Chrétiennes Series, no. 11 (Paris: Éditions du Cerf, 1968), 84–86, which collates two Latin versions at this point; cf. Paul F. Bradshaw, Maxwell E. Johnson, and L. Edward Phillips, eds., *The Apostolic Tradition: A Commentary*. Hermeneia Commentary Series. (Minneapolis: Fortress Press, 2002), 116–18.

82. Hymn 57 from the first sequence of hymns in John and Charles Wesley, *Hymns on the Lord's Supper* (1749; in Osborn, 3:256).

83. Cf. John Calvin, *Institutes*, IV.17.10–12 (in McNeill and Battles, eds., *Calvin: Institutes*, 2:1370–73). McNeill used the term "virtualism" to describe Calvin's sacramental views in this edition of Calvin's *Institutes* (2:1370, n. 27); cf. Campbell, *Christian Confessions*, 181–83.

84. Ibid., hymn 66, stanza 2 (Osborn, 3:264) and hymn 116, stanza 5 (in Osborn, 3:302).

85. Hymn 57 from the first sequence of hymns in John and Charles Wesley, *Hymns on the Lord's Supper* (1749; in Osborn, 3:256).

86. Jones, *United Methodist Doctrine*, 265–66; cf. Campbell, *Methodist Doctrine*, 76–77. Mark Stamm has offered a theological rationale for the practice of open communion in *Let Every Soul Be Jesus' Guest: A Theology of the Open Table* (Nashville: Abingdon Press, 2005).

87. Jones, *United Methodist Doctrine*, 266.

88. WCC Faith and Order Commission, *Baptism, Eucharist and Ministry*, 10–15.

89. John Wesley, "Letter to a Roman Catholic," ¶ 10 (in Jackson, ed., *Works*, 10:82).

90. The Nicene Creed is quoted from the *Catechism for the Use of the People Called Methodists* (1989), qu. 55, p. 28.

91. James H. Moorhead, *World without End: Mainstream American Protestant Visions of the Last Things, 1880–1925* (Bloomington: Indiana University Press, 1999), xiii–xiv.

92. Solomon Jacob Gamertsfelder, *Systematic Theology* (Cleveland: C. Hauser, 1913), 115–19.

93. Ibid., 567–73.

94. Harris Franklin Rall, *Modern Premillennialism and the Christian Hope* (New York: Abingdon Press, 1920), 245–53; and *Was John Wesley a Premillennialist?* Ryerson Essays, no. 1 (Toronto: Methodist Book and Publishing House, 1921). Wesley's *Explanatory Notes upon the New Testament* includes lengthy notes on Revelation 20, verses 2 and 4, in which Wesley explained that there was not simply one but actually two separate millennia described in these verses: "During the former [millennium], the promises concerning the flourishing state of the Church (Rev. x. 7) shall be fulfilled; during the latter, while saints reign with Christ in heaven, men on earth will be careless and secure" (the term "secure" here carries the archaic sense of "overconfident"; in the 1948 printing of the *Notes*, pp. 1037, 1038–39).

Rall demonstrated that Wesley's source for this, as for many of his *Notes*, was the work of the German text critic Johann Albrecht Bengel, whose *Gnomon Novi Testamenti* (1742) was one of the first works to employ a critical examination of the manuscript sources of the New Testament: cf. Bengel, *Gnomon Novi Testamenti*, comments on Revelation 20:2 and 20:4, 3rd ed. (London: David Nutt and Williams and Norgate; Edinburgh: Williams and Norgate; Cambridge: Macmillan and Associates and Deighton and Associates; and Oxford: J. H. Parker and Parker, 1862), 1055–56, 1057.

95. Embossed in Lucy Rider Meyer's own handwriting on the cover of Isabelle Horton, *High Adventure: The Life of Lucy Rider Meyer* (New York: Methodist Book Concern, 1928).

96. Ibid., 117.

97. Ibid., 77.

98. Runyon, *The New Creation*, 5, 168–221.

99. M. Douglas Meeks, ed., *Wesleyan Perspectives on the New Creation* (Nashville: Kingswood Books, 2004).

CONCLUSION

1. The Bishops' Address, in *The Journal of the General Conference of The Methodist Episcopal Church, South* (Nashville: Publishing House of The Methodist Episcopal Church, South, 1894), 25; Address of the Bishops, in the *Journal of the General Conference of The Methodist Episcopal Church* (New York: Eaton and Mains; and Cincinnati: Curts and Jennings, 1896), 38.

2. John Wesley, "The Scripture Way of Salvation," III:18 (in Outler, ed., *Sermons*, 2:168).

3. The Latin term *traditio* is a substantive derived from the verb *tradere*, "to hand on" or "hand over." Similarly, the Greek παράδοσις ("tradition") is a substantive derived from the verb παραδίδωμι, "to hand on" or "hand over." Cf. Gerhard Kittel, ed., *Theological Dictionary of the New Testament*, trans. and ed. Geoffrey W. Bromiley (Grand Rapids: William B. Eerdmans Publishing Co., 1964), s.v. "δίδωμι," 2:171–72 (sections on "παραδοῦναι" and "παράδοσις").

4. The issue of continuity and change in the development of a Christian tradition was the subject of Newman's *Essay on the Development of Christian Doctrine* (1845) and has remained a consistent focus of historical and theological reflection; for an overview, see John E. Thiel, "Perspectives on Tradition" in *Catholic Theological Society of America Proceedings* 54 (1999): 1–18.

5. Fourth World Conference on Faith and Order (Montreal 1963), report "Scripture, Tradition, and traditions," ¶ 39; in Gassmann, ed., *Documentary History of Faith and Order, 1963–1993*, 10–18.

6. Langford, *Practical Divinity* (1998), 1:247–58.

7. John Wesley, "Catholic Spirit," III:1 (in Outler, ed., *Sermons*, 2:93; in Jackson, ed., *Works*, 5:502).

8. Ibid., III:4 (in Outler, ed., *Sermons*, 2:94; in Jackson, ed., *Works*, 5:503).

9. Charles Wesley, "Catholic Love," published in 1755 (a critical edition of the traditional [not modernized] text; Randy L. Maddox, ed.; Durham, N.C.: Duke Center for Studies in the Wesleyan Tradition, 2007).

10. In Clarke, *Memoirs of the Wesley Family*, 281.

11. Charles Wesley, stanza from hymn 46, in a sequence of "Hymns for Christian Friends," in *Hymns and Sacred Poems* (1749), 2:322 (in Osborn, 5:466).

12. World Methodist Council, "Wesleyan Essentials of Christian Faith," section on "Our Common Life" (in WMC *Handbook of Information 2007–2011*, 98).

13. Charles Wesley, stanza from hymn 203, in "Hymns for Christian Friends," in *Hymns and Sacred Poems* (1749), 2:279 (in Osborn, 5:423). The language is altered as in the contemporary British Methodist hymnal *Hymns and Psalms*, no. 374.

BIBLIOGRAPHY

Ad Hoc Committee on E.U.B. Union of The Methodist Church and The Commission on Union of The Evangelical United Brethren Church. *The United Methodist Church: The Plan of Union as adopted by the General Conferences, November 1966, and the Annual Conferences, 1967, of The Methodist Church and The Evangelical United Brethren Church.* N.p.: 1967.

African Methodist Episcopal Church Hymnal. Also known as the "AMEC Bicentennial Hymnal." Nashville: African Methodist Episcopal Church, 1984.

Ames, William. *The Marrow of Theology.* Translated by John Dykstra Eusden. The United Church Press, 1968. Reprint edition. Durham, N.C.: The Labyrinth Press, 1983.

Andrews, William, ed. *Sisters of the Spirit: Three Black Women's Autobiographies of the Nineteenth Century.* Bloomington: Indiana University Press, 1986.

Apess, William. *On Our Own Ground: The Complete Writings of William Apess, a Pequot.* Edited by Barry O'Connell. Amherst: University of Massachusetts Press, 1992.

The Apostolic Tradition: A Commentary. Hermeneia. Edited by Paul F. Bradshaw, Maxwell E. Johnson, and L. Edward Phillips. Minneapolis: Fortress Press, 2002.

The Apostolic Tradition. Hippolyte de Rome: La Tradition Apostolique d'après les anciennes Versions. Edited by Bernard Botte. Sources chrétiennes series, no. 11. Paris: Éditions du Cerf, 1968.

Baker, Frank. *John Wesley and the Church of England.* Nashville: Abingdon Press, 1970.

Bangs, Nathan. *A History of The Methodist Episcopal Church.* 4 vols. New York: T. Mason and G. Lane, 1839.

Bengel, Johann Albrecht. *Gnomon Novi Testament.* 3rd ed. London: David Nutt and Williams and Norgate; Edinburgh: Williams and Norgate; Cambridge: Macmillan and Associates and Deighton and Associates; and Oxford: J. H. Parker and Parker, 1862.

Black, James M., ed. *Songs of the Soul, No. 2: For Use in Sunday Evening Congregations, Revivals, Camp Meetings, Social Services, and Young People's Meetings.* Cincinnati: Curts and Jennings; and New York: Eaton and Mains, 1896.

Bondi, Roberta C. *To Love as God Loves: Conversations with the Early Church.* Philadelphia: Fortress Press, 1987.

———. "The Meeting of Oriental Orthodoxy and United Methodism." In *Christ in East and West*, edited by Paul Fries and Tiran Nersoyan, 171–84. Macon, Ga.: Mercer University Press, 1987.

———. "The Role of the Holy Spirit from a United Methodist Perspective." *Greek Orthodox Theological Review* 31, no. 3–4 (1986): 351–60.

———. *To Pray and to Love: Conversations on Prayer with the Early Church.* Minneapolis: Fortress Press, 1991.

The Book of Common Prayer: 1662 Version. Everyman's Library, no. 241. London: David Campbell Publishers. 1999.

The Book of Discipline of the Methodist Church in India, 2nd ed. Bombay: Methodist Church in India, n.d. [after 1982].

The Book of Discipline of The United Methodist Church 1968. Nashville: The Methodist Publishing House, 1968.

The Book of Discipline of The United Methodist Church 2008. Nashville: United Methodist Publishing House, 2008.

Borgen, Ole. *John Wesley on the Sacraments: A Definitive Study of John Wesley's Theology of Worship.* Grand Rapids: Francis Asbury Press, 1985.

Brantley, Richard E. *Locke, Wesley, and the Method of English Romanticism.* Gainesville: University Press of Florida, 1984.

Brightman, Edgar Sheffield. *The Finding of God.* New York: Abingdon Press, 1931.

———. *The Problem of God.* New York: Abingdon Press, 1930.

Bryant, Barry E. "Trinity and Hymnody: The Doctrine of the Trinity in the Hymns of Charles Wesley." *Wesleyan Theological Journal* 25, no. 2 (Fall 1990): 64–73.

Buckley, James M. *History of Methodists in the United States.* New York: Christian Literature Co., 1896.

Bundy, David. "Christian Virtue: John Wesley and the Alexandrian Tradition." *Wesleyan Theological Journal* 26, no. 1 (Spring 1991): 139–63.

"By Water and the Spirit: A United Methodist Understanding of Baptism." Nashville: General Board of Discipleship of The United Methodist Church, 1996.

Calvin, John. *Institutes of the Christian Religion.* Library of Christian Classics Series. In *Calvin: Institutes of the Christian Religion.* Edited by John T. McNeill and Lewis Ford Battles. 2 vols. Philadelphia: Westminster Press, 1960.

Campbell, Ted A. "Charles Wesley, Theologos." In *Charles Wesley: Life, Literature and Legacy.* Edited by Kenneth G. C. Newport and Ted A. Campbell , 264–77. Peterborough: Epworth Press, 2007.

———. *Christian Confessions.* Louisville: Westminster John Knox Press, 1996.

———. "Conversion and Baptism in Wesleyan Spirituality." In *Conversion in the Wesleyan Tradition.* Edited by Kenneth J. Collins and John H. Tyson, 160–74.

———. *The Gospel in Christian Traditions.* New York: Oxford University Press, 2008.

———. *John Wesley and Christian Antiquity: Religious Vision and Cultural Change.* Nashville: Kingswood Books, 1991.

———. "John Wesley and the Legacy of Methodist Theology." *Bulletin of the John Rylands University Library of Manchester* 85, no. 2–3: 405–20.

————. "John Wesley on the Mission of the Church." In *The Mission of the Church in Methodist Perspective*. Edited by Alan G. Padgett, 45–62. Studies in the History of Missions, 10. Lewiston: The Edwin Mellen Press, 1992.

————. *Methodist Doctrine: The Essentials*. Nashville: Abingdon Press, 1999.

————. "Methodist Ecclesiologies and Methodist Sacred Spaces." In *Orthodox and Wesleyan Ecclesiology*. Edited by S T Kimbrough, 215–25. Crestwood, New York: St. Vladimir's Theological Seminary Press, 2007.

————. "The Mystery of the First Article of Religion, and the Mystery of Divine Passibility." *OXFORDnotes* 4, no. 1 (24 May 1996): 5.

————. "'Pure, Unbounded Love': Doctrine about God in Historic Wesleyan Communities." In *Trinity, Community and Power: Mapping Trajectories in Wesleyan Theology*. Edited by M. Douglas Meeks, 85–109. Nashville: Kingswood Books, 2000.

————. *The Religion of the Heart: A Study of European Religious Life in the Seventeenth and Eighteenth Centuries*. Columbia: University of South Carolina Press, 1991.

————. "The Shape of Wesleyan Thought: The Question of John Wesley's 'Essential' Christian Doctrines." *Asbury Theological Journal* 59, no. 1–2 (Spring and Fall 2004): 27–48.

————. "The 'Way of Salvation' and the Methodist Ethos beyond John Wesley: A Study in Formal Consensus and Popular Reception." *Asbury Theological Journal* 63, no. 1 (Spring 2008): 5–31.

Cannon, William R. *The Theology of John Wesley, with Special Reference to the Doctrine of Justification*. Nashville: Abingdon-Cokesbury Press, 1946.

The Catechism (Formerly *"The Turner Catechism"*) *of the A.M.E. Church*. Nashville: A.M.E.C. Sunday School Union; reprint edition of 2000.

A Catechism for the Use of Children. London: T. Cordeux, 1817.

A Catechism for the Use of the People Called Methodists. Peterborough: Methodist Publishing House, [1989].

Catechisms of the Wesleyan Methodists: Compiled and Published by Order of the Conference. No. 2, "For Children of Seven Years of Age and Upward." Toronto: Samuel Rose, 1867.

The Catechisms of the Wesleyan Methodists. No. 1, "For Children of Tender Years." New York: J. Emory and B. Waugh, 1829.

The Catechisms of the Wesleyan Methodists. No. 2, "For Children of Seven Years of Age and Upward." Nashville: Southern Methodist Publishing House, 1883.

Chadwick, Owen. *The Reformation*. Pelican History of the Church. Harmondsworth: Penguin Books, 1972.

Chalmers, Thomas. *Sermons and Discourses*. 2 vols. New York: Robert Carter, 1844.

Chiles, Robert E. *Theological Transition in American Methodism, 1790–1935*. New York: Abingdon Press, 1965.

Christensen, Michael. "John Wesley: Christian Perfection as Faith Filled with the Energy of Love." In *Partakes of the Divine Nature: The History and Development of Deification in Christian Traditions*. Edited by Michael Christensen, 219–29. Madison, N.J.: Farleigh Dickinson University Press, 2007.

Clapper, Gregory S. *John Wesley on Religious Affections: His Views on Experience and Emotion and Their Role in the Christian Life and Theology*. Metuchen, N.J.: The Scarecrow Press, 1989.

Clark, Elmer T., ed. *What Happened at Aldersgate.* Nashville: Methodist Publishing Corporation, 1938.

Clarke, Adam. *The Holy Bible, Containing the Old and New Testaments, the Text Carefully Printed from the Most Correct Copies of the Present Authorised Translation, Including the Marginal Readings and Parallel Texts, with a Commentary and Critical Notes.* London: Thomas Tegg and Son, 1836.

———. *Memoirs of the Wesley Family.* 2nd ed. New York: Lane and Tippett, 1848.

Cobb, John B. Jr. *God and the World.* Philadelphia: Westminster Press, 1969.

Coke, Thomas, and Henry Moore. *The Life of the Rev. John Wesley, A.M.: Including an Account of the Great Revival of Religion, in Europe and America, of which He Was the First and Chief Instrument.* London: G. Paramore, 1793.

Cokesbury Worship Hymnal. Nashville: Cokesbury Press, 1938. Reprint edition, Nashville: Abingdon Press, 1986.

Collection of Hymns for the Use of the Methodist Episcopal Church, Principally from the Collection of the Rev. John Wesley. New York: Bangs and Emory, 1825.

Collins, Kenneth J., *John Wesley's Theology: Holy Love and the Shape of Grace.* Nashville: Abingdon Press, 2007.

———. *The Scripture Way of Salvation: The Heart of John Wesley's Theology.* Nashville: Abingdon Press, 1997.

Collins, Kenneth J., and John H. Tyson, eds. *Conversion in the Wesleyan Tradition.* Nashville: Abingdon Press, 2001.

Constitutional Practice and Discipline of The Methodist Church. Volume 2. Peterborough: Methodist Publishing, 2009.

Cracknell, Kenneth, and Susan J. White. *An Introduction to World Methodism.* Cambridge: Cambridge University Press, 2005.

Davies, Horton. *The English Free Churches.* London: Oxford University Press, 1952.

Davies, Rupert E. *Methodism.* Harmondsworth: Penguin Books, 1963.

Deschner, John. *Wesley's Christology: An Interpretation,* rev. ed. Dallas: Southern Methodist University Press, 1985.

The Doctrines and Discipline of the African Methodist Episcopal Church 2004. Nashville: AMEC Publishing House, 2005.

The Doctrines and Discipline of The Methodist Episcopal Church. New York: Hunt and Eaton; Cincinnati: Cranston and Curts, 1892.

The Doctrines and Discipline of The Methodist Episcopal Church. New York: Eaton and Mains; Cincinnati: Curts and Jennings, 1896.

Dreyer, Frederick. "Faith and Experience in the Thought of John Wesley." *American Historical Review* 88 (1983): 12–30.

du Buc [Bucanus], Guillaume. *Institutiones Theologicae seu Locorum Communium Christianae Religionis ex Dei Verbo et Praestantissimorum Theologorum Orthodoxo Consensu Expositorum Analysis.* Geneva, 1609.

Dunlap, E. Dale. "Methodist Theology in Great Britain in the Nineteenth Century: With Special Reference to the Theology of Adam Clarke, Richard Watson, and William Burt Pope." PhD diss., Yale University, 1956; repr. ed.: Ann Arbor, Mich.: University Microfilms International.

Earle, Jesse A., and Dorothea Derrig. "Akron, Ohio." In *Encyclopedia of World Methodism.* Edited by Nolan B. Harmon, 1:73. Nashville: United Methodist Publishing House, 1974.

Episcopal-United Methodist Dialogue Team. *Make Us One with Christ: The Study*

Guide Version. N.p.: Office of Ecumenical and Interfaith Relations of the Episcopal Church in the USA and the General Commission on Christian Unity and Interreligious Concerns of The United Methodist Church, 2006.

Felton, Gayle Carlton. *This Gift of Water: The Practice and Theology of Baptism among Methodists in America*. Nashville: Abingdon Press, 1993.

A Form of Discipline for the Ministers, Preachers, and Members of the Methodist Episcopal Church in America, Considered and Approved at a Conference held at Baltimore, in the State of Maryland, On Monday the 27th of December, 1784. New York: W. Ross, 1787.

Free Methodist Hymnal: Published by Authority of the General Conference of the Free Methodist Church in North America. Chicago: The Free Methodist Publishing House, 1910.

Gamertsfelder, Solomon Jacob. *Systematic Theology*. Cleveland: C. Hauser, 1913.

Gassmann, Günther, ed. *Documentary History of Faith and Order, 1963–1993*. Faith and Order Paper no. 159. Geneva: World Council of Churches, 1993.

George, A. Raymond. "Foundational Documents of the Faith: IX. Methodist Statements." *Expository Times* 91 (June 1980): 260–63.

Gibson, William. *The Church of England 1688–1832: Unity and Accord*. London: Routledge, 2001.

Griffin, Eric Richard. "Daniel Brevint and the Eucharistic Calvinism of the Caroline Church of England, 1603–1674." ThD thesis, University of Toronto, 2000.

Gunter, W. Stephen, Scott J. Jones, Ted A. Campbell, Rebekah Miles, and Randy L. Maddox. *Wesley and the Quadrilateral: Renewing the Conversation*. Nashville: Abingdon Press, 1997.

Haller, William. *The Rise of Puritanism, Or, The Way to the New Jerusalem as Set Forth in Pulpit and Press from Thomas Cartwright to John Lilburne and John Milton, 1570–1643*. New York: Columbia University Press, 1938.

Harmon, Nolan B. "The Creeds in American Methodism." In *Encyclopedia of World Methodism*, s.v. "Confession of Faith," 1:563.

———, ed. *Encyclopedia of World Methodism*. 2 vols. Nashville: United Methodist Publishing House, 1974.

Hatch, Nathan. *The Democratization of American Christianity*. New Haven: Yale University Press, 1989.

Heitzenrater, Richard P. "'At Full Liberty': Doctrinal Standards in Early American Methodism." In *Mirror and Memory: Reflections on Early Methodism* (Nashville: Kingswood Books, 1989), 189–204.

———. *Mirror and Memory: Reflections on Early Methodism*. Nashville: Kingswood Books, 1989.

———. *Wesley and the People Called Methodists*. Nashville: Abingdon Press, 1995.

Hempton, David. *Methodism: Empire of the Spirit*. New Haven: Yale University Press, 2005.

Heppe, Heinrich. *Reformed Dogmatics: Set Out and Illustrated from the Sources*. Edited by Ernst Bizer. Translated by G. T. Thompson. London: Allen and Unwin, 1950.

———. *Reformierte Dogmatik*. Kreis Moers: Buchhandlung des Erziehungsvereins, 1935.

Hohenstein, Charles R. "New Birth through Water and the Spirit: A Reply to Ted A. Campbell." *Quarterly Review* 11, no. 2 (Summer 1991): 103–12.

———. "The Revisions of the Rites of Baptism in The Methodist Episcopal Church, 1784–1939," PhD diss., Notre Dame University, 1990.

Holland, Bernard G. *Baptism in Early Methodism.* London: Epworth Press, 1970.

Horton, Isabelle. *High Adventure: The Life of Lucy Rider Meyer.* New York: Methodist Book Concern, 1928.

Hughes, Hugh Price. *Social Christianity: Sermons Delivered in St. James Hall, London.* London: Hodder and Stoughton, 1890.

Hymn Book of The Methodist Protestant Church: Compiled by the Authority of the General Conference, 14th ed. Baltimore: Book Concern, Methodist Protestant Church, 1852; original printing was 1837.

Hymnal of The Methodist Episcopal Church. Cincinnati: Cranston and Stowe, 1878.

Hymns and Psalms: A Methodist and Ecumenical Hymn Book, rev. ed. London: Methodist Publishing House, 1984.

Hymns for the Use of The Methodist Episcopal Church. New York: Carlton and Porter, 1849.

Hymns for the Use of The Methodist Episcopal Church with Tunes for Congregational Worship. New York: Carlton and Porter, 1857.

James, William. *The Varieties of Religious Experience: A Study in Human Nature.* New York: The Modern Library, 1902.

Joint Commission between the Roman Catholic Church and the World Methodist Council. *The Apostolic Tradition: Report of the Joint Commission between the Roman Catholic Church and World Methodist Council: 1986–1991, Fifth Series.* Singapore: World Methodist Council, 1991.

Joint Commissions on Church Union between The Methodist Church and The Evangelical United Brethren Church. *Plan of Union: Report to the General Conferences, November 1966 of The Methodist Church and The Evangelical United Brethren Church.* N.p.: 1966.

Jones, Scott J. *John Wesley's Conception and Use of Scripture.* Nashville: Kingswood Books, 1998.

———. *United Methodist Doctrine: The Extreme Center.* Nashville: Abingdon Press, 2002.

Journal of the General Conference of The Methodist Episcopal Church. New York: Eaton and Mains; and Cincinnati: Curts and Jennings, 1896.

Journal of the General Conference of The Methodist Episcopal Church, South. Nashville: Publishing House of The Methodist Episcopal Church, South, 1894.

The Junior Catechism. Memphis: C.M.E. Church Publishing House, n.d.

The Junior Catechism of The Methodist Episcopal Church and The Methodist Episcopal Church, South. New York: The Methodist Book Concern, [1932].

Kirkpatrick, Dow, ed. *The Doctrine of the Church.* Nashville: Abingdon Press, 1964.

Kittel, Gerhard, ed. *Theological Dictionary of the New Testament.* Translated and edited by Geoffrey W. Bromiley. Grand Rapids: William B. Eerdmans Publishing Co., 1964.

Knudson, Albert C. *The Doctrine of God.* Nashville: Cokesbury Press, 1930.

———. "Henry Clay Sheldon—Theologian." In *Practical Divinity: Theology in the Wesleyan Tradition.* 2 vols. Nashville: Abingdon Press, 1998, 2:125–36.

Kostof, Spiro. *A History of Architecture: Settings and Rituals.* New York: Oxford University Press, 1995.

Langford, Thomas A. *Practical Divinity: Theology in the Wesleyan Tradition,* rev. ed. 2 vols. Nashville: Abingdon Press, 1998.

Lavely, John H. "Edgar Sheffield Brightman: Good-and-Evil and the Finite-Infinite God," in *The Boston Personalist Tradition in Philosophy, Social Ethics, and Theology.* Edited by Paul Deats and Carol Robb, 121–45. Macon, Ga.: Mercer University Press, 1986.

Lee, Umphrey. "The Historical Backgrounds of Early Methodist Enthusiasm." PhD diss., Columbia University, 1931.

———. *John Wesley and Modern Religion.* Nashville: Cokesbury Press, 1936.

Leith, John, ed. *Creeds of the Churches.* 3rd rev. ed. Atlanta: John Knox Press, 1982.

Lenton, John. *John Wesley's Preachers: A Social and Statistical Analysis of the British and Irish Preachers Who Entered the Methodist Itinerancy before 1791.* Milton Keynes: Paternoster Press, 2009.

Lindberg, Carter. *The European Reformations.* Oxford: Basil Blackwell, 1996.

Lloyd, Gareth. *Charles Wesley and the Struggle for Methodist Identity.* Oxford: Oxford University Press, 2007.

Long, D. Stephen. *John Wesley's Moral Theology: The Quest for God and Goodness.* Nashville: Abingdon Press, 2005.

Macquarrie, John. *Principles of Christian Theology.* 2nd ed. New York: Charles Scribner's Sons, 1977.

Maddox, Randy L., ed. *Aldersgate Reconsidered.* Nashville: Kingswood Books, 1990.

———. *Responsible Grace: John Wesley's Practical Theology.* Nashville: Kingswood Books, 1994.

Manual of the Laws and Discipline of the Methodist Church in Southern Africa. 6th ed. N.p.: Methodist Church of Southern Africa Publishing House and Book Depot, 1981.

Manual of the Pentecostal Church of the Nazarene: Published by Authority of the General Assembly Held at Pilot Point, Texas, 1908. Los Angeles: Nazarene Publishing Co., 1908.

Mathews, James K. *A Global Odyssey: The Autobiography of James K. Mathews.* Nashville: Abingdon Press, 2000.

Matthews, Rex Dale. "'Religion and Reason Joined': A Study in the Theology of John Wesley." PhD diss., Harvard University, 1986.

McCaine, Alexander. *The History and Mystery of Methodist Episcopacy; Or, A Glance at "The Institutions of the Church As We Received Them From Our Fathers."* Baltimore: Richard J. Matchett, 1827.

———. *Letters on the Organization and Early History of the Methodist Episcopal Church.* Boston: Thomas F. Norris, Olive Branch Office, 1850.

McCormick, Kelley Steve. "Theosis in Chrysostom and Wesley: An Eastern Paradigm on Faith and Love." *Wesleyan Theological Journal* 26, no. 1 (Spring 1991): 38–103.

Meeks, M. Douglas, ed. *The Future of the Methodist Theological Traditions.* Conference papers, Seventh Oxford Institute of Methodist Theological Studies, Oxford, England, 1982; Nashville: Abingdon Press, 1985.

———. "Trinity, Community, and Power." In *Trinity, Community and Power:*

Mapping Trajectories in Wesleyan Theology. Edited by M. Douglas Meeks, 15–31. Nashville: Kingswood Books, 2000.

———, ed. *Trinity, Community and Power: Mapping Trajectories in Wesleyan Theology.* Nashville: Kingswood Books, 2000.

———, ed. *Wesleyan Perspectives on the New Creation.* Nashville: Kingswood Books, 2004.

———, ed. *What Should Methodists Teach? Wesleyan Tradition and Modern Diversity.* Nashville: Kingswood Books, 1990.

Meredith, Lawrence. "Essential Doctrine in the Theology of John Wesley with Special Attention to the Methodist Standards of Doctrine." PhD diss., Harvard University, 1962.

Methodist Catechism: Compiled by Order of the Conference of the Methodist Church in Ireland. London: The Epworth Press, [1948].

Methodist Church Nigeria Constitution 1990. A typescript document with no further bibliographical data consulted at the archives of the World Methodist Council in Lake Junaluska, North Carolina.

The Methodist Hymnal: Official Hymnal of The Methodist Church. Baltimore: The Methodist Publishing House, 1935.

The Methodist Hymnal: Official Hymnal of The Methodist Church. Nashville: The Methodist Publishing House, 1964. Subsequently published by The United Methodist Publishing House as *The Book of Hymns.*

The Methodist Hymnal: Official Hymnal of The Methodist Episcopal Church and The Methodist Episcopal Church, South. New York: Methodist Book Concern, 1905.

The Methodist Hymn-Book. London: Wesleyan Conference Office, 1933.

Methodist Worship Book. Peterborough: The Methodist Publishing House, 1999.

Miley, John. *Systematic Theology.* 2 vols. New York: Hunt and Eaton, 1892–94.

Monk, Robert C. *John Wesley: His Puritan Heritage: A Study of the Christian Life.* 2nd rev. ed. Lanham, Md., and London: Scarecrow Press, 1999.

Moorhead, James H. *World without End: Mainstream American Protestant Visions of the Last Things, 1880–1925.* Bloomington: Indiana University Press, 1999.

Muller, Richard A. "'Perkins' *A Golden Chaine*: Predestinarian System or Schematized *Ordo Salutis*?" *Sixteenth Century Journal* 9, no. 1 (1978): 69–81.

Newport, Kenneth G. C., and Ted A. Campbell, eds. *Charles Wesley: Life, Literature and Legacy.* Peterborough: Epworth Press, 2007.

Nicholson, William. *A Plain, but Full Exposition of the Catechism of the Church of England.* Oxford: John Henry Parker, 1842.

Norwood, Frederick A. *The Story of American Methodism.* Nashville: Abingdon Press, 1974.

Oden, Thomas C. *Doctrinal Standards in the Wesleyan Tradition.* 2nd rev. ed. Nashville: Abingdon Press, 2008.

Ogden, Schubert M. "Evil and Belief in God: The Distinctive Relevance of a 'Process Theology'." *Perkins School of Theology Journal* 31 (1978): 29–34.

An Ordinal: The United Methodist Church: Adopted for Official Alternative Use by the 1980 General Conference. Nashville: United Methodist Publishing House, 1980.

Outler, Albert C. "Do Methodists Have a Doctrine of the Church?" In *The Doctrine of the Church.* Edited by Dow Kirkpatrick, 11–28. Nashville: Abingdon Press, 1964.

———. "The Reformation and the Vitality of Classical Protestantism," in *Albert C. Outler as Historian and Interpreter of the Christian Tradition.* Edited by Ted A. Campbell, 223–28. Anderson, Ind.: Bristol Books, 2003.

———. *Theology in the Wesleyan Spirit.* Nashville: Discipleship Resources, 1975.

Padgett, Alan G., ed. *The Mission of the Church in Methodist Perspective.* Studies in the History of Missions Series. Vol. 10. Lewiston: Edwin Mellen Press, 1992.

Pearson, John. *An Exposition of the Creed.* New York: D. Appleton and Co., 1851.

Pelikan, Jaroslav. *Credo: Historical and Theological Guide to Creeds and Confessions of Faith in the Christian Tradition.* New Haven: Yale University Press, 2003.

Pelikan, Jaroslav, and Valerie Hotchkiss, eds. *Creeds and Confessions of Faith in the Christian Tradition.* 3 vols., with a collection of source material in original languages on CD-ROM. New Haven: Yale University Press, 2003.

Perkins, William. *A Golden Chaine, or The Description of Theologie, Containing the Order of the Causes of Salvation and Damnation, according to God's Word.* 2nd ed.; Cambridge: John Legate, 1597.

———. *A Treatise Tending unto a Declaration, Whether a Man Be in the Estate of Damnation, or in the Estate of Grace.* London: John Porter, 1597.

The Pictorial Catechism of The Methodist Episcopal Church. New York: Carlton and Phillips, 1855.

Piette, Maximin. *John Wesley in the Evolution of Protestantism.* Translated by J. B. Howard. New York: Sheed and Ward, 1937.

Pliny the Younger. *C. Plini Caecili: Epistularum Libri Decem.* Edited by R. A. B. Mynors. Oxford: Clarendon Press, 1963.

A Pocket Hymn Book: Designed as a Constant Companion for the Pious, Collected from Various Authors. Philadelphia: Henry Tuckniss, 1800; original printing, 1793.

Polišenský, Josef V. *War and Society in Europe, 1618–1648.* Cambridge: Cambridge University Press, 1978.

Pope, William Burt. *A Compendium of Christian Theology: Being Analytical Outlines of Theological Study; Biblical, Dogmatic, and Historical.* 3 vols. New York: Phillips and Hunt; Cincinnati: Walden and Stowe, 1881.

Powell, Sam. "The Doctrine of the Trinity in Nineteenth-Century American Wesleyanism, 1850–1900." *Wesleyan Theological Journal* 18, no. 2 (Fall 1983): 33–46.

Praise Evangel: For Sunday-Schools, Revivals, Singing Schools, Conventions, and General Use in Christian Work and Worship. Lawrenceburg, Tenn.: James D. Vaughn, 1919.

Probationer's Manual of The Methodist Episcopal Church: Prepared under the Authorization of the General Conference. New York: Methodist Book Concern, 1914.

Quantrille, Wilma J. "The Triune God in the Hymns of Charles Wesley." PhD diss., Drew University, 1989.

Rack, Henry D. "Early Methodist Visions of the Trinity." *Proceedings of the Wesley Historical Society* 45:38–44, 46:57–69.

———. *Reasonable Enthusiast: John Wesley and the Rise of Methodism.* Philadelphia: Trinity Press International, 1989.

Rall, Harris Franklin. *Modern Premillennialism and the Christian Hope.* New York: Abingdon Press, 1920.

————. *Was John Wesley a Premillennialist?* The Ryerson Essays, no. 1. Toronto: Methodist Book and Publishing House, 1921.

Ralston, Thomas N. *Elements of Divinity; Or, A Concise and Comprehensive View of Bible Theology, Comprising the Doctrines, Evidences, Morals, and Institutions of Christianity, with Appropriate Questions Appended to Each Chapter.* Edited by Thomas O. Summers. Nashville: Cokesbury Press, 1928.

Rattenbury, J. Ernest. *The Evangelical Doctrines of Charles Wesley's Hymns.* 3rd ed. London: Epworth Press, 1954.

Raymond, Miner. *Systematic Theology.* 3 vols. Cincinnati: Hitchcock and Walden; New York: Phillips and Hunt, 1879.

Richey, Russell E. *Doctrine in Experience: A Methodist Theology of Church and Ministry.* Nashville: Kingswood Books, 2009.

————. *Early American Methodism.* Bloomington: Indiana University Press, 1991.

————. *The Methodist Conference in America: A History.* Nashville: Kingswood Books, 1996.

Rigg, James H. *Was John Wesley a High Churchman? A Dialogue for the Times.* London: The Wesleyan Methodist Book Room, 1882.

Roberts, Alexander, and James Donaldson, eds., *The Ante-Nicene Fathers.* Buffalo: Christian Literature Publishing Co., 1885. Reprint edition: Grand Rapids: William B. Eerdmans Publishing Co., 1971.

Runyon, Theodore. *The New Creation: John Wesley's Theology Today.* Nashville: Abingdon Press, 1998.

Rusch, William G. *Reception: An Ecumenical Problem.* Philadelphia: Fortress Press in cooperation with the Lutheran World Federation, 1988.

Ruth, Lester, ed. *Early Methodist Life and Spirituality: A Reader.* Nashville: Kingswood Books, 2005.

Schmidt, Jean Miller. "'Strangely Warmed': The Place of Aldersgate in the Methodist Canon." In *Aldersgate Reconsidered.* Edited by Randy L. Maddox, 109–19. Nashville: Kingswood Books, 1990.

Schmidt, Leigh Eric. *Holy Fairs: Scottish Communions and American Revivals in the Early Modern Period.* Princeton, N.J.: Princeton University Press, 1989.

Semmel, Bernard. *The Methodist Revolution.* New York: Basic Books, 1973.

The Senior Catechism of The Methodist Church. London: Methodist Publishing House, 1952.

A Short Scriptural Catechism Intended for the Use of The Methodist Episcopal Church. Philadelphia: Henry Tuckniss, 1795; originally published 1793.

Simpson, Mathew. *A Hundred Years of Methodism.* New York: Nelson and Phillips; Cincinnati: Hitchcock and Walden, 1876.

Sing to the Lord: Hymnal. Kansas City: Lillenas Publishing Company, 1993.

Stamm, Mark. *Let Every Soul Be Jesus' Guest: A Theology of the Open Table.* Nashville: Abingdon Press, 2005.

Starkey, Lycurgun M. Jr. "The Holy Trinity." In *Encyclopedia of World Methodism,* s.v. "Trinity," 2:2366–77.

Stevens, Abel. *A Compendious History of American Methodism: Abridged from the Author's "History of The Methodist Episcopal Church."* New York: Phillips and Hunt, and Cincinnati: Walden and Stowe, 1867 (although a preface printed in the book carries the date 1868).

Stone, Lawrence. *The Causes of the English Revolution, 1529–1642.* New York: Harper and Row, 1972.

Stookey, Laurence H. *Baptism: Christ's Act in the Church.* Nashville: Abingdon Press, 1982.

———. *Eucharist: Christ's Feast with the Church.* Nashville: Abingdon Press, 1993.

Summers, Thomas O. *Systematic Theology: A Complete Body of Wesleyan Arminian Divinity Consisting of Lectures on the Twenty-Five Articles of Religion.* Nashville: Publishing House of The Methodist Episcopal Church, South, 1888.

Taves, Ann. *Fits, Trances, and Visions: Experiencing Religion and Explaining Experience from Wesley to James.* Princeton: Princeton University Press, 1999.

Thiel, John E. "Perspectives on Tradition" in *Catholic Theological Society of America Proceedings* 54 (1999): 1–18.

Thorsen, Donald. *The Wesleyan Quadrilateral: Scripture, Tradition, Reason and Experience as a Model of Evangelical Theology.* Grand Rapids: Zondervan Publishing House, 1990.

Thrall, Homer S. *History of Methodism in Texas.* Houston: E. H. Cushing, 1872.

Tripp, David. "Methodism's Trinitarian Hymnody: A Sampling, 1780 and 1989, and Some Questions." *Quarterly Review* 14, no. 4 (1994): 359–85.

Tucker, Karen B. Westerfield. *American Methodist Worship.* New York: Oxford University Press, 2001.

———. "'Plain and Decent': Octagonal Space and Methodist Worship." *Studia Liturgica* 24, no. 2 (1994): 129–44.

Turner, Henry McNeal. *The Genius and Theory of Methodist Polity; Or, the Machinery of Methodism: Practically Illustrated through a Series of Questions and Answers.* Philadelphia: Publication Department, A.M.E. Church, [1885].

Tyson, John R. *Charles Wesley on Sanctification: A Biographical and Theological Study.* Grand Rapids: Francis Asbury Press, 1986.

———. "The Lord of Life Is Risen: Theological Reflections on *Hymns for Our Lord's Resurrection*, 1746." *Proceedings of the Charles Wesley Society* 7 (2001): 81–99.

United Methodist Book of Worship. Nashville: United Methodist Publishing House, 1992.

United Methodist Hymnal: Book of United Methodist Worship. Nashville: United Methodist Publishing House, 1989.

Urlin, Richard Denny. *John Wesley's Place in Church History: Determined with the Aid of Facts and Documents Unknown to, or Unnoticed by, His Biographers.* London: Rivingtons, 1870.

Vedder, Henry C. Review of *History of Methodists in the United States*, 1899 ed.; in J. M. Buckley. *American Journal of Theology* (1900): 200–203.

Vickers, Jason E. *Invocation and Assent: The Making and Remaking of Trinitarian Theology.* Grand Rapids: William B. Eerdmans Publishing Co., 2008.

The Voice of Praise: A Compilation of the Very Best Sacred Songs for Use in Sunday Schools and Praise Services. Philadelphia: Hall-Mack Company, 1904.

Wainwright, Geoffrey. "Ecclesial Location and Ecumenical Vocation." In *The Future of the Methodist Theological Traditions.* Edited by M. Douglas Meeks, 93–129. Nashville: Abingdon Press, 1985.

———. "Methodism and Apostolic Faith." In *What Should Methodists Teach? Wesleyan Tradition and Modern Diversity.* Edited by M. Douglas Meeks, 101–17. Nashville: Kingswood Books, 1990.

Walsh, John, Colin Haydon, and Stephen Taylor, eds. *The Church of England, c. 1689–c. 1833: From Toleration to Tractarianism*. Cambridge: Cambridge University Press, 1993.

Watson, J. R. *The English Hymn: A Critical and Historical Study*. Oxford: Oxford University Press, 1997.

Watson, Richard. *Theological Institutes; Or, A View of the Evidences, Doctrines, Morals, and Institutions of Christianity*. Edited by John McClintock. New York: Carlton and Phillips, 1854.

———. *Theological Institutes; Or, A View of the Evidences, Doctrines, Morals, and Institutions of Christianity*. Edited by Thomas O. Summers. Nashville: Stevenson and Owen, 1857.

Wesley, Charles. "Catholic Love" [1755]. Edited by Randy L. Maddox, Durham, N.C.: Duke Center for Studies in the Wesleyan Tradition, 2007.

———. *Funeral Hymns*. Bristol: William Pine, 1769.

———. *Gloria Patri, etc . . . Hymns on the Trinity*. London: [William Strahan], 1746.

———. *Hymns for Children*. Bristol: Felix Farley, 1763.

———. *Hymns for Our Lord's Resurrection*. London: William Strahan, 1746.

———. *Hymns for the Nativity of Our Lord*. n.d [believed to be 1745], n.p.

———. *Hymns for the Use of Families and on Various Occasions*. Bristol: William Pine, 1767.

———. *Hymns for Those That Seek and Those That Have Redemption in the Blood of Jesus Christ*. Bristol: Felix Farley, 1747.

———. *Hymns on God's Everlasting Love*. London: W. Strahan, n.d. [believed to be 1742].

———. *Hymns on the Trinity*. Edited by Wilma J. Quantrille. Bristol: Felix Farley, 1767. Reprint edition, Madison, N.J.: The Charles Wesley Society, 1998.

Wesley, Charles, and John Wesley. *The Eucharistic Hymns of John and Charles Wesley*. [*Hymns on the Lord's Supper*, 1749.] Edited by J. Ernest Rattenbury. London: Epworth Press, 1948.

———. *Hymns and Sacred Poems*. London: William Strahan, 1739.

———. *Hymns and Sacred Poems*. London: W. Strahan, 1740.

———. *Hymns and Sacred Poems*. Bristol: Felix Farley, 1742.

———. *Hymns and Sacred Poems in Two Volumes*. 2 Vols. Bristol: Felix Farley, 1749.

———. *Hymns on the Four Gospels, and the Acts of the Apostles*. A collection of hymns and poems on passages from the Gospels and Acts, published posthumously in Osborn's edition of *The Poetical Works of John and Charles Wesley*.

———. *The Poetical Works of John and Charles Wesley*. Edited by George Osborn. London: Wesleyan Conference Office, 1868.

Wesley, John. *The Appeals to Men of Reason and Religion and Certain Related Open Letters*. Oxford/Bicentennial Edition of the Works of John Wesley 11. Edited by Gerald R. Cragg. Oxford: Oxford University Press, 1975.

———. *A Collection of Hymns for the Use of the People Called Methodists*. Bicentennial Edition of the Works of John Wesley 7. Edited by Franz Hildebrandt and Oliver Beckerlegge. Nashville: Abingdon Press, 1983.

———. *A Collection of Psalms and Hymns*. Charleston, S.C.: Lewis Timothy, 1737.

———. *A Compend of Wesley's Theology*. Edited by Robert W. Burtner and Robert E. Chiles. New York and Nashville: Abingdon Press, 1954.

———. *Explanatory Notes upon the New Testament*. Naperville, Ill.: Alec R. Allenson, Inc.; and London: Epworth Press, 1950.

———. *Instructions for Children*. London: M. Cooper, 1745.

———. *John Wesley: A Representative Collection of His Writings*. A Library of Protestant Thought. Edited by Albert C. Outler. New York: Oxford University Press, 1964.

———. *Journal and Diaries*. Bicentennial Edition of the Works of John Wesley. Edited by W. Reginald Ward and Richard P. Heitzenrater. Nashville: Abingdon Press, 1988–2003.

———. *The Journal of the Rev. John Wesley, A.M., Sometime Fellow of Lincoln College, Oxford*. "Standard Edition" of the Works of John Wesley. 8 vols. Edited by Nehemiah Curnock. London: Epworth Press, 1906–19.

———. *Letters*. Bicentennial Edition of the Works of John Wesley. Edited by Frank Baker. Oxford: Oxford University Press. 2 vols. to date, 1980 and 1982.

———. *The Letters of the Rev. John Wesley, A.M.* 8 vols. "Standard Edition" of the Works of John Wesley. Edited by John Telford. London: Epworth Press, 1931.

———. *The Methodist Societies: History, Nature, and Design*. Bicentennial Edition of the Works of John Wesley 9. Edited by Rupert E. Davies. Nashville: Abingdon Press, 1989.

———. *Sermons*. Bicentennial Edition of the Works of John Wesley. 4 vols. Edited by Albert C. Outler. Nashville: Abingdon Press, 1984–87.

———. *The Sunday Service of the Methodists in North America*. London: [Strahan], 1784.

———. *Wesley's Standard Sermons*. "Standard Edition" of the Works of John Wesley. 2 vols. 3rd ed. Edited by Edward H. Sugden. London: Epworth Press, 1951.

———. *The Works of the Reverend John Wesley, A.M.* 14 vols. Edited by Thomas Jackson. London: Wesleyan Conference Office, 1873.

Wesley, Susanna. *Susanna Wesley: The Complete Writings*. Edited by Charles Wallace Jr. Oxford: Oxford University Press, 1997.

Westerkamp, Marilyn J. *The Triumph of the Laity: Scots-Irish Piety and the Great Awakening, 1625–1760*. New York: Oxford University Press, 1988.

Whitefield, George. *Select Sermons of George Whitefield*. London: Banner of Truth Trust, 1959.

———. *Sermons on Important Subjects: With a Memoir of the Author, by Samuel Drew, and a Dissertation on His Character, Preaching, &c., by the Rev. Joseph Smith*. London: H. Fisher, Son, and P. Jackson, 1828.

Whitehead, John. *The Life of the Rev. John Wesley, M.A., Sometime Fellows of Lincoln College, Oxford*. 2 vols. London: Stephen Couchman, 1793, 1796.

Wigger, John H. *Taking Heaven by Storm: Methodism and the Rise of Popular Christianity in America*. Urbana: University of Illinois Press, 1998.

Wiley, H. Orton. *Christian Theology*. 3 vols. Kansas City, Mo.: Beacon Hill Press, 1962–63.

Wilken, Robert L. "The Christians as the Romans (and Greeks) Saw Them." In *Jewish and Christian Self-Definition*. 3 vols. Edited by E. P. Sanders. Philadelphia: Fortress Press, 1980–82, 1:100–125.

Williams, Colin W. *John Wesley's Theology Today*. Nashville: Abingdon Press, 1960.

Williams, Rowan. Letter of commendation in the first issue of *The Oxford Theologian* 1 (Spring 2010): 6–7.

Wood, Robert. *The Early History of the Walk to Emmaus.* Nashville: Upper Room Books, 2001.

Workman, Herbert Brook. *The Place of Methodism in the Catholic Church.* Rev. and enl. ed. of 1921. London: Epworth Press; first edition was 1909.

World Council of Churches Faith and Order Commission. *Baptism, Eucharist and Ministry.* Faith and Order Paper no. 111. Geneva: World Council of Churches, 1982.

———. *Confessing the One Faith: An Ecumenical Explication of the Apostolic Faith as It Is Confessed in the Nicene-Constantinopolitan Creed (381).* Faith and Order Paper no. 153. Geneva: World Council of Churches, 1991.

———. *The Nature and Mission of the Church: A Stage on the Way to a Common Statement.* Faith and Order Paper no. 198. Geneva: World Council of Churches, 2005.

World Methodist Council. "Methodist Statement of Association with the Joint Declaration on the Doctrine of Justification," approved by the World Methodist Council on 23 July 2006, http://worldmethodistcouncil.org/index.php?option=com_docman&task=doc_download&gid=45.

———. "Wesleyan Essentials of Christian Faith." *In World Methodist Council Handbook of Information 2007–2011.* Lake Junaluska, N.C.: World Methodist Council, 2007, 95–98.

Young, Carlton R. *An Introduction to the New Methodist Hymnal.* Nashville: Methodist Publishing House/Graded Press, 1966.

Yrigoyen, Charles Jr. *Praising the God of Grace: The Theology of Charles Wesley's Hymns.* Nashville: Abingdon Press, 2005.

INDEX

LaVergne, TN USA
02 October 2010
199238LV00005B/2/P

9 781426 711367